D0712147

lightner
witmer

lightner witmer

his life and times

PAUL McREYNOLDS

American Psychological Association
Washington, DC

Published by
American Psychological Association
750 First Street, NE
Washington, DC 20002

Copies may be ordered from
APA Order Department
P.O. Box 92984
Washington, DC 20090-2984

In the UK and Europe, copies may be ordered from
American Psychological Association
3 Henrietta Street
Covent Garden, London
WC2E 8LU England

Typeset in Garamond Regular by EPS Group Inc., Easton, MD

Cover photograph: Lightner Witmer, 1910, by Elias Goldensky, Philadelphia.
    Courtesy of the University of Pennsylvania Archives.
Printer: Royal Book Manufacturing Inc., Norwich, CT
Cover Designer: Archie Ferguson, New York
Technical/Production Editor: Catherine R. Worth

Library of Congress Cataloging-in-Publication Data

McReynolds, Paul, 1919–
    Lightner Witmer : his life and times / Paul McReynolds.
        p.   cm.
    Includes bibliographical references and indexes.
    ISBN 1-55798-444-1
        1. Witmer, Lightner, 1867–1956.   2. Psychologists—United States—
Biography.   I. Title.
BF109.W57M38   1997
150'.92—dc21
[B]   97-17508
                                                                                           CIP

British Library Cataloguing-in-Publication Data
A CIP record is available from the British Library

Printed in the United States of America
First Edition

To
the former
associates and students
of Lightner Witmer,
who generously
shared their remembrances
with me

CONTENTS

ILLUSTRATIONS

PREFACE

This book chronicles the life and times of a major figure in early American psychology, a man whose influence, although diluted over the passage of time, nevertheless touches the shape of current Western culture. Lightner Witmer, widely recognized as the founder of clinical psychology, also can be considered the primary pioneer of school psychology and a major figure in the development of special education. Further, in a role associated with these accomplishments but going beyond them, Witmer was an early, outspoken, and effective advocate for the rights and improved treatment of children. It is in the sense that these several callings are important and pervasive in modern society that I referred to the persisting influence of Witmer's work.

The seminal event in Witmer's founding of clinical psychology was his establishment, in 1896—over a century ago—of the world's first psychological clinic, at the University of Pennsylvania. This date was only 17 years after Wilhelm Wundt (under whom Witmer had studied) had established, in Leipzig, Germany, what is generally considered to have been psychology's first experimental laboratory, and it was 4 years before Sigmund Freud's *Interpretation of Dreams*.

Although his founding of the first psychological clinic was an important achievement, and the kind of dramatic event that is easily identified, it was by no means Witmer's only contribution to the new profession, and a number of his other actions that are reviewed in this book are of equal historic significance. Perhaps the most important of these is the fact that Witmer was the first to put forth the *idea* that the fruits of scientific psychology could have practical benefits for human beings—that is, that scientific psychology could be mobilized to help people having personal difficulties in living. Witmer lived at a time when psychology was becoming scientific and, in the process, was declaring its separation from, and its independence of, philosophy. Witmer was a pioneering part of that movement, but he was also the first to go beyond the transition from philosophical to scientific psychology and to maintain that psychology, in addition to being a science, could also form the basis for a new helping profession.

I first became interested in Witmer about 30 years ago, when I picked up a copy of his *Analytical Psychology* at a used book store. I had earlier developed a serious interest in the history of psychology, especially biographies. As a clinical psychologist, I was intrigued by Witmer's role in the origins of clinical psychology, but when I looked into it, I found that almost nothing had been written about him. Thus stimulated, I began a search, first on a casual basis and later as a serious, scholarly enterprise, to learn as much as possible about Witmer's life and career. This project, carried on over a period of years while I was primarily engaged in regular professorial and research functions at the University of Nevada, involved extensive correspondence; contacts with various institutions and archives; and inquiries to trace, and then trips to meet and interview, surviving former students and associates of Witmer or his wife, Emma Repplier Witmer. As the result of these extended efforts, I was able to accumulate an extensive collection of Witmer material. Some of this material was included in earlier articles, but extensive new data about Witmer and early clinical psychology are presented in this volume.

I have organized this book so as to present Witmer's life in a primarily chronological, narrative fashion. Although the text includes numerous accounts of personal events and circumstances, as befits a biography, I have given particular attention to the professional, scientific, and academic side of Witmer's life course—including the development of his clinic and his school, his publications, his students, his clinical approach, and similar substantive themes.

It is important, in constructing a biography, to keep in mind that the person did not exist in splendid isolation, but rather lived in a particular historical period, and in a particular unique culture nexus. It is essential, if the subject is in some sense to come alive in the pages of text, that these important background features be appropriately presented. Although Witmer's era, in the long historical sense, was not so very far in the past, it was nevertheless an era in many ways foreign to the contemporary world. Accordingly, I have provided brief views of the economic

and political backdrop in which Witmer thrived. In the same sense, and
to a somewhat greater degree, I have included certain general descriptions of overall developments in the discipline of psychology during
Witmer's time.

This book is intended as a contribution to the historical record and
as the definitive biography of clinical psychology's founder. Although I
have endeavored to tell the Witmer story in an engaging way, my main
commitment has been to Clio, the Muse of history. Thus, my aims have
been accuracy, objectivity, and as much comprehensiveness as can be
brought within the covers of a book of reasonable length. It is my hope
that the book will be of interest not only to clinical and school psychologists but also to general historians of psychology. Witmer, after all,
was in the first generation of scientific psychologists in America and was
a charter member—and the last of these to die—of the American Psychological Association. Beyond this, the book, I believe, should have
some value to historians of American culture. Finally, the life story of
Witmer, with his unique personal characteristics and trailblazing career
accomplishments, is of considerable interest in its own right.

For their support and encouragement in the development of this book,
I owe so much to so many. First, I am indebted, beyond measure, to
the numerous former students and associates of Witmer, many of whom
I came to know personally, who by their enthusiasm for my project
inspired me to bring this volume to its completion. It is a pleasure to
dedicate the book to them. For encouragement in the writing of this
volume, I thank Wendell Carlson, Thomas K. Fagan, Hamilton Elliott,
Robert C. Jenkins, John A. Popplestone, Donald K. Routh, Martin E.
P. Seligman, and Charles D. Spielberger. My colleagues John Altrocchi,
Nancy Taylor, and Duane Varble read a draft of the entire manuscript
and offered numerous helpful suggestions, for which I am extremely
appreciative. My sincere thanks go to Theodore J. Baroody and
Catherine R. Worth of APA Books for their patience and skill in turning
a complex manuscript into a finished book. Most of all, I am deeply
grateful to my wife, Billie. She was a constant source of support, encouragement, and wise counsel throughout the entire project that culminated in this volume, and her outstanding editorial assistance in the
preparation of the book itself was invaluable.

SOURCES AND ACKNOWLEDGMENTS

This biography could not have been written without the helpfulness of numerous individuals who provided important personal data, and the support of various institutions that furnished essential archival data, and which together provided the basic information from which a particular life could be transformed into words. Specific credits are indicated in the Notes, but to give an overall picture, I list here my major sources of primary data.

A special collection of Witmer's papers does not exist, but numerous records, documents, and newspaper clippings relating to Witmer and his period are in the holdings of the Archives of the University of Pennsylvania, Philadelphia. I am grateful to the Director and staff of the University of Pennsylvania Archives and Records Center for their courtesy in making a wide range of data available to me. In particular, I deeply appreciate the tireless and expert efforts of Gail M. Pietrzyk, Public Services Archivist, in tracking down the answers to endless questions relating to Witmer. I also greatly appreciate the valuable information furnished by John A. Popplestone, Director, Archives of the History of American Psychology at the University of Akron. Additional important data were generously provided by the following data sources: Archives of the American Medical Association; Department of Rare Books and Manuscripts, Boston Public Library; Miriam Coffin Canaday Library, Bryn Mawr College; Rare Books and Manuscripts Library, Columbia University; Rare and Manuscripts Collections, Cornell University

Library; Devereux Foundation; Harvard University Archives; Archives of the Karl Marx Universität (now University of Leipzig); Special Collections, Lehigh University Libraries; Library of Congress, Manuscript Division; Archives and Special Collections on Women in Medicine, Florence A. Moore Library of Medicine, Medical College of Pennsylvania; Getchell Library, University of Nevada; Special Collections Department, University of Pennsylvania Libraries; Joseph W. England Library, Philadelphia College of Pharmacy and Science; Lane Medical Library, Stanford University; United States Office of Personnel Management; and Manuscripts and Archives, Yale University Library. Vital statistics (e.g., births, marriages, and deaths) were obtained from a number of public agencies.

Valuable information was also furnished by the Historical Society of Pennsylvania; the Mennonite Conference Historical Society of Lancaster County, Pennsylvania; the Lancaster County Historical Society; the American Philosophical Society; the American Psychological Association; the Pennsylvania Psychological Association; and the Laurel Hill and West Laurel Hill Cemeteries, both in the Philadelphia area. Essential data were also provided by officials from the Epworth Academy; the Agnes Irwin School; the Friends' Central School; the Elwyn Institutes (all in or near Philadelphia); the Bancroft School in Haddonfield, New Jersey; and the Philadelphia City Troop of the Pennsylvania National Guard. Three genealogists, Millicent Berghaus, Millicent Cooper, and David Tritchler, uncovered important family data.

Julius Wishner, head of the clinical program at the University of Pennsylvania when I began my project, and a friend of long standing, made available to me the microfilms of the accumulated cases of Witmer's psychological Clinic. Mildred Sylvester, the last Executive Officer of the Clinic during Witmer's tenure, donated to me a large collection of Witmer materials, as did Helen Backus Graber, Witmer's secretary in the 1920s. Genevieve McDermott Murphy, a stalwart at both the Clinic and the Witmer School, gave me valuable Witmer items and took me to see the facilities that had been the Witmer School. Important gifts of their Witmer-related memorabilia were also made by Marion Mack and Helen Ford Joyce. I conducted extended interviews with Sylvester, Graber, Murphy, Frank Irwin, Morris Viteles, Marion Braumgard Graham, Carolyn Ambler Walter, and John Walter, and a telephone interview with Joyce, all of whom had known Witmer or his wife. The Walters kindly shared with me certain Witmer items that they had inherited, and John Walter, an attorney, obtained for me copies of various relevant legal documents, including Witmer's will.

Numerous former students and associates of Witmer sent me detailed reminiscences; these persons, in addition to those covered above or in the Preface, included Wendell Carlson (an old friend), Margaret A. Forrest, Olive Logan, John R. Martin, Jay L. Otis, and Kingsley R. Smith. For various translations I thank Klaus Ludwig, Ingrid Moore, and Catherine Mary. Other individuals who contributed in important ways include John D. Abbate, Geraldine Jonçich Clifford, Rachel Cox, F. J. Dallett, Thomas K. Fagan, Raymond D. Fowler, Isabelle M. Friedman, Joseph L. French, Ernest R. Hilgard, Paul Hollingsworth, Melvin J. Horst, Maryellen C. Kaminsky, Dorothy Lynn, Scott Nearing, Sheila Ochsenhirt, John M. O'Donnell, Sidney Repplier, Saul Rosenzweig, John Saltmarsh, Winifred L. Tillery, Robert Waller, and Robert I. Watson. I thank David Ambler, Carolyn Ambler Walter, Natalie Elder Passmore, and Mary Elder Spencer for permission to quote from Witmer's letters and documents; Roberta Yerkes Blanshard for permission to quote from a letter by Robert Yerkes; Scott Murphy for permission to quote from a letter by Miles Murphy; Peter Forbes for permission to quote from a letter by Scott Nearing; and Catherine Parsons Smith for permission to quote from the memoir of Frances Holsopple Parsons.

I am indebted to the Research Advisory Board of the University of Nevada, Reno, for travel support in connection with my Witmer project. In research for this book, I collected much more materials than could be included in the book, and I regret that I was unable to utilize all the contributions provided by others. The above comments do not include the numerous books and articles used in my writing. These are listed in the References, but I note here four books that were especially helpful: Nathaniel Burt's *The Perennial Philadelphians*, Edward P. Cheyney's *History of the University of Pennsylvania: 1740–1940*, John M. Reisman's *A History of Clinical Psychology*, and Donald K. Routh's *Clinical Psychology Since 1917.*

1

Early Life

$\mathbf{L}$ightner Witmer's earliest years were lived in the aftermath of the great cataclysm that was the American Civil War. Born on June 28, 1867, just two years after the close of that war, Lightner was a member of the immediate postwar generation, whose formative years were experienced in the atmosphere of relief, remorse, anxiety, and hope that followed that terrible convulsion.[1] Philadelphia, where he was born, had been on the Union side in the war, and Gettysburg—where the pivotal battle had been fought but four years before and where Lincoln, in the same year, had delivered the words that were to become immortal, "Fourscore and seven years ago . . ."—was only a little over a hundred miles to the west and even closer to the ancestral Witmer settlement in the Lancaster area.

Although it is impossible to firmly identify any specific effects of the postwar cultural climate on Witmer's developing personality, it is not implausible to speculate that the idealism and strong feeling for justice that were to characterize his later, adult years may have had their origins, at least in part, in public discussions of the war and Reconstruction policies. Similarly, Witmer's later deep admiration for the works of Walt Whitman, some of whose more poignant poems concerned the war, may have been nurtured in this period.

Some further sense of the period in which Witmer entered the scene can be garnered from the following observations. People were still living, when he was born, whose lives overlapped with those of Franklin, Washington, and Jefferson. In Washington, Andrew Johnson was president and Ulysses S. Grant was waiting in the wings to take office the next year. The overwhelming portion of Americans lived on farms, and ordinary transportation was by horse-drawn vehicles. Although the era of the railroad was well under way, the Pennsylvania Railroad, which was to play a large role in the future affairs of the state, had only in 1861 completed its line from Philadelphia to Pittsburgh. The majority of people had only an eighth-grade education, or less, and attendance at college was unusual except among the upper classes and was limited almost entirely to men.

The city of Philadelphia, then as now, was one of the nation's great cities and was an outstanding center of culture, as indeed it had been since the days of Benjamin Franklin. Intensely conscious of the fact that it was the city in which America had achieved its nationhood and famous for a string of important "firsts"—including the first public library in the United States, the first public hospital, and the first scientific society (all founded by Benjamin Franklin)—Philadelphia has always been somewhat unique among American cities.[2] In part, this uniqueness, the feeling of being somehow special, that its citizens enjoyed in Witmer's era, and perhaps to some extent still do, flowed from its history. There are countless places in the city and its environs where important events, going back to the prerevolutionary era, occurred, and Philadelphians have never overlooked this fact—an attitude that has tended to imbue contemporary events in a rich historical patina.

An additional characteristic of Philadelphia, particularly during the period of Witmer's growth and maturity, was the emphasis on society. I mean this in the sense of social status, of position, of who one is and knows. This theme of a patrician upper class, with its aura of the "best" schools, the "right" clubs, and the like, was of course related to the historical orientation noted above, and when combined with the spirit of down-to-earth practicality highlighted earlier by Franklin himself, resulted in the development of a number of cultural institutions, including the Academy of Natural Sciences, founded in 1812, and the Franklin Institute, established in 1824. Another important and even older facet of the city into which Witmer was born was the University of Pennsylvania. This historic institution was in that period, as it is today, one of the country's outstanding centers of learning. It was also a part, through its historical, financial, and social ties, of the greater network of Philadelphia institutions and opportunities that beckoned to intelligent and aspiring young men of that time and place.

This, then, was the city of Lightner Witmer. He was, among other categories in terms of which he could later be labeled, such as psychologist, educator, husband, and war veteran, always a Philadelphian. Except for the period of his doctoral education in Leipzig, Germany, and for two relatively short periods in war service, and, of course, for numerous vacation and business trips, he would never leave the environs of Philadelphia. The characteristics of this location, along with the period in which he lived, were major factors in determining the kind of person that Witmer was to become and the nature of the things that he was to accomplish.

LIGHTNER WITMER'S DIRECT FORBEAR, on his father's side, was Benjamin Weitmer (as the name was then spelled), who immigrated to America from his native Switzerland in 1716 and settled in Lancaster County, PA, as a representative of the London Land Company.[3] Benjamin brought with him from Switzerland his wife and their son Abraham, and a second son, John, was born in Pennsylvania in 1719. In 1722, Benjamin received a patent from the London Company for 265 acres several miles east of the city of Lancaster, and in 1733, he built a home in East Lampeter Township along the road known as the King's Highway. In 1739, Abraham went to Philadelphia to be naturalized as an Englishman—the fee was two pounds two shillings. This procedure was, of course, not necessary in John's case, because he was born in an English colony.

The Weitmers had been German speaking in Switzerland, and the family continued to write their name in German characters long after transferring to Pennsylvania. They were an early part of that movement into eastern Pennsylvania of people known as the *Pennsylvania Dutch*. A little earlier history may be helpful here. In 1681, in England, the reigning monarch, Charles II, granted to William Penn, a prominent English Quaker, a charter for a vast expanse of territory west of the Delaware River between New York and Maryland. The area, which was in payment for funds that the King had owed Penn's late father, was given the name "Pennsylvania," which, roughly translated, means "Penn's Woods."

William Penn was a strong proponent of religious freedom, and he opened the area not only to Quakers seeking a place of tolerance for their religious views but also to other groups in search of a religious haven. Penn died in 1718, but the colony continued under the tutelage of his sons and grandsons until the Revolutionary period. Among the early settlers, as already noted, were the Pennsylvania Dutch; most of these people came from the German Rhineland and the German-oriented part of Switzerland, but some were French Huguenots. Despite what they were called, none, or at any rate very few, were from the Netherlands; the word *Dutch* was simply a misinterpretation of *deutsch* (German). Most of this surge of settlers belonged to the Lutheran or Reformed churches, but quite a number were members of faiths that grew out of the earlier European pietistic movement: These included the Amish and the Mennonites, groups that rejected church formalities and emphasized plain ways of living. The Witmers were part of this latter group.

Benjamin Witmer had a number of descendants, and the Witmers have been prominent in communities in the Lancaster area ever since the early days. Currently, there are numerous Witmers listed in the telephone directory for Lancaster and nearby towns, some of which have charming names, such as Paradise, Bird-in-Hand, and Intercourse, and yes, there is even a town named Witmer.[4] The area was, and continues to this day to be, a prosperous and beautiful farming area, and the Amish and Mennonites are still very prominent. Because of the plain but unusual styles of these groups—the Amish, in particular, reject modern conveniences and still use horses for farm power, drive buggies rather than cars, and wear simple clothes—the area has become something of a tourist center. There are also other reasons for the historical significance of the whole Lancaster region. In the Conestoga Valley, in the first half of the eighteenth century, German settlers invented and developed the famous Conestoga wagons, which later became famous as the covered wagons, or "prairie schooners," that led the way to the West. In the Revolutionary period, most American population centers were on the Atlantic coast; Lancaster was the most inland city of the entire 13 colonies. It was also the national capital for one day, September 27, 1777, when Congress stopped there after fleeing from Philadelphia after the battle of Brandywine. At the time of the Revolution, Philadelphia was the largest city in America and one of the largest English-speaking cities in the world.

Back now to the early eighteenth century and the genealogy of Lightner Witmer. As noted above, Benjamin Weitmer (Witmer) had two sons, Abraham and John. Abraham evidently never married, but John Witmer married Fronika (Frances) Roland, who had been born in Switzerland and had come to this country with her parents in 1727, when she was only 7 years old. Seven children were born to this union. One of these, John Jr., grew up to be a member of George Washington's staff of observation in the Revolutionary War. Another, David, who was born on December 15, 1752, is, however, in the line of interest here. David was married to Esther Kendig in 1774, and they had nine children. David is remembered as the man who founded and named the town of Paradise. He was a highly prominent figure in his time: He was involved in farming, milling, road construction, running a newspaper, and politics and was a partner in operating a stage line called the "Stage Dispatch." He is said to have been a friend of George Washington, presumably through his brother, and is reported to have gone to Philadelphia to meet Washington in 1789, when the newly elected president was on his way to New York for the inauguration. Later, in 1794, Washington visited the Lancaster area.

David Witmer was clearly the energetic, organizing type of person who is appropriately considered a pillar of the community. He helped to construct a stone wall around the local graveyard and was responsible for having a brick schoolhouse built in Paradise, directly across from the Mennonite Church. In 1806, David provided the land for a meeting house for the Mennonite Society and donated $80 toward the $400 cost of the building. However, the Society refused to accept him because his home was too fancy and his carriage had springs. After this experience, David turned to the Episcopal Church, which he joined in 1812. He died in 1835, at the age of 82.

The eldest son of the children of David and Esther Witmer was David Jr. He was born in 1778 and, thus, grew up thinking of himself as a citizen of a new country. Like his parents, David Jr. lived in Paradise, where he was the postmaster, and helped erect the building that served as the Episcopal Church—thus carrying on the separation from the Mennonite denomination began by his father. In 1800, the first year of the new century—or the last year of the old one–on the 29th of April, David Jr. took as his bride Jane Lightner, the daughter of Adam Lightner of Lancaster, and the couple journeyed to Philadelphia, some 60 miles away, for their honeymoon. The couple had eight or nine children (the record is not altogether clear), of whom one, a son named Elam, born in 1812, was destined to be the grandfather of Lightner Witmer.

Elam married Maria Musselman of Paradise. Her parents were Michael and Barbara; he was a distiller and miller and operated a copper shop. It is interesting to note that the Musselman home was purchased early in the 1850s, by a prominent Lancaster lawyer and politician, James Buchanan, for his brother, who was then rector of the Paradise Episcopal Church. Later, in 1856, Buchanan was elected president.

Shortly after their marriage—probably in the latter 1830s—Elam and Maria Witmer left the Lancaster area and moved to Germantown, a historic village a few miles northwest of Philadelphia. Germantown had been founded in 1683 by a group of German Pietists from the Rhineland and, later, during the Revolution, was the site of the battle of Germantown. When the Witmers moved there, it had long since ceased to be an exclusively German community, although this ethnic group was still highly prominent. At this time, Germantown was a thriving and beautiful suburb of Philadelphia. In 1854, it had became of the larger city and is marked today by Germantown Avenue.

Elam and Maria Witmer were the parents of three boys and three girls. One of the boys, the third-born child, was given the name David Lightner, the first name after his grandfather and the second after his grandmother. This David, who was born in 1841, was married, on July 26, 1866, in Philadelphia, to Katherine Huckel. David was 25 at the time, and Katherine was 24. The ceremony was conducted by the Reverend William N. Diehl, of the Germantown Episcopal Church.

THE FIRST CHILD OF David and Katherine (in one record, Katherine is referred to as Kate; presumably, this is the way she was known to her friends) was born in the parents' home, at 1505 North 7th Street, with Dr. Ellwood Wilson in attendance. The date, as noted earlier, was June 28, 1867. The name recorded for the child was David L. Witmer, Jr., but he seems to have been called Lightner from the first. In 1917, when he was 50 years old, Lightner went to the Bureau of Health in

Philadelphia and had his recorded name officially changed to Lightner Witmer, stating that although his name originally had been recorded as David L. Jr., it was later changed—presumably by his parents—to Lightner.[5]

Lightner's father, David, was a pharmacist. He had graduated from the Philadelphia College of Pharmacy, which was then located at 147 North Tenth Street, in 1862, with the PhG (graduate in pharmacy) degree. This school, in a manner analogous to so many other institutions in Philadelphia, was the first college of pharmacy in the nation, dating its origin from 1821. Students in David's day were required, as part of the graduation requirements, to write an inaugural essay. The title of David's was "Helianthamum Canadensis."[6] After graduation, at the age of 25, David entered the retail pharmacy business and, some time later, took on his younger brother Horace as partner, and the firm became known as D. L. Witmer and Brother.

Years later, in 1921, when David died at the age of 80, a newspaper obituary stated that he had "founded a wholesale drug business over fifty years ago with his brother, Horace J. Witmer, at Germantown and Montgomery Avenues" and, further, that "until recent years Mr. Witmer was active head of the firm which bears his name."[7]

Some further insight into Lightner's father is provided in the same brief obituary:

> During the Brumbaugh administration, Mr. Witmer suggested to the Governor many preventive measures to safeguard children from temptations that beset them in large cities. Among these was the suggestion [that] a law be passed obliging railroad companies to enclose tracks with fences to keep children from playing in the paths of fast trains. He also suggested the passage of laws preventing boys under eighteen from smoking.

Martin G. Brumbaugh was governor of Pennsylvania from 1915 to 1919, so these suggestions would have been made when David Witmer was in his mid or late 70s. It is unlikely that a man at this age would for the first time engage himself in the public scene, and it would be interesting to know what kinds of political or petitionary activities in which he may have been involved when Lightner was growing up. The quotation above—which brings to mind conceptions of the period when people traveled chiefly by train, when the steam locomotive was king and railroad companies were very powerful politically—is also interesting in that it indicates the concern of the older man for the welfare of children. Was this something he picked up from his son, the Lightner of this biography, or from the general political temper of the times? Or was it perhaps representative of an earlier, intrinsic interest, in which case it may have contributed to Lightner's own deep interest in children? Although these are idle questions, it is not too far-fetched to suspect some relation between the father's and son's interests in the welfare of children. Further, with some imagination and willingness to speculate, one can see in this David Witmer something of the assertiveness of the two earlier Davids in the family line and perhaps also something of the rugged and opinionated independence that was to characterize his son Lightner.

Lightner's mother, Katherine, remains an unclear figure. This is unfortunate, since her influence on Lightner, both biologically and psychologically, was probably at least of the same order as that of his father. Her maiden name, Huckel, is not Mennonite, though it is probably German. It is known, from 1870 census data, that her father, Joseph Huckel, was at that time a bank clerk. Years after both she and David had died, Joseph Collins, who was probably the closest friend Lightner ever had, and who undoubtedly knew both of Lightner's parents, stated that "he [Lightner Witmer] owes his adornments to his mother and his limitations to his father. The former were largely in the field of the intellect, the latter in the affect."[8]

It is easy—probably too easy—to read quite a bit into these rather cryptic comments. Lightner was destined to be both brilliant and, at times, difficult, and what Collins seems to be suggesting is that the first of these traits was due primarily to his mother and the second mainly to his father. Even if this is what he meant, it may, of course, not be true, although it clearly does say something about the favorable impression that Kate had made on Collins.

In 1869, a second child, who received the name of Albert Ferree, was born to the Witmers.[9] The date was April 28, which meant that Albert Ferree was 22 months younger than Lightner. At this time, the family lived at 1514 North 8th Street. About 5 years later—on October 9, 1874—a third child, a girl, arrived. She was given the name of Lilly Evelyn. Then, in 1876, on September 5, their fourth and last child, a boy who was named Paul DeLancey, came along.[10]

All four children would eventually earn higher degrees and have professional careers. This could hardly have happened without a supportive and encouraging attitude on the part of the parents. All in all, it seems reasonable to conclude, from the facts noted above plus other circumstantial evidence, that the home environment provided by David and Katherine Witmer stressed honesty and personal integrity, hard work, achievement—especially intellectual achievement—and social advancement of the kind that can be obtained through professional careers. Further, it appears that the family was fairly prosperous; after all, they lived in a nice part of town, and it took a certain amount of money to finance the education of several children. In sum, it may be assumed that the Witmer family, which included the young Lightner, although by no means a part of the city's higher society or of its core business and political establishment, was in its own limited way a contributor to the city's prosperity and vitality. Briefly, the family could be described as middle class, solid, respectable, and upwardly mobile.

Something of the senior Witmers' lifestyle and social ambitions for their children is revealed by the fact that they sent Lightner, as a young boy (and possibly the younger children later), to a dance school to learn the proper social graces. An embarrassing experience in this class was remembered by Lightner many years later. It seems, as he recalled it, that he didn't like the girls and he didn't like the dancing class, but he was required to attend. For certain exercises, the students would form two lines facing each other, then they would take hands—boy, girl, boy, girl—and dance toward each other and then back. On one particular occasion, they had finished the dance, and the teacher was talking to them when suddenly someone looked at Lightner and snickered. He realized he was still holding the girl's hands and hadn't dropped them, and all the other boys had dropped their hands![11]

Lightner's paternal grandparents, Elam and Maria Witmer, probably lived nearby while he was growing up, and perhaps this was true of his maternal grandparents, Joseph and Mary Huckel, as well. Then there was his father's brother, Uncle Horace, who was his father's partner in the pharmaceutical business, and probably other relatives as well. It also seems likely that from time to time, the Witmer family traveled, by train, to the Lancaster area to visit with their numerous relatives living there.

PHILADELPHIA, IN 1876, mounted a world's fair to celebrate the 100th anniversary of the signing of the American Declaration of Independence. The affair was called the Centennial Exposition. It attracted over 10 million visitors, one of whom, it may safely be assumed, was the 9-year-old Lightner Witmer. Here, he may have seen, among the mechanical and scientific exhibits, such newfangled devices as the telephone (Alexander Graham Bell[12] had only just transmitted the first message on the device in March, and here in June he was demonstrating it for the first time); the typewriter (a practical commercial machine that had been on the market for only 2 years); the self-binding reaper; the sewing machine; and young Thomas Edison's duplex telegraph. The Philadelphia Museum of Art also had its beginnings in this Exposition.

In the same period, the Pennsylvania Railroad attained the dominance that it was to maintain for so long. In the 1870s and 1880s, too, the exclusive and famous suburban residential area to the west of Philadelphia, known familiarly as the "Main Line," had its real beginnings. The term *Main Line*, which was to become, and remain, as commonplace to Philadelphians as *the Peninsula* is to San Franciscans, had its origin from the earlier Main Line of Public Works, a complex plan for connecting Philadelphia and Pittsburgh. The area was served by the Pennsylvania Railroad, which was active in developing and publicizing it.

Because of the inherent beauty of the region, the elegance of many of the estates that grew up in it, and the social level of many of the inhabitants, the term Main Line rather shortly came to have a social as well as a geographical significance; thus, to say that one lived on the Main Line was to say something about who one was as well as about where one resided. Among the stops along the Main Line were—and are—Overbrook, Merion, Haverford, Bryn Mawr, Villanova, and Devon. Several of these, particularly the last one, were later to play important roles in Witmer's life.

IN JUNE OF 1880, Lightner turned 13. A growing youth, physically characterized by an abundance of energy and a bodily stature shorter than most of his peers, he had completed his elementary schooling and looked forward now to his college preparatory work.

The school that had been chosen for this important period of his life was the Episcopal Academy of Philadelphia. This famous school, con-

sidered one of the top prep schools in America, was located, during the
period that Witmer attended it, on the southwest corner of Locust and
Juniper Streets, in the midst of the city's finest residential district. The
school had been founded in 1785 by a group of Episcopalians led by
William White, rector of Christ Church and the first bishop of Pennsylvania. The same men were instrumental during the same period in
organizing the American Protestant Episcopal Church as independent of
its Anglican ancestry. Originally located on 4th Street below Market, the
Episcopal Academy moved to its Locust Street site in 1850 and stayed
there until 1921, when it moved to Overbrook, on the Main Line. It is
presently located in Merion and Devon.

The Episcopal Academy, then a day school for boys (it is now coeducational), was in Witmer's period the most prestigious secondary school,
both socially and scholastically, in the area. It has always been considered
a proper school for solid young Philadelphians. That Lightner was enrolled there tells us something, not only about Lightner but also about
his family. As already observed, his parents were hardly important figures
in Philadelphia society or governing circles, and certainly they were not
of old Philadelphia stock. They were, however, industrious, and his father
was a successful merchant. The selection of the Episcopal Academy for
Lightner suggests parents who placed great value on the role of education, who were dedicated to doing their best for their children, and who
inculcated in their children, perhaps especially in their firstborn child,
the importance of high achievement.

Lightner entered the academy in September of 1880 and graduated
on June 30, 1884, having just turned 17. The school records list his
parent as Mrs. D. L. Witmer.[13] The fact that it was Lightner's mother
who represented the family to the Academy suggests, although of course
it does not confirm, that it was his mother who provided the main
stimulus and encouragement for the children's educational goals.

The Witmers lived about $2^1/_2$ miles from the Episcopal Academy.
There is a surviving anecdote that suggests that Lightner walked to
school, at least some of the way. The students, so the story goes, were
all required to follow a strict dress code; this included dark trousers,
which, however, did not reach to the shoes, thus revealing conspicuous
regulation white stockings. Sometimes on the way to school, bigger boys
reviled and chased young Lightner because of the stockings. Lightner
solved the problem by taking off the stockings before coming to the

danger area, stuffing them in his pocket, and then putting them back on just before arriving at school.[14]

This experience probably occurred early in Witmer's period at the Academy. Another anecdote appears to have harkened back to a later episode and offers a glimpse of a more assured young man. Three boys, Lightner and two others, were each going to build a canoe, for which they had the materials and the instructions. The two other boys started arguing about who would be the first to get his canoe finished, but Lightner just listened to them and didn't say anything. He thought (as he recalled later) that he wanted his to be the last, because they'd make mistakes and then they'd learn how to do it, and the second would be better, but the third would be the best in the end![15]

These anecdotes tell us something about Lightner as a boy. Both are based on Witmer's later reminiscences, and the fact that he reported and shared them, quite aside from their exact accuracy, is of considerable interest. Notably, both narratives, as remembered or reconstructed by Witmer, highlight the role of intelligence in the solution of problems and suggest a certain shrewdness in dealing with others, as well as a somewhat introverted nature.

The curriculum at the Episcopal Academy was strictly traditional— "solid but stodgy" is the way it was described for that period by Charles Latham, Jr.,[16] a historical minded member of the school's staff, in 1981—and comprised the usual classical subjects, including Latin and Greek. The headmaster was a clergyman, and the program included religious instruction and daily chapel services.

Lightner received a good grounding in the basic educational areas and in the classics at the Episcopal Academy. This inference is based in part on his future academic successes (e.g., his later prizes in Latin and Greek in college). It can also be conjectured, although with perhaps less assurance, that enrollment at such an exclusive school as the Episcopal Academy occasioned considerable pride in Lightner, all the more so because of his own middle-class background. It is my impression that social status and prestige were of considerably more than passing importance to Witmer, particularly in the first half of his life. Probably this attitude was more or less inevitable in a brilliant youngster from an upwardly mobile family in the Philadelphia of that era.

Joseph Collins, who in his adult years was Witmer's closest friend, in 1931 described Witmer's early years in the following way:

As a boy he was what is known as a good mixer, but he was a careful chooser. . . . While in school, he was keen for games of skill and strength and he played them well. He had an opportunity to make good in football, but forced to choose between that and books, he gave up football. . . . His constitution was what the French call *type musculaire* and the Germans "athletic type."[17]

Since Collins did not know Witmer when both were boys, it follows that this description was based largely on comments made either by Witmer himself in later years or by his parents.

IT NEVER OCCURRED TO Lightner Witmer, when he was a student at the Episcopal Academy, that he might grow up to be a psychologist. One can be certain of this, since at that time the area of psychology, as a discipline that one might follow and identify with, was only just in the process of coming into being.

In 1879, at the University of Leipzig, in Germany, Wilhelm Wundt, a professor of philosophy whose primary interests were in psychological issues, had founded the first psychology research laboratory and, in so doing, had made the crucial advance in emancipating psychology from philosophy and in establishing psychology as a scientific discipline. Although there is some uncertainty about just what is meant in this instance by *founding* and also some dispute among historians about Wundt's priority, the psychological investigations by Wundt, and the year 1879, have come to be accepted as symbolic of the emergence of psychology as a science. Beginning in the 1880s, Leipzig, for at least two decades, was the mecca for individuals aspiring to this new science. A number of Americans traveled to Germany to study with Wundt and came back proclaiming themselves to be psychologists. Most of these, it seems likely, would have gone into some other scholarly or scientific discipline had not Wundt's laboratory and doctoral program existed and, in a sense, beckoned.

So it was that the foundations of the new field that Witmer was eventually to follow were being laid in the period just before and during his prep school years. All this was of course unknown to him, but it is of prime importance in understanding the cultural context of which his life was to be a part.

Psychology as a field of study, as distinct from its identity as an empirical and experimental science and before general adoption of the appellation *psychology*, is, of course, much older than Wundt's time. Indeed, one may safely assume that people have always been interested in and curious about the behaviors, motives, and emotions of themselves and their fellows. In the eighteenth and early nineteenth centuries, a number of philosophers, including David Hume, David Hartley, Jeremy Bentham, and Herbert Spencer, developed highly astute conceptualizations of human behavior, based on their own introspections and observations. However, these interpretations, because they were not based on systematic empirical data, were necessarily speculative, tentative, and not subject to confirmation. In this prescientific era, what we now think of as psychology was generally referred to as *mental philosophy*. The gropings that eventually were to lead to a data-based, scientific psychology had their beginnings in the following way.[18]

In 1796, Nevil Maskelyne, the astronomer royal at Greenwich, England, noted that he and his assistant came up with slightly different readings in observing stellar transits across a wire in the field of a telescope, a basic procedure in calibrating the Greenwich clock. Eventually, it was learned that rather marked individual differences can be expected among individuals on this task, and further, it became evident that the problem is a human and not a mechanical one. In the first half of the nineteenth century, astronomers made a number of attempts to deal with these observer differences, which they referred to as the *personal equation*. In the 1860s, F. C. Donders, a Dutch physiologist, took on the problem. He developed the reaction time method, the time it takes a person to react to a given stimulus, and elaborated it to study a variety of mental processes. His work and derivations from it constituted a major contribution to the shortly-to-emerge new discipline.

Another important forerunner was the anatomist–physiologist Ernst Weber at the University of Leipzig. In 1846, he published an important work,[19] based on empirical data, on the sense of touch. Weber's research took him away from pure anatomy and physiology and into the realm of sensation and perception (i.e., into psychology). Among other things, Weber reported that the smallest actual difference between two weights that could be perceived as a difference was a function, not of the magnitude of the weights, but of the ratio between them. This theme was taken up later by Gustav Fechner, one of the great figures in the history of psychology, and the immediate forerunner, at Leipzig, of Wilhelm Wundt, who was to arrive there in 1874.

Fechner merits a little more biographical space here because, as will be evident later, his work was tied to that of Witmer in a special and somewhat personal way. Fechner was a brilliant, complex, and rather eccentric man. He began his career by taking a degree in medicine, but then his interests changed to physics and mathematics, and by the age of 33, he found himself professor of physics at Leipzig. His real inclination, however, was increasingly shifting toward philosophy, especially to broad metaphysical issues. Fechner conceived that the central question was how to understand the relation, in an empirical sense, between the two worlds of mind and matter. His inspiration for solving the riddle was to determine the relationship between physical magnitudes and perceived intensities, and he suspected that this relationship might take the form of an identifiable ratio between the physical stimulus and the mental reaction. Fechner evidently came to this insight independently of Weber's work, but once he noted the similarity of his and Weber's ideas, he christened the relationship, which he was able to state in precise mathematical terms, as *Weber's law* (modern psychologists refer to it as the *Weber–Fechner law*). During the next decade, Fechner carried out extensive research in the new area, to which he gave the name *psychophysics* (because it related the psychical and the physical), and in 1860, his classic *Elements of Psychophysics*[20] appeared.

Work on psychophysics was not Fechner's only contribution to the incipient discipline of scientific psychology. He was also the founder of the field of experimental aesthetics. This field is concerned with identifying and describing the factors that cause some objects to be perceived as more pleasing than other objects, that is, with the dynamics of beauty. Fechner began by studying the ancient question of the most pleasing ratio between the length and width of rectangles. Later, he became interested in the question of which of two Madonnas, both reputedly painted by Hans Holbein the younger, was the more beautiful. In 1876, his pioneering book in the area, *Vorschule der Aesthetik*,[21] appeared; later, this work would prove important in Witmer's dissertation.

PROBABLY, IT HAD LONG since been decided that Lightner would go on to college; presumably, this was one of the chief reasons for his attending the Episcopal Academy. There were two old and premier universities in the area to which he might apply: the University of Pennsylvania (Penn), in Philadelphia, and Princeton, about 50 miles to the northeast.[22] Though Princeton was in New Jersey, it was considered a "Philadelphia college," and most of the sons of the "old Philadelphians," as well as those aspiring to such status or to professional careers, went to either Penn or Princeton. Other nearby colleges included Haverford, Swarthmore, and Lehigh. Temple University, in Philadelphia, was scheduled to open in 1884. All of these were men's schools, though a new college for women, at Bryn Mawr on the Main Line, would have its first students in 1885.

2

College Years

In the fall of 1884, at the age of 17, Lightner Witmer entered the University of Pennsylvania as a freshman in arts, in the university's college department. Although the reasons for his choice of Penn, as opposed, say, to Princeton, are not now known, the decision was logical enough: Penn was close, a fine university, and probably—everything considered—less expensive. The fact that Witmer did select Penn reinforces the assumption that at this period in his life he had no conception of going into psychology, because if he had planned to do so, he probably would have opted for Princeton, where James McCosh, probably then the best known authority in America in *mental philosophy* (as psychology was then known) offered courses.

As the University of Pennsylvania was then organized, the College Department included what today would generally be called Arts and Sciences.[1] The expenses for a student for the school year were estimated to range from $100 to $200 for tuition, $10 to $50 for textbooks, $30 to $100 for clothing, and $25 to $100 for extras. Recommended boarding houses near the university charged $5–$7 per week.[2]

The University of Pennsylvania is located in West Philadelphia, as it was in Witmer's student days. The grounds of the campus are arboreal and serene, as they were—although no doubt to a lesser degree, since the campus was fairly new then—in Witmer's college years. Over everything hovers the ghost of Benjamin Franklin, who is considered the principal founder of the institution.[3] The classic, ivy-covered central building of the campus is College Hall, begun in 1871 and completed in 1872, which in its time has served innumerable uses. It was here, very likely, that Witmer took most of his courses as an undergraduate, and it was here that the Psychological Clinic would later be housed. The University of Pennsylvania began as a charity school in 1740, was expanded into an academy in 1753, and became the College and Academy of Philadelphia in 1755. In 1765, it inaugurated the first medical school in the New World, and in 1779, it formally adopted the title of university—the first American institution to do so. Until 1872, the university was located in central Philadelphia. By that time, however, it had outgrown its limited quarters and so moved to its present location, then a large open space on the west side of the Schuylkill River.

The early years in the new campus thus coincided with Witmer's boyhood, and only 11 previous classes had attended there when he entered in the fall of 1884. We may assume, then, that for the city, for the faculty, and for the students themselves, including Witmer, the campus still had an aura of newness in Witmer's student days. The fact that he maintained his affiliation with the university over so many succeeding decades, as the trees grew larger and numerous new buildings appeared, must have given him the feeling of maturing and aging apace with the "new" Penn.

In addition to the movement of the campus, a number of other important academic changes occurred during the 1870s and 1880s. In 1872, the Towne Scientific School was established to provide training in chemistry, mining, engineering and architecture, and in 1874, the new University Hospital was dedicated. Courses in music were instituted in 1875; a Dental School was set in operation in 1878; and the Wharton School—the nation's first university school of business, and still one of the best—began functioning in 1881.[4]

These various developments, which on their face might seem to have little to do with Witmer's career, illustrate the general point that the University of Pennsylvania, shortly before Witmer entered it, was engaged in a period of rapid and dramatic growth, an expansion that was to continue during Witmer's early years on the faculty. Further, this pioneering and developing atmosphere may have been instrumental in shaping Witmer's own attitudes toward academic achievement and, in particular, toward his own opening of new paths, as exemplified later in his founding of the Psychological Clinic. Similarly, the boosterlike growth philosophy that characterized the university in that period may well have enhanced the institution's acceptance of and its enthusiasm for his Clinic.

In the period under review, the clinic was of course well into the future. In the 1880s, the most important of the new developments in the university—the one, that is, that was to prove most significant for Witmer's career—was the establishment of the Graduate School. This took place in several stages: The idea was approved by the Trustees in 1881, a circular announcing graduate instruction was issued in 1884, and the first students were enrolled in 1885–1886. The "leading spirit"[5] in the organization of the graduate school was Professor Edmund J. James, and the first dean was E. Otis Kendall. However, the "first really active Dean, who superseded Professor Kendall in 1888, was Professor George S. Fullerton . . . one of the most able of the younger men of the Faculty."[6] Two of these men, James and Fullerton (especially the latter), were to be important figures in Witmer's development.

The concept of a "graduate school," so named because persons studying there would already be college graduates and would be seeking advanced learning, was relatively new in American education, but the establishment of such programs was a conspicuous trend among top American universities at this time. The practice of awarding the doctor of philosophy (PhD) degree came from Germany, where graduate training, in the sense of intensive independent research contributing to the advancement of knowledge, originated. In 1876, a new university, Johns Hopkins, was founded in Baltimore, MD, with the stated primary aim of providing education at the graduate level, including the terminal PhD, in imitation of the German model. At Pennsylvania, as at other American universities, the graduate school did not have a separate faculty, as did the medical school and the law school, but rather, instruction was typically provided by faculty also offering undergraduate courses. From its inception, both the master of arts (MA) and PhD degrees were offered, and men and women were admitted on an equal basis. Both the graduate faculty and the number of students grew very slowly, with only 40 or 50 being enrolled by the mid 1890s. In 1895, the school was aided tremendously by a gift of $500,000 from Charles C. Harrison, then the

university provost, to set up an endowment for graduate scholarships
and fellowships.

LIGHTNER WITMER'S ADMISSION TO the University of
Pennsylvania as an undergraduate, in 1884, was not automatic but required that he pass examinations in Greek, Latin, English, Geography,
History, and Mathematics.[7] Presumably, his work at the Episcopal Academy had given him good skills in these areas. There were 24 students
—all men, since women were not yet admitted to the College—in
Witmer's freshman class in the Arts program, and a total of 380 undergraduates in the entire University. The academic year was divided into
two terms. The curriculum for the freshman and sophomore years was
essentially set, but the latter two years offered the opportunity for various
electives. In his first year, Witmer, as required, studied Greek, Latin,
English, History, and Mathematics (algebra, geometry, and trigonome-
try). During his sophomore year he completed the required courses in
Greek Language and Literature, Latin Language and Literature, Rhetoric
and the English Language, English Composition and Declamation,
Higher Mathematics, and Chemistry, as well as an elective in German.[8]
    The modern reader will be struck by the strong classical emphasis in
the first two college years. This was characteristic of most of the better
known universities of that time, but it was evidently not wholly satisfying
to the young Witmer. For his junior and senior years he transferred from
Arts to the Wharton School of Finance and Economy, which had been
established five years before. Courses in this school provided one of the
few opportunities for undergraduates to get into the applied world. It
should be remembered that Lightner's father, David Witmer, was a successful business man, and it is quite possible that the son was at this
stage of life considering following a career in business. The shift in academic emphasis can also be seen, in retrospect, as presaging Witmer's
later strong interest in the practical side of life. During his junior year
Witmer took work in Ethics, Logic and Philosophy, Physics, American
History, Constitutional Law, Political Science, Political Economy, Mer-
centile Practice, and Declamation. It is noteworthy that Witmer took
several courses in the sciences, a fact that perhaps both foreshadowed
and contributed to his later interest in experimental psychology and his
eventual insistence on a scientific orientation in psychology.

Records for his senior year have not survived, but Witmer himself, in a reminiscence many years later, stated that "I took in my last two years the Wharton School courses in finance and political economy."[9] During his last two college years Witmer was strongly attracted to, and influenced by, two faculty members mentioned earlier, Edmund J. James and George S. Fullerton.[10] James was the professor of finance and administration, and Fullerton taught the courses in philosophy, logic, and ethics, and was well-read in the new psychology. James had graduated from the University of Illinois and then taken his doctorate in political science in Germany. In 1896 he would move to the University of Chicago, and later would become president of Northwestern University, and eventually of the University of Illinois, his alma mater.

Fullerton had done his undergraduate work at the University of Pennsylvania, after which he attended the Princeton Theological Seminary and then earned his PhD at Yale, in 1883, just one year before Witmer entered Penn as a freshman. Witmer took his courses in Ethics and in Logic and Philosophy with Fullerton; further, it is almost certain that he also completed Fullerton's offerings in Intellectual and Moral Philosophy and in Logic and Psychology.[11] One of the texts in the latter course was *Outlines of Psychology*, by the German philosopher-psychologist Rudolf H. Lotze[12]; this was probably the most sophisticated statement of psychology then available, and one may suppose that Fullerton used it in part to keep up on the field himself. Although primarily a philosopher, Fullerton was something of a transitional figure in the new scientific psychology that was just coming into being; indeed, he would later be one of the founders, and still later the fifth President, of the American Psychological Association. Many years later, Lightner remembered Fullerton as "a brilliant teacher, thinker, and talker" who employed the Socratic method of quizzing a student."[13]

By today's conventions, and even in comparison with some other colleges of that period, Penn was a relatively small institution during Witmer's college years. Undoubtedly, he knew many of the other students, and developed close friendships with some of them, as is the perennial way among college students. Two other students of that period had later careers that would overlap with that of Witmer. These were Joseph Penniman, who was destined years later to become Provost of the University, and William Newbold, whose early career would in many ways parallel that of Witmer.

A small school, such as Penn was then, has many advantages. Most important, perhaps, it affords the intelligent and energetic student an opportunity to participate widely and to develop habits of leadership. Lightner Witmer, it appears, was such a student. He was elected president of the freshman class, and joined the Philomathean Society, a prestigious literary society dating back to 1813, and won some of its prizes for orations and essays. He was also awarded honors during his undergraduate years in Latin, Greek, English, philosophy and declamation. In addition, he served as editor of the *Pennsylvanian*, and was class Prophet and Valedictorian of his class.[14]

All in all, Witmer was a busy, involved, committed, and achieving young man, evidently of the active type which, while by no means common on college campuses, is nevertheless familiar to every experienced teacher. When it goes well, as it evidently did for Lightner, this period can be a wonderful prelude in a person's life: the world is full of excitement, promise, and opportunity, all waiting to be mastered. Here is a reminiscence of what Witmer was like in his college years, made many years later by his classmate Joseph Penniman. The young Witmer, Penniman wrote,

> took intellectual and spiritual life ideas very seriously and was never in his addresses and debates willing to accept without proof the views of others, but was always endeavoring to find a satisfactory reason for his opinions. The volumes to which he often referred and the authors he quoted during those Friday evening meetings in the rooms of the Philomathean Society made a distinct impression upon the writer of these paragraphs. Lightner Witmer revealed to his younger associates, as well as to his own classmates, evidences of intellectual power that were at once an example and stimulus to those who met him in debate. There was serious thinking and earnest intellectual effort on the part of the boys in that old society, and many look back to its meetings as valuable in their contribution to the development of powers of independent thought.
>
> Lightner Witmer's mental attitude toward the current thought of college life was critical and analytical. He had an intellectual honesty of opinion, and bluntness and fearlessness of expression that sometimes was mistaken for an antagonistic attitude, which in fact it was, but not toward persons. Those who knew him realized that he was quite as ready to criticize and correct his own opinions, as he was to criticize and correct the opinions of others.[15]

The general picture suggested by these remarks is that of a young man with a brilliant and wide-ranging intellect, a strong mental independence, and an assertive, even outspoken, interpersonal style.

In 1888 Witmer passed two milestones: he received his AB degree
and celebrated his 21st birthday—the latter an age that, in males, conferred the right to vote, and which in general, was a considerably more
meaningful dividing line than it is today. To help the reader empathize
with the year 1888, here are a few markers: Grover Cleveland was then
President of the United States (in his first term), and Queen Victoria
was the ruler of the British Empire. In his laboratory at West Orange,
in nearby New Jersey, Thomas Edison had just completed the world's
first large technological laboratory, and in 1888 he was perfecting his
phonograph, and also working on a device that would make pictures
appear to move, and which he was to patent a few years later. He had
invented a practical incandescent light bulb only nine years before, and
the electrification of America was slowly beginning. Automobiles were
still well in the future. Walt Whitman, the great U.S. poet and the author
of *Leaves of Grass*, was still alive, and was living across the Delaware
River in Camden, New Jersey.

LIGHTNER'S BROTHER, FERREE, AND his sister, Evelyn (this
is apparently the way they were usually addressed), were also moving
forward in their education.[16] Ferree, like his elder brother, took his college preparatory work at the Episcopal Academy and then entered the
Philadelphia College of Pharmacy in September 1888. It will be recalled
that David Witmer was a graduate of the Philadelphia College of Pharmacy, so Ferree's enrollment there was an instance of a son following in
his father's footsteps. The school was still located in the same place,
during Ferree's years, as when his father went there, and like his father,
Ferree had to write an inaugural essay. The title of Ferree's essay was
"Neutral Ground Between Botany and Zoology."[17]
    Evelyn, 5 years younger than Ferree and 7 years junior to Lightner,
was also educated in private schools. Her first 2 years were in a French
school, then there were 4 years in an English school, after which she
entered Friends' Central School for college preparatory work.
    Friends' Central, which still exists, was (and is) an outstanding sec-
ondary school. During the period that Evelyn attended, it was located
at 15th and Race Streets, next to the Quaker Meeting House. Founded
in 1845 by the Society of Friends, the institution from its beginning
welcomed both boys and girls. In Evelyn's day, there were two principals,

one for the boys and one for the girls; the classes were separate and on different floors. Although very few girls attended college in that era, the school did have a college preparatory course for girls. According to Clayton Farraday, an authority on the history of Friends' Central, the principal of the girls' department at that time was "a dynamic Quaker and vibrant teacher of the natural sciences."[18]

From her attendance at Friends' Central, as well as from the example of her brothers, one may presume that Evelyn too was looking forward to college. Three options in the area would in principle be open to her when her turn came: first, the recently (1885) opened college for women at Bryn Mawr; second, the Biology School of the University of Pennsylvania, which since its establishment in 1884 had admitted women on the same basis as men; and the Philadelphia College of Pharmacy, which had been coeducational since 1876.

As for Lightner, in the fall of 1888 (the same year that Ferree entered the College of Pharmacy), he took a position teaching English and history at the Rugby Academy for Boys, a preparatory school in Philadelphia. Several factors that may have influenced Lightner in accepting a position at Rugby can be suggested. Prominent among these is the probability that he did not yet know what career he wished to follow and was, in a sense, marking time. Teaching at the academy gave him the opportunity, too (whether or not this was consciously intended), to try out, in a limited way, one career option, that of academia. Then, too, teaching at the Rugby Academy provided an independent income, with the financial and psychological independence that such a salary represented.

The Rugby Academy for Boys, established in 1865, was located at 1415 Locust Street. It included three schools, designated lower, middle, and upper, and its curriculum was designed to prepare students for employment in business, for technical schools, or for entrance into college. Witmer's classes were in the upper school. He taught at the Rugby Academy for 2 years.[19]

During the first of these years, 1888–1889, Lightner, in addition to his work at the Rugby Academy, took certain courses in the Department (as it was then titled) of Law at the University of Pennsylvania, although he was not officially enrolled in this department.[20] In the fall of 1889, while continuing to teach at the Rugby Academy, he entered the graduate school of the University of Pennsylvania in the Department of

Philosophy, with the intention of working toward an advanced degree in political science.[21] The attraction that pulled him in this direction was doubtless Professor Edmund James, with whom he had studied as an undergraduate.

Apparently, at this period in his life, Witmer was going through considerable inner searching, perhaps experiencing something of a mild crisis, as to what career to go into. He does not appear to have considered medicine, but it is evident from his flirting with the law—and his remembering this some 60 years later[22]—that the legal profession, perhaps in part because of his skill in debate, held a notable appeal for him. Then there were the courses he took in finance, suggesting his consideration of a business career. Finally, we can note his interest in political science, which presumably would have meant, had Witmer chosen to follow it up, an academic position teaching that discipline.

Actually, of course, the field in which Witmer was eventually to locate—academic psychology—was only just then emerging, and the specific profession that he was to follow—clinical psychology—did not yet exist even in primitive form and would not until some years later, when Witmer himself would inaugurate it.

There was, however, one episode during his teaching at the Rugby Academy that clearly foreshadowed Witmer's later clinical interest. In a 1907 article describing the field of clinical psychology, Witmer reported his experiences in 1889 with a boy in one of his English classes who had serious language deficiencies.[23] Witmer undertook to give the lad special tutoring and discovered that although the youth had acute hearing, he had difficulty distinguishing between two similar sounding words. Witmer referred to this condition as *verbal deafness* and attributed it to a defect in articulation. He therefore concentrated on the student's oral articulation and his ability to note differences in similar sounds. The result of Witmer's remedial work was to bring about sufficient improvement in the boy's verbal skills to enable him to enter the University of Pennsylvania the next year.

This is an interesting report. The boy was evidently bright enough but suffered from certain specific verbal difficulties.[24] Today, the boy's problem might be diagnosed as *dyslexia*. Witmer's role in the episode is instructive in revealing several significant things about him. First, it indicates that as early as 1889, Witmer was developing a clinical psychological orientation. Second, it provides some advance hints of Witmer's eventual clinical approach: an emphasis on practical results, on effecting behavioral changes that help the person involved meet real-life goals; an orientation, in doing this, to identify and deal with the immediate maintaining causes of the disturbance; and a willingness to be innovative in seeking methods to effect change.

IT IS UNLIKELY THAT Wilhelm Wundt, when he founded the world's first Laboratory of Psychology at the University of Leipzig in 1879, was aware of the far-reaching scientific revolution that he was ushering in—specifically, the field of systematic experimental psychology. In the same year, 1879, in England, Francis Galton, whose orientation was radically different from that of Wundt, inaugurated a separate but equally important channel in the development of scientific psychology: the study of individual differences. To say that this approach got under way in the year 1879 is, to be sure, an oversimplification of a complex development, yet there is no doubt that Galton was the chief figure in this new direction, and it is also true that 1879 is an appropriate date to mark Galton's pioneering efforts in the study of individual differences, since during that year, he published six papers on psychological topics, and these papers reflected the shift of his interests to psychology from other topics.[25] Unlike Wundt, Galton was not affiliated with a university; rather, he was financially independent, and carried on a long sequence of psychological investigations through his own resources.

It is important to an understanding of the development of scientific psychology in the 1880s and 1890s—and of Witmer's role in the discipline that he was to enter—to emphasize the distinction between the orientations of Wundt and Galton. Although the dichotomy was not new with them, they stand out as prominent examples of the two sides of scientific psychology. These two sides are, first, the study of the psychological nature of humans in general and, second, the study of psychological differences among people. The former approach, which exemplifies the primary orientation of Wundt, is sometimes referred to, for short, as *experimental psychology*, and the latter, which applies to the work of Galton, is typically designated as the field of *individual differences*. The former approach searches for the general laws of behavior—as, for example, the Weber–Fechner law discussed earlier, or the laws of human learning, or the laws of perception, or of other areas, the latter approach, in contrast, aims at the description of individuals and is interested in measuring the various traits and personality dimensions on which people differ. Both approaches are scientifically valid, and in a full portrait of psychology, they are complementary to each other.[26] It will be evident, as this book traces the career of Witmer, that he had a foot in both camps, so to speak, with the emphasis on the experimental side early in his career and on the individual differences side later in—and during most of—his professional life.

The new scientific psychology, especially as espoused by Wundt, found fertile grounds in America during the 1880s—the period during which Witmer was completing his secondary and college education. Three figures, each of whom would play a role in Witmer's career, stand out in retrospect. These three, listed by seniority, are William James, G. Stanley Hall, and James McKeen Cattell. Of the three, Cattell was destined to have the most influence on Witmer.

William James, who would become America's best known psychologist and philosopher, was born in New York City in 1842. His brother, Henry, the future novelist, was born the next year. The family made numerous trips to Europe, and William grew up in a highly intellectual and cosmopolitan atmosphere. He was first inclined to be an artist, but deciding that he lacked the requisite talent, he turned to science, and thence to medicine. He received the doctor of medicine (MD) degree at Harvard in 1869 but was becoming more interested in philosophy. In 1872 he began teaching philosophy at Harvard. His interest in physiology and philosophy coalescing to some degree, he developed and began offering a course, in 1875–1876, titled "The Relations Between Physiology and Psychology."

Two years later, in 1878, he signed a contract with Henry Holt and Company to write a book on psychology. His first paper in the field, "Are We Automata?"[27] was published in 1879, the same year in which Wundt established his laboratory and Galton published in the area of individual differences. Several other papers by James on psychological topics appeared in the 1880s. Although he met Wundt during his travels in Germany and found the meeting pleasant enough, he had little sympathy with Wundt's emphasis on introspective laboratory procedures, feeling that they were mostly a waste of time. In 1889, James was given the title of professor of psychology at Harvard. Note that his interests were not limited, during this period, to psychology in the strict scientific sense; for example, he was instrumental in founding, in the mid-1880's, a society for the study of psychical research—a topic that was to attract him throughout his career.

G. (Granville) Stanley Hall was born in 1844 in a rural community in Massachusetts. After graduating from Williams College in 1867, he spent a year at the Union Theological Seminary in New York. From 1868 to 1871, he studied in Germany, and in 1872, he took a teaching position at Antioch College. While there, he read the first volume of Wundt's new *Grundzüge der Physiologischen Psychologie* and, greatly attracted by it, decided to return to Germany to study with Wundt. However, when he was offered a position as instructor of English at Harvard, he found it expeditious to take that instead. While at Harvard, he got to know James, carried out a study on the muscular perception of space, and received his PhD in psychology—the first in America.

In the same year, 1878, Hall journeyed back to Germany and Wundt. Although not a student in the usual sense, Hall was the first American to study with Wundt. He was somewhat disappointed with Wundt, however, and by 1880, he was back at Cambridge, MA, although without a position. Fortunately, President Eliot of Harvard invited him to give a series of Saturday lectures on education. These were very well received, and as a result, President Gilman of the recently founded (1876) Johns Hopkins University invited Hall to come to Baltimore, MD, as lecturer in psychology. Then, in 1884, Hall was appointed professor of psychology and pedagogy at Johns Hopkins University. In 1887, he founded the *American Journal of Psychology*, America's first technical outlet in the new discipline, and in 1888, he moved to Worcester, MA, as the first president of the newly established Clark University.

JAMES MCKEEN CATTELL was the third and youngest of the key American psychological pioneers listed above. He was born in 1860 and, thus, was 16 years junior to Hall. More at home in the "new psychology" than either Hall or James, he was to be especially significant in the early career of Lightner Witmer.

Cattell's father, William C. Cattell, was a graduate of Princeton University and of the Princeton Theological Seminary. After several years teaching in a college preparatory school, he took a position as professor of ancient languages at Lafayette College in Easton, PA, located about

60 miles north of Philadelphia. While teaching at Lafayette College, William Cattell met and married Elizabeth McKeen, whose maiden name explains the middle name of their first son, James McKeen. Shortly before this birth, however, the family moved to Harrisburg, PA, where the father had accepted a pastorate. The family was there during the fateful battle of Gettysburg (1863) of the Civil War, and the elder Cattell helped take care of the wounded in hospitals at nearby Harrisburg. Later in the same year, after the Confederate forces had retreated, William Cattell, answering an urgent request from the trustees of Lafayette College, returned to that institution as its president.[28]

James McKeen, or Jim, as he was known, entered Lafayette College as a freshman in 1876. After graduating 4 years later, he found himself uncertain as to what field he should follow and, accordingly, left for a year in Europe, evidently hopeful that a period in Europe would help him find a meaningful direction to pursue. During the year abroad, Cattell, then 20 years old, spent most of his time at Göttingen, Germany, where he was greatly impressed by the lectures on psychology given by Rudolf Hermann Lotze. However, Lotze died later in the year, and so Cattell, deciding to spend another year in Europe, went to the University of Leipzig, where he heard lectures by Wundt. However, he did not enroll in the doctoral program at this time.

Largely through the efforts of his father, who was a personal friend of President Gilman of Johns Hopkins University, Cattell was awarded a fellowship in philosophy at Johns Hopkins for the 1882–1883 academic year. Cattell registered for Hall's advanced course in experimental psychology, and during this semester, he made the decision to become a psychologist. When his fellowship was not renewed for the next year, he decided to go back to Leipzig and to work for his PhD with Wundt.

Cattell was a student in the doctoral program at Leipzig from the fall of 1883 until the spring of 1886, when he received his PhD. He was the first of a number of Americans (Hall's earlier stay being largely perfunctory) who journeyed to Germany in the latter part of the century to study experimental psychology with the master. Note that this general trend was a phenomenon not limited to psychology. As observed earlier, PhD-level graduate schools were developed in Germany in the latter half of the nineteenth century, and it was only in certain German and Austrian universities that advanced training in most sciences and in the medical specialties could be obtained. Even when this was not the case, such German training carried with it considerable prestige. Thus, by 1880, about 400 Americans were registered in graduate work in Germany and Austria, equaling the number of such students in the United States.[29] Further, it has been estimated that between the middle of the nineteenth century and World War I, about 50,000 Americans sought higher degrees in German and Austrian universities.[30] Cattell, in choosing to study in Germany, was thus in tune with the times, although a pioneer insofar as psychology was concerned.

Cattell's period at Leipzig was highly successful. He carried out a number of experiments and proved adept in improving and developing various items of laboratory instrumentation. Less than a month after he began his studies, Wundt invited him to dinner at his home, and this was repeated many times. Eventually, Cattell taught Wundt's daughter, Lolo, to skate and later took Wundt's family rowing on the same river on which they had skated.

In July 1885, Professor Wundt asked Cattell to become his laboratory assistant. Although the position carried no pay, it was a distinct honor, especially in that Cattell was to be the first such assistant, and Cattell was glad to accept the offer.[31] His duties, however, were not to begin until the fall semester, and in the interim, Cattell returned briefly to the United States and also spent some time in England. During the latter period, he met Francis Galton, whose work on the psychology of individual differences was by now attracting considerable attention. Back at Leipzig, Cattell had the tasks of directing the new students in the laboratory and of completing his own dissertation and exams.

After completing his work at Leipzig, Cattell went to Cambridge University, in England, where he fell in with James Ward and other faculty interested in the new psychology. He helped set up a psychology laboratory at Cambridge and might have stayed there permanently had such a position been available. However, he was also hopeful that something might turn up at the University of Pennsylvania, in part because his parents had now settled in Philadelphia. His father, too, was strongly desirous that Jim might obtain a position at Penn, and he had approached the provost, William Pepper, whom he knew from his own college presidency.

The major influence on Cattell during his period in England was Francis Galton. Indeed, the appeal to Cattell of the scientific orientation of Galton proved stronger than that of Wundt. Cattell, working with

Galton at the latter's laboratory in South Kensington, England, became deeply imbued with Galton's approach, which included several key features. First, data were typically collected from a large number of persons on multiple variables; second, the measures obtained included both simple anthropometric (e.g., height, weight, and maximum dynamometer, or squeeze pressure) and sensory (e.g., reaction time and visual judgment) variables; and third, the data were analyzed statistically, to point up central tendencies and dispersions of individual values and any interrelationships among variables.[32]

In late 1886, while in England, Cattell received word of his appointment to the University of Pennsylvania as lecturer on psychophysics. As it turned out, however, he did not actually leave England until December 1887, to offer his lectures. Then, in April 1888, as soon as the spring term ended, Cattell returned to Cambridge University to resume his work there and also to be near his English fiancée, Josephine Owen (Cattell and Owen were married in December of that year). In November 1888, Cattell received word from Fullerton that the University of Pennsylvania had established a professorship in psychology, and that he, Cattell, was in line for the position. Cattell accepted the offer, and the appointment was made official by the Board of Trustees on January 1, 1889.[33]

Thus it was that when Lightner Witmer enrolled for graduate work at the University of Pennsylvania in the fall of 1889, there was a new man, James McKeen Cattell, with the title of professor of psychology, on the faculty of the philosophy department.[34]

3

Philadelphia and Leipzig

The new man at the University of Pennsylvania, Professor Cattell, was at the time the best trained psychologist to be found anywhere; he was the only expert in the new psychology to have studied with both Wundt and Galton. He had already published several papers and was personally acquainted with most of the top psychologists in Germany, England, and the United States. Along with Professor Fullerton, whose training was in philosophy but who was also well read in the new psychology, Cattell's appointment made the University of Pennsylvania probably the strongest university in America in the field of psychology.

When Witmer entered the graduate school in the fall of 1889, he also held his teaching position at Rugby Academy for Boys; he was thus in the same position as are many contemporary graduate students, in that he had to work while going to school. In returning to Pennsylvania as a matriculate in the Department of Philosophy, Witmer's intention, as already noted, was to major in political science under Professor Edmund James. It is not clear when or under exactly what circumstances this aim was modified. It is possible that Witmer interested himself immediately in the offerings of the new Professor Cattell.[1] Further, recall that Witmer had previously taken work with Fullerton and was positively impressed by him. It is reasonable to suppose, then, that possibilities for Witmer in experimental psychology became evident to him in a positive way early in the 1889–1890 school year. At the very least, Cattell's presence furnished definitive evidence of the existence of a vocational field, experimental psychology, that Witmer almost certainly had never previously considered and also provided an outstanding role model for that vocation.

Then, too, there was the practical problem of earning a living. The previous year, right after graduation with his AB, Witmer had taught at the Rugby Academy for Boys, and he was doing so now while in graduate school, but as many later students were to discover, this is a difficult situation under which to do serious study. What would be desirable would be a paying assistantship. Such positions were very rare then, but one was available for Cattell to dispense. Fullerton played the key role in steering Witmer into it. In Witmer's words, "He it was who asked me to become an assistant in psychology, to Cattell, one condition being that I change my major from Political Science under James to Experimental Psychology."[2]

This assistantship, to become effective June 1890, was for the next school year, 1890–1891, and the catalog listings for that year, under "Instructors: in the College Department," include the entry "Lightner Witmer, AB, Assistant in Psychology."[3] Quite possibly, Witmer was the first student in the United States—the first in a very long and distinguished line—to hold the formal position of psychology assistant (as distinct from a fellowship). The special stipulation—that Witmer, if he were to be the assistant in psychology, must have that as his major— was certainly reasonable, but it is interesting also in that it indicates that Witmer's actual entry into psychology was occasioned in part by the very down-to-earth need for the additional income that would be provided by an assistantship. This observation is not to suggest that his attraction to psychology was not genuine, but it does illustrate that the crucial choice points of a person's life are governed not only by one's interests and aspirations but also by the circumstances that unexpectedly present themselves.

The influence of Cattell on Witmer's decision to enter the new field of psychology was doubtless very great, and probably decisive. As a friend of Witmer was to write many years later, Cattell "fired young Witmer's imagination to such a degree that the student determined to follow in the footsteps of the teacher."[4] Thus, it seems very likely that if Cattell had not come to the University of Pennsylvania when he did, Witmer would not have become a psychologist.

In June of 1890, Lightner's brother, Ferree, completed his work at the Philadelphia College of Pharmacy and received the PhG degree. Then that fall, at the same time that Lightner began his year as psychology assistant, Ferree entered the University of Pennsylvania's School of Medicine. Both brothers listed their address as 1734 Park Avenue; probably this means that they were living together away from their parents' home.[5]

Cattell, when he received his appointment as professor, had immediately set about planning for a psychology laboratory at the University of Pennsylvania, and even while still in Europe, he arranged for the purchase of certain key apparatus from Carl Krille, Wundt's instrument maker. The university contributed $500 toward equipment, and Fuller and Cattell managed to raise nearly $3,000 from private sources,[6] plus some support from the Seybert fund and a grant from the Bache fund, for additional instrumentation. Thus it was that Witmer found himself working in what was doubtless the best equipped laboratory in the world except for that at Leipzig. Probably, Witmer himself, under Cattell's direction, helped arrange and calibrate the new instruments.

The new laboratory, along with relevant graduate instruction, was housed in two rooms on the second floor of the new (since 1884) Biological Hall.[7] Cattell modeled the laboratory after that of Wundt's facility at Leipzig, and although the research program that he inaugurated included further work on psychophysics, some of the work clearly showed the influence of Galton. Thus, Witmer, as assistant, was assigned to collect data on individual differences—using "all classes of persons"[8] as subjects—in reaction time.

Cattell's growing commitment to the Galtonian paradigm was further reflected in an important article that he published in 1890 in the British journal *Mind*. The article was titled "Mental Tests and Measurements" and set forth in some detail a proposed battery of mental tests.[9] From the historical perspective, this article was a classic: It paved the way for the development and expansion of the psychological study of individual differences in the United States, and it added a term, *mental tests*, to the psychological vocabulary. In the article, Cattell recommended specific test measures on which individuals could be compared.[10]

During the 1890–1891 academic year, Witmer, we may assume, was deeply involved in his graduate studies in psychology. Although it is not known precisely in which of Cattell's courses he was a student, most likely these included Scientific Methods in Psychology, Experimental Psychology, Special Psychological Problems, and Advanced Psychology. In addition to his course work, he was carrying out research under the direction of Cattell and performing such duties in his role as psychology assistant as were assigned. Witmer was one of four students in the new graduate program in psychology at the University of Pennsylvania, and the only one primarily interested in psychology (two of the four were clergymen, and the other was a student of philosophy).[11] It is not surprising that he was the one given the assistantship.

At this point one would be inclined to suppose—certainly Witmer must have so supposed—that his life now had a certain predictable direction: He would proceed in his work with Cattell, eventually writing his dissertation, and then, with his University of Pennsylvania PhD, he would seek a teaching position. This reasonable expectation, however, was not to be realized. In the fall of 1890, Cattell was approached by authorities from Columbia University in New York and invited to join their faculty as professor of experimental psychology, at the outstanding salary of $2,500 per year, a dramatic advance over his salary at the University of Pennsylvania. After some hesitation, Cattell accepted the offer, with the resignation from the University of Pennsylvania to be effective in June 1891.

Several possibilities, in principle, were now open to Witmer: He could continue in graduate school at Penn, working with Fullerton and James; he could go to Columbia University with Cattell; or he could seek some kind of employment. The University of Pennsylvania also faced a problem. Having made the decision to offer graduate work in psychology and having invested considerable effort and funding in this area, there was undoubtedly a reluctance to suddenly terminate the program.

THE SOLUTION THAT WAS worked out was that Witmer would go to Leipzig to seek his PhD under Wundt—it was conceived that this would take about 18 months beyond his graduate work at Penn—and then, if successful, would return to direct the psychology laboratory at Penn. It is not clear whose idea this was or just what negotiations were involved, although two influences are obvious: First, it was something that Witmer was willing to do; and second, both Cattell and Fullerton thought very highly of Witmer. Fullerton had known Witmer for some time, was very involved in the psychology program, and—one can assume—would have hated to see it fold. Cattell, for his part, had invested considerably of himself in the Pennsylvania laboratory and undoubtedly wished it to continue, especially since he was leaving the university somewhat in the lurch by going to Columbia. If he were to be replaced, who was to be selected? Experts in the new psychology were very rare, and Witmer, who was well along in his doctoral studies, was a known quantity and was familiar with the Pennsylvania laboratory. One essential part Cattell himself must have carried out: He was the one who knew Wundt, and it can be surmised that he must have corresponded directly with Professor Wundt and strongly recommended Witmer to him.

All in all, the plan seems to have been very sensible. Witmer's salary as an assistant for the period that he was in Germany was to be raised to $800 per year so that he could afford to go.[12] To Witmer, the arrangement, once the disappointment of not working with Cattell had passed, must have seemed an extraordinary visitation of good fortune.

Before leaving for Germany, Witmer had completed four semesters of graduate work in psychology under Cattell, four in philosophy with George Fullerton, four under Edmund James in political science, and two with Edward Reichert (of the medical faculty) in physiology.[13]

WITMER LEFT THE UNIVERSITY of Pennsylvania in February 1891 and set out for Germany.[14] The steamer on which he booked passage was *The Russia*, bound for Hamburg. He was assigned to share a cabin with a stranger, who proved to be a man named Joseph Collins, a young physician from New York who was on his way to do graduate work in medicine at Frankfurt. Here is the way Collins, some 40 years later, described this initial meeting:

> The cabin to which I was assigned was empty and I went to bed and to sleep. When I awakened in the morning, I saw in the bunk opposite mine what seemed to be a fair and beardless youth. He was sleeping soundly so I thought it cruel to disturb him, so I tried to be the traditional mouse while dressing. I was opening the door stealthily when the sleeper called out, "Why hurry, you won't get there for a fortnight." That was my introduction to Lightner Witmer.[15]

At this time, Witmer was 23 years of age, and Collins was 24. The two young men became good, and eventually close, friends. During their stay in Europe, they kept in touch with each other and toured certain regions together. The fact that Collins, like Witmer, was traveling to Europe to engage in advanced study illustrates the fact, noted earlier, that in this period of history a large number of Americans were taking advantage of the advanced status of many German academic institutions. Collins's aim was to learn more about the brain and nervous system. In addition to studying at Frankfurt, he would also spend some time at the nearby University of Heidelberg.

While there are no personal letters or reminiscences to frame the occasion, it seems probable that Witmer was very favorably received by Wilhelm Wundt at Leipzig. After all, James McKeen Cattell, who in a sense was Witmer's sponsor, had been one of Wundt's favorite students. Further, Witmer was arriving as an advanced student, already familiar with many of Wundt's conceptions and laboratory procedures.

WUNDT IS TYPICALLY PRESENTED in textbooks as a pedantic, authoritarian, and altogether *professorial* person (in the more compulsive connotation of this label). Whereas there is some truth to this characterization, it is also true that Wundt could be very warm, took great personal interest in his students, sometimes had them to his home for Sunday dinners and on holidays, and followed their later careers with avid interest. In keeping with the pattern of the German university system, Professor Wundt was both a commanding and a demanding figure, to be approached by his students with considerable deference and formality. There was never any doubt who was in charge of his laboratory. Yet within the context of this implicitly recognized differential status, Wundt could be extremely supportive. For example, Charles H. Judd, who obtained his PhD under Wundt in 1896, wrote the following in a later reminiscence:

> I suppose I should never forget my examination. . . . I had done the proper thing of course and appeared at two P.M. in a dress suit and white gloves. The gloves ripped just as I went into the examination. . . . I doubt whether I should ever have come through if there had not been some very good psychology exhibited on the part of my first examiner [Wundt]. He asked me as his first question what

part of the United States I came from. Fortunately I knew the answer to this question.[16]

Wundt was born in Germany in 1832. He obtained an MD degree from Heidelberg in 1856 and in the next year was appointed *Dozent* (lecturer) at the same institution. In 1862, in a preliminary indication of an interest in psychology, he offered a course titled Psychology as a Natural Science. Then in 1873–1874, Wundt published his monumental *Grundzüge der physiologischen Psychologie*, and in 1875, after a period at the University of Zurich, in Switzerland, he was called to the philosophy chair at Leipzig. Although Wundt began experimental work in his first year at Leipzig, the formal opening of his *Psychologisches Institut* (Psychological Institute) is usually accepted as 1879, as noted earlier. During Wundt's early years at Leipzig, Gustav Theodor Fechner was also living there, although he was to die in 1887. In its early period, Wundt's laboratory was very primitive, but eventually it achieved a level of sophistication, in terms of equipment and space, that made it the model of later psychological laboratories throughout the world.[17]

Wundt himself was a tall, somewhat slender man. His facial features were rugged and clear-cut, and he wore thick, heavy glasses and a full beard. His usual suit color was dark gray, and he walked with a slight stoop. He was strongly committed, not only to his laboratory and the experimental approach that it reflected but also to the theoretical system that he was developing.[18]

One aspect of his system concerned the concept of attention. To study the various facets of attention, Wundt undertook to measure the time required for different mental processes, through the determination of reaction times under certain different conditions. For example, suppose a person is instructed to press a button when a light goes on. The reaction time tends to be longer when the person's attention is directed toward the anticipated sense impression than when it is focused on the movement that is to be made. Strenuous efforts were expended to increase the precision of the apparatus for measuring small units of time. The primary instrument in this endeavor was the Hipp chronoscope, which had been designed and manufactured by Mathias Hipp, a German watchmaker, and was calibrated for measures in terms of milliseconds. An important characteristic of Wundt's research approach was the assumption that people could be trained to take and maintain given mental sets and to report accurately, from their own conscious introspections, on certain mental processes.

It was Wundt's custom, when a new group of students arrived, to assign each of them a preliminary laboratory project to work on. These projects, not surprisingly, typically derived from his own theoretical system. Generally, he had a dozen or more new graduate students each year. Other American students whose periods at Leipzig overlapped with that of Witmer were Frank Angell, who left as Witmer was arriving; Howard C. Warren; Edward B. Titchener; E. A. Pace; and Edward Wheeler Scripture. The general practice was for the students to serve as subjects for each other. The type of projects conducted in Wundt's laboratory, based as it was on the man in general rather than on the individual-differences paradigm, typically required only a few subjects, sometimes only one or two.

WITMER MATRICULATED IN philosophy at the University of Leipzig on April 17, 1891, and established residence at R. Schumann-strasse 4.[19] In his first semester (termed summer 1891), he took seminars on Experimental Psychology (Wundt), History of Educational Theory (Richter), and Pedagogy (Masius) and courses on Introduction to Experimental Psychology (Külpe), History of Monarchy, Aristocracy and Democracy (Roscher), Aesthetics (Seydal), and Psychology (not otherwise identified; Strümpell). Quite a heavy schedule! Of these various instructors, Wundt was, of course, head of the Psychological Institute, although the department was still designated as philosophy, not psychology. Külpe, then 29 years of age, had completed his doctorate under Wundt in 1887, and was destined later to leave Leipzig and gain considerable eminence in his own right; he was now *Dozent* and assistant in the Psychological Institute, having succeeded Cattell in this position. Strümpell was a rather famous pedagogist in the tradition of Johann Friedrich Herbart. It is interesting that Witmer, during his first semester, engaged in the study of aesthetics, which was later to be the subject of his dissertation.

During his second semester (winter 1891–1892), Witmer was enrolled in the History of Modern Philosophy and in the Psychological Laboratory, both with Wundt; two courses in education, under Professors Masius and Richter; a course in Psychology (not otherwise identified) by Dr. Külpe; and a course on the Philosophy of Law, under Professor Fricker. In his final semester (summer 1892), Witmer took only one formal course, Introduction to Philosophy and Logic, under Wundt. He was, of course, busily occupied on his dissertation during this period.

In looking over this overall curriculum, one is struck by the emphasis that Witmer devoted to education, or *pedagogy*, as it was then known. It may be presumed that this emphasis was not unrelated to Witmer's later strong interest in educational issues, in general, and in working with the behavior problems of children, in particular. One notes also the course on law, suggesting that Witmer's earlier interest in this area had not entirely disappeared. With respect to Wundt, many psychologists might be surprised to note how many courses he taught outside the strict boundaries of experimental psychology.

At the University of Pennsylvania, Witmer had worked on an assignment from Cattell, collecting reaction time data from a large number of subjects in the individual differences paradigm. Evidently, he proposed to Wundt that he continue something along this line at Leipzig, perhaps for his dissertation. However, Wundt, as Witmer wrote later, "wouldn't hear of this being a psychological problem and banned it immediately, his idea being that experimental psychology was really based on the conscious reaction of subjects and required concurrent introspection."[20] Actually, this reminiscence, written many years later, seems hardly fair to Wundt in view of the fact that the dissertation that Witmer eventually conducted, which was suggested to him by Wundt himself, did not focus on introspection (in the usual psychological meaning of this term) and gave considerable attention to individual differences, as will be seen shortly.

Witmer's feelings toward Wundt were ambivalent. On the positive side, he clearly had great respect for the older man and for his rigorous research methods, as indicated by various positive remarks that he made about Wundt early in his teaching career at Penn. On the negative side, he was genuinely repelled by what he saw as Wundt's dogmatic insistence on his own perspective. In the 1948 letter to E. G. Boring, Witmer recalled that Wundt

made Titchener do over again an investigation on reaction time because the results obtained by Titchener were not such as he, Wundt, had anticipated. Also, he excluded me as a subject, or rather my reaction times when I worked for Titchener because in his opinion my sensory reaction to sound and touch was too short to be a true sensory reaction. He advised me to get a cardboard pendulum and practice so as to increase my reaction time and presumably make it truly sensory. I was disgusted at this suggestion; it seemed to me that if my sensory reaction time was X-sigma, I could easily learn to delay the reaction making it X plus Y sigma.[21]

Witmer also made the following comment in the same letter:

I certainly owe one thing to Wundt. He suggested as an experimental thesis an investigation of the aesthetic value of the 'Golden Section' in simple geometric forms. I not only made up a lot of the material myself, but I went to see Fechner's widow and secured from her some of his material which I still have.[22]

Fechner, it may be recalled, was the founder of the fields of psychophysics and of experimental aesthetics. A longtime professor at Leipzig, Fechner was particularly interested in aesthetics when Wundt arrived there in 1875. Wundt had long had great respect for Fechner, who was 31 years his senior, and it is not surprising that he suggested a continuation of Fechner's research on aesthetics to Witmer. Fechner had died in 1887, 4 years before Witmer arrived.

WITMER'S DISSERTATION WAS published, in two articles, in Wundt's journal *Philosophische Studien,* under the title "Zur experimentallen Aesthetik einfacher räumlicher Formverhältnisse" [On the Experimental Aesthetics of Simple Spatial Relationships of Form].[23] Witmer indicated his indebtedness to Herrn Professor Wundt, "under whose supervision this research was conducted," and also acknowledged the help of Herrn Assistenten Dr. Külpe and Herrn Mitgliedern of the Psychological Institute.[24] In addition, Witmer expressed his appreciation to Frau Professor Fechner and Professor Dr. Kuntze, Fechner's literary executor, for providing him with unpublished manuscripts on aesthetics by Fechner.[25] In addition to these articles in German, Witmer wrote a long abstract of his research in English for the *Psychological Review,* a new American journal that Cattell and James Mark Baldwin had founded in 1894.[26]

In the first of his two articles in *Philosophische Studien,* Witmer reviewed Fechner's work establishing the field of experimental aesthetics and summarized certain previously unpublished work of Fechner.[27] In describing a key experiment on form perception by Fechner, Witmer reported that Fechner used as subjects 228 men and 119 women. This is a very considerable number of subjects. Presumably, the reason that Fechner made use of so many participants was that not everyone responded in the same way. This suggests that the common assumption among historians of psychology—that German psychology of that period was completely antagonistic to the recognition of individual differences—is misguided. To be sure, Fechner was not primarily interested in individual differences as such, yet clearly he was well aware of their importance.

The purpose of Witmer's study was to investigate the aesthetic value of different visual forms as a function of ratios among certain of their dimensions. Although a variety of forms, including lines and crosses, were used, the emphasis was on rectangles. Since the time of the classical Greeks, there has been a notion that the degree of aesthetic pleasure to be derived from a line or a geometric figure (e.g., a rectangle) is in some manner a function of the relative proportions of its dimensions. The alleged ideal ratio has traditionally been referred to as the *golden section*; this is defined as obtaining when the ratio of the smaller dimension is to the larger dimension as the larger is to the sum of the dimensions, or, as it works out, .618. Thus, to have the golden section in a rectangle, the width of the figure should be .618 of the length. Fechner constructed rectangles of varying proportions and determined which ratio subjects reported most pleasing. His results, as already indicated, showed notable individual differences, but the mode was a ratio of .62.[28]

Whereas Fechner's primary method had been to present the subject with two figures and ask which he or she preferred, Witmer laid a number of figures before the subject, who stood looking down at them, and asked him (Witmer's subjects were evidently all men) to indicate the one that he found most pleasing. Witmer used eight different series of figures, some cut out of cardboard and others drawn with black ink on white paper. The eight series included enclosed figures (rectangles, triangles, and ellipses); a straight line (55 mm) divided into two segments at various points; right angles with different lengths of lines; horizontal lines with a perpendicular drawn at various points; and several more complex figures.

Witmer used a total of 14 subjects, but not all participants evaluated all stimuli. To assess the stability of the evaluations, Witmer presented the same rows of stimuli two or three times with large temporal spacing, so that the participants' memories of their original choices would presumably be erased. He concluded, however, that the choices were so stable that the replicative procedure seemed superfluous, and accordingly, only 6 of the participants evaluated all stimuli more than once.

Witmer found two modes of judgments for the most pleasing proportions: One of these was when the sides of the rectangle were equal, that is to say, a square; the second was when the ratios of the shorter to the longer side ranged from .57 to .65 for the different experimental series, with an overall average of .61 (essentially the same as reported by Fechner and as the classical golden mean, or a ratio of approximately 3 to 5). Witmer concluded that it was best to conceive of a range of preferred ratios, rather than a single point, because the curve of aesthetic preference fell very slowly on either side of its apex. He rejected the notion that the most pleasing proportion was due to some mystical principle in the universe manifested in mathematical relationships and suggested that future research would probably reveal a multiplicity of causal physiological and psychological factors.

The significance of individual differences in the proportions judged to have maximal aesthetic value was particularly interesting to Witmer, due in part, no doubt, to his earlier training under Cattell. He wrote that "individual personalities became a factor"[29] in the choice of ratios judged most pleasing, and provided a figure to illustrate graphically the range and variations in aesthetic preference among subjects. Witmer also speculated as to the causes of individual differences. At one point, he suggested that "the obtained individual differences could possibly be explained by physiological differences in the functioning of the organs of individuals (e.g., eye movements)."[30] On a more idiographic level, Witmer noted that one participant reported that he could not see a cross (one of his stimuli) without surrounding it with flowers; another subject might see a cross and be reminded of a cross in his hometown square.[31] As another example of idiosyncratic factors contributing to individual differences in perception, Witmer observed that if a picture of a person was shown to a tailor, the tailor might find it pleasing simply because the person was well dressed. From a broader perspective, the education and social standing of a subject, Witmer suggested, might influence his aesthetic preferences.

Although hardly epochal in its ramifications, Witmer's dissertation was a solid piece of research, performed at a point in the history of psychology when rigorous, painstaking, precise data gathering and data analysis had only recently come into vogue.[32] Probably, the main thing that Witmer himself got out of his dissertation—this, probably, is true of most new doctorates—was a heightened respect for rigorous experimental standards and some special skills in how to conduct research.

Witmer's dissertation was adjudged to be highly praiseworthy (*admodum laudabilis*). His doctoral orals were administered on July 18, 1892, by a committee composed of Wundt, Masius, and Fricker. His performance earned him the distinction of magna cum laude. The formal doctoral diploma was awarded on March 29, 1893, at the end of the academic year. By this time, Witmer had, of course, long since been back in the United States. Along with the PhD degree, Witmer received the title of *Magister* (master). This is the basis on which Witmer, in later biographical entries, properly listed himself as having received the MA degree in Leipzig in 1892, the same year he completed his doctorate. At the University of Leipzig, the two distinctions had been combined for some time.

WITMER WAS A TOURIST and visitor, as well as a student, during his period in Europe. On one occasion, he journeyed to Munich, Germany, where he saw Baron Carl DuPrel, who was then a leader in the popular spiritualistic movement.[33] It is doubtful that he went to Munich solely to see DuPrel, since Witmer was not attracted to the tenets of spiritualism. Nevertheless, he obviously was sufficiently intrigued by the spiritualistic perspective to take the opportunity to talk with one of its leaders. It is important, as a way of putting this whole matter in some perspective, to point out that during this period in history, there was a tremendous interest in spiritualism in both Europe and America. One manifestation of this vogue was the bequest, in 1883, of $60,000 (a tremendous sum in those days) to the University of Pennsylvania by Henry Seybert, with the understanding that the fund would be used, in part, to conduct a systematic study of spiritualism. Witmer commented later on his contact with DuPrel:

> I was interested even then in what I later called Clinical Psychology, so I told DuPrel that I was there in Germany studying experimental psychology under

Wundt on the Seybert fund, to which his reaction was that the income of the
Seybert fund was being stolen by Dr. Pepper for purposes alien to the fund.[34]

The striking part of this statement is the revelation that Witmer, even
while studying experimental psychology, was interested in the yet unborn
field of clinical psychology. Of course, one does not know the degree of
his interest, and his comment is in any event a retrospective one, but it
is certainly an interesting remark. DuPrel's charge that Pepper, the university provost, was out of line in supporting Witmer on the Seybert
fund, as he evidently was, seems not to have been justified, because
Pepper had been given considerable latitude in expending the fund. Further, the university had in fact set up a committee, under the chairman-
ship of Pepper and including Fullerton and Weir Mitchell (a well-known
Philadelphia neurologist), which conscientiously examined the claims of
spiritualism and later issued a detailed negative report.[35]

Witmer also took advantage of his period in Europe to visit some of
the famous cultural highlights with his new friend Joseph Collins. Later,
in recalling some of their experiences together, Collins wrote the following:

I would rather walk the Louvre or the Uffizi with Witmer than anyone I know.
Had I never heard of Giordano Bruno or Pico della Mirandola, I know of no
one who could inform me so lucidly of what they represented than he.[36]

This interesting comment identifies an aspect of Witmer's personality—
an interest in artistic and humanistic matters—not previously observed
in these pages.

In addition to Collins, there was another friend of Witmer's in Europe
at this time: William Newbold (briefly mentioned in chapter 2). He had
been an undergraduate at the University of Pennsylvania during the same
period as Witmer and had graduated a year ahead of Witmer. Newbold
had then taught Latin for 2 years at the Cheltenham Military Academy
and, at the same time, was enrolled in graduate work in philosophy at
the University of Pennsylvania. In June 1891, he had received his PhD
for his dissertation, "Prolegomena to a Theory of Belief," and was now
at the University of Berlin for further study.[37] Berlin is not far from
Leipzig, and it seems probable that Newbold and Witmer may have seen
each other and possibly traveled together during their period in Europe.

In addition to the students in Wundt's program who were later to
become eminent psychologists, there were two whose period at Leipzig

overlapped with that of Witmer but who were later to follow quite different careers. One of these was the American Lincoln Steffens, who was later to make his mark as a journalist focusing on sociological issues and whose *Autobiography*[38] would be an important contribution to American letters. Steffens, as a young man seeking basic answers to fundamental ethical and personal issues and having failed to find these in his philosophical courses at the University of California, had now come to the mecca of the new psychology in Leipzig. Unfortunately, he was again disappointed.[39]

The other student whose presence in Wundt's laboratory seems, in retrospect, somewhat unexpected was the German Hugo Eckener. This remarkable young man (he was 1 year younger than Witmer) did his doctoral research on the rate of fluctuation of attention.[40] Becoming interested in the design and construction of airships (this was, of course, before the Wright brothers and airplanes), he joined Count Ferdinand Graf von Zeppelin's firm and later played the leading role in the extensive development and use of Zeppelins early in the twentieth century. Eckener commanded the *Los Angeles* in its trans-Atlantic flight in 1924, as well as the *Graf Zeppelin* in its historic globe-circling flight in 1929 and was in command of the ill-fated *Hindenberg* (although not on board) when it exploded and burned at Lakehurst, NJ, in 1937. Witmer and Eckener maintained contact over the years, and Eckener came to visit Witmer in Philadelphia on at least one occasion.[41]

Witmer was 25 when he completed his work at Leipzig in 1892 and headed for home. He did not go directly back to the United States, however, but paused in London, in August, to attend the meetings of the International Congress of Experimental Psychology. This was the second international meeting of the budding new science. The first had been held in 1889, at Paris, and was known as the International Congress of Physiological Psychology. Later congresses are referred to simply as International Congresses of Psychology. At the 1892 London Congress, Witmer presented a paper, his first as a professional psychologist, based on his dissertation research, "The Aesthetic Value of the Mathematical Proportions of Simple Figures:—A Contribution of an Experimental Aesthetic."[42]

WITMER'S TRIP FROM LONDON back to the states and the University of Pennsylvania represented for him a brief transition between the ending of one chapter of his life and the beginning of another. Blessed now with the imprimatur of a PhD from the world's leading Psychological Institute, his vocational decision now irrevocably behind him, and looking forward to working with the facilities of an excellently equipped laboratory, Witmer, it may be surmised, must have felt considerable satisfaction and enthusiasm as he anticipated the new academic year at the University of Pennsylvania.

4

Professional Beginnings

American psychology continued its rapid growth in the early 1890s, and in the spring of 1892, G. Stanley Hall, in his third year as president of Clark University, sent invitations to at least 26 persons interested in the new psychology to come to Clark on July 8, to consider the formation of a national organization. The meeting was accordingly held, probably in Hall's study, although the attendance was very sparse, with most of those invited being unable, or perhaps in a few cases not wishing, to be present.[1] Among those in attendance, in addition to Hall, were Fullerton, who served as chairman, and Joseph Jastrow, who was appointed secretary. A committee, to consist of Hall, Fullerton, Jastrow, James, Cattell, James Mark Baldwin, and George T. Ladd,[2] was set up to make further plans; additionally, it was decided, on invitation from Professor Fullerton, to hold the first annual meeting of the new organization at the University of Pennsylvania in the coming December (1892).

It was further determined at the organizational meeting that in addition to those present, all persons who had responded positively to the original invitations would be considered as charter members of the association. Witmer was listed in the later proceedings of the association[3] as such a member, from which it can be inferred either that he had sent his acceptance by mail from Germany or—what is probably more likely—that Fullerton had accepted on his behalf.[4]

The year 1892 also marked important changes in university psychology programs, not only at the University of Pennsylvania but also at Harvard, Stanford, and Cornell. The change at Penn was, of course, the beginning of the stewardship of Witmer. At Harvard, the important event was the arrival of Hugo Münsterberg, to take over the direction of the psychology laboratory.

It will be recalled that William James had agreed in 1878 to do a book on psychology and that in 1889, his academic title had been changed to professor of psychology. This was the year before the book finally appeared, in 1890, so that James was identified in the book by his new title.[5] The work, *Principles of Psychology*,[6] encompassed two volumes and was recognized immediately as something of a classic—as, indeed, it is still, over a century later. William, like his brother Henry, was a masterful writer, so that he could put psychological issues, and their possible resolutions, in ways that grabbed and held the reader's attention. Curious about, and tremendously insightful into, every facet of human nature, James approached psychology with a kind of sophisticated common sense.[7] He reported relevant experimental and empirical data whenever they seemed pertinent and available but did not feel dependent on them.

Although James did not feel at home in the psychological laboratory and felt that much of the experimental work going on in the field was pointless, he did accept, at least in principle, the importance of objective research. Too, he felt a great deal of loyalty to Harvard, and it was important to him that Harvard be second to none in the new experimental psychology. Further, after completing the *Principles*, James's primary scholarly interest shifted from psychology to philosophy. For all of these reasons, he wished to bring in someone to take over the psychology laboratory at Harvard, so that he could concentrate on philosophy. The man he selected for this choice position was Hugo Münsterberg.

Münsterberg, a native of Germany, had earned his PhD under Wundt in 1885 and had then gone to the University of Heidelberg, where, in 1887, he received his MD. He then took a position at the University of Freiberg, in Germany, where he engaged in a scientific dispute with Wundt that led to certain ill feelings between them. James, in spite of —or perhaps in part because of—this antipathy of Münsterberg toward

Wundt, evaluated Münsterberg very highly and invited him to come for a 3-year appointment at Harvard.[8] Münsterberg accepted, and in August 1892, he sailed for America.

The American student Frank Angell, who had been at Leipzig before Witmer, and who left there with his doctorate shortly after Witmer arrived, took a position at Cornell. This was in 1891. In the same year, a new university, Stanford, was established in California. Stanford's president, David Starr Jordan, who, perhaps incidentally, had been a student at Cornell, wished to develop a psychology program at Stanford, and in 1892, he invited Angell to become its head. Angell accepted and went there the same year.[9] To take his place at Cornell, Angell recommended Edward Titchener, an English student with whom he had come to be quite friendly during their overlapping periods under Wundt at Leipzig. Titchener accordingly was invited to Cornell and accepted the position there. Although Titchener had begun at Leipzig well before Witmer, he completed his doctorate there the same year, 1892 (presumably because Witmer had done prior graduate work), and he arrived at Cornell in time for the fall session.

It thus happened that in 1892, four university psychology laboratories —those at Pennsylvania, Harvard, Stanford, and Cornell—were taken over or inaugurated by Wundt graduates. In addition, Cattell was already at Columbia, and Hall, who had studied briefly with Wundt, was at Clark. Further, within the next few years (before 1900) H. K. Wolfe, E. A. Pace, E. W. Scripture, H. C. Warren, H. Gale, G. T. W. Patrick, G. M. Stratton, C. H. Judd, and G. A. Tawney, Wundt students all, would be going, respectively, to Nebraska, Catholic University, Yale, Princeton, Minnesota, Iowa, California, Chicago, and Beloit.[10] It would seem, certainly, that American psychology was being constructed on a solid Wundtian base. In fact, this was to prove true only in part: The Americans enthusiastically imported Wundt's passion for experimentation, for objectivity, and for scientific rigor; however, the substantive and theoretical directions that they were to pursue, after their first few years away from Leipzig, were hardly those of Wundt. Instead, these would be shaped by new ideas, new discoveries, new fashions in thought, and, perhaps most of all, by the deeper ethos of the American culture.

WITMER RETURNED TO Philadelphia in time for the 1892 fall term. His new title was lecturer in experimental psychology.[11] The *Uni-*

versity of Pennsylvania Catalog for 1892–1893 indicates that during the first term, he offered a course on mental measurements, to include "lectures, reports and advanced work in the laboratory," and, in the second term, he offered a course on experimental psychology, described as including lectures and laboratory work, and another course on experimental aesthetics, described as including lectures with demonstrations and experiments.[12] This latter course was clearly a follow-up of his dissertation interests and probably included some of the experimental procedures he had developed in Leipzig.

Witmer's new residential address was 4215 Chester Avenue,[13] on the university side of the Schuylkill River. Probably he took rooms at this location to be nearer the university than he had been before going abroad. It seems almost certain that his residence was separate from that of his parents, because it was a long way from his father's business. Possibly, Lightner and Albert lived together at this new address. Albert was now in his last year of medical school. This calls our attention to the fact that the senior Witmers, during the previous 2 years, had two sons in graduate school at the same time, one in Germany and one in Philadelphia: a family circumstance that must have been very rare in those days, which also must have constituted something of a burden on the family finances, especially since their daughter, Evelyn, was attending a private school. The situation had, of course, been helped considerably by the fact that Lightner had been on the salary of an assistant, an arrangement that amounted to his having a fellowship, during his period in Germany.

Although Lightner had already entertained certain thoughts that later, in retrospect, he would identify as having presaged his ultimate interest in applied psychology, he was, at this point, the new man from Leipzig, a strictly experimental psychologist, enthusiastically imbued with the spirit of laboratory research. These conclusions are evident from his work and publications during his first few years on the University of Pennsylvania faculty.

Soon after his return, Witmer resumed experimental work in the psychology laboratory.[14] It is noteworthy that he presented two experimental papers at the first meeting of the APA, which took place at the University of Pennsylvania in December. Conceivably, he may have collected additional experimental data after his return from Leipzig, before the meeting.

The first meeting of the new national organization, which covered two days (December 27 and 28, 1892), was a historic one. It was here that the name American Psychological Association was formally adopted. Annual dues were set at $3. Several new members, including William Newbold of the University of Pennsylvania philosophy faculty, were elected. G. Stanley Hall was chosen as president, and George T. Ladd was chosen as vice president. A total of 12 papers were presented at the Philadelphia gathering.[15] Of these, one was by Hall[16] ("Historical Prospects of Experimental Psychology in America"), and this served as the presidential address. Another was presented by Cattell[17] ("Errors of Observation in Physics and Psychology"). Other papers, in addition to the two by Witmer (reviewed below), included one by Jastrow[18] ("Experimental Psychology at the World's Fair") and one by Münsterberg[19] ("The Problems of Experimental Psychology").

Before discussing Witmer's papers, a few comments may be made about Jastrow's interesting presentation, the content of which helps frame the historical period. Jastrow had been a student of Hall's at Johns Hopkins at the same time that Cattell was there. After taking his doctorate there in 1886, he had gone, in 1888, to the University of Wisconsin as professor of psychology. By 1892, he, like Cattell, had become very interested in mental testing, along the lines pioneered by Galton. Now it happened that in 1893, Chicago was to host a world's fair, called the Columbia Exposition, to mark the 400th anniversary of Columbus's discovery of America. The various sciences were invited to set up exhibits, and the one on psychology was to be directed by Jastrow. The exhibit would include not only various devices used in psychology laboratories but also—and more dramatically—facilities by which visitors to the fair, for a small fee, could be tested on such individual-differences variables as dermal sensation, accuracy of movements without the guidance of the eye, accuracy of vision, memory, and quickness of perception. As in the earlier work of Galton and Cattell, these measures were concerned mainly with the simpler sensory and motor functions and had little to do with the higher mental processes. The Chicago exhibit was patterned after Galton's earlier collection of data at South Kensington and was an indication of the growing interest in mental testing in America.[20]

Witmer's two papers at the December APA meeting in Philadelphia constituted, in effect, his introduction to the American psychological community. Although he had previously presented a paper at the Lon-

don International Congress, as reported in the preceding chapter, the
APA papers were more significant in that they were on his home ground.
Copies of the two papers do not survive—indeed, they may have been
delivered extemporaneously, from notes. However, the abstracts in the
Proceedings provide a summary of each paper's contents. The first paper,
titled "Some Experiments Upon the Aesthetics of Simple Visual Form,"
reported some follow-up research on Witmer's dissertation topic, although it is unclear whether the research had been performed at Leipzig,
after completion of his dissertation, or in Philadelphia, after his return.[21]
The summary in the *Proceedings* is not informative with respect to methodology or subjects, but it does report certain factors that Witmer felt
affected the pleasingness of a perceived figure. His main conclusion was
that "a figure of less pleasing proportions falling within a border of
similar proportions (the border of the sheet of paper on which the figure
is drawn, for example) will be chosen rather than a figure of more pleasing proportions within a border with whose proportions those of the
figure do not correspond."[22] In other words (although Witmer did not
put it in quite these terms, which came into use only later), the pleasingness of a figure is a function, not just of the figure as such, but also
of the ground on which it appears. Witmer also suggested that eye movements might be crucially involved in aesthetic judgments.

The second of Witmer's APA presentation, titled "The Chronoscopic
Measurement of Simple Reactions on all Classes of Persons," was a report on the investigation under way in the University of Pennsylvania
laboratory on the reaction times of "all classes of persons."[23] This research was probably an extension of the work that Witmer had been
conducting under Cattell's supervision before going to Leipzig. The specific question addressed by the data that Witmer presented concerned
the comparative reaction times of persons to stimuli of sound, light, and
electric shock. Although the study was incomplete, the preliminary research indicated that the reaction time to electric shock was shortest
(i.e., fastest) and to light stimulus was longest (i.e., slowest), with the
auditory stimulus in the middle. These findings were in accord with
what earlier investigators had found, and Witmer never published his
data beyond the values given in the abstract.

IN THE FALL OF 1892 and early in 1893, Witmer found himself
faced with an unexpected academic problem. The difficulty, which prob-

ably caused considerable—albeit only transient—stress, concerned the status of his work with Wundt at Leipzig. Though he had completed his work there, and his dissertation had been scheduled for publication in *Philosophische Studien*, he had not yet received (so one may infer from the available correspondence) formal notification of the acceptance of his dissertation and, thus, of his degree. On November 10, 1892, Witmer wrote (in German) a letter of inquiry to Wundt. In it, he stated that he had received word from Germany "according to which someone heard in Leipzig that my work had been of so little value that there was doubt that I would receive the doctorate with the dissertation. May I ask you to inform me in this matter. I have received the impression that you judged my work as being of scientific value."[24]

Witmer went on, in this letter, to comment on affairs at the University of Pennsylvania. He wrote that he had been "so occupied with college and preparations that scientific research is minimal and accompanied with great difficulties. Two classes are keeping me busy; one postgraduate class, candidates for the doctorate of philosophy, 12 students in number, of whom three are able to carry out independent research, and one undergraduate class of 20 students."

On January 18, 1893, Witmer wrote again to Wundt. Since his earlier letter, he had received a postcard from Wundt that indicated that a letter was following. Witmer now wrote, however, that he had not received that letter and thought it might somehow have been lost, particularly since he—Witmer—currently had two apartments and mail was being delivered to both (presumably this meant that he was in the process of changing residences). This little episode, with its quaintly human overtones, illustrates also something of the delays in trans-Atlantic communication in that long-ago era. In the letter, Witmer also reported to Wundt on the just-concluded meetings of the APA, noting that a number of Leipzig alumni were in attendance. In addition, he commented at some length on his developing research program at the University of Pennsylvania and on a special pendulum that he had constructed for his Hipp chronoscope. There were, according to Witmer, 10 projects currently under way in his laboratory, half for student exercises and half for research. "As a whole," he concluded, "I am content with the number and the quality of the students. In the beginning we can only follow very slowly the pace of the Leipzig laboratory."

Although further correspondence is not available, and possibly never existed, the matter that had concerned Witmer proved groundless: He received his doctorate, and his dissertation was published. Presumably, the clarifying letter from Wundt arrived shortly, despite the problem of two apartments. One is left wondering, though, as to the source of Witmer's concern about his status.

AT PHILADELPHIA, WITMER, with Cattell having moved to Columbia, was the only experimentalist, although his friend Titchener was at Cornell. Another experimentalist with whom Witmer developed a personal relationship was Hugo Münsterberg, the German psychologist who, as noted earlier, had accepted William James's invitation to join the faculty at Harvard on a 3-year trial basis and had begun his tenure there in the fall of 1892, at the same time Witmer was taking over at Penn. A number of letters, from Witmer to Münsterberg, which help to delineate this relationship and which throw additional light on Witmer's activities during this period, have been preserved.

It is possible that Witmer and Münsterberg, who was Witmer's senior by 4 years, met while Witmer was still in Germany, and it is even conceivable that they traveled on the same ship to the United States in August of 1892. In any event, they certainly came in contact with each other at the inaugural meeting of the APA, held—as noted earlier—at the University of Pennsylvania in December 1892. Münsterberg was welcomed as a guest in America and was asked to address the meeting. In his remarks,[25] he took the position that experimental psychology should become broader and should investigate "the entire circle of psychological problems."[26]

Witmer's letters to Münsterberg during 1893, from which the following selections are drawn, were nine in number, ranging in time from January 10, 1893, to the following July 14.[27] In the first of these, only a couple of weeks after the APA meeting, Witmer, recalling that Münsterberg planned to travel "southward," invited him to stop in Philadelphia and stay at the University Club as his (Witmer's) guest. For some reason, however, Münsterberg postponed his trip, and Witmer, after receiving Münsterberg's response, wrote (January 31) expressing his disappointment and suggesting that Münsterberg come early in March, when they could go on to Washington and see the inauguration of Grover Cleveland as the President. Witmer also commented on some work he was doing on attention, which he would like to discuss with Münsterberg.

A brief period ensued during which Münsterberg was ill. Then, after receiving word from Mrs. Münsterberg that her husband was recovering and was thinking of visiting New York, Witmer wrote to Münsterberg (March 6) that "I am afraid you have been working too hard. You put to blush even Americans by the amount of work you can do." He offered to meet Münsterberg in New York but urged him to spend a week in the warmer climate of Philadelphia. Further correspondence (March 10 and March 14) implies that the two young psychologists, along with Münsterberg's wife, did meet and dine together in New York.

Witmer's next letter (March 30) leads to the inference that Münsterberg raised with Witmer the possibility of Witmer's coming to Harvard, presumably in a letter now destroyed. The position, one gathers, would have been under Münsterberg, working in his experimental program, and on a year-to-year basis. It is impossible now to know whether Münsterberg's invitation to Witmer was firm, based on consultations with James, or merely an opening discussion. In any event, Witmer took it as a serious proposition. The following excerpts are selected from Witmer's long letter of response (March 30):

My dear Professor,

I have taken a long time to consider the proposition made by you in your recent letter—too long you may think. But you made it impossible for me to talk the matter over with anyone, and I found it required much thinking over to arrive at a decision. I believe I now see quite clearly my answer to your proposal. I have decided that I cannot accept the instructorship at Harvard if offered me. My reasons are two in number.

1. I signed a contract with the University of Pennsylvania, the terms of which are somewhat as follows. I agreed to study abroad for a year and a half receiving $800 a year. At the completion of this time, I agreed to teach psychology at the Univ. of Penn. for three years: two years at a fixed salary as lecturer, the third year as Ass. Prof. with salary undetermined. This is the first year of my term of instruction. Considering the fact that the Univ. of Penn. maintained me abroad for 1½ years, I feel morally bound by the terms of this contract. . . .

2. Another consideration—a personal one—also influences my decision. I fully appreciate all the advantages of the position in question—a connection with Harvard University, the opportunity for original research, the possibility of succeeding you. . . . the opportunities for original research in your laboratory are surpassed nowhere; if I had means, I would willingly devote my life to original research excessively. . . . Your offer is consequently very attractive to me. I feel too

that I could work *with* you with pleasure and profit. But I cannot work *under* anyone—not even under you. The feeling of independence is something, and I have just discovered that it would be unpleasant, even impossible, for me to give up the freedom I enjoy here. It isn't that I am Director of the laboratory and represent experimental psych.—I care but little for official position. But here I am completely my own master—the work in exp. psych. is in my own hands. I am compelled to account to none but those who selected me. . . .

In conclusion, I have to express my appreciation of the honor you have done me, and the pleasure your high opinion of me gives me. I thank you greatly for the offer you have made me, which I value so highly that it was only after much deliberation, that I was able to reach the decision that I have just communicated to you.

Münsterberg, after receiving Witmer's letter, again wrote him urging him to come to Harvard, and Witmer again declined (April 9), referring, among other things, to the greater security he had at Penn. In a letter of May 27, Witmer commented enthusiastically on the World's Fair in Chicago, from which he had just returned and which the Münsterbergs were planning to visit. In the final letter in the series (July 14), Witmer remarked at length on some more personal matters:

I am down here at the [word unclear] Biological laboratory of the University, where I have a room for myself. I am dissecting a human head—working out especially the muscles of expression with their vascular and nervous supplies. I am also at work on the [word unclear] general physiology. I want to study the mental accompaniment of any physiological excitation. Later I propose experimenting on myself and others with drugs to study the accompanying feelings. In psychology proper, I am at work on the emotions and the will [here Witmer briefly comments on some theorizing by Münsterberg on pleasure and pain, and then proceeds as follows].

I am using myself as *Versuch* [next word unclear, but the obvious meaning is "experimental subject"] in experiments on pleasure and pain. I let a horse throw me from his back, allowing me to drop on my shoulder and head. I showed a beautiful loss of consciousness before the act. I was thrown while mounting— that is, the horse ran about 50 yds. while I tried to get my seat, and then threw me over his head. I not only do not remember mounting and the horse running, but I forget almost everything that happened that evening. . . . Besides this, I have cut my foot badly and have a few other ills and aches. The psychological side of my afflictions will form the basis of at least three lectures next Fall.

These letters from Witmer to Münsterberg during 1893 provide a fascinating glimpse into Witmer's personal life during his first year as a faculty member at the University of Pennsylvania. And while it is unfortunate that Münsterberg's letters to Witmer were not also preserved, it seems evident, from Witmer's letters (including what may be read between the lines) that both men were making overtures toward what they hoped would be a permanent friendship.

As noted earlier, Münsterberg, in 1892, had accepted a 3-year trial appointment at Harvard. As 1895 approached, the question of Münsterberg's status naturally arose. In a confidential letter to Harvard's president Eliot, dated February 21, 1895, James discussed, in a very candid way, the possible men who might be offered the position.[28] Münsterberg, he felt, was clearly the top choice, with Baldwin a close second. Cattell he didn't seriously consider because he would probably not wish to leave Columbia. Witmer he described as "energetic, intelligent, but not heavy weight." Titchener was seen as "very energetic and reputedly a great success as a teacher, but apparently not original in the way of ideas and (although from Oxford) quite a barbarian in his scientific and literary manners, and quarrelsome in the extreme." Jastrow had "a narrowish intellect," and Scripture was "energetic but shallow, and a complete barbarian."

As it happened, Münsterberg went back to Freiburg for 2 years but returned to Harvard on a permanent basis in 1897.

FOR WITMER, THE NEXT few years were a time of adapting to the new role of a university faculty member. The transition from graduate student to staff is a fairly straightforward one, since the two roles include many overlapping behaviors, yet there are also major differences in the two roles—in responsibilities, prestige, and self-image, and as well as in behind-the-scene politics and competitions. No doubt Witmer, especially because he was in charge of an excellent laboratory and had experienced the ego-boosting correspondence with Münsterberg, found the change both exciting and rewarding. His salary for the 1893–1894 academic year was $1,500, which, while not munificent, was a notable increase over the $800 he had received as an assistant.[29] In a letter to Cattell, Witmer remarked (in a complaint that has been echoed by innumerable beginning academics) that although he liked teaching, his classes left little time for original work, especially because he was endeavoring to get his students started on their own experimental research.[30]

In his second faculty year, 1893–1894, Witmer offered two undergraduate courses on Experimental Psychology, one including material on the physiology of the nervous system and sensation and the other focusing on perception, and the same two advanced courses (Experimental Psychology and Experimental Aesthetics) that he had given the previous year.[31] Probably, it was in connection with these courses that Witmer began the preparation of a set of illustrative experiments that later would result in the publication of a manual for students in experimental courses. In 1894–1895, Witmer and William Newbold, who had joined the faculty the same year that Witmer had, were both promoted to the rank of assistant professor.[32] Together with Fullerton, as chairman, Witmer and Newbold constituted the faculty of the Department of Philosophy. Newbold's title was assistant professor of philosophy; Witmer's title was assistant professor of psychology. The catalog for the 1894–1895 school year listed, in the college offerings, General Psychology under Newbold and Experimental Psychology under Witmer. Witmer also offered, at a more advanced level, a Systematic Course in Experimental Psychology, Special Topics for Class Experimentation, a Seminary [seminar] for the Study of Child-Psychology, and Individual Laboratory Work.[33]

Attention is drawn, in particular, to the third of these, the Seminar for the Study of Child-Psychology (hyphen in original). This is the first formal evidence of Witmer's special interest in children. The 1894–1895 university catalog does not offer a description of the seminar, but the 1895–1896 catalog, which lists the same course, includes a one-paragraph synopsis, which states that the course is "for teachers, and others who have special opportunities of observing children." Students were expected to do experimental work with children either in the schoolroom or in the laboratory, and the topics chosen were to be "such as have an immediate bearing upon pedagogical psychology."[34]

One of the students, in particular, in Witmer's summer 1895 class in child psychology made a lasting impression on Witmer. This was George Twitmyer, then principal of the Honesdale, PA, schools. As Witmer wrote many years later:

In 1895 I was conducting courses in child psychology and making a few tentative efforts toward the clinical study of individual children. Dr. Twitmyer was not only the most active and appreciative student of that year's summer school, but he himself seized upon the clinical method and applied it himself subsequently in the schools of Bethlehem and Wilmington.[35]

In the years ahead, George Twitmyer's son, Edwin B. Twitmyer, would become Witmer's closest and most valued collaborator.

For the 1895–1896 year, Witmer added a course titled, "Reading of a German Work on Psychology." The book to be read was *Zur Analyse der Empfindungen*,[36] by Ernst Mach. This book, originally published in 1886, was a highly provocative work—actually, it is still considered important—focusing on the analysis of sensations from the positivistic perspective. The book is essentially a methodological tome and argues that sensations, based on direct observation, constitute the basic data of science.

Although Fullerton was the department chairman during this period, he left the running of the laboratory to Witmer, and all of the more advanced courses in psychology, after Witmer arrived, were given by him. Further, Fullerton, who had been dean of the graduate faculty since 1888, became, in 1894, dean of the college and vice provost. Although he stepped down from the deanship in 1896, he continued as vice provost.

In addition to his regular classes, as just discussed, Witmer took an active part in a special program that the university inaugurated in 1893 to provide continued education for local public school teachers. These classes, for the convenience of the teachers, were given in the evenings and on Saturdays. It was his participation in these classes (as is elaborated in the next chapter) that provided the catalyst for the origins of his Psychological Clinic.

In 1893, the university of Pennsylvania had granted its first PhD in psychology. The recipient was Caspar Wistar Miller. Miller had earned his bachelor of philosophy degree at the University of Pennsylvania in 1890 and in 1894 would receive an MD from the same institution. It is evident that he was working on his PhD and his MD at the same time. After 1894, he would leave psychology and spend his entire career in the medical area.[37] Nevertheless, his brief period in psychology, because of his dissertation and his relation to Witmer, is of considerable interest.[38]

In the fall of 1892, Witmer had just returned from Europe and begun his tenure as a faculty member. Fresh in his mind was his dissertation research on the pleasingness of various figures, which, although completed, had not yet been published. In some manner that cannot now be reconstructed, Miller became interested in Witmer's topic and decided to undertake his own research in the area. Very probably, Miller had already taken graduate psychology courses with Fullerton, and it is conceivable that he was, so to speak, looking for a dissertation topic when Witmer returned. It is also possible that Witmer and Miller had been acquainted even before Witmer went to Europe.

Miller's dissertation examined individuals' reported preferences for rectangles of various proportions, horizontal lines intersected at various points, and vertical lines intersected at various points (crosses).[39] In accord with Witmer's emphasis on the importance of individual differences, Miller gathered a large number of subjects—731 in all, comprising 496 males and 235 females, including students at the University of Pennsylvania, the Episcopal Academy, the Pennsylvania Academy of Fine Arts, the Carlisle Indian School, Philadelphia's House of Refuge and Almshouse, and a local grammar school. Miller found large individual differences and observed no support for the classical golden section. In general, the square was the most pleasing figure, especially for younger subjects.

THIS WAS A TIME IN Western thought during which there was tremendous interest in certain esoteric perspectives on human nature. This interest was particularly prominent in France, where the theoretical formulations of Jean-Martin Charcot, Pierre Janet, and Alfred Binet and others on hypnosis, hysteria, and dissociation, received wide attention. Notions such as the subconscious, the unconscious, automatic processes, and hypnotic phenomena were widespread in the intellectual world, although Freudian theory had not yet emerged to exploit such concepts. For the most part, these themes did not appeal to Witmer.[40] The one excursion that he made into the realm of unusual mental phenomena was the development of an interest in hypnosis, which he was later to employ occasionally in his practice.

At the theoretical level, Witmer turned his attention, in 1893–1894, to the psychology of pleasure and pain. Although it is not known specifically why these areas so attracted Witmer, it is notable that they were highly topical in psychology at that time.[41]

On February 16, 1894, Witmer delivered a talk on pleasure and pain before the Section on Neurology of the New York Academy of Medicine. His remarks, which were summarized in the March 15 issue of the *American Medico-Surgical Bulletin*, were directed at clarifying certain interpretations made by neurologists as to psychologists' conceptions of pleasure and pain.[42] Following Witmer's presentation there were three discussants—H. R. Marshall, C. L. Dana, and Joseph Collins—whose remarks were also published in brief. The fact that Witmer's friend Collins was one of the discussants leads to the speculation that Witmer's invitation to speak may have been arranged by Collins.

A longer, and presumably complete, version of Witmer's New York Academy paper was published in the April issue of the *Journal of Nervous and Mental Diseases*, under the title "The Psychological Analysis and Physical Basis of Pleasure and Pain."[43] Before examining the substance of this paper, a few words of background are in order. There was, at this time, great interest in the concept of "sensation." Sensations were considered by many psychologists to be the basic elements of awareness and were conceived to have the dimensions of *quality* (in the sense, e.g., that the visual sensing of blue is different from the auditory sensing of a tone) and *intensity*. This analysis was congruent with a wide range of phenomenal experiencing, but a knotty problem arose: Are pains and pleasures sensations? Or are they better viewed as a third dimension, conceptualized as a *pleasure–pain* variable, of all sensations? Marshall,[44] during the period under discussion, was the strongest exponent of the position that a hedonic quality, some feeling of agreeableness or disagreeableness, was an integral part of all sensations. He referred to this conception, which he derived primarily from introspective analysis, as the *quale theory*.

Witmer objected strongly to this theory. In particular, he criticized the notion that the matter could be adequately resolved by introspective analysis. He argued that it was just as reasonable to conceive of pains as sensations in their own right as it was to think of, say, visual phenomena as sensations. He was also very skeptical of the conception, represented in quale theory, that pleasures and pain represent, in some basic sense, different points on the same underlying feeling continuum. In the past several years, there had been a great deal of physiological research on the issue of pain receptors and neural tracts, and Witmer's paper showed familiarity with this technical literature.

The Second Annual Meeting of the American Psychological Association, as noted above, was held in New York in 1893. Witmer attended this meeting, although he did not present a paper. The third annual meeting, in December of 1894, took place in Princeton. Witmer did not attend, and the minutes state that papers offered by Jastrow, Delabarre, Titchener, Pierce, and Witmer were not read. Witmer did attend the fourth APA meeting, held on the University of Pennsylvania campus in December of 1895. Cattell was president of APA at the time, and he gave the presidential address.[45] Fullerton was elected president for 1896. Witmer presented a paper titled "Variations in the Patellar Reflex as an Aid to the Mental Analysis," but he evidently failed to send an abstract to APA's secretary in time for it to be printed in the proceedings.[46] This is unfortunate, because it would be interesting to know the precise nature of Witmer's paper, especially since a few years later Edwin B. Twitmyer would do his dissertation on the patellar reflex. Witmer also sponsored a paper by his student Oliver Cornman on the processes of ideation.[47]

The 1895 APA annual meeting also saw the appointment of an important committee on psychological tests. Cattell, following his 1890 paper on mental tests, had strongly espoused the development and use of tests to measure various physical and mental capacities, and after arriving at Columbia, he organized a research project to further this aim. Indeed, at this same APA meeting, Cattell's younger associate at Columbia, Livingston Farrand, gave a preliminary report on the Columbia project.[48] In a number of other psychology departments around the country, too, interest with tests was growing. The interest was, of course, an aspect of the broader individual differences movement. The purpose of the committee was "to consider the feasibility of cooperation among the various psychological laboratories in the collection of mental and physical statistics."[49] The members of the committee were to be Baldwin, Jastrow, Sanford, Witmer, and Cattell, with the last serving as chairman. Note that the *tests* referred to were not tests in the later sense of intelligence tests, personality tests, and the like. Rather, following Galton, they were primarily sensorimotor tasks (e.g., reaction time, sensory discrimination, and speed of movement).

In 1894, Witmer published an article in the new *Psychological Review* on a control instrument for the Hipp chronoscope.[50] To explain the modification that Witmer proposed, a few introductory comments on this famous instrument will be helpful. Early experimental psychology placed strong emphasis on the measurement of reaction times, and the premier instrument for this task was the Hipp chronoscope, which was calibrated in $1/1,000$ of a second. This instrument was found in all the better psychological laboratories of the period. The Hipp chronoscope, in appearance, was about 2 feet high. It consisted of a square wooden base, with beautifully beveled wood columns at the corners; at the top of the columns was a platform on which stood the clockwork. A weight, which furnished the motive power for the apparatus, descended from the midst of the clockwork, in the center of the supporting columns. The movements in the clockwork were regulated by a spring adjusted to make 1,000 vibrations per second. The apparatus included two electromagnets, wired in such a way that they governed the beginning and ending of the passage of recorded time. Additional, complementary instrumentation was required to transduce stimulus onsets and response onsets to the chronoscope.[51]

To operate the Hipp chronoscope in a reliable manner, it was necessary to assess its accuracy periodically to correct for any constant error. This had conventionally been done by recording the time it took an object to fall a given distance, a technique of this sort having been developed by Cattell. Witmer now designed and constructed a metal pendulum to serve the same control purpose. As well as can be judged from his article, the pendulum worked successfully and was used thereafter at the University of Pennsylvania, at least to some extent at Columbia, and perhaps elsewhere.

During 1895, Witmer published a highly critical review of two articles by van Biervliet that had appeared in *Philosophische Studien*.[52] The purpose of van Biervliet's studies was to investigate the relation of reaction times to pulse rates, and his conclusion, according to Witmer, was that in general, reaction time diminished as pulse rate increased. Witmer argued, however, that this conclusion was not justified, because of the large variations in the data.

This completes the survey of Witmer's publications through 1895. Note that although the greater part of his overall career would be devoted to clinical psychology, he had, by 1896, established a solid reputation in experimental psychology.

THIS CHAPTER FOCUSED ON Witmer's early career in academic psychology. From the narrative perspective, however, this was not the only current of importance to Lightner in the mid-1890s. There were also significant family matters. His younger brother, Albert Ferree, who was a student in the University of Pennsylvania Medical School when Lightner returned from Europe, graduated with his MD degree in 1893,[53] and in the fall of the same year, Evelyn Witmer entered the Biology School of the University of Pennsylvania.[54] In 1894, Ferree took a position as instructor in physiology at the University of Pennsylvania. This meant that for a period, three of the Witmer children were associated with the University of Pennsylvania, and all in Biological Hall: Ferree as instructor in physiology, Evelyn as an undergraduate student in biology, and Lightner as assistant professor of psychology. The fourth sibling, Paul, did not attend the University of Pennsylvania, although he later earned a doctoral degree in pharmacy.

One gathers that the younger Witmers were all extremely bright; their academic achievements, certainly, would suggest this. Their parents must have been pleased with them and proud of their own sense of accomplishment through their children's advances. There were other familial changes too. Grandmother Maria Witmer died in 1895; her husband, Grandfather Elam, had died 9 years earlier, in 1886.[55] In 1895, also, the senior Witmer, David, had switched from a retail pharmacy to the wholesale pharmaceutical business.[56] Evidently he was doing well.

By 1894, Lightner's friend Joseph Collins had settled in New York City and set up a medical practice. Because Collins is a major figure in the present account, a few words about his background will be helpful. He was born in Brookfield, CT, in 1866 and, thus, was a year older than Witmer. After being raised on a farm and attending public schools, Collins spent 3 years teaching in a boys' private school in Danbury, CT. He then attended the University of Michigan in 1884–1885, but transfered to New York University the next year. Here, he received the MD degree in 1888. After several years of general practice, Collins went to Europe (as recounted earlier), to engage in graduate study of the nervous system. This topic continued to challenge him after his return to New York, and eventually, in the latter 1890s, it became his major field of practice.

It is through a reminiscence of Collins, many years later, that we can gain some additional insight into what Witmer was like in the 1890s. Collins, looking backward in 1931, wrote of Lightner as follows:

> For many years, we spent our holidays together. When we returned from Germany, we went to and through the Adirondacks on bicycles which, in those days, were devoid of brakes. His favorite method of going down steep hills was with legs on the handlebar. When we went to a livery in the Berkshires or in South Carolina to hire saddle horses, I would ask for a gentle, sure-footed beast and he would ask for one with a bad reputation. I have seem him shoot the rapids of the Allagash River in a canoe when it seemed to me and to my guide that it was an even bet that he could not possibly go through without a spill. He was keen on play those days: tennis, golf, riding, tramping, and best of all loafing.[57]

5

The First
Psychological Clinic

During the early years of his tenure at the University of Pennsylvania, Witmer had structured his career strictly in the mainstream of the new experimental psychology. His articles and presentations had been frequent and well received. He was a charter member of APA, and although still quite young (he was only 28 in 1895), he had been appointed to an important APA committee. Further, he held one of the more prestigious chairs in American psychology and was in line for eventual promotion to full professor.

Certainly, it would have been predicted at this time that Witmer would continue working from an experimental, laboratory-oriented perspective and probably would become one of the leaders in the new scientific psychology. Indeed, such a prediction would not have been altogether amiss. He did continue with laboratory work, and as late as 1904, he presented a paper on psychophysics at the 13th Annual Meeting of the American Psychological Association.[1] Further, as is evident in the chapters to follow, Witmer always maintained, in his own mind at least, a strong identification with laboratory-based research.

Nevertheless, there also existed in Witmer this other, this more practical, more person-oriented interest that has been noted earlier in previous chapters. Here, briefly, is a summary of the earlier indications of Witmer's interest in working directly with people in some kind of helping relationship. First, there was his inclination toward a career in the law, a motivation so strong that he remembered it vividly in his latter years. Even his passing undergraduate flirtation with business and political science bespeaks an orientation toward an applied career. Next, there was his interest, when he was teaching at the Rugby Academy, in working with a boy who had learning problems. Later, when he had had this same boy in a class at the University of Pennsylvania in 1894–1895, he was again intrigued and challenged by the young man's limitations. Then, according to his later testimony, Witmer, while in Germany, was thinking of what was later to become clinical psychology. These early clues to his future course, based as they were on his recollection some years later, may have been somewhat altered in the process of recall; however, they were not at all implausible. Indeed, the implausible thing would be for Witmer's interest in an applied, helping vocation to have appeared suddenly, without a prior period of incubation.

Although this applied perspective in Witmer's thinking had lain dormant since 1890, when he became assistant in psychology under Cattell, it now began to reassert itself. One manifestation of this interest was a focus on child psychology. As already noted, Witmer began offering a seminar in this area in the 1894–1895 school year.[2] Interest in the psychology of children was not unique with Witmer, as it was an emerging field in the early to mid 1890s, stimulated largely by the broader child study movement. While Witmer himself had never taken a course in child psychology as such, his courses in educational psychology at Leipzig undoubtedly included extensive material on developmental psychology. These courses should be given considerable weight in tracing the process of Witmer's professional development. Before he went to Germany, he had no training whatsoever in practical, applied psychology; at Leipzig, however, he took four courses in education, and educational psychology is preeminently an applied discipline. Further, Germany was then probably the leading center for the study of pedagogical principles. Although specific information on the content of the four courses that Witmer took in education is not available, it can be assumed that they included material on the views of such preeminent educational reformers as Johann Heinrich Pestalozzi and Friedrich Froebel and of the influential pedagogical psychologist Johann Friedrich Herbart.[3] One of Witmer's instructors, Ludwig Strümpell, was a well-known pedagogist and a follower of Herbart. Most important, the courses differed strikingly from those of Cattell and Wundt in that they focused on the whole person rather than on psychological processes as such. This earlier academic history, then, can be seen as presaging the shift in Witmer's central interests that was to occur in 1896. This shift was from an exclusive commitment to psychology as a pure science—experimental psychology—to a parallel, and eventually stronger, commitment to psychology as a practical, helping profession.

This chapter focuses on the year 1896, in particular on Witmer's founding, during that year, of a psychological clinic at the University of Pennsylvania. The establishment of the Clinic (as it was called), the world's first, was a major event in the history of psychology, especially in the history of clinical psychology. Thus, it ranks as one of those symbolic points, like Wundt's establishment of the first psychological laboratory 17 years earlier, that will always stand as an important marker in the history of the discipline. This chapter reviews and reconstructs the various events and circumstances involved in the Clinic's beginning. First, however, it will be helpful to briefly consider the overall cultural milieu in which Witmer worked, which provided the intellectual climate in which his innovative ideas could take root and prosper.

COMPLEX EVENTS, SUCH AS the establishment of the first psychological clinic, are invariably multidetermined. Frequently, the critical precursors are the confluence of favorable circumstances in the prevailing cultural currents and the presence of a dynamic, catalytic individual with the insight and verve to make things happen. From this perspective, the characteristics of the larger American society in the 1890s are now reviewed, to point out the factors that made the times propitious for the beginning of a psychological clinic, a facility that had not existed before but that a half-century later would be commonplace.

Benjamin Harrison was president when the decade began. He was succeeded by Grover Cleveland (his second term) in 1893, and William McKinley served from 1897 to 1901, when he was assassinated and succeeded in office by Theodore Roosevelt. Not only chronologically and symbolically, but in actuality as well, the 1890s represented a transitional period in American history. Thus, the historian Henry Steele Commager referred to "the decade of the nineties as the watershed of American history,"[4] before which the nation was primarily agricultural and concerned with domestic problems and after which the primary focus was urban and industrial and on the nation's place in the international community. Similarly, H. Wayne Morgan observed that the 1890s brought a sense of change, along with a feeling of national unity. "Many Americans," he wrote, "sought a larger 'civilizing' mission beyond material success to sustain national vitality."[5]

As the new century approached, the political, economic, and psychological traumas of the Civil War were fading into the past. "Already," wrote Commager, "the war was becoming a romantic memory: its grand figures were writing their stately memoirs, and novelists were celebrating its heroic virtues."[6] Although the nation was not without certain economic stresses, the overall mood of the decade was one of optimism, spiritedness, and vigor. Excitement in the "new psychology" matched the ferment in other fields, and the discipline of psychology was rapidly becoming established as a major area of study in American universities.[7] The production of PhDs in the top American departments was increasing rapidly, with a consequent drastic decrease in the number of Americans going to German universities. At the same time, American universities, including the University of Pennsylvania, were expanding rapidly, especially at the graduate level, and tended to be receptive to new programs and directions. It would seem, then, that the peculiar cultural qualities of the 1890s, particularly in academic circles, provided a welcoming atmosphere for professional innovations, such as Witmer's Clinic was to be.

Another cultural verity, this one particularly endemic to the American ethos, that facilitated Witmer's inception of his Clinic was a pervasive concern with the practical value of actions. It is instructive to note that in 1896, Witmer published an article titled "Practical Work in Psychology"[8] and later in the same year presented a paper on "The Organization of Practical Work in Psychology"[9] at the Fifth Annual Meeting of the American Psychological Association (these two papers are reviewed in the next section). The theme of looking to the practical value of knowledge, of fostering the useful, the utilitarian, was—and is—deeply ingrained in the American psyche, possibly having descended in part from the struggles of the early pioneers in converting a wilderness to a nation. As examples of this national spirit in Witmer's day, there was the practical work of Thomas Edison in nearby New Jersey and the development of pragmatic philosophy in the hands of Charles Pierce and William James.[10] This interpretation can help explain not only the origins of the Psychological Clinic but also the positive reception received by the Clinic and other, similar facilities early in the twentieth century.

A PARTICULARLY IMPORTANT TREND in the wider society that helped set the stage for the emergence of a psychological clinic was the rise, in the 1880s and 1890s, of what came to be known as the *child study movement.* Although interest in the systematic study of children can be traced back to Pestalozzi, in the late eighteenth century, and to Froebel and Herbart, in the early nineteenth century, the more immediate antecedents of the child study movement were Charles Darwin's record of his infant son's development[11] and Wilhelm Preyer's influential *Die Seele des Kindes.* In this latter work, translated as *The Mind of the Child,*[12] Preyer reported detailed observations on the early development of his own child. His book led to a number of biographical, diary-like studies of infant and child development by other investigators.

One of the earliest of these observational studies was conducted by Kathleen Carter Moore, a doctoral student in psychology at the University of Pennsylvania. For her dissertation, "The Mental Development of a Child," Moore carried out systematic observations on her infant son throughout the first 24 months of his life.[13] Although her study was patterned after that of Preyer, it contained considerable original material and can still be read with interest and profit. Moore received her PhD in 1896, the same year in which Witmer founded the first psychological clinic.[14]

Witmer's role, if any, in suggesting, advising, or directing Moore in her study is not known. She was married in 1892 to John Percy Moore, an instructor in geology, and was conducting her research during Witmer's early period on the faculty. He had recently returned from Germany and was doubtless more familiar with child psychology and with Preyer's work than anyone else on the faculty. It is plausible, then, to assume, at the very least, that Moore discussed her research with Witmer and possibly was a student in his seminars on child psychology.

Studies such as those by Preyer and Moore, while of interest primarily to professionals, had little direct influence on the broader child study movement, which swept across the nation in the 1890s. The leading figure in this movement was G. Stanley Hall. Hall's special area of interest was the psychology of children and adolescents, and in 1891, he established the journal *Pedagogical Seminary*. In 1893, he was instrumental in founding the National Association for the Study of Childhood. Once under way, the interest in child study spread rapidly, as numerous groups for the advancement of child welfare and for the study of children were formed throughout the nation. The movement was especially prominent in educational circles, and elementary and secondary school teachers were encouraged to undertake studies of children's behaviors, attitudes, and feelings. Many did so, and although the scientific payoff of these efforts was minimal (for the most part, the studies were marked more by the zeal of the investigators than by the rigor of their method, as indeed was largely true of the research by Hall himself), the effects of the teachers' involvement were to enhance the quality of elementary education and to accentuate the demands for improved education of teachers.[15]

Whether inspired by the peripheral winds of the child study movement or by a broader Zeitgeist, the University of Pennsylvania in 1894 established a chair of pedagogy, which was filled by Martin Brumbaugh. Brumbaugh much later became governor of Pennsylvania, and it is he to whom Witmer's father made the suggestion that railroad tracks be enclosed with fences to protect children. The child study movement can perhaps best be seen as part of a broader movement in Western society for the increased valuation of children and concern for their welfare. Another manifestation of this cultural trend was the establishment, in January 1896, of a new medical journal, *Pediatrics*, devoted to the diseases of infants and children.

Witmer was not personally involved in the child study movement as such; indeed, his personality was not such as suited him to be a follower in any movement. Yet the movement was important in several ways to his founding of the Clinic and his subsequent work with children. Thus, it helped create the public atmosphere in which the idea and acceptance of a child clinic could flourish: This had never been true before. More specifically, the rising interest in the psychology of children was probably instrumental in Witmer's instituting his seminar (as noted earlier) in child psychology in the 1894–1895 academic year. Finally, it was a public school teacher who, imbued with the spirit of the times, first sought Witmer's help (as will shortly be related) in coping with the unusual learning problem manifested by one of her students and thus inaugurated the specific sequence of events that culminated in Witmer's Clinic.

THIS SECTION EXAMINES IN some detail the founding of the Psychological Clinic in the seminal year 1896. One could perhaps quarrel slightly with the use of the word *founding* in this context, if by that term one were to mean a deliberate, carefully planned, formal establishment and announcement of a new venture. There is certainly no evidence that Witmer inaugurated the Clinic in such a public, official sense; nor, indeed, could he have, since its beginnings were necessarily tentative and gradual. Yet it is clear that by the close of 1896, an ongoing clinic, with plans for its continuance, had been established.

It will be recalled that Witmer participated in the special program that his university had set up, to provide special classes for local public school teachers. In the 1895–1896 academic year, he offered an introductory course on psychology for teachers, and six students enrolled.[16] This number is of more than passing interest, because the catalog description of courses for teachers stated that "should the number of students taking a course fall below six, the course may be discontinued."[17] It is intriguing to conjecture that if only five or fewer students had enrolled in Witmer's class, it might have been canceled, with the beginnings of the Clinic quite different than as described below.

The following paragraphs trace, in a month-to-month scenario, insofar as this is possible, the sequence of steps that led to the first psychological clinic. These steps can also be taken to reflect developments in Witmer's thinking during the year.

February 1896. At some point during this month Witmer gave a talk before the Educational Club of Philadelphia. Possibly the invitation to give this talk was stimulated by his course for teachers in the 1895–1896 school year. The contents of this presentation can be inferred from a paper that Witmer published in the following July; this paper, summarized below, included a note that a portion of it had been read at the February meeting of the Educational Club.[18] More important than the content of the talk was the likelihood that it brought him in contact with a wide range of school personnel and thus may have led indirectly to later referrals to him of problem children.

March 1896. Sometime during the month following Witmer's talk a student in one of his classes, who was also a teacher in a Philadelphia grammar school, described to Witmer a difficult problem presented by one of her students. Here is the way Edward P. Cheyney, the eminent historian of the University of Pennsylvania, reported the occasion:

> It was in a course on child psychology given in the winter of 1895–96 by Prof. Lightner Witmer, Professor Cattell's successor, to a class principally of school teachers, that the germ of the Psychological Clinic appeared. One of these teachers described the curious case of a pupil, an intelligent boy, who yet could not learn to read. At the professors request he was brought out for examination and became a long standing problem of much interest.[19]

The name of this insightful teacher was Margaret T. Maguire. According to Witmer, "She was imbued with [the] idea that a psychologist should be able, through examination, to ascertain the causes of a deficiency in spelling and to recommend the appropriate pedagogical treatment for its amelioration or cure."[20]

With this case in March 1896, the work of the Psychological Clinic was begun. At that time, as Witmer was to write later,

> I could not find that the science of psychology had ever addressed itself to the ascertainment of the causes and treatment of the causes and treatment of a deficiency in spelling. Yet here was a simple developmental defect of memory; and memory is a mental process of which the science of psychology is the only authoritative knowledge. It appeared to me that if psychology was worth anything to me or to others it should be able to assist the efforts of a teacher in a retarded case of this kind.[21]

The boy with the spelling problem may be referred to as *Charles Gilman*, the pseudonym used by Witmer himself. Gilman's problem, as it turned out, was not a simple spelling problem but instead was much more complex, as is elaborated in the next section; today it would be termed *dyslexia*, or learning disability. The first case in the history of clinical psychology was thus a boy with a learning disability. Although this diagnosis lacks the high drama of Freud's first case, Anna O., in the history of psychoanalysis—which, interestingly enough, had been reported in just the previous year, 1895[22]—or of the hysterical patients of

Jean-Martin Charcot in the previous decade, it does suggest, by the very fact that it refers to an all-too-common human affliction, the wide range of human difficulties that would come to be addressed by clinical psychology.

Not a great deal is known about this catalytic woman, Margaret T. Maguire.[23] In 1907, Witmer referred to her as "now the supervising principal of a grammar school in Philadelphia."[24] Many years later, in 1931, she was in a still different position, as revealed in this paragraph from a Philadelphia newspaper:

> The woman who offered the first human want and specimen to Dr. Witmer's consideration was Margaret T. Maguire, the red-haired and vigorous principal of the McCall Vocational School at 7th and DeLancey streets, known in public school circles as a militant for better and more specialized pedagogic methods.[25]

Evidently Maguire had lost nothing of her innovative style and caring attitude over the years.

Spring 1896. Gilman was the first, but not the only, problem child that Witmer saw in the spring of 1896. Later Witmer wrote that during that early period, "I saw several other cases of children suffering from the retardation of some special function, like that of spelling, or from general retardation, and I undertook the training of these children for a certain number of hours each week."[26]

July 1896. Under the auspices of the American Society for the Extension of University Teaching, Witmer offered a laboratory course, from July 6 through July 31, on the Methods and Results of Child-Psychology, with a particular focus on the characteristics of defective children and the special methods of training them. Here is the complete course description:

> This course is intended for teachers and students of psychology interested in the modern methods of observing the mental and physical characteristics of children at all periods of their development. Class and individual experiments will be made, not upon children but upon members of the class, serving the purpose of illustrating the methods of experimentation. A feature of the work will be visits to institutions for the training of defective children, for the purpose of studying types of children and the psychology of the special methods of instructing the imbecile and the idiot, the deaf and dumb, the blind and the youthful criminal.[27]

This brief summer course can be seen as a transition between the seminar Witmer had offered earlier on child psychology and the more clearly clinical course he would offer in the summer of 1897. More broadly, it reflects Witmer's growing commitment to practical, helping work with children.

Also in July, Witmer published the paper on the teaching of psychology to teachers that was referred to above in connection with his February talk before the Educational Club.[28] The article included a brief summary of the bright boy with a spelling problem seen in March and also quoted a college president who had attended the July extension course on child behavior to the effect that he had never known that such problems were discussed in psychology. For the most part, however, the article, which paid tribute to Hall and Galton, was a rather academic discussion of the aspects of contemporary psychology that Witmer felt should have a place in psychology courses for teachers. The significance of the article is that it was Witmer's first publication relating psychology to educational practices, a theme that would be prominent throughout the rest of his career.

October 1896. The October 15 issue of the new journal *Pediatrics* carried an editorial by Witmer titled "The Common Interests of Child Psychology and Pediatrics."[29] This paper related psychology to medicine, just as his July paper had related psychology to education. Further, it suggested that psychology should have a key role in working with problem children. Toward this end, Witmer concluded, the pediatrist, the psychologist, and the pedagogue should join forces.

November 1896. In an article in *Pediatrics* one month later, Witmer was more explicit about a possible helping role for psychologists. The article, "Practical Work in Psychology," begins with these prescient words:

> The practical side of psychology deserves serious attention from professional psychologists. The practice of psychology may become as well defined a pursuit of a trained professional class as is the practice of medicine.[30]

Witmer suggested four contributions that "practical psychology can offer in the study of the results of mental training"[31]: first, "the examination of the physical and mental conditions of school children"[32]; second, "the study of defective children"[33]; third, "a psychological museum"; and fourth, "an experimental training school."[34] In the third of these, the psychological museum, Witmer had in mind collections of work done by defective children, apparatus used in teaching them, and research results, exhibited in the form of tables and graphs.

Following the general discussion of the practical contributions that psychology can make in work with children, Witmer presented, by way of illustration, a fairly detailed case study (although not called that) by Mary E. Marvin. The subject was a 10-year-old boy referred to as *P*. Marvin, who had what Witmer referred to as a *cooperative association* with the University of Pennsylvania's Department of Psychology—which meant, of course, with Witmer himself—had developed a specialty in teaching mentally defective children and also in teaching oral speech to the deaf. She had begun working with P in 1892, when he was 7. At that time, the only words he spoke were *papa* and *mama*, and these were spoken inarticulately and without any evident idea of their meaning. His sense of smell was acute, and when his hand came in contact with an object he hastily withdrew it and carried it to his nose. Away from home, he was uncontrollable, and the first impulse, on given any object, was to destroy it with his fingers. His attention span was incredibly brief, but Marvin did discover two activities that held his interest: stringing buttons and playing with balls. He also was greatly attracted by music, and it was said that he could hum most of the tunes he had ever heard.

During the 4 years that Marvin worked with P (typically 3 hours a day, 5 days a week) he made very notable progress. By playing with him, she had gradually gained his affection and then began teaching him speech through music. By June 1894, he could sing "Way Down Upon the Swanee River." Using candy as a reward, she taught him to count to 5. By June 1896, he was able to write all of the alphabet to dictation and could frame simple sentences. Although it is impossible from this distance to form a definitive diagnosis of P, it seems probable that today the child would be characterized as having autistic disorder. Note that Witmer, much later—in 1920—described another child who appears to have been autistic.[35]

Although Witmer does not specifically state that he saw P, it can be assumed that he did, although P was clearly Marvin's case. The important point is that the case made a strong impression on Witmer and, along with the case of Charles Gilman, contributed at a critical juncture to Witmer's growing vision of a new helping role for psychology.

December 1896. On December 29–30, 1896, APA held its Fifth An-

nual Meeting in Boston and Cambridge, with 45 members in attendance. George Fullerton, now the APA president, gave an address on
"The 'Knower' in Psychology".[36] Witmer, on December 29, presented a
paper titled "The Organization of Practical Work in Psychology."[37] This
paper, which called for the application of scientific psychology to practical affairs and which included the first usage anywhere of the term
psychological clinic, has generally—and correctly—been considered as
marking the first call for a new helping profession, although the more
formal designation of *clinical psychology* was 11 years away.[38] Under the
rubric of practical work in psychology, Witmer included the following:

> 1. The direct application, whether by professional psychologists; practicing
> physicians or teachers, of psychological principles to therapeutics and to education.
> 2. Such psychophysical investigation of mental conditions and processes as may
> serve to throw light upon the problems that confront humanity in the practice
> of medicine or teaching.
> 3. The offering of instruction in psychology, to students of medicine or to
> teachers, that contains a promise of future usefulness to them in their respective
> professions.[39]

It is evident from these introductory themes that Witmer had not yet
fully conceptualized, or at least was not yet prepared to announce, his
conception of a separate applied psychological profession. Nevertheless,
we see in the three functions listed above the attributes of practice,
research, and teaching that were later to characterize clinical psychology.
Witmer went on to recommend that a university psychology department
should have a close relationship with the medical school and should have
access to all classes and grades of children, in order to conduct appropriate physical and mental tests. Under the concept of "an experimental
training school" he proposed:

> a. Independent schools or homes for such children as can afford to pay for
> expert psychological and pedagogical treatment.
> b. A psychological clinic and dispensary.
> c. Special or ungraded training schools for children who are backward or phys-
> ically defective [to be controlled by public schools authorities but related to the
> Psychology Department of the local university].[40]

The second of these, a psychological clinic, was already in development at Penn under Witmer's auspices. The first, special private schools

or homes, was possibly suggested in part by Mary Marvin's experience and plans and was some years later to be realized in Witmer's own schools.

Witmer's brief paper, the harbinger of a later large and flourishing field in psychology and modern culture, was, according to widely accepted lore, poorly received by the audience, with the only reaction to his presentation being a few raised eyebrows.[41] This retrospective negative evaluation, however, apparently is due in its entirety to the following sentence in the brief biography by Collins, written in 1931: "The only reaction he [Witmer] got from his audience was a slight elevation of the eyebrows on the part of a few of the older members."[42] It seems obvious that Collins, who by this time was a well-known author of popular books, was exercising a certain literary license in his phraseology. Since he was not present at the 1896 meeting, it follows that his interpretation of the reception of Witmer's paper came either from Witmer himself or from his own belief that the profession had not adequately appreciated Witmer—a view clearly indicated in his later comments in the article. It is also conceivable—perhaps even probable—that Collins did not intend his comment to be taken literally but meant it simply as a metaphorical allusion to point out the importance of Witmer's overall contribution to clinical psychology by emphasizing the modesty of its beginning.

In fact, it is simply not known how the audience received Witmer's seminal paper. One suspects that the paper, like most short papers at scientific meetings, was received rather blandly, with no general enthusiasm one way or the other.[43] It was not, after all, a major address, but was one of 21 brief presentations.

Overall Caseload in 1896. After his examination of Charles Gilman in March, Witmer, as already reported, examined several other children in the spring of 1896. Thus initiated, his pioneering clinical work continued throughout the year. I now briefly review the cases that he saw in 1896. This summary is based on the available case records of Witmer's Psychological Clinic, which have been preserved on microfilm.[44] The surviving records for 1896 are extremely sparse, but it is possible to discern or to infer from them certain features of Witmer's case contacts during that year.

A few words may be interjected at this point on the case records that were maintained in the Psychological Clinic. Each new case was assigned a number, based on the chronological order in which the child or adult was first seen, and the data for successive cases were filed in separate folders. It is these records that are now on microfilm. I do not know when this systematic numbering system was instituted, but it was certainly not in place at the beginning, and may not have been organized for some years. My supposition is that it was developed after the Clinic was clearly a going concern, and that at this time the early cases were assigned numbers retrospectively—a procedure hardly immune from error—with Gilman being assigned the number 0001.

Returning now to the data for 1896, it is evident, from a perusal of the records, that they were not very systematic and that Witmer had not yet thought through just what the case records should contain or (probably) even that he would keep systematic case records. For the most part, the records consist of abbreviated, informal notes that Witmer made for his own use and of exercises (e.g., writing, spelling, or addition) presumably intended to provide some idea of a child's mental functioning.[45] Case 0008, however, included a six-page typed form with blanks for the insertion of data concerning the examination, family data, physical health history and status, pedagogical history, speech, hearing, reading, and understanding of verbal commands. This form was not used in any other 1896 cases for which records survive. For Cases 0009 and 0013, Witmer's longhand notes were written on a one-page form with "Observation" printed at the top and "University of Pennsylvania/Psychological Laboratory" printed at the upper left.

How many cases did Witmer see during 1896? Although a definitive answer is not possible, a good estimate can be derived from the case numbers, even though the case numbers were not assigned until some time—possibly some years—later. Many of the records, including the first one, are not dated, but Case 0023 is dated November 10, 1896,[46] and Case 0027 is dated January 14, 1897. From these data, it can be inferred that from 23 to 26 cases were seen by Witmer in 1896. Such a conclusion, however, is somewhat problematic because of the paucity of data in the preserved records; further it can be deduced, on internal evidence, that 2 of the cases were actually initiated later and should not have been included in the 1896 file.[47] It is thus possible to settle on 24 as perhaps the most likely (but still highly uncertain) number of cases seen by Witmer in 1896.

Most of the case contacts appear to have been in the nature of consultations, probably occupying only a single session. Probably, in most instances, a child was brought to Witmer's office, according to prior arrangement, by a parent or teacher. Witmer interviewed and examined the child, considered whatever other data had been provided, and then made such recommendations as he deemed appropriate. Of the 24 cases referred to above, data are completely missing on 3; of the remaining 21, 1 (Case 0023) was an adult, and the remaining 20 cases were children, comprising 14 boys and 6 girls. Referrals, when indicated, were from public schools, a nursery, and at least one from a physician. The most general cause of referral appears to have been concern by a teacher, nurse, or parent concerning a child's developmental progress—in learning, speech, or motor functions—or with respect to possible overall mental deficiency. One child was described as "chronic chorea," and another, in today's terminology, would probably be referred to as "hyperactive." Still another child had previously been labeled "hydrocephalic," although Witmer was evidently skeptical of this diagnosis.[48]

The adult case (Case 0023) was a woman with reported neurasthenia and delusions of persecution. Witmer did not see the woman herself but was consulted by two men, one a physician, concerning the possibility that the woman's refusal to visit her mother was due to hypnotic occult influences that others were exercising on her. Witmer rejected this possibility and advised that the only way to restore the relation between mother and daughter would be to win the confidence of the daughter and then persuade her to see her mother.

Despite this adult consultation, Witmer's central interest was in working with problem children. In doing this, he had few tools with which to proceed. Even rudimentary tests of intelligence did not yet exist, and Witmer necessarily fell back on informal assessments of verbal and numerical ability. Despite his feeling that scientific psychology should have something important to offer in helping problem children, in fact, it had very little to provide. Further, Witmer's own training and clinical experience were also severely limited. It is not surprising, then, to learn that in his early cases he placed great emphasis on a child's developmental history and on physical characteristics that might possibly be etiologically involved in the child's status.

BECAUSE OF ITS HISTORIC importance, Witmer's first case, the case of Charles Gilman, merits a closer look. The information to be presented is abstracted from Witmer's 1907 case report, published under the title "A Case of Chronic Bad Spelling—Amnesia Visualis Verbalis, Due to Arrest of Post-Natal Development."[49] Description of this case will take the reader up to the year 1907, but it seems best to summarize the entire case history here rather than to postpone aspects of it until later chapters.

Gilman, at the time he first came to Witmer's attention in March 1896, was 14 years of age, in apparent good health, and a pupil in a Philadelphia grammar school. In the opinion of his teacher, however, he was endowed with at least normal intelligence but nevertheless was three grades retarded. His problem, as Maguire saw it, was a specific difficulty in spelling.

Witmer's initial examination confirmed the boy's difficulty in spelling and revealed an equal problem in reading. The only written words that Charles could pronounce without first spelling them were *an, the,* and a few other monosyllables. He was unable to recognize such a simple word as *house* on sight. When copying a word from the blackboard, he could never copy more than one syllable at a time, and his copy showed many blunders. In geography, he had some difficulty locating places on a map, but he was good at drawing and was reported to be remarkably good in history and in science, where he was quick to find causes for observed effects. He was able to make logical inferences and expressed himself well in spoken language. Witmer concluded that Charles was of at least average intelligence. He had good memory for sounds, as well as good visual memory for colors, single figures, and even separate letters; however, he could not visualize the appearance of whole words. Witmer's first thought was that Charles's problems were due to inefficient school training, and accordingly in the spring of 1896, he arranged for Charles to have special exercises in the rapid apprehension of words, to improve his visual memory. When the teacher was unable to find adequate time for this, Charles came regularly to the university for special treatment by Witmer himself.

Witmer identified certain specific errors; for example, he learned that Charles would read "was" for "saw" and "weather" for "water." Further, he discovered that Charles was afflicted with a problem of double vision and referred him to an oculist. The oculist determined that although Charles had practically normal vision in each eye, there was a tendency, due to a defect in the ocular muscles, for the one eye to focus slightly lower than the right. This problem was largely alleviated by prescription glasses. Despite this correction, Charles could not spell or read any better than before. Witmer felt, however, that educative processes could now be undertaken with some hope of success, and both he and Maguire renewed their efforts. For some time, Charles still had to spell each word before recognizing it, but on December 7, 1896, he recognized by sight two words: *happy* and *following*. He continued to progress, and by March 1897, he could recognize many words and could even read something from newspapers. Regular training ceased in April, but when Witmer saw him in May, Charles still showed certain curious confusions and transpositions (e.g., he would read "especially" for "particularly," or vice versa, and he would write "htat" for "that").

In October 1897 an operation was performed to improve Charles's vision, but when Witmer saw him on December 31, 1897, he showed only very little improvement in reading from the time the special training had ceased in April. In June 1899, when Charles was 17 years of age, he graduated from grammar school and enrolled in a school of industrial arts, where, because of his talent for drawing, he did excellent work in a textile department. However, he unfortunately developed tuberculosis of the muscles and joints, and when Witmer saw him on July 9, 1903, his physical condition was serious. Although Charles was over 6 feet tall, he weighed only 120 pounds and was easily fatigued. He reported, however, that he greatly enjoyed his recently acquired ability to read. He reported that he had read Dumas and Balzac, and he successfully read a passage for Witmer. His conversation was that of an entirely normal young man. In January 1907, Charles died of tuberculosis.

Witmer's final conception of the boy's basic problem was that he was deficient in the ability to call up visual images of words, a condition that Witmer labeled *verbal visual amnesia*; such stored visual word memories, Witmer theorized, were necessary for a person to readily identify perceived words. Charles, Witmer speculated, had from infancy been affected with an ocular muscular limitation that had prevented him from building up a normal repertoire of visual word images until its correction, or near correction, by wearing glasses at the age of 14. In today's nosological system, Charles's affliction, on the basis of the information available, would be termed *dyslexia*.[50]

The summary above is based on Witmer's 1907 case report. The surviving material in the microfilm record for the case of Charles Gilman

(Case 0001) is extremely meager. Of the four sheets (all undated), three include brief samples of spelling and arithmetic, and the other is limited to physical measures. Most interesting is a typed note added by GGI on February 17, 1919. GGI undoubtedly refers to Gladys Geneva Ide, who took her doctorate under Witmer in 1919. It seems probable that Ide, in looking over the early records in 1919, noted that the folder for the first case was largely vacant and inserted a note referring to a lecture by Witmer in which she had heard him describe his first case as a bad speller.[51] In his lecture, as recalled by Ide, Witmer attributed the boy's problem to weak eye muscles and stated that with glasses, eye surgery, and teaching at the Clinic, the boy was able to read for pleasure in 6 months. This is a much more casual and sanguine picture than that in the 1907 case report. Whether this difference is due to Witmer's later imperfect recollection or more likely to Ide's reconstruction of it cannot be determined, but in any event, the detailed 1907 report should be considered the more accurate.

THE TWO PRECEDING SECTIONS were devoted to the origins, during 1896, of what later became known formally as the Psychological Clinic. The pioneering steps, all taken by Witmer before he was 30 (his 30th birthday would come in June 1897) were, from the biographical perspective, obviously the major events of the year. However, there were also other developments, in the latter part of 1896, that are of interest.

Although Witmer's role at the 1896 APA Meetings in Boston and Cambridge is memorable chiefly because of his paper on practical work in psychology, his presence was also notable in other respects. One such respect was the presentations by two of his students, Albert L. Lewis[52] and Mary P. Harmon,[53] of experimental papers. Both of these papers reported research on reaction times and muscle movements. The reader will recall that in 1890, when Witmer was a graduate student and Cattell's assistant, Cattell had assigned him the task of collecting reaction times on ordinary persons and that Witmer had continued this line of research after his return from Leipzig, and, further, that he had presented a provisional summary of his findings on individual differences in reaction time at the meetings in 1892 in Philadelphia.

The papers by Lewis and Harmon at Boston were follow-ups of this general line of research.[54] Lewis, who had obtained his bachelor of arts degree (BA) in 1894 and who was destined to become a prominent Philadelphia attorney in later years, compared four groups, described as American men, American women, Negroes, and Indians, on reaction times to light, sound, and touch and on free-arm movements (extension and flexion). No meaningful overall group differences were found, but a relationship between reaction time and rate of movement was reported. Harmon obtained a variety of physical and mental measurements on 100 women in a normal school and on 34 boys and 63 girls in a kindergarten. This study was conceived as part of a broader plan to obtain extensive normative data on a wide range of subjects.[55]

The 1896 APA meeting also received the Preliminary Report of the Cattell Committee on mental and physical tests.[56] The committee, which included Witmer, had looked into the various sensorimotor tests, or—as they were tending to be called—physical and mental, or psychophysical, tests. The report set forth 25 tests and types of measurements (plus a background data form), which it felt merited further study and use. Among the test procedures considered—to give a brief sampling—were keenness of vision, color vision, sensitiveness to pain, dynamic pressure, and reaction time for sound, memory, and imagery. Witmer was identified as being involved in the appraisal of most of the 25 and as being particularly interested in speed of movement, will power, voluntary attention, and modifiability of the knee jerk (patellar reflex).[57]

The business session of the 1896 APA meeting brought up some contentious issues. These revolved around the question of the general purpose of the association and the related question of criteria for membership. The fact is that APA, as its membership increased, was undergoing growing pains. The underlying issue was whether the organization should encompass all interests, including philosophical psychology, under its umbrella or whether it should focus on the newer, scientifically oriented experimental psychology. The matter had arisen at the 1895 meeting in Philadelphia, with the result that at the 1896 meetings, philosophical papers were grouped together in their own session. This adjustment, however, was not deemed adequate by the experimentalists, which included Witmer. Their aim was to complete the divorce between philosophy and scientific psychology. To this end, Witmer, at the 1896 business session,[58] offered three motions, which can be summarized as follows: first, that only psychological papers be accepted for the annual meetings; second, that a plan be made for the organization of an American Philosophical Association; and third, that election to membership in APA be made more selective. The motions were referred to the APA Council (its governing body), but no formal action was taken.

It is notable, however, that at the Sixth Annual Meeting of the American Psychological Association, at Cornell, more stringent membership requirements were adopted. This change, however, did not fully satisfy Witmer, as shown by the fact that a few months later he wrote to Hall proposing the formation of a new society exclusively for experimental psychologists. Witmer's letter has not survived, but we know of its existence through a letter from Hall to Titchener in March 1898, which included the following:

> A line from Witmer says that he wants to join you, me and others in forming a new Psychological organization which shall put the lab on a proper basis and exclude half-breeds and extremists. Do you want to consider it?[59]

As Goodwin puts it, "This Witmer-led revolt failed to materialize,"[60] primarily because Titchener opposed it. Although Titchener was doubtless the most passionate of the group in espousing the cause of the experimentalists, he felt that setting up a new society, at least at that time, would be divisive and injurious to the fledgling APA.

The reader may be surprised to learn that Witmer, even while he was in the process of developing what would come to be known as clinical psychology, should so strongly have championed the banner of experimental psychology in its strict laboratory sense. The fact that he did so is clear evidence, if any were needed, that at this point in his career Witmer not only considered himself an experimentalist but also considered his approach to practical psychology, as presented in his 1896 APA presentation, to be fully in keeping with a scientific orientation.

The episode also tells something about Witmer as a person. He was not only forceful and strong-willed but also quite willing—more willing than his friend Titchener, evidently—to undertake a move that would be unpopular among many of his colleagues, if he considered it to be the right action to take.

IN OCTOBER 1896, the *North American Review* published an article by R. Osgood Mason titled "Educational Uses of Hypnosis."[61] In this article, Mason, a physician, held that hypnosis had already demonstrated its usefulness in therapeutics and psychological research and argued that it could also be of value in educational practice. Witmer, who had gained familiarity with hypnosis, took a skeptical view of Mason's article, which he considered uncritical, and wrote a strong, but courteous, response to it, "The Use of Hypnosis in Education."[62]

The most interesting part of Witmer's article is the revelation that he had a 27-year-old college woman under treatment for stuttering, and that he had used hypnosis in her treatment. It was his opinion, however, that hypnosis could provide only transient benefit for her affliction. For more permanent improvement, he felt she needed to develop greater self-confidence. For this reason he had assigned her to receive special lessons in articulation from an instructor trained in teaching the deaf to speak.[63]

It is conceivable, perhaps even probable, that this case was one of those seen in the latter part of 1896 for which no written record remains.

FOR WITMER, 1896 HAD been a year of transition. As such, it was the second major transition of his adult life—the first having been when he decided, some 6 years earlier—to enter into the field of psychology. This second transition, which drastically changed the course of his life, was in his decision, along with its resulting actions, to enlarge the borders of scientific psychology to include the evaluation and treatment of individuals with mental and behavioral problems. The emphasis was on children and adolescents, as it was to be throughout his career, but even in this first year, adult cases were seen, and the idea of making psychology practical, as well as scientific, applied, in principle, to adults as well as to younger persons.

Witmer's radical step was without precedent. He was, of course, in no sense the first person to attempt to help psychologically limited and distressed individuals: Certainly teachers, physicians, pastors, and others had given generously of themselves to this end since time immemorial. What was unique about Witmer's action was that he took on the helping role in his capacity as a psychologist. No psychologist had put forth this idea before Witmer. Some, like Hall, had espoused the scientific understanding of children, and others, like Cattell, had pioneered psychological assessment, but it had remained for Witmer to propose that the scientific study of human behavior could be brought directly to bear on the alleviation of human problems.

6

At the Turn of the Century

Lightner Witmer, in 1897, was an active young professional with a lot of irons in the fire. He can be visualized in this way: a man of very modest height (say, about 5 feet, 6 or 7 inches) with an athletic build, blue eyes, well-groomed with dark hair parted in the center, typically wearing a dark suit with high shirt collar and tie,[1] and hurrying from one task to another in the excitement and challenge of his many commitments.

At the University of Pennsylvania, Witmer had his classes, his research and writing, the graduate program in psychology, and his growing clinical work. He had also undertaken, beginning in the 1896–1897 school year, to teach part-time at nearby Bryn Mawr College for women, offering one course each semester.[2] Witmer's contract with Byrn Mawr required him to lecture 3 hours weekly during the fall semester of 1896, for a salary of $250—a nice addition to his income at Penn. He titled his course at Bryn Mawr Physiological and Experimental Psychology and had his students perform simple experiments—probably some of the exercises that were to appear later, in 1902, in his book on experimental psychology. It is fascinating to learn too that Witmer furnished each student with three models of the brain and that the class examined prepared specimens of human and ox brains. Witmer also taught in the spring semester of 1897, with a focus on perception. For this class, the college made funds available for the purchase of basic experimental apparatus, and this amounted, in effect, to the establishment of a psychological laboratory at Byrn Mawr.

Witmer used the occasion to gather research data as well. Assisted by a graduate student, presumably from Penn, he collected systematic data on 100 women (the undergraduates at Penn were, at this point, all men) on reaction times to sound, rate of movement, sensitivity to pain, fineness of discrimination for lifted weights, and minimal pressure stimuli. He was reengaged for the 1897–1898 year, and he offered a course on child study in the first semester and a course on modern psychological theory in the spring semester. At this point, his period at Bryn Mawr ended, because the college was able to employ a full-time faculty member in psychology.

The *University of Pennsylvania Catalog* for 1896–1897 listed a 2-year course by Assistant Professor Witmer open to teachers and titled simply Psychology, with the first year devoted to introductory material and the second to child development.[3] In the regular psychology offerings, Witmer was listed for four courses, the first three for $1\frac{1}{2}$ hours weekly and the fourth for 2 hours. The listings were Modern Psychological Theory, Special Topics for Class Experimentation, Seminary for the Study of Child-Psychology, and Individual Laboratory Work.[4] The first of these courses was especially geared to graduate work. This course was based on Wundt's (1873–1874) *Grundzüge der Physiologischen Psychologie.*

For the 1897–1898 school year, Witmer was listed for eight offerings (although, of course, not all were to be given in the same semester or year). These were Physiological Psychology, Sensation and Perception, Complex Mental Processes, Experimental Psychology, Modern Psychological Theory, Selected Themes in Experimental Psychology, Seminary in Child Psychology, and Individual Laboratory Work.[5] These titles are not dissimilar to what one might find in a contemporary university catalog. The most interesting new statements, in the description for the Seminary in Child Psychology, are these: "Opportunity is given for studying classes of children that deviate more or less widely from the normal. A *psychological clinic* will supplement schoolroom observation in the study of special cases of retarded or unusual mental development" (emphasis added).[6]

Equally interesting is the addition in 1897 of two new men to the psychology staff: Lightner's younger brother Ferree and Lightner's student A. L. Lewis.[7] Lewis, it will be recalled, had presented a paper on reaction time at the Fifth Annual Meeting of the American Psychological Association, in 1896 in Boston. He was now named assistant in the Psychology Laboratory, and Ferree, who had been an instructor in physiology, was now appointed assistant demonstrator of physiology and assistant in physiological psychology.[8] He thus assisted his older brother in teaching Physiological Psychology. It is also of interest to note that Ferree, in 1897, published a paper on epilepsy in *Pediatrics*.[9]

Along with his classes, Witmer pushed ahead with his clinical program. Not only did he continue to see cases but in the summer of 1897 he again gave a 4-week course on child psychology under the auspices of the American Society for the Extension of University Teaching (following its inception in summer 1896, as noted in chapter 5). This offering, however, was conspicuously different from the 1896 presentation. Here, in Witmer's own words, written in 1907, is a description of the 1897 summer course:

> In addition to lecture and laboratory courses in experimental and physiological psychology, a course in child psychology was given to demonstrate the various methods of child psychology, but especially the clinical method. The psychological clinic was conducted daily, and a training school was in operation in which a number of children were under the daily instruction of Miss Mary E. Marvin. At the clinic, cases were presented of children suffering from defects of the eye, the ear, deficiency in motor ability, or in memory and attention; and in the training school, children were taught throughout the session of the Summer School, receiving pedagogical treatment for the cure of stammering and other speech defects, for defects of written language (such as bad spelling), and for motor defects.[10]

The clinical aspects of this 1897 summer course are striking, and the offering can appropriately be thought of as constituting the first formal instruction in clinical psychology. It was then followed, in the regular academic year, by the child seminary described above, and with this, the path of ongoing education in the clinical area, which extends down to the present day, can be said to have begun, even though the new profession, as such, had not yet been formally christened.

Direct clinical service (i.e., examination of children) was combined with teaching. Thus, Cheyney, the University of Pennsylvania historian, commented that "in his course that opened in the Fall of 1896 more children were brought than could be examined by one person and another teacher had to be appointed for that special work. Interested persons were found who contributed to the expenses of the clinic. No fees were charged. ...."[11] Who this additional teacher was it is now impossible to say. However, one thinks in this connection of Mary E. Marvin, because Witmer is known to have valued her highly and because she had helped in the summer clinical work, as noted in the quotation above from Witmer. Cheyney does not say that the appointment was full-time, and probably it was not. One may, however, conceive of this person—whoever it was—as the first in a long line of individuals employed for rendering direct service in the Clinic, separate and distinct from regular teaching in the department.[12] Despite this assistance, direct clinical services were rendered on only a modest basis in 1897, and this was to be the case for several future years as well. The preserved clinical records include 15 new cases in 1897, most of which were described in somewhat more detail than those of 1896.

The year 1897 was notable, in the Witmer family, for another milestone. In the fall of this year, Evelyn Witmer, having just received a bachelor of science degree in biology from the University of Pennsylvania, entered (as an advanced student) the Woman's Medical College of Pennsylvania.[13]

ALSO IN 1897, Witmer, in the continuation of a strong interest, published a long chapter on pain in a prominent medical encyclopedia.[14] The chapter was a strong one—topical, readable, strong on scholarship, and rigorous in its critical examination of central issues. There are, Witmer pointed out, two different approaches to the study of pain, one subjective and one objective. In the former approach, the pain is experienced by the person under study, who can report directly on the nature of the phenomenal feeling; in the objective method, in contrast, the pain is in another person, and "the investigator has to depend upon bodily movements as the expressive symbol of something unseen, unfelt, unexperienced."[15] Further, research on pain can follow any of three paths: the psychological, which examines pain as a mental phenomenon; the psychophysical, which considers pain in terms of physical causes or precipitating stimuli; and the psychophysiological, which investigates pain as related to bodily processes.

Witmer examined the relation of the concept of pain to the concept of disagreeableness and rejected the notion that pain was simply the extreme on a pleasant–unpleasant dimension. Similarly, he rejected the then somewhat prominent quale theory, which held that pain never exists as a sensation in its own right but always as a constituent of some other sensation or mental state. On the contrary, Witmer argued, pain is "presented in consciousness with the distinctness, difference, vividness, and isolation that characterize simple sensations."[16] After reviewing the views of Fechner, Wundt, James, Münsterberg, Strong, Lange, and other contemporary theorists on pain, the chapter turned to the problem of the physical causes of pain.

"Much has been made,"[17] Witmer observed, of the fact that there is no specific stimulus for pain. Nevertheless, it is possible to identify the stimuli leading to pain; thus, apparently all or most stimuli that act on the body are capable, at appropriate intensities, of eliciting pain. As an illustration of this generalization, Witmer reported that in his own research on dermal sensations, he had found that "minimal pressure stimulus of 1 or 2 gm. will give a sensation of touch; greater intensity of the same stimulus ranging from 20 gm. to 15 kgm. will give a sensation of pressure; 5 kgm. to 15 kgm. will give both pressure and pain, while maximal stimuli above 15 kgm. give rise to pain only."[18]

The longest section of the article concerns the psychophysiological bases of pain. Although much of the technical content of this section has long since become dated, the chapter reveals an excellent command of the neural anatomy and physiology of the day. Witmer posited a specialized pain tract in the spinal cord and conceived that this tract, along with a hypothesized special region in the somaesthetic area of the cerebral cortex, constituted, in effect, a center for the perception of pain.

In the same year, in a further expression of his interest in the education of teachers, Witmer published a long article, in two parts, in the *Educational Review*.[19] The theme of the article was that elementary and secondary school teachers would benefit greatly from exposure to the new scientific psychology. Witmer proposed, in considerable detail, four courses that would provide proper psychological training for teachers, and he inveighed strongly against the inclusion of philosophical and metaphysical speculations in such courses. He further stated that the courses now offered at the Philadelphia Normal School were modeled after his general plan.

ON OCTOBER 15, 1897, Witmer was elected a member of the American Philosophical Society. This organization goes back, as might be expected, to the fine hand of Philadelphia's Benjamin Franklin, in 1743. The word *philosophical*, in this case, carries the meaning of wisdom or knowledge, and in fact, the membership is primarily a society of scientists and supporters of science—the first scientific association in the New World. Within its membership rolls can be found such names as Franklin, Washington, Darwin, Pasteur, and Einstein. The society met (and still meets) in its original home, Philosophical Hall, which dates from 1789 and is located close to the venerated Independence Hall.[20]

IN THE 1890s, the island of Cuba, less than 200 miles off the coast of Florida, was part of the dwindling Spanish empire in the Americas. The same was true of the island of Puerto Rico. In 1895, a movement for independence from Spain erupted in Cuba, and the United States, both because of extensive investments in and trade with the island and of sympathy with a people seeking independence, strongly favored the Cuban insurgents.

The civil war in Cuba steadily became more intense, and following severe rioting in Havana in December 1897, President William McKinley sent the battleship *Maine* to the port of Havana to provide protection, if needed, for U.S. citizens. On February 15, 1898, there was a huge explosion on the battleship, causing the death of 260 members of the crew. Although the cause of the explosion was never definitively determined, Spain was blamed, and many Americans, led by an eager press, adopted the war cry "Remember the Maine." After a vociferous national debate, the U.S. Congress, to support the insurgents, declared war on Spain on April 25, 1898. Although most of the fighting took place in Cuba, there was also limited action in Puerto Rico and later in the Philippine Islands, which had also been a part of the Spanish empire.

The American forces were made up of regular army troops plus volunteers, and in Philadelphia, Witmer, along with many others, volunteered for service. He was mustered into the U.S. Army as a private on

June 11. According to a later reminiscence of Collins, Witmer "wanted
to see how men behaved in battle and how he would behave himself.
Real danger tended to increase the desirability of life, and therefore
attracted him."[21] Witmer was attached to the First Troop, Philadelphia
City Cavalry, and served in Puerto Rico, under the commands of Major
Generals Nelson Miles and John Brooke.[22]

The First Troop, or—as it was ordinarily known in Philadelphia—
the City Troop, did not actually meet the enemy in Puerto Rico. As
recounted by Nathaniel Burt, "Just as its members were preparing for
battle a messenger galloped up to tell them the war was off, and they
had to go home."[23]

The fact was that the American invasion of Puerto Rico met almost
no opposition, and the war itself was over very shortly. Witmer was
discharged from the service on November 11, 1898. The war with Spain,
coming 33 years after the end of the Civil War and 83 years after the
last foreign war, was significant, both symbolically and actually, in marking the emergence of the United States as a world power.

The City Troop, like so many institutions in Philadelphia, has a long
history. It was the first voluntary cavalry corps in America, going back to
1774. Its greatest moment of glory was in the Battle of Princeton, during
the Revolutionary War. By Witmer's time, the City Troop had attained
the status of a venerable and beloved Philadelphia organization. During
peacetime, it served primarily as a private club or society, although of
course with regular drills. Burt described its peacetime role as "one long
picnic of rigorous but jolly training periods in camps, parades, usually to
escort Presidents through the city streets, and a perpetual round of dinners
and dances,"[24] often carried out in very dashing uniforms.

In other words, membership in the City Troop was a matter not just
of patriotic duty but also (and perhaps even more) of considerable distinction in the social fabric of Philadelphia life. Witmer, during his war
service, was only a temporary member of the City Troop; permanent
membership could come about only by election by the regular members.
It must therefore have been a matter of great satisfaction when he was
elected a permanent member, with the rank of private, on January 3,
1899.[25]

WHEN WITMER BEGAN MILITARY duty, he of course did not
know how long the war would last. Fortunately, it was a brief con-

flict. This meant that he could return to his academic duties after only a short absence, a fact that was probably of considerable relief to the graduate students in the department, since by the late 1890s Witmer's doctoral program in psychology was in full swing. Three students, in particular, were actively working toward their degrees; these were Oliver Perry Cornman, Anna Jane McKeag, and Edwin Burket Twitmyer. It is convenient to consider this trio as a group, even though this takes us a little in advance of the main narrative.

Cornman received his PhD in 1899. He was particularly interested in the educational problems of children and taught the course on Child Psychology in the 1898–1899 academic year.[26] His research, directed by Witmer, was on the relation of proficiency in spelling to the method of instruction, the age and intelligence of the students, and other factors.[27] After graduation, Cornman took a position in the Philadelphia public schools and eventually became an authority on the education of backward children and a national leader in the development of classes in special education. When he died in 1930, at the age of 64, he was associate superintendent of schools in Philadelphia. His obituary in the *Philadelphia Inquirer* stated that "Dr. Cornman collaborated with Dr. Lightner Witmer, of the University of Pennsylvania, in introducing modern psychological methods into the public schools."[28]

The next student to receive the doctorate in psychology at the University of Pennsylvania was Anna Jane McKeag, who was awarded the degree in 1900. McKeag had come to the University of Pennsylvania in 1897, after receiving her AB from Wilson College at Chambersburg, PA. She was evidently a highly precocious young woman—indeed, she had become an instructor at Wilson even while a college sophomore. She continued to teach there after graduation, taking leave to attend Penn from 1897 to 1900. McKeag's dissertation, directed by Witmer, was an experimental follow-up of Witmer's theoretical position that pain is a sensation in its own right, and not merely an aspect of other sensations.[29] Her results, based on sophisticated laboratory procedures, supported that interpretation. As in the case of Cornman, there will be little occasion, in the remainder of this volume, to examine the life of McKeag, so her later career may be summarized at this point. After her PhD, McKeag returned to Wilson College as dean; then in 1903, she moved to Wellesley and, by 1909, had attained the rank of professor of education. In 1912, at the age of 48, she returned to Wilson College as president. In

1915, however, she returned to Wellesley. She retired in 1932 and died in 1947.[30]

Edwin Burket Twitmyer, the son of George Twitmyer, who was referred to earlier, arrived at the University of Pennsylvania in 1897, the same year as McKeag. Edwin had received his PhB and MA degrees at Lafayette College and was appointed an instructor in psychology at Penn. In the 1898–1899 school year, he taught the Psychology of Perception course with Witmer.[31] Twitmyer's doctoral research, which led to his PhD in 1902, was on the patellar reflex and can be described, in retrospect, as something of a historical what-might-have-been.[32]

Witmer had studied the patellar reflex in the mid-1890s and had given a paper on the topic at the 1895 APA meeting, and it can be assumed that his interest in the reflex played a significant role in Twitmyer's choice of a research topic.[33] Witmer was not the first investigator to be concerned with the patellar reflex, however. Lombard, in 1887, had published an article on the topic,[34] and James, in his 1890 *Principles of Psychology*, had called attention to the phenomenon.[35] Weir Mitchell, an eminent Philadelphia neurologist and a friend and supporter of Witmer, had also previously studied the patellar reflex.[36]

Twitmyer intended his research to be in part a replication of Lombard's work. Whereas Lombard had used only himself as a subject, Twitmyer used a number of subjects. A further change in methodology was that with some of his subjects the hammer taps that elicited the reflex were preceded by a signal bell. Twitmyer's great and crucial discovery, even though quite adventitious, was that after a considerable number of trials, the signal bell itself would elicit the reflex, before the hammer tap. This phenomenon is, of course, what later became known as the *conditioned reflex*.

At about the same time, Ivan Petrovich Pavlov, a Russian physiologist, independently discovered the same phenomenon in his work on salivation in dogs. It was Pavlov who followed it up, named it, and explored the phenomenon in depth; and it was Pavlov who thus provided a major influence on the course of theoretical psychology.[37]

Why was Twitmyer's discovery not recognized as the scientific breakthrough that it in fact was? Twitmyer—to look ahead—presented the crucial part of his investigation at the Meeting of the American Psychological Association held at the University of Pennsylvania in 1904.[38] His paper, however, elicited no discussion, even though William James, who was presiding, as well as presumably Witmer himself, were present, and was soon largely forgotten.

Various reasons have been advanced to account for the obscurity into which Twitmyer's discovery descended.[39] These include the ideas that American psychology was not yet ready to grasp the import of the discovery and that Twitmyer himself did not follow up his research. Certainly the latter is true, since Twitmyer in fact did not extend his research. The question, though, is why didn't he? Dallenbach concluded that Twitmyer "missed the boat" because he was young, inexperienced, and not a promoter.[40] But these characteristics, even if true, cannot explain why Twitmyer failed to continue his research on the patellar reflex. For this, however, a very good explanation can be put forth: Bluntly put, Twitmyer's interests shifted from the experimental to the applied area. There seems little doubt that this was so, since in the years under discussion, he was actually working with Witmer on clinical cases and since his entire career, after graduation, was devoted to the applied area. Twitmyer would concentrate, in his clinical work, on speech pathology. In this connection, it is interesting to note that Mary Marvin, who was the very earliest of Witmer's coworkers, was continuing to work with Witmer and that her special field of expertise was speech problems. To anticipate a bit, Twitmyer and Marvin, in 1907, would be married.

BY THE TURN OF THE century, Witmer had attained a position of considerable status at the university and was frequently invited to give lectures in the community. Thus, in 1898, he offered a series of three lectures at the Pennsylvania College for Women. The topic of the first lecture, probably on April 23, was "Imagination: What we think." During the next day, he presented two talks, the first concerning experiments in the speed of thought (based, presumably, on research on reaction time) and the second on "Aesthetics, or the Psychology of the Beautiful." The *Pittsburgh News* commented that "Dr. Witmer is a graceful and fluent speaker, and his lecture was listened to throughout with interest." The newspaper account also reported that "advance sheets of Dr. Witmer's new book on psychology are out, and have been favorably received by Prof. James [of] Harvard."[41]

Later in the same year, Witmer was interviewed by a reporter from the *Philadelphia Inquirer* concerning Weber's law. The reporter had read that a Professor Titchener of Cornell had claimed to have discovered that this law held true with respect to the sense of smell, even as today some findings, or alleged findings, in psychology often hit the popular press, and the reporter interviewed Witmer to question him about Titchener's claim. The article stated that Witmer "is not very enthusiastic over the alleged discovery of Professor E. B. Litchener [*sic*] of Cornell University, that 'Weber's Law' holds with respect to the sense of smell. 'I know Litchener [*sic*] very well,' said Professor Witmer yesterday. 'He was with me at Leipsic University.' " After explaining Weber's law at some length, Witmer concluded by saying that "Professor Joseph Jastrow and Professor James of Harvard, the latter one of the leading psychologists of the country, have little faith in it, and for myself, I have never thought investigation along that line was worth the trouble."[42]

This interview is illuminating in revealing not only Witmer's attitude toward Weber's law—an important theme in the experimental psychology of the day—but also his tendency to hold strong opinions and to speak out bluntly, even when disagreeing with a friend, as Titchener was.

On the evening of February 3, 1899, Witmer spoke on "The Faculty of Language and Its Development" at the Church of the Sure Foundation in West Chester, PA, a town about 35 miles west of Philadelphia. He reviewed the current state of knowledge on the language center in the brain, rejected the claims of phrenology, and discussed the role of visual memory in learning to spell—a theme tied in with his ongoing clinical work with Charles Gilman. He pointed to the process of learning how to ride a bicycle (a vehicle then newly in vogue) to illustrate how aspects of awareness in motor performance eventually become automatic. To make the point that verbal memory can often be enhanced by oral repetition, he commented that "at Byrn Mawr College I asked a class of one hundred young ladies how many could learn the Constitution of the United States without speaking it. Very few of them thought they could do it. Yet we keep children's mouths closed in school and expect them to learn."[43]

THE MAIN COURSE OF this narrative has now reached the transitional year 1900. Here are several markers to help put that date in historical perspective. On January 4, 1900, in Rome, Giacomo Puccini's opera *Tosca* had its first performance. In the same year Sigmund Freud's seminal work, *The Interpretation of Dreams*, was published; the famous philosopher, Friedrich Nietzsche, died; the physicist Max Planck set forth the quantum theory; and William McKinley was reelected President of the United States.

This was also the year that, in Philadelphia, Lightner's sister Evelyn received an MD degree from the Woman's Medical College of Pennsylvania, and at the University of Pennsylvania Anna Jane McKeag—as already noted—received her PhD under Lightner's tutelage. For Lightner himself there was no such dramatic personal milestone, but he was busy with his classes and his public presentations, and undoubtedly was deeply involved in working on his experimental manual.

Because of his range of knowledge and his tendency to speak bluntly and authoritatively, Witmer had become a favorite source for newspaper reporters, and he was asked, early in the year, to give his opinion on spiritualism. Professor James Hyslop of Columbia University had given a lecture in New York on spiritualism and, in particular, on a famous medium known as Mrs. Piper. Reports of the lecture were picked up by the *Philadelphia Inquirer*, and the newspaper sent a reporter to interview Witmer about Hyslop's claims and about spiritualism generally.[44]

To put this episode in proper context, it will be helpful to interpolate a few words about the popularity of spiritualism in the latter part of the nineteenth and early in the twentieth centuries. The term *spiritualism* refers to the doctrine that it is possible, through appropriate means, to communicate with the spirits of the dead. This communication is ordinarily accomplished through the intermediation of a person, called the medium, who has a special gift for reaching the spirits of the departed. The setting in which the medium practices is termed a *seance* and typically takes place in darkness or reduced light. Typically, the medium enters into an apparent trance state during the seance. Frequently, mediums are under the "control" of another person, who typically arranges sittings and handles procedural matters.

The beginnings of the spiritualistic movement in America can be traced to occurrences in a New York State farmhouse in March 1848. Loud rappings were interpreted to come from the spirit of a man said to have been murdered in the house. Although later discredited, this episode set off a rash of interest in spiritualistic phenomena, and by the turn of the century, the spiritualistic movement constituted a significant current in the popular culture of America and Western Europe.[45]

Although the general attitude of the public was one of skepticism, there were at the same time many intelligent and open-minded observers who felt, with varying degrees of conviction, that there was in some sense a core of truth in spiritualistic claims. These eventually included such figures as the eminent English physicist Sir Oliver Lodge; the creator of Sherlock Holmes, Sir Authur Conan Doyle; and, in the chronological period on which we are now focusing, Professors William James of Harvard and James Hyslop of Columbia. James is already known to the reader; Hyslop, a well-known philosopher, was, among other distinctions, a founder of the American Society for Psychical Research. As for Witmer himself, he was skeptical, even disdainful, of the pretensions of the spiritualists.[46]

The most famous medium in the United States during the latter 1880s and the 1890s was Leonora E. Piper of Boston, known everywhere simply as Mrs. Piper. William James, who had an intense interest in paranormal phenomena, attended a large number of seances with Mrs. Piper and considered her to have some kind of "supernormal powers."[47]

The *Philadelphia Inquirer* featured the reporter's interview with Witmer under a two-column headline: "Hyslop's Spirit Talk Is Viewed Skeptically," with the subhead "Professor Witmer, of the University of Pennsylvania, Says There Is a Large Element of Doubt in Mrs. Piper's Spiritualistic Seances." In his lecture, Hyslop had said that he visited Mrs. Piper disguised by a mask, with his voice changed, and that during the seance, she told him many remarkable things about his dead relatives: Witmer, after paying tribute to Professor Hyslop's stature as a philosopher and logician, raised a number of questions concerning the validity of his conclusions. For example, Dr. Hodgson (Mrs. Piper's control), who knew Hyslop, if only slightly, was present at the sitting. Further, Witmer pointed out, it would be necessary, to draw any scientific conclusions, to consider many sittings, and "since Mrs. Piper charges a considerable sum for each sitting, the affair becomes expensive." Speaking more generally about mediumistic reports, Witmer was reported to say that "no experimental psychologist, whether here or abroad, has spoken favorably of the tests. We demand conditions which, it seems, the mediums and their earthly guides refuse to grant us. Can Professor Hyslop's conclusions be verified? That is the whole business in a nutshell."[48]

In May of 1900, Witmer, in a letter to his friend Hugo Münsterberg at Harvard, offered to organize some functions in Philadelphia at which both Münsterberg and the German ambassador would speak. The relevance of this proposal was that Münsterberg, who was by now chairman of philosophy (which included psychology) at Harvard, was highly active in efforts to improve cultural relations between Germany and the United States. In closing his letter, Witmer conveyed "kindest regards to Mrs. Münsterberg and my 'nieces'" (implying that they saw him as their uncle).[49]

In August of the same year, Witmer began a series of talks on "Child Study" at Pottstown, PA, a small town about 31 miles northwest of Philadelphia.[50] The occasion was sponsored by the Pennsylvania Sunday School Assembly, and the burden of Witmer's first lecture was to stress the role of bodily development, specifically in athletics, along with the nurturing of the mind. His second lecture was on mental growth and moral conduct in children.

"A large percentage of the so-called lies for which children are punished by their parents and teachers are no lies at all." This is the quotation that the *Philadelphia North American* used to open its headlined report of a talk by Witmer before the Philadelphia Normal School for Girls on November 15, 1900. In his talk, Witmer focused on the role of imagination in children. As an instance, Witmer related the following little episode:

> Not long ago a mother told me that her boy came home from a walk with his nurse and told her that he had seen an elephant. The nurse declared that they had not seen an animal of any kind, and for fear of making the boy tell another story, he was not questioned further. But a few days later the mother and the boy walked along the same street in which he had declared that he had seen the elephant. Suddenly he cried: "There's the same elephant," and sure enough there was the picture of an elephant on the fence. The boy had seen it, and the nurse hadn't, and for that reason it was natural for older people to think that he was not telling the truth.[51]

EARLY IN THE NEW CENTURY, Witmer's thoughts went beyond the Philadelphia area. In a letter to Cattell on May 24, 1901, he wrote,

> I have a fair chance of being appointed dean of the School of Pedagogy of the New York University. My work in the school would be in the various psychologies. ... Will you help me by writing a letter to Chancellor H. M.

MacCracken? . . . I am not yet certain in my own mind that I will accept what they may offer me, but under certain conditions I believe that I would have a great opportunity to develop a side of psychology in which I am much interested, and to contribute toward the establishment of a standard of professional training for teachers.[52]

It comes as something of a surprise to learn that Witmer, even while by all accounts doing well at Penn, should have considered moving to New York. However, the tentative offer, to the extent one can draw inferences from Witmer's letter, would apparently have been an academic advance and might have afforded him the opportunity to put some of his prized ideas into practice.

Nothing further is known about this episode in Witmer's career except that on June 1 he wrote to Cattell thanking him for his letter to Mac-Cracken. For one reason or another, Witmer did not go to New York. The history of clinical psychology might be different if he had done so.

Meanwhile, at Penn, Witmer was moving forward on his book in experimental psychology. This was published in 1902, under the title *Analytical Psychology: A Practical Manual for Colleges and Normal Schools.*[53] Note the word *practical* in the book's title. The orientation implied by this term thus evidently reflected Witmer's perspective in the laboratory as well as in the Clinic. The manual's origins went back to 1893, when Witmer had begun developing a series of illustrative experiments to accompany his lectures. Successive classes at the University of Pennsylvania and Byrn Mawr had used the growing set of experiments. Anna McKeag, then a professor at Wilson, and a "Miss Pritchard," psychology instructor at the Philadelphia Normal School, had also used the procedures and had made helpful suggestions.

The book was not a text of psychology nor a laboratory manual in the usual sense. Rather, as described in the preface, "This Manual comprises a series of experiments that can be performed by untrained students of psychology without supplementary explanation on the part of the teacher and without costly and complicated apparatus." It further stated that "the experiments are not intended primarily to constitute a manual of experimental psychology. Their purpose is to illustrate the facts and principles of psychology by leading the student . . . to discover for himself the psychological facts upon which are based the principles of the science."[54]

The book thus occupied a rather unusual niche. Although intended for use by instructors to supplement their lectures in those instances in which complex laboratory equipment was not available, it was also a kind of self-guide for strongly interested students. For these reasons the book was not a real competitor with Titchener's more sophisticated laboratory manual for college instruction, which was brought out in two volumes in 1901 and 1905.[55]

The contents of *Analytical Psychology* are particularly interesting in that the book includes highly elaborate visual material, including numerous charts, graphs, sketches, and photographs. Some of the presentations are in color and involve page overlaps. This was one of the very first technical books—and the first in psychology—to be so profusely illustrated. A total of 50 experiments are described. They include the psychological areas of apperception, attention, association, perception of space, psychophysiology, psychophysics, and sensation. As might be expected, a number of visual illusions, such as the inverted staircase and the Necker cube (common to modern elementary texts) are presented. For each of the experiments, there is a detailed description of materials needed, procedures to follow, and an interpretative discussion.

Lightner sent a complimentary copy of the volume to his former mentor, along with a letter beginning "My dear Cattell." The letter included the following passage:

> I hope you will accept [the book] as an expression of my indebtedness to you who were my first instructor in experimental psychology, and in recollection of those first experiments in which I assisted in the performance of some twelve years ago. The book is a very little thing, but I put good work into it—and I hope to have given expression to a certain ideal of method in the teaching of psychology to beginners.[56]

There were two printings of the book, in 1902 and 1907. It was never revised, although Witmer considered revising it in 1917. The book remained in the publisher's listing until 1935. Initially, its price was $1.50; by 1935, this had risen to $2.60.[57] The manual was in partial use at the University of Pennsylvania at least into the early 1920s.[58]

In addition to his book, Witmer arranged, during 1902, for a publication outlet for selected researches by his students. This was to be in the form of occasional monographs under the title *Experimental Studies in Psychology and Pedagogy*, with himself as editor. Ginn and Company was the publisher.

The first monograph in the new series, published in 1902, was the doctoral research of Oliver Cornman, with a brief preface by Witmer.[59] The second, published simultaneously, was Anna McKeag's dissertation.[60] The next in the series did not appear until 1908; this was a study of statistical methods in psychophysics. The author, F. M. Urban, gave credit to Professor Witmer for stimulating the work.[61]

WITMER WAS AN ACTIVE member of the APA Committee on Physical and Mental Tests. Further, he had been a student of Cattell, who was the leading proponent of such tests, and Cattell, at Columbia, was now carrying out extensive research on such tests on college students. It is not surprising, then, to find that Witmer also desired to study application of these tests with students. In an 1897 letter to Cattell, he asked where he could obtain descriptions of the tests developed by Jastrow and also of Franz Boas's anthropological tests.[62] (Cattell gave him the information.) In July 1902, in further letters to Cattell, Witmer remarked that he and his laboratory were now located in College Hall, in the former physics laboratory, and that he planned to essentially duplicate the testing program that Cattell was carrying out at Columbia.[63] To what extent he did so cannot now be determined; it is unlikely, however, that his efforts were carried to full fruition. In 1901, Wissler, a Cattell student, had reported strikingly negative results in efforts at Columbia to predict college performance on the basis of the Galton-Cattell-like psychophysical tests: These findings cast an immediate pall over the wide enthusiasm among psychologists for sensorimotor tests.[64]

At its meeting on May 5, 1903, the University Trustees promoted Witmer to the rank of full professor. This was 9 years after he became assistant professor; he never held the rank of associate professor.

In the fall of the same year, Witmer began a 2-year part-time period at Lehigh University, with the rank of Professor. This was in addition to his regular duties at the University of Pennsylvania. Lehigh is located in Bethlehem, PA, about 50 miles north of Philadelphia. The Lehigh catalogs for 1903–1904 and 1904–1905 listed courses in Analytic Psychology, Physiological Psychology, Genetic Psychology, and Experimental Psychology, and Pedagogy. It is not clear which of these courses Witmer actually taught during his 2 years at Lehigh, but it can be assumed that he was deeply involved in the laboratory courses, because he had just published a book in that area. Further, during his period at Lehigh, Witmer established a psychology laboratory.[65] He was assisted in teaching by William H. Davis, who was at the same time working on his doctorate under Cattell at Columbia. Witmer thought highly of Davis, and partly through his influence, Davis replaced him, on a full-time basis, at Lehigh in 1905.

At this point, a brief digression concerning Lightner's brothers and sister. Ferree, as already reported, was affiliated with the University of Pennsylvania after receiving his MD degree in 1893. On at least two occasions during this period, he treated cases of children referred to him by Lightner.[66] By 1904, and possibly before, Ferree had moved to a position as a neurologist in the out-patient department of the Hospital for Ruptured and Crippled in New York City. Evelyn, after completing her medical training and doing advanced study in bacteriology in Berlin, had begun practice in Philadelphia. The fourth sibling, Paul, elected to go into the same field as his father and in which Ferree had earned a PhG degree. In 1905, Paul was awarded a PD (doctor of pharmacy) degree at the Philadelphia College of Pharmacy.[67] This achievement meant that all four of the Witmer children had now earned doctoral degrees—a family accomplishment that would be extremely rare today and that must have seemed incredible in 1905.

IN 1895, E. W. SCRIPTURE, head of psychology at Yale, had brought out a book titled *Thinking, Feeling, Doing*.[68] Edward Titchener, at Cornell, discovered that in two chapters, Scripture had borrowed heavily, without including what Titchener considered sufficient attribution, from a translation, by J. E. Creighton and himself, of a work by Wundt. Titchener requested that the APA Council censure or expel Scripture as guilty of plagiarism. However, the Council took no action, and in protest Titchener resigned from APA. The Scripture incident was probably not the only factor leading to Titchener's rupture with the APA. For some time, he had been dissatisfied with the directions that major segments of American psychology, as reflected in APA, were taking and had toyed with the idea of setting up a separate organization to enlist the true experimentalists. Witmer, as recounted earlier, sympathized with this view and, in 1898, had proposed the formation of such an alternative organization. At that time, however, Titchener was reluctant to take this step, because of his feeling that although he had left APA, he hesitated to injure it further by leading a rival organization.

By 1904, however, Titchener concluded that a separate experimental society was essential. To avoid harm to APA, this new group would be very informal: no officers, no dues, no committees, and no publications. Instead, it would be simply an annual get-together, social as well as professional, of like-minded experimentalists who could chat informally about common interests. In essence, what Titchener had in mind was something more like a club than a scientific society. In January 1904, he sent out invitations to a number of men, suggesting that they get together at Cornell sometime in the coming spring. Here is the reply he received (January 20) from Witmer:

> My dear Titchener:
>
> I have received your circular letter of January 15th. I am heartily in sympathy with your proposal which you will remember we have discussed informally on one or two occasions. Although you can rely on me to assist in making the Society for Advancement of Experimental Psychology a success, I do not care to engage in the project unless there is a prospect of some measure of success attending our efforts. I shall wait with interest to hear from you who will take part in the formation of the new society. In my opinion, the membership should be limited distinctly to experimentalists, and the papers and discussion should be restricted to those having an experimental basis.[69]

That Titchener evidently replied immediately is evident, since Witmer's next letter is dated January 25. This was a $2^1/_2$-page, double-spaced letter, which read in part as follows:

> Dear Titchener,
>
> I am very much pleased with the way in which you have gone about to form the Society of Experimentalists. I do not think that the least suspicion of self-seeking on your part can arise, and I believe that you are the best man to lead in this movement, and I shall be very glad to give you my hearty co-operation.
>
> I think that you would be wise to limit the number invited to take part until after we have had some opportunity to settle upon the plan of organization. I am inclined to think that certain men, prominent in the field of Experimental Psychology, are apt to addle the egg. Even Cattell, for whom as an experimentalist I have the highest regard, is so much of a society politician that his influence in the organization would tend to guide its activity with reference to other larger interests. I cannot conceive of Baldwin working with us except for his own personal interests and advantage. Münsterberg would tie us to his high flying kite of

philosophy and meta-physics. If these three men share in the organization, particularly if we make any compromise in order to get them in for the supposed
benefit of their influence, you may be sure that they will be running the society
in the course of a year. I feel myself in sympathy with your methods as an
experimentalist and with what you stand for in the field of Psychology. . . .

I also approve of your informal club meetings. I am quite positive in my
objection to inviting women. Your suggestion that they should be told that if we
include them they are likely to come into a smoke charged and coatless atmosphere is one that will not work out in practice. I should regret to exclude by
this a number of very capable experimentalists, but I am sure from experience,
that you cannot run an informal meeting of men and women. We want a small
vigorous association where we can speak out our minds with perfect freedom. I
shall like, if I feel inclined to attack your views and results vigorously without
being misunderstood by others at the meeting as I know I should not be misunderstood by you. The larger and more heterogeneous the organization the more
likely is vigorous discussion to be misinterpreted and to be taken as an offence
by individuals who may happen to be attacked. I think that the presence of
women in the organization adds greatly to this danger, owing to the personal
attitude which they usually take even in scientific discussions. I favor a small
association, no invited guests, and no women members.[70]

Perhaps the most striking feature of this letter, from the modern perspective, is the strong attitude of both Titchener and Witmer against the
acceptance of women into the experimental group. This attitude, however, clearly did not reflect a belief, on the part of either man, that
women could not make good experimentalists—indeed, Titchener's first
PhD, Margaret Floy Washburn, was a woman, and Witmer, as we saw
earlier, had been involved, probably as the major professor, in the doctorates of Kathleen Carter Moore and Anna McKeag. It is also of interest
to observe that later that very same year, 1904, a woman, Mary Calkins
of Wellesley College, was elected president of APA. Note further that 4
years earlier, Witmer's sister, Evelyn, had earned an MD degree; that
Witmer's entry into the clinical arena had been preceded by his classes
for public school teachers (comprising, very probably, primarily women);
that two women, Margaret Maguire and Mary Marvin, had been important catalytic agents in Witmer's own professional development; and
that he had taught with pride at Byrn Mawr, a women's college.

There is, then, something seemingly paradoxical about Witmer's spir-
ited objection to including women in the new experimental group when
contrasted with his close association with women in his own work. The
answer appears to have been a kind of compartmentalization in Witmer's

mind, based on certain cultural mores of his time—specifically, that men and women were sufficiently different temperamentally as to make free and easy social intercourse between them difficult. This was an era in which, after a polite dinner, the men and women would retire to different rooms, the men to smoke and talk "men's talk" and the women to chat about womanly topics. Women, of course, could not (certainly did not) smoke, and the very term *smoker* designated an informal but exclusive men's group. What Titchener and Witmer wanted was a get-together in which the men could light up, take off their coats, and utter a few strong words if they wished—all of which would be quite unacceptable if women were present.

For the first meeting of the experimental group, Witmer proposed, on March 21, to talk on "The Laboratory Investigation of Backward Children" and mentioned a couple of other possibilities, one concerning the shortest reaction times, and the other the distinction between sensory and muscular reaction times, on which he could present.[71] Evidently, Titchener opted to include all three, judging from Witmer's next letter, March 31, from which the following is a brief excerpt:

> Great Scott! I did not expect you to put me on the programme for three papers. I intended to contribute on only one of the three and gave you a choice, expressing my preference for the "Laboratory Investigation of Backward Children." I do not see how I can possibly live up to the requirements of that programme, and I think there is too much Witmer for Monday, April 4th. I would much prefer to take all the time that you can possibly allow me for one of the three subjects.[72]

The first meeting of the new, nameless, informal gathering of experimentalists took place at Cornell on April 4th and 5th, with Titchener serving as host.[73] Witmer presented two papers, "The Laboratory Investigation of Backward Children" and "Shortest Reaction Values, and Sensory and Muscular Reactions."[74] Because the latter paper evidently included both of the additional themes on which Witmer had said he would be prepared, it appears that Titchener's will prevailed in this instance. Witmer's role in helping found the Society of Experimental Psychologists indicates clearly that as of 1904, he still conceived of himself as an experimental psychologist. Further, the topic of his first paper, "backward" children, shows that he considered this kind of research to be properly within the bounds of experimental psychology.

TO THIS POINT IN THE present chronicle, Lightner was single. This status changed in 1904. The marriage took place on June 11—17 days before Witmer's 37th birthday and about 2 months after the Cornell meetings. His bride was Emma Repplier, 26, of Philadelphia.

Repplier was a member of a socially prominent and well-to-do Philadelphia family. She was a highly accomplished young woman and—if one may judge from pictures—also quite attractive. Her grandfather, John Repplier, and her great uncle, George Repplier, were important Philadelphians in an earlier period and had helped establish a historic Catholic Church on 13th Street near Market. Her father, George Repplier, and her mother, Fanny (Levy) Repplier, lived in New York, but when Emma was 14, she was sent to Philadelphia to enter the Agnes Irwin School on the Main Line.[75] This was a well regarded finishing school for girls, especially for daughters of families of means. Emma was there for the 1891, 1892, and 1893 academic years. During this period, the school was at 2011 Delancey Place. The school had been founded by Agnes Irwin in 1869 (she was a direct descendant of Benjamin Franklin), and Irwin was still directing the school when Repplier was a student. Irwin left the following year, however, to become the first dean of the newly established Radcliffe College in Cambridge.

The curriculum at Agnes Irwin included Latin, French, and German, as well as English grammar and composition, along with other subjects. It was clearly effective in Repplier's case, because she later became a highly articulate and graceful writer. Part of this skill may have been achieved in emulation of her famous aunt, Agnes Repplier (her father's half-sister), who was one of the best known essayists of her time and, indeed, in the entire history of American letters. Agnes Repplier published in the better magazines of the day and was the author of numerous positively reviewed books. She and her niece, Emma, were quite close.

In 1899, Emma Repplier joined the staff of the Library of the American Philosophical Society. The Librarian, I. Minis Hays, assigned her the task of preparing a calendar of the correspondence concerning the Revolutionary War of George Weedon, Richard Henry Lee, Arthur Lee, and Nathaniel Green.[76] Later, she was asked to develop a calendar of the papers of Benjamin Franklin in the collection of the American Philosophical Society. Before completing this project, however, Emma left her position at the Library, presumably because of her impending marriage.[77] In 1906, two historical papers by Repplier, one on Benjamin Franklin[78] and one on John Paul Jones,[79] were published; data for both were collected at the Library of the American Philosophical Association.

It is not known how Lightner and Emma met. However, a plausible guess would be that it was through their mutual involvement with the American Philosophical Society. Witmer, it will be recalled, had been inducted into membership in this organization in 1897.

The Witmer–Repplier wedding took place at the Eaglesmere Hotel, in the Pocono Mountains, a favorite Philadelphian resort area about 100 miles north of the city. Lightner and Emma carried out the ceremony in an unusual way. Instead of their leaving after the vows and the reception, they had the guests come to the hotel, and after the reception, the couple stayed and the guests left. The Eaglesmere Hotel was one of the grand old mountain resort hotels of the time.[80]

Somewhere along the line, possibly when she was at Agnes Irwin, or even earlier, Emma had come to be called Fifi by her friends, and she will from time to time be referred to by this name in the pages that follow.

The Episcopal Academy (Philadelphia), as it was when Lightner was a student.

Witmer's graduation portrait; AB University of Pennsylvania, 1888. (Courtesy of the Archives of the University of Pennsylvania)

WILHELM WUNDT

BORN AUGUST 16, 1832

James McKeen Cattell, Witmer's major professor at the University of Pennsylvania. (Courtesy of the Archives of the History of American Psychology)

Wilhelm Wundt, Witmer's major professor at the University of Leipzig. (Courtesy of the Archives of the History of American Psychology)

Part of Cattell's laboratory at the University of Pennsylvania. (Courtesy of the Archives of the University of Pennsylvania)

Drexel Grammar School (Philadelphia), where Witmer examined Cases 0032-0035, in 1897. (Courtesy of Winifred L. Tillery; the photograph is ca. 1960)

Witmer as a young faculty member. (Courtesy of the Archives of the University of Pennsylvania)

Emma and Lightner at their wedding reception, 1904. (Courtesy of Carolyn Ambler Walter)

ANALYTICAL PSYCHOLOGY

A PRACTICAL MANUAL FOR COLLEGES
AND NORMAL SCHOOLS

PRESENTING THE FACTS AND PRINCIPLES OF

MENTAL ANALYSIS

*IN THE FORM OF SIMPLE ILLUSTRATIONS AND EXPERI-
MENTS, WITH 42 FIGURES IN THE TEXT
AND 39 EXPERIMENTAL CHARTS*

BY

LIGHTNER WITMER

GINN AND COMPANY
BOSTON · NEW YORK · CHICAGO · LONDON
ATLANTA · DALLAS · COLUMBUS · SAN FRANCISCO

Title page of Witmer's experimental
psychology text, *Analytical
Psychology,* 1902.

Cover of the first issue of the journal
The Psychological Clinic, 1907.

Vol. I, No. 1.   March 15, 1907.

THE PSYCHOLOGICAL CLINIC

*A Journal for the Study and Treatment
of Mental Retardation and Deviation*

Editor:
LIGHTNER WITMER, Ph. D.,
University of Pennsylvania.

Associate Editor: Associate Editor:
HERBERT STOTESBURY, Ph. D.,   JOSEPH COLLINS, M. D.,
The Temple College,   Post Graduate Medical College,
Philadelphia.   New York.

CONTENTS

THE PSYCHOLOGICAL CLINIC PRESS
WEST PHILADELPHIA STATION, PHILADELPHIA, PA.

Edwin B. Twitmyer, Witmer's
closest collaborator at the
University of Pennsylvania.
(Courtesy of the Archives of
the University of Pennsylvania)

Arthur Holmes, Assistant Director
of the Psychological Clinic in its
formative years. (Courtesy of the
Archives of the University of
Pennsylvania)

Witmer's school at Rose Valley, Pennsylvania, in winter.

"Flotsam," the Witmers' vacation home in Nova Scotia

A teaching-demonstration clinic at the Psychological Clinic, 1916 (courtesy of the Archives of the University of Pennsylvania).

Boy illustrating test materials in the Psychological Clinic (courtesy of the Archives of the University of Pennsylvania).

The Witmer Formboard Test.

The Witmer Cylinders Test.

Lightner and Emma in their middle years (Photograph of Emma, Courtesy of Carolyn Ambler Walter).

Frances Holsopple Parsons, a Witmer student, circa 1920. (Courtesy of Catherine Parsons Smith). See her reminiscences of Witmer as a teacher (chapter 10).

Three members of the Psychological Clinic staff at the clinic entrance, circa 1923. From l. to r.: Helen Backus (later Graber), Karl G. Miller, Alice M. Jones (later Rockwell).

Morris Viteles (top) and Miles Murphy, Witmer's close associates in the 1920s and 1930s. (Viteles portrait courtesy of the Archives of the University of Pennsylvania; Murphy portrait courtesy of Scott Murphy)

President Gates of the University of Pennsylvania, presenting Witmer with a commemorative book, *Clinical Psychology*, in 1931.

Mildred Sylvester, Executive Officer of the Psychological Clinic in the 1930s.

Witmer in later years.

Cover of brochure advertising
the Witmer School, in Devon,
Pennsylvania.

SCHOOL RESIDENCE

The WITMER SCHOOL

A RESIDENCE SCHOOL for not more than fifteen children.

A DAY SCHOOL for not more than ten children.

AN OBSERVATION SCHOOL for the psychological examination of children
who may need corrective or educational guidance at home or at school.

AT DEVON, PA.

Near Devon station on the Main Line of the Pennsylvania Railroad, forty minutes by
train from Philadelphia, and on the Lincoln Highway just west of the Devon Horse
Show Grounds and the Waterloo Road.

PRESENTED BY
LIGHTNER WITMER, PH. D. (Leipzig), SC. D. (Pennsylvania)
FOUNDER and DIRECTOR

1937

7

A New Profession:
Clinical Psychology

In December 1904, APA held its Annual Meeting at the University of Pennsylvania. The presidential address was delivered by William James, who spoke on "The Experience of Activity."[1] At the business meeting, Mary Whiton Calkins, of Wellesley College, was elected president of the association for 1905—she was the first woman to receive this honor—and two members—Professors Lightner Witmer and George Stratton, the latter from Johns Hopkins—were elected to 3-year terms on the APA council. The newly elected secretary and treasurer was William Harper Davis, who had succeeded Witmer at Lehigh.[2]

Among those presenting papers at the meeting were Witmer, Twitmyer, and Münsterberg. Twitmyer's presentation, on the patellar reflex, was reviewed in the previous chapter.[3] Münsterberg discussed tone sensations,[4] and Witmer reported research on the psychophysics of comparative weights.

In Witmer's study, known only through an abstract,[5] the standard weight was 100 grams, and the comparison weights were 100, 102, 104, 106, and 108 grams. There were three subjects; each subject made 200 judgments (referred to in that era as *experiments*) of a comparison stimulus with the standard as to which was the heavier. The innovative aspect of Witmer's study was that the participants also rated each judgment in terms of their level of confidence. The main significance of this study in Witmer's overall career was not so much that it demonstrated his continuing expertise in psychophysics as that it was his last reported formal study in experimental psychology.[6]

THIS SECTION BRINGS THE record up-to-date on continuing developments in the Psychological Clinic, which Witmer had founded (although without the imprimatur of a formal dedication) in 1896 and which has been rather bypassed in the reporting of other biographical events and transitions.

Most of the information available on the early Clinic years is what is preserved in the microfilmed case files. Although this information, by later Clinic standards (not to mention by today's criteria), is, with a few exceptions, rather meager, it is nevertheless quite revealing. Perhaps the real wonder is that anything at all is preserved from those formative years. Examination of the Clinic records for the decade after its inception shows clearly that the activity of the Clinic, during the years 1897–1906, was very modest. One may therefore ask: Why was there this 10-year plateau, during which the Clinic failed to grow but instead remained in an essentially level, or even reduced, status?

There are, of course, many possible personal reasons—Witmer's involvement in the Spanish-American War, his efforts to build up the department, supervision of graduate students, the preparation of his 1902 book, his marriage—yet one suspects that there was also a more profound reason, namely, that these were the years in which Witmer was getting his feet wet, so to speak, in working with problem children. The period was, in effect, a learning experience for Witmer (i.e., learning how to be a clinical psychologist).[7]

It should be remembered that in 1896, when Witmer inaugurated the Clinic, he had no experience in, or meaningful training for, clinical work. His key idea, that scientific psychology should and could also be practical, was essentially an abstract conception, based on very little actual experience. The present suggestion, then, is that the 10 years between 1897 and 1907 were years in which Witmer, through numerous contacts with problem children and their parents, as well as a few adult cases, accumulated sufficient clinical experience to feel expert enough to undertake bigger things and, in effect, to attempt to carry through the several points listed in his December 1896 paper before APA.

The year 1907 marked the beginning of new and more ambitious developments for Witmer, comparable, in historical importance, to his pioneering work of 1896. But more on these developments later in this chapter; at this point, it is important to review Witmer's clinical experience in the intervening years.

With respect to how clinical work was organized during this period, there is a fair amount of information. The following lines from a brief history of the Clinic written in 1931 by Samuel Fernberger (then a colleague of Witmer at the University of Pennsylvania) provide a succinct, albeit limited, picture:

> During the academic year 1896–97 cases were seen for a few hours only one day each week. During the summer of 1897 a daily clinic was run for a four-weeks period, and that same autumn a daily clinic was instituted at which about three cases were seen each day. In this way the Psychological Clinic continued for some ten years. Professor Witmer did most of the clinical examination of the cases himself.[8]

This statement is helpful in getting a feeling for Witmer's clinical activities during the 10 years following the pivotal first year, but it should not be taken as fully accurate in detail. Thus, it is highly unlikely that Witmer routinely saw three cases daily, although he may have done so for occasional periods. If, however, Fernberger's statement, which may well have been based on casual remarks by Witmer some 30 years later, is interpreted to mean that Witmer spent up to 3 hours daily, during the academic year, on new cases and continuing sessions; contacts with parents, physicians, teachers, and other referral sources; correspondence; and relevant administrative work, then the statement is probably not too far off the mark.

According to the numbering system used in the preserved clinical records, it appears that a total of 93 cases had been seen by the end of 1906. This number comprised, as best as can be determined, up to 24 cases in 1896, 14 in 1897, 7 in 1898 (2 cases assigned here to 1898 could have been 1899 cases), 7 in 1899, 0 cases in 1900, 3 in 1901, 4 in 1902, 11 in 1903, 11 in 1904, 8 in 1905, and 4 in 1906. These specific figures, because of the imprecise nature of the records,[9] are necessarily somewhat problematic; however, both the overall total and the general year-by-year trend are probably not too far off the mark. In this context, attention is directed in particular to the values for 1900 and 1901, which included a total of only 3 cases. This severe decrement can most plausibly be explained by assuming that Witmer was more or less wholly involved, in these years, in working with his publishers on his *Analytical Psychology*, which was published in early 1902.

For the estimated 93 cases prior to 1907, the files are completely empty on 9, and many of the others contain extremely minimal data. In contrast, some of the case files are fairly extensive, running up to several dozen pages. Frequently there are brief longhand notes, some undecipherable, made by Witmer during an interview; most of the inclusions, however, are typed. There is great variation among the files as to what they contain, including data provided by teachers, parents, or physicians; letters, judgments, and recommendations reached by Witmer; and longhand spelling and mathematical exercises performed by the child under examination. In a few instances, there is a typed form with blanks filled in. It is important to remember, in considering these case files, that they were not intended as finished case reports, much less for the perusal of posterity; rather, they represented folders in which relevant case data, some of them casual and haphazard, were accumulated for Clinic use.

Although the referral sources are not always listed, it is evident that they included schools, parents, physicians, and community social authorities. Margaret Maguire, who was responsible for Witmer's first case, made at least two other referrals. Mary Marvin, who was operating a small residential school for problem children, also figured in at least two of Witmer's cases in this period. Most of the cases were children, but several were adults, and of course, in the case of children, their parents were also typically involved. (In the reports from the Clinic, and generally in Witmer's day, the term *children* often included young persons who, in a later era, would be called *adolescents*.) The presenting problems covered a wide range and included academic learning problems, speech problems, developmental problems, and behavioral problems. Among the presenting concerns were delayed speech, stammering, aggressive behaviors (e.g., fighting or throwing a knife), sleep disturbances, crying to excess, refusing to stay in school, overexcitability (now referred to as *hyperactivity*), refusing to eat (now *anorexia*), melancholia, nervousness, fearfulness, vacant staring, and laughter without cause.

The most common questions asked of Witmer by persons making referrals were, What is the mental capacity of this child? Is the child inherently backward? If so, how backward? These were, however, by no means the only types of questions addressed to Witmer in these early years, and it would be a mistake to assume that Witmer was interested solely in backward children. Several cases were referred for evaluation of probable brain injury, and several had been afflicted with disability disorders or arrested physical development, including epilepsy and cerebral palsy. A number of boys were referred for delinquent or antisocial behaviors, in some instances approaching or surpassing incorrigibility. Many referrals were clearly calls for help in coping with problem children or with an adult's personal anxieties and fears.

Witmer's evaluations of children were based on material gathered from parents, teachers, physicians, and others; on talking with the child; on the child's performance in various cognitive tasks; and on historical and familial data. In addition to information of a psychological nature, Witmer typically collected a wide array of physical data: weight, height, body build, posture, nasopharyngeal characteristics, and visual and auditory factors. He was very sensitive, particularly in this early period, to the possibility of relevant medical problems in the children he saw and frequently referred children to an oculist, neurologist, or other physician for specific examinations.[10]

One of the more common reasons for referring a child for a medical consultation was suspicion of enlarged adenoids. The idea that infected or enlarged adenoids could have deleterious mental and developmental effects in children was part of the accepted medical knowledge of the time,[11] and was taken for granted by educators, as indicated in an influential work by Terman.[12] Witmer, in his early period, not only accepted the relationship, but reported in a number of instances that a child's behavior improved after surgical removal of his or her adenoids. Such improvements may, of course, have been due to a kind of placebo effect.

Witmer's conclusions, following the examination of a child and depending on the purpose of the examination, were sometimes in the form of a diagnosis, such as "high-grade feeble-minded," and sometimes in the form of specific recommendations, such as transfer to a special school or specific instructions to parents. In a limited number of cases, Witmer himself undertook treatment. The great majority of the examinations and interviews were conducted in his office and laboratory, but a few were carried out in a home or a school setting. The children seen were mostly White but included occasional African American children.

During this early learning period, Witmer, of course, had no master mentor or clinical supervisor, because none existed, but one gathers, in looking over the records, that there were a number of physicians, teachers, and school principals with whom he discussed his cases, as well as, presumably, a few budding psychologists, including Oliver Cornman and Edwin Twitmyer.

After 1906 there was a marked increment in the number of cases seen in the Psychological Clinic. Approximately 75 new cases were examined in 1907, and—to anticipate a bit—this volume would itself grow markedly in the years ahead.

At this point, to bring the drama of real people to the overall chronology just recounted, several widely different Clinic case reports in the 1896–1907 period are summarized briefly. On May 31, 1897, Witmer examined four children (Cases 0032 through 0035) at the Drexel Grammar School in Philadelphia. The four children, boys varying in reported ages from 5 to 9, had evidently been referred by their teachers—probably through the principal—for intellectual and behavioral evaluations. Witmer interviewed each child, asked him to perform certain spelling or arithmetic tasks (some preserved in the records), observed behavioral and physical characteristics, and typed his report (by "L.W.") on printed sheets labeled "Observation." It is clear from the preserved data that Witmer discussed the cases with the teachers before conducting his examinations and no doubt afterward as well. Although his evaluations were primitive by his later standards, these very early cases are of considerable importance in the history of school psychology, in the sense that in these evaluations, Witmer, without benefit of title or official designation, performed tasks that later would be considered in the province of school psychologists. Witmer can thus be properly considered the first school psychologist.[13]

The record for Case 39, seen in 1897, was much longer: It comprised some 62 pages, mostly correspondence to and from Witmer. The case concerned a 19-year-old youth who was irresponsible and had limited mental capacity. Witmer arranged for the youth to live in Mary Marvin's Home School, which was only three blocks from the campus, and arranged a low-level job for him in Biological Hall. Witmer also arranged for a complete medical examination and even saw that the boy had adequate clothes. Despite extensive, time-consuming involvement, Witmer charged the mother no fee, on the ground that he had not helped the boy as much as he had hoped.

Case 64, a boy, was treated for a speech problem in 1903. A follow-up note in the file some 20 years later stated that the young man now held a well-paying professional position and had no noticeable speech defect. Case 135, seen in 1907, was a 7-year-old girl with a history of developmental problems. She had suffered a possible head injury at age 3 weeks and had a history of unconscious spasms. She was markedly delayed in sitting up and walking, and her current vocabulary was limited to *papa, mama, clock,* and *yes.* She was unable to feed herself but was able to hold a glass with both hands. She appeared insensitive to pain and sometimes showed brief paroxysmal patterns. Witmer examined the child twice, focusing primarily on historical and neurological questions, and the child was also seen by Seymour D. Ludlum, a physician with whom Witmer often collaborated.[14]

Although he was primarily interested in children and adolescents, Witmer did occasionally see an adult. One such instance was a case seen in 1907, a man referred to him by a physician, who complained of nervousness, disturbed sleep, accelerated heart action, and fear bordering on terror, with associated melancholia. Witmer put the man into a morris chair (an easy chair with an adjustable back) and made certain suggestions—without, however, intending to hypnotize him—to the effect that he would sleep well that night. This turned out to be the case, and the treatment was repeated the next day, with the same result. On the third day, Witmer attempted a total hypnosis, but without success.[15]

A word on nomenclature: Witmer did not use the word *patient* to refer to the persons he saw professionally. He did use *case,* although sparingly; generally he simply spoke of *the child,* or used the person's name (child or adult). He did adopt the terms *diagnosis, prognosis,* and *treatment* from medicine.

IN EXAMINING THE CASE records for the early period, I discovered, filed with the document for Case 0090 but having nothing to do with that case, a 4$\frac{1}{2}$-page, untitled typed paper by Witmer concerning his clinical experience up to that point. This brief manuscript looks very much like the beginning of a serious article, and it is not implausible to assume that Witmer intended it as such; but for some reason never completed it (it ends abruptly, just before a planned case description), and that it somehow was filed in the 0090 folder. The manuscript is not dated, but my judgment is that it was probably written in 1903 or 1904,[16] and for reference purposes I refer to it as Witmer's "1904 Clinical Perspective."[17]

The paper begins in this way:

> Since March 1896 I have been conducting a Psychological Clinic in connection with the Laboratory of Psychology under my direction at the University of Pennsylvania. Children who are suffering from various degrees of mental retardation have been sent to me, for examination and to suggest psychological treatment, by teachers in the schools, some though not all taking courses with me in Genetic Psychology, and by parents and physicians. On Saturday mornings I give a course in Genetic Psychology to advanced students, the work of which is restricted chiefly to the study of the phenomena and causes of retardation. These students assist in the examination and some of them in the treatment.

Witmer then restated the goals he had set forth in his 1896 presentation to the APA for the practical application of psychology, but now he emphasized more clearly the need for a new profession. Thus, he stated, as one goal, "The training of students of Psychology for a new profession, that of the practicing psychological expert." He noted that little progress had so far been made in such professional training, although there had been some contributions of value to "any scientific clinical psychology."[18]

"The first question that concerns us when a child is brought into the Clinic is the ascertainment of the physical and mental status," he wrote. After noting that it was relatively easy to obtain basic physical measurements, although there was a lack of adequate normative data, he wrote the following:

> It is a very difficult matter to state with any measure of accuracy and definiteness the variations in mental status from the hypothetical normal. At first I had a great deal of confidence in the exacter psychophysical tests, the measurement of reaction-time, rate of movement, and the various sensory capacities, but I am [now] inclined to think that these give us little more than we already know.

Witmer suggested that mental retardation was perhaps best revealed by backwardness in schoolwork, although this was not always a safe guide. "It is notably unsafe," he commented, "to trust the judgment of parents and perhaps of teachers." He had found that he could pretty much tell, by having a child rise in class and read for 1 minute and then rating the child on a 5-point scale, how intelligent the teacher would consider the child. But such snap judgments, he observed, are unsatisfactory for either scientific purposes or for treatment.

Laboratory methods, such as reaction-time, may be overrefined for use with children, he suggested, and, in any event, were extremely difficult to implement.

> I still believe . . . in exact measurement[s, but] these must begin on a basis of rougher estimations. The psychology of the individual is in such a primitive condition, that I do not believe that we have, as yet, a satisfactory psychology for determining the mental status in the same terms in which a physician even can determine the status from a physical examination for purposes of diagnosis.

This brief manuscript provides a glimpse into Witmer's developing conception of clinical psychology. It is of particular interest in that it reveals a shift away from his enthusiasm for Galton-like psychophysical tests.

AS WITMER'S INTEREST IN the clinical area developed, his professional role came to extend beyond the university setting. Beginning back in 1896, he had had some degree of affiliation with the Pennsylvania Training School for Feeble-Minded Children, an institution primarily for the care and education of feebleminded children, located in Elwyn, PA, a community about 17 miles southwest of Philadelphia, and this relationship was formalized in 1906. This school was founded in 1854, and in 1856, Edouard Seguin, then a refugee from France and a famous pioneer in the education of the mentally retarded, served briefly as its educational director. The school, which has a distinguished record of service, still exists and is now known as the Elwyn Institutes. According to the preserved records at the Elwyn Institutes, Witmer was listed as psychologist from 1906 to 1956, a period of 50 years. His role with the Pennsylvania Training School was as a consultant rather than as a staff psychologist.[19] It is thus accurate to say that he was one of the nation's first psychological consultants to an independent mental institution.

In addition to his affiliation with the Pennsylvania Training School, Witmer, at least by 1907 and probably considerably earlier, held two other consultant relationships. One of these was with Mary Marvin's Home School in West Philadelphia, and the other was with the Haddonfield Training School for the Mentally Deficient and Peculiarly Backward, located in the town of Haddonfield, NJ, near Camden, across the Delaware River from Philadelphia. The reader will recognize the name of Mary Marvin, whose collaboration with Witmer went back to 1896, but a few words are in order on the Haddonfield facility. It had been founded by Margaret Bancroft in 1883. Bancroft had been a public school teacher in Philadelphia, who had developed a strong interest in backward children. The Haddonfield School was a leader in the training and care of backward and disturbed children, as indeed it still is, under its current name of Bancroft.[20]

SOMETIME IN THE AUTUMN or early winter of 1906, Lightner and Fifi called on Mrs. J. Lewis (Mary L.) Crozer at her home in Chester, PA (Chester is about 10 miles southwest of Philadelphia). The Crozers were a wealthy couple who from time to time made grants to causes that they considered worthy. Among the institutions that had found the favor of the Crozers' philanthropy were the Homeopathic Hospital of Chester and a facility called the Home for Incurables. They were also seriously interested in the relatively new Temple College (it had been founded in 1884). Although it is not known how it happened that Witmer knew about and eventually met Mrs. Crozer, a good guess would be that it was through the intermediation of Herbert Stotesbury. Stotesbury was the faculty member responsible for psychology at Temple, and he was Mrs. Crozer's nephew. Witmer and Stotesbury had become acquainted through common professional interests and became close and enduring friends.[21]

It is evident that Witmer's hope and desire, in meeting and getting to know Mrs. Crozer, were that eventually she might be willing to provide some financial assistance toward his plans for expansion in the range of his clinical applications. Prior to the meeting in question, Witmer had sent Mrs. Crozer a copy of an unpublished paper he had written, "The Fifteen Months' Training of a Feeble-Minded Child."[22]

It will be recalled that in his seminal 1896 paper before APA, Witmer had recommended the establishment of special facilities for troubled and backward children. These early, rather loose, ideas had never left his vision and by now had matured considerably; however, it would clearly require extensive financial support—well beyond what the university could provide—to get them under way.

In December, after his meeting with Mrs. Crozer, Witmer left for a trip to Chicago, Denver, and St. Paul. The main purpose of the trip was to address Penn alumni in banquets in Denver and St. Paul.[23] Witmer attended the banquets as the official representative of the university, and in his remarks, he pointed out that the university's Medical School was the largest in the country and extolled in particular the Wharton School and the laboratories of physics, zoology, botany, and psychology. He related that

> a well known medical professor returned from the Yale Bi-centennial celebration, where he had seen the Yale Laboratory of Psychology, filled with the idea that we must establish at Pennsylvania a similar institution, ignorant of the fact that the Laboratory of Psychology at the University of Pennsylvania was in existence several years before that at Yale University was founded; that Pennsylvania, in fact, boasts the oldest laboratory in continuous existence in the United States and that the first chair to be restrictedly entitled a "professorship of psychology" was founded at the University of Pennsylvania before such chair existed at any other institution in the world.[24]

The fact that Witmer represented the university on these occasions indicates his esteem within the academic administration. The trip was also significant in introducing Witmer to the West. He came to love the Rocky Mountains and would return in later years to sample them more directly. Finally, and most significant from the professional perspective, he took the occasion, on his trip, to visit the juvenile courts in Denver, St. Paul, and Chicago. He was impressed with the efforts in these facilities to rehabilitate delinquent youth. In Chicago, Witmer observed, the juvenile court had the support of a bureau conducted by a psychologist who examined children brought before the court for truancy, incorrigibility, or backwardness. Probably this "bureau" (Witmer's term) was the forerunner of the historically famous Juvenile Psychopathic Institute.

These visits reflected and reinforced Witmer's growing interest in the problem of delinquency.

On January 12, 1907, Witmer addressed an eight-page letter to Mrs. Crozer. The opening paragraph read as follows:

> My dear Mrs. Crozer:
>
> I am going to take the liberty of asking you for a considerable sum of money, i.e., ten thousand dollars, for an object which I believe will appeal to you as strongly as it does to me. Provost Harrison and I are trying to raise a large sum of money to place the work of the Department of Psychology of the University of Pennsylvania in a position to render assistance to a large class of most deserving children; those who, by reason of mental deficiency or physical defects, are likely, when they reach adult life, to find themselves at a great disadvantage in comparison with their more normally endowed brothers and sisters. All of the class of children to which I refer can be greatly helped by proper treatment, and many of them can be advanced to normal mental and moral capacity.[25]

In 1907, $10,000 was a tremendous amount of money. This was an era in which stamps for ordinary letters cost 2¢ and textbooks sold for $1.50. The $10,000 which Witmer asked from Mrs. Crozer would probably amount, in today's terms, to around $150,000. The request, then, was a very substantial one.

Witmer, in continuing the letter, noted that Mrs. Crozer had been "interested this fall and winter in some of my work." Then, calling attention to the generosity that she and her husband had shown in the alleviation of human suffering, he indicated his belief that this generosity had made her "particularly able to understand the motives of one who desires to make his scientific knowledge as great a benefit as possible to humanity."

After briefly reviewing his recent work with children, Witmer stated that "this seems to be the psychological moment" for the kind of expansion in treatment facilities that could only be realized with significant additional funding. He stated that he would like to rent a house in the city for the examination and treatment of problem children; this would be a research as well as a treatment center and would be coordinated with appropriate juvenile court and school authorities. Witmer offered to give up his summer vacation to get these several programs under way if the funding should be forthcoming.

Finally, Witmer emphasized in his letter the need for a periodical that would cover and disseminate the kinds of work carried on in these and other similar facilities. The importance to Witmer of this aspect of his request was indicated by the fact that he proposed to reserve half of the $10,000, should it be made available, for the support of the proposed journal and a supplementary series of monographs.

In addition to the letter's appealing substantive content, Witmer pointed out that he would invite Herbert Stotesbury, the psychology professor at Temple College, and Mrs. Crozer's nephew, to serve as associate editor of the planned new journal. He also noted that the National Educational Association would be meeting in the summer in Philadelphia, with the implication that this fact helped make the present year, 1907, an ideal time for expansion in local clinical facilities.

Witmer's letter to Mrs. Crozer, as noted above, was dated January 12; the reply from Mrs. Crozer came in a brief letter dated January 14. In it, she indicated that she would very much like to give him the $10,000 that he sought but that she was simply unable to do so. She did, however, say that she would be glad to give him $1,000 after his work started.

This response must have been highly disappointing to Witmer. However, this was not the end of the story. Two days later, Mrs. Crozer changed her mind and decided to contribute the full $10,000 requested, $5,000 in February and $5,000 on July 1. Witmer notified Provost C. C. Harrison of this pleasant development, in a memorandum dated January 16, and also called on Harrison. However, Harrison was away from his office at the time. In a note to Witmer, on January 17, delivered to Witmer's home at 2426 Spruce Street, Harrison congratulated Witmer on the grant and wrote that he would be pleased to accept an invitation, tendered by Mrs. Witmer, to have luncheon with the Witmers on the forthcoming Saturday.[26]

Mrs. Crozer's handsome gift made a tremendous impact on the projects that Witmer wished to carry out. In an indirect, but very important sense, Mrs. L. Lewis Crozer can be considered a true heroine in advancing the welfare of children and in the early history of clinical psychology.

In March 1907, in his 40th year, Witmer launched the journal that he had discussed in his grant request to Mrs. Crozer. He titled the new publication *The Psychological Clinic*, with the subtitle *A Journal for the Study and Treatment of Mental Retardation and Deviation*. As will be evident throughout the rest of this narrative, this journal was destined to play a major role, during the early decades of the twentieth century, in the development of clinical psychology and special education.

The first issue was dated March 15, 1907, only a little over a month after reception of the first half of Crozer's gift, which made the publication possible. From the brevity of this interlude, it can reasonably be inferred that Witmer had his plans for a journal well advanced before writing to Crozer. Getting a new journal under way is naturally an expensive proposition, and without the Crozer grant, *The Psychological Clinic* might never have taken wing. In a letter to Cattell, Witmer stated that he planned to distribute 10,000 copies of the journal among universities, physicians, educators, and teachers of special education as a means of publicizing the new journal.[27]

In the first issue's lead article, Witmer explained the reason for inaugurating the journal. After referring to his work in the clinical area in 1896 and 1897, he wrote the following:

> From that time until the present I have continued the examination and treatment of children in the psychological clinic. The number of cases seen each week has been limited, because the means were not at hand for satisfactorily treating a large number of cases. I felt, also, that before offering to treat these children on a large scale I needed some years of experience and extensive study, which could only be obtained through the prolonged observation of a few cases. Above all, I appreciated the great necessity of training a group of students upon whose assistance I could rely. The time has now come for a wider development of this work. To further this object and to provide for the adequate publication of the results that are being obtained in this new field of psychological investigation, it was determined to found this journal, *The Psychological Clinic.*[28]

Other possible reasons for establishing the journal may also have influenced Witmer. First of all, the establishment of a journal is a time-honored way of formally and publicly announcing a new movement or area of specialization, in this case, the new discipline and profession of clinical psychology. Further, by editing the new journal, Witmer would tend to establish himself as the leading figure in the new profession. In this latter sense, Witmer's role was somewhat analogous to that of Wundt, who edited the *Philosophische Studien*, of Hall, with his *Pedagogical Seminary*, and of Titchener, who largely controlled the *American Journal of Psychology*. Another reason for establishing the journal could have been as a way of encouraging research on retarded and disturbed children; certainly clinicians are more likely to adopt a research stance when there is a good opportunity for reporting their investigations to their peers. Finally, another possible payoff was that the journal might help publicize the clinical training program at the University of Pennsylvania, and thus serve to bring in graduate students interested in the clinical area.

The cover page of the first issue of *The Psychological Clinic* listed Witmer as editor, with Herbert Stotesbury, PhD, and Joseph Collins, MD, as associate editors. Collins, of course, was Witmer's neurologist friend in New York, and Stotesbury, also a friend, was the psychologist at Temple College (now University) identified in Witmer's letter to Crozer. The first issue of the journal, in addition to the opening article by Witmer (summarized in the next section), included a paper on infantile stammer in a 12-year-old boy, by Clara Harrison Town,[29] who would receive her doctorate at Penn in 1909; a brief case study of a juvenile delinquent by Edward A. Huntington,[30] a Philadelphia school principal; a detailed description, by Witmer, of the offerings in the university's psychology department;[31] an unsigned review, but probably by Witmer, of a recent article in the *Psychological Bulletin*; and a final section, "News and Comment," which included items concerning forthcoming conferences in the United States and Europe and relevant academic psychology appointments and promotions. The inside back cover advertised the monographs edited by Witmer (these were now available from the Psychological Clinic Press), and the outside back cover listed the courses in psychology to be offered in the forthcoming Pennsylvania Summer School, including a course titled The Psychological Clinic.

Subscription matters were set forth on the inside cover page. The journal, it was announced, would be published monthly except July, August, and September (the academic summer months) thus making nine issues per volume. Each volume was to cover parts of two calendar years, with the first issue dated March, and the ninth issue dated February of the following year. The annual subscription price was $1.00, and single issues sold for 20¢. The address was given as the Psychological Clinic Press, West Philadelphia Station, Philadelphia.

THE LEAD ARTICLE IN the inaugural issue of the new journal, titled simply "Clinical Psychology,"[32] is perhaps the most important document in the history of clinical psychology. It formally announced the new profession; gave it the name of "clinical psychology"; specified its independence from medicine and education; implicitly set the requirement that it would be a doctoral level profession concerned with the prevention, diagnosis, and treatment of mental and behavioral deviations and that it would be founded on a scientific basis and would have close academic ties.

This article can be viewed both as an editorial announcing the birth of a new journal—this is the context in which it was considered in the preceding section—and as the call for a new profession—this is the sense in which it is now examined. Witmer began the article with an autobiographical account of the origins and development of "what I have called 'a psychological clinic'"[33] and of the key experiences that led him to this direction in his career.

Witmer pointed out that clinical psychology, as he envisaged it, was closely related to medicine, sociology, and pedagogy. However, he added this qualification:

> While the field of clinical psychology is to some extent occupied by the physician, especially by the psychiatrist, and while I expect to rely in a great measure upon the educator and social worker for the more important contributions to this branch of psychology, it is nevertheless true that none of these has quite the training necessary for this kind of work. For that matter, neither has the psychologist, unless he has acquired this training from other sources than the usual course of instruction in psychology.[34]

One can imagine that Witmer gave considerable thought, before writing this article, as to what name to give the prospective profession. Probably the expression "clinical psychology" had been in his mind for some time, since he referred to "scientific clinical psychology" in his 1904 prospectus.[35] In discussing the new term, Witmer wrote:

> The phraseology of "clinical psychology" and "psychological clinic" will doubtless strike many as an odd juxtaposition of terms relating to quite disparate subjects. . . . I have borrowed the term "clinical" from medicine, because it is the best term I can find to indicate the character of the method I deem necessary for this work.[36]

Although his earlier clinical work had emphasized the problem of mental retardation, Witmer saw the proper role of clinical psychology as much broader, as indicated in the article's final paragraph:

> I would not have it thought that the method of clinical psychology is limited necessarily to mentally and morally retarded children. . . . The methods of clinical psychology are necessarily invoked wherever the status of an individual mind is determined by observation and experiment, and pedagogical treatment applied to effect a change, i.e., the development of such individual mind. Whether the subject be a child or an adult, the examination and treatment may be conducted and their results expressed in the terms of the clinical method.[37]

It is worth speculating briefly on the ramifications of the term *clinical psychology*. Words do carry important connotations, and titles, or labels, can be extremely significant in their implications. By calling the new profession *clinical psychology*, Witmer clearly designated it a branch of psychology, and this classification was further reinforced by the fact that Witmer himself was a professor in a major psychological department.

What alternative names might Witmer have considered? One possibility, no doubt, was *practical psychology*—the appellation he had used in 1896. Presumably, *applied psychology* may also have been considered. In his unpublished 1904 paper, Witmer had spoken of "the practicing psychological expert," but this does not easily translate to the name of a profession. Doubtless, Witmer engaged in considerable thought before centering on *clinical psychology*, but in any event his selection of this term was a masterstroke. Juxtaposition of the words *clinical* and *psychology*, although it may have seemed odd back in 1907, today evokes the aura of a sophisticated, individually oriented helping profession.

ALTHOUGH WITMER WAS THE first to use the term *clinical psychology* in the sense of a distinct profession, and the first to use it in any sense in the English language, and, in those respects, can be said to have invented the term, he was not actually the first person to join together the words *clinical* and *psychology*. This distinction, as pointed out in 1983 by Robert A. Butler, belongs to French psychopathology in the latter 1890s.[38]

More specifically, the expression *la psychologie clinique* appeared in a short-lived French journal that was published in Paris from December 1897 till December 1901, several years before Witmer's introduction of the term *clinical psychology*. Butler's source for this information was a 1968 article by Claude M. Prévost, from which the following excerpt, using Butler's (1983) translation, is taken:

> It is probably well-known that French psychopathology at the end of the 19th century—the time of Charcot and Bernhem—was the foremost in the world; what is less well-known is that during this period the expression "clinical psychology" was very commonly used. The proof of what we are claiming is the weekly publication, more than ten years before the journal of Witmer, of the *Journal of Clinical and Therapeutic Psychology* (*Revue de Psychologie Clinique et Thérapeutique*) in Paris, from December 1897 till December 1901.[39]

This discovery of a pre-Witmer use of the phrase *clinical psychology* is of considerable historical interest,[40] but it should not be interpreted to depreciate the importance of Witmer's own coining of the term. There are distinct differences in the context and meanings of Witmer's and the early French usage. The *Revue* was published by two hospital physicians, Paul Hartenburg and Paul Valentine, for physicians, and can best be seen as one manifestation of the intense interest in psychopathology in French medical circles around the advent of the twentieth century. There is no evidence that the journal's terminology had any continuing effect or—and most relevant—that it led to, or was associated in any way, with the development of a new profession, independent of medicine. In contrast, Witmer's term *clinical psychology* was conceived precisely to delineate a distinct new professional area, and it is from this terminological beginning that the present, many-faceted profession and discipline has grown.

As ALREADY NOTED, the first issue of *The Psychological Clinic*, in addition to Witmer's lead editorial on clinical psychology, included an article by him on university offerings in psychology.[41] The first part of the article presented Witmer's philosophical rationale for a university department of psychology. Because Witmer was the head of the Pennsylvania program, his conception of how a department should be organized and the needs it should meet is of considerable historical interest.

The two opening sentences summarize his overall orientation: "What the department of psychology in a modern university teaches is quite as important as what it contributes to science in the way of original research. The exclusive pursuit of either teaching or research will result in something less than the largest measure of effectiveness."[42] Later, in the same paragraph, he stated that "the most effective teaching of psychology will be done by those who gain their inspiration and knowledge from contact with the phenomena of mind, as these are studied by the experimental method."[43]

The role of psychology in a university, in addition to training psychologists, was, in Witmer's view, to enrich offerings in "the so-called humanities," to contribute, "at least implicitly," to the professional education of teachers, physicians, and social workers, as well as "to instruct and educate the community."[44]

Witmer then turned to a brief survey of several university psychology departments. He was lavish in his praise of the Clark University program, under President Hall, and that at Columbia, headed by Cattell. Both, he said, "have understood the vital importance of an appeal to those who felt a practical need of psychology."[45] The program at Penn, he stated, was animated by the impulse to establish child psychology "upon a secure foundation"[46] and was characterized by the development of the clinical method; further, it was organized to provide "the kind of training that can be utilized by students either in practical pursuits or in the service of original investigation."[47]

Standing in contrast to these three departments, all of which emphasized comparative psychology (individual differences), including child psychology, were, in Witmer's opinion, those of Harvard and Cornell:

> I must not minimize the fact that there are psychologists who do not share the belief in the importance of comparative work in child psychology for the science of psychology and for the teacher. Thus the Harvard department of psychology maintains that experimental psychology is not only of no use to the teacher, but, in the words of the director of the Harvard laboratory, a positive "danger." That experimental psychology may be useless,—even dangerous,—to the teacher is doubtless true, but it is true only of that type of psychology represented by the Harvard laboratory, i.e., a psychology dominated by philosophical ideas. And the Cornell laboratory, which has not been excelled in this country in the scientific quality of its experimental work, stands out frankly as a laboratory for experimental introspection within the field of the psychophysics of the individual consciousness.[48]

Although Witmer added that he did not wish "to discredit or even to criticize"[49] the attitude of the Harvard and Cornell programs, it is

clear that his sympathies were in a different direction. Whereas his comments on the Cornell laboratory, directed by his friend Titchener, were,
despite a difference in orientation, actually highly positive, his remarks
on the Harvard program, directed by his friend Münsterberg, were in
fact extremely negative.

The article concluded with a detailed description of the courses in
psychology now offered at Penn. These included Psychology 1 (Modern
Psychology), taught by Twitmyer; Psychology 2 (Child Psychology),
taught by Witmer; Psychology 3 (Genetic Psychology), taught by
Stotesbury; Psychology 4 (Educational Psychology), taught by a number
of local or nearby school authorities; Psychology 5 (Analytical Psychology), taught by Stotesbury; Psychology 6 (Physiological Psychology),
taught by Twitmyer; Psychology 7 (Advanced Experimental Psychology),
taught by Twitmyer; and Psychology 8 (The Psychological Clinic), taught
by Witmer and his assistants and medical specialists. This course included daily clinics and field work.

THE QUESTION MUST HAVE arisen in Witmer's mind, how
would Münsterberg react to the criticisms that he—Witmer—had made
(despite his disclaimer) in *The Psychological Clinic*? The answer was not
long in coming. In a letter written on March 26, which unfortunately
has not survived, Münsterberg took strong exception to Witmer's published comments. Witmer answered immediately. In his letter, dated
March 28 (and from which the content of Münsterberg's March 26 letter
can be inferred), he first apologized for being tardy in responding to a
letter of March 17, in which Münsterberg had evidently sought information on the most efficient tests for the examination of children.[50]
Then he turned to the issue at hand:

> I received this morning your favor [letter] of March 26, written after you had
> read in the "Psychological Clinic" my reference to the attitude of the Harvard
> Laboratory toward Child Psychology. I regret extremely that you take my remarks
> as in the nature of a personal attack. I beg to assure you that I hope there will
> be no change in our personal relations. I made the statement to which you take
> exception because I thought it justified from your article in the "Atlantic Monthly"
> on the *Danger from Experimental Psychology*, which is so far as I know, you have
> never retracted. I am willing to publish any communication on the subject that
> you care to send me to be inserted in the forthcoming number of the "Psycho-

logical Clinic." If I have misrepresented the attitude of the Harvard Laboratory, I should be glad to have you convince me and the educational public of the fact.[51]

Münsterberg's article in the *Atlantic Monthly*,[52] to which Witmer's note referred, had belittled the relevance of experimental psychology to education and had concluded in a statement that Witmer, with his commitment to scientific education for teachers, must have found particularly galling: "I look on psychology as a whole and say with full assurance to all teachers: This rush toward experimental psychology is an absurdity."[53] Witmer was not the first to object to Münsterberg's position. His old mentor, Cattell, had previously assailed Münsterberg's (1898) *Atlantic Monthly* article,[54] and this fact may have encouraged Witmer's own reaction. Even earlier, in 1895, Hall and Münsterberg had clashed on the role of psychology in the education of teachers, with Hall taking the view that Witmer later espoused.[55]

Witmer's hope that his friendship with Münsterberg might continue despite his published criticism of the program that Münsterberg directed, although probably sincere rather than disingenuous, was naive. After all, Münsterberg, a man of considerable status and self-importance, and known to be hypersensitive to criticism, could hardly have avoided seeing Witmer's negative evaluation of his program as a reflection on him personally.[56]

A few weeks later, on April 17 and 18, the experimental group held its fourth annual gathering at the University of Pennsylvania. According to the report in the *American Journal of Psychology*, "Professor Witmer entertained the psychologists most hospitably at the University Club, and then conducted them on tours of inspection through his unusually well-appointed laboratory."[57] Witmer did not present, but papers were given by Twitmyer, J. D. Heilman, and F. M. Urban of the University of Pennsylvania's psychology department.

Münsterberg did not attend, but he had invited the group to hold its next meeting (i.e., for 1908) at Harvard. In a letter dated May 17, 1907, Witmer, acting in his role as temporary chairman of the group, wrote to Münsterberg informing him that they had talked the matter over and agreed to accept Münsterberg's invitation:

I therefore have the pleasure of conveying to you the official acceptance of your invitation. I want to add for my own part, that if the feelings which you harbor toward me will make it unpleasant or impossible for you to invite me to attend the meeting next spring, I trust that you will apprize [*sic*] me of the fact at the present time.[58]

How—and whether—Münsterberg responded to this letter is not known, although it is clear that he was quite provoked with Witmer. As for the 1908 Harvard meeting of experimental psychologists, it occurred as planned, but Witmer was not in attendance. The University of Pennsylvania was represented by Urban.[59]

Seen in the context of the earlier warm relationship between Witmer and Münsterberg, the break in their friendship comes as a sudden and sharp surprise. It is possible, of course, that their rift was precipitated by unpleasant personal interactions between them, known only to them.[60] Be this as it may, however, the underlying cause of the break was probably pretty much as seen by Witmer: that is scientific and professional differences. Whereas early in the friendship both were aspiring young experimentalists and had similar theoretical orientations, their conceptions of the nature of psychology had now come to differ drastically.

The immediate matter that brought Witmer and Münsterberg to the parting of ways, at least from Witmer's perspective, was their differing conceptions of the place of child psychology and practical applications in the psychology programs they headed at Penn and Harvard, respectively. There were, however, more basic underlying differences. One of these was their respective attitudes toward the process of science. Whereas Witmer was a strong believer in the experimental method, Münsterberg held a different view of the nature of science. Witmer, in this respect a true follower of Wundt, was basically a positivist, devoted, when possible and as an ideal, to objective measuring and counting. Münsterberg, in contrast, insisted that it was impossible to measure "psychical facts"[61] and that reliance on the whole armamentarium of the new experimental psychology for practical purposes was misguided.

Another, related point that nettled Witmer was Münsterberg's increasingly philosophical emphasis. Although James had originally brought Münsterberg to Harvard to take over the experimental laboratory so that he, James, could concentrate on philosophy, things had not worked out quite as planned. As the years had passed, Münsterberg, although he continued to direct the laboratory, largely turned it over to others and became more and more devoted to speculative philosophy.[62] Whereas

Witmer and most other psychologists of the time were keenly committed to psychology's emergence from the cover of philosophy, Münsterberg, at Harvard, insisted that the two disciplines be kept together.

Despite their substantive and methodological differences, the paths followed by Witmer and Münsterberg were in some respects similar. Thus Witmer, although he paid strong allegiance to formal experimentation, had in fact shifted his attention almost entirely to the clinical, helping area. Much the same was true of Münsterberg; although formally head of the Harvard laboratory, his interests were turning increasingly to the applied sphere, including forensic psychology and personnel selection, and some historians have considered him the founder of applied psychology.[63] In addition, he was extremely active, under the banner of his MD degree, in psychotherapy. Further, both men reached out from their university chairs to the wider public—Witmer by interviews and public presentations primarily in the Philadelphia area and Münsterberg by numerous books and articles in magazines such as the *Atlantic* and *McClure's*. Finally, both men, in their personality structures, were inner driven, strong willed, opinionated, and ambitious.[64]

The May 1907 issue of *The Psychological Clinic* included two items of particular interest. First, there was a full-page advertisement[65] calling attention to Münsterberg's 1906 edited volume *Harvard Psychological Studies*.[66] The text of the advertisement, which may well have been written by Münsterberg himself, emphasized the breadth of the Harvard laboratory, including its relevance to the practical problems of education. Whether this advertisement was placed in response to Witmer's earlier criticism cannot be known, but Witmer could not resist assuming something of a victory. Thus, the second relevant item, appearing in the "News and Comment" section, most likely written by Witmer, reads in part as follows:

It is reported that the director of the Harvard Psychological laboratory is about to make the laboratory useful in the direction of an examination and classification of the backward children of Cambridge. The advertisement of the "Harvard Psychological Studies," found on one of the cover pages of this number of *The Psychological Clinic*, is also in evidence to show that Professor Münsterberg has recently seen a great light. The Psychological Clinic does not flatter itself that it has been the sole cause of what must appear to many to be a marked change in Professor Münsterberg's attitude on the question of the relation of psychology to education.[67]

The fact that the heads of psychology at Penn and Harvard were now on unfriendly terms, as the news got around, must have occasioned comment in the various halls of academia. Some evidence of this is provided in a letter from Robert Yerkes, then a young experimentalist at Harvard, to Titchener:

> I think Witmer was unfair and I feel that if he is a gentleman as well as a scholar he will apologize sometime. It is not a question of truth. I am not especially concerned about that for I think M and W are different and that there [sic] laboratories also are different, without being worthy of damnation. I am sorry I could not attend the meetings for I should very much like to talk the matter over with Witmer quietly. His Clinic should be an excellent institution.[68]

The Witmer–Münsterberg matter also came up in correspondence between Witmer and Titchener, and in a 1908 letter to Titchener, in words that simultaneously expressed and denied antagonism toward Münsterberg, Witmer wrote:

> As to Münsterberg there never was any rift excepting what was caused in his mind by my criticism in "The Psychological Clinic." I haven't got any personal feeling against Münsterberg and hope I shall never have cause for any, but I can't stand some of his public utterances and if he continues to make a mess of applied psychology, I may have to give expression to some protest. But as I wrote to you before, I do not see why this should have anything to do with our personal relations.[69]

The Witmer–Münsterberg episode, as just recounted, reveals in striking fashion Witmer's growing self-assurance and assertiveness and highlights in particular his tendency to express himself plainly and bluntly, even when it was impolitic to do so. The episode also underlines his strong commitment to, and indeed identification with, his own personal vision of the nature of psychology and the importance in his vision of practical work with children.

While the break in friendship was a loss for both men, it had little effect on the directions of their respective careers. Both men continued, enthusiastically and successfully, on the courses they had chosen.

8

The Restoration of Children

As long ago as 1896, in his presentation at the APA meeting, Witmer had recommended the establishment of a small residential facility to provide "expert psychological and pedagogical treatment"[1] for children in need of intensive care. Now, in 1907, with the support of the Crozer fund, he was able to implement this goal on an experimental basis. For this purpose, he obtained the use of a house near the university, large enough for 10 children at any one time, plus two resident nurses. Witmer referred to the new facility as a Hospital School, to emphasize that its object was to keep children for a brief period to restore them to a condition in which normal development would be possible.[2]

The specific aim of the facility was to provide a 24-hour environment in which the children could be provided with expert psychological and pedagogical training. A second but related purpose was to provide opportunities for proper diagnosis and prognosis. Witmer felt that observation over a period of days, or even much longer, was frequently required to understand a child adequately. The general idea of the Hospital School grew out of the summer clinics that Witmer had carried out on a smaller basis since 1896.

The Hospital School opened in July 1907, only a few months after the receipt of the Crozer grant.[3] Each child was given a psychological examination by Witmer and a neurological examination by his neurologist friend, Samuel Ludlum. A number of professional staff people, including advanced graduate students under Witmer, were selected to help operate the school. Each morning during the summer, the children were taken for special instruction, including manual training, to rooms that had been set up at College Hall on the university campus. Some of the children, for example, those with speech defects, required individual treatment. On occasion, the children were taken to Fairmont Park for play in the open air. When the summer session ended, most of the children who had spent time there were sent home, but the school resumed activity on a limited basis in October, and Witmer's intention was to continue it as long as available funding permitted.

The further history of the Hospital School is obscure. It is clear that it continued, though doubtless on a much smaller basis, for several years, since Witmer referred to it in discusions of several cases that he saw through 1910,[4] and the facility was described briefly in the *Courses in Psychology* bulletin for the 1911 summer school.[5] From the beginning of the Hospital School there had been two classes of children in residence: those receiving free services and those supported by their parents. Income from this latter source, probably plus occasional small subsidies, evidently kept the facility in operation—at least for a period—after the Crozer funds were exhausted.[6]

At some point in 1908, Witmer elected to establish his own private residential school, under his own ownership and direction, for the education and treatment of backward and troubled children. Probably some of the staff, as well as some of the children in the Hospital School at the time of its closure, were transferred to the new private school. This school, inaugurated sometime in 1908, was entirely independent of the university, although some of Witmer's clinical students gained experience there. The school was financed primarily by fees from the parents of the children in residence; a limited number of fee-free children were also treated. The school was located in what was then the country, in the Wallingford–Moylan–Rose Valley area, not far from Elwyn, about 15 or 20 miles southwest of the university. It was generally known as the Rose Valley School, or, by some, as the Rose Valley–Moylan School.[7]

The Rose Valley Home and School was located in an attractive three-story mansion, set in a beautiful tree-lined area. It is not known how much time Lightner and Emma spent at Rose Valley, but it must have been considerable, in view of Witmer's emphasis on creating a 24-hour therapeutic environment. Witmer was to operate the Rose Valley School until 1921, when he would move the facility to Devon, PA. In 1937, in a brochure advertising his school, he wrote the following:

> Since 1908 I have had under my supervision and control at my country place a home and school for a small group of children whom I have examined in my private practice and who have been entrusted to me by their parents for educational treatment.[8]

It is important to emphasize the significance, in Witmer's overall life story, of his operation of a small private school for problem children. After having undertaken the school at Rose Valley, he devoted himself assiduously to such a facility for the rest of his career, indeed for some years after his retirement from the university. The operation of a private treatment facility, including full responsibility for its organization, professional care, and business management, was in addition to, and quite separate from, his affiliation with the University of Pennsylvania. It was, in effect, a second, although closely related, career track.

THE FIRST ISSUE OF Volume 2 of *The Psychological Clinic* appeared in March 1908. A statement on the inside front cover stated that "more than two hundred new subscribers read *The Psychological Clinic.*" Stotesbury and Collins were no longer listed as associate editors (i.e., Witmer was the sole editor). The issue opened with a four-page editorial by Witmer "Retrospect and Prospect."[9] This brief piece, concerned with the status and progress of the journal, was very positive and even self-congratulatory. The journal's readers, according to Witmer, "include practising physicians and medical specialists, professors of pedagogy and psychology, superintendents of education, grade teachers and teachers of defective children, social workers, and others interested in modern philanthropic work for the relief of poor children."[10] One notes the absence in this listing of clinical psychologists, a profession not yet fully formed.

The editorial was largely a plea for greater public concern with the welfare of children. The goal was to enable each child to reach that child's full potential, including gifted as well as retarded children. The school, in Witmer's view, should take a leadership role in advancing toward this goal:

> If insufficient food and unhealthful environment make the progress of a child impossible, the school must bring these facts to the attention of the public, and must see that some satisfactory solution is offered.[11]

The emphasis here on the overall welfare of children was a new strand, and somewhat of a transition, in Witmer's perspective; whereas earlier he had focused on the role of psychologists in helping children, he now added a broader social concern.

Witmer also revealed something of his research philosophy in this editorial. With respect to the factors that influenced the development of adult efficiency, he wrote these words:

> It is my belief that we shall more profitably investigate these causes by the study of the individual than by the study of the masses. A statistical inquiry doubtless must be undertaken before conclusions of general applicability can be formed, but the most convincing statistics will be obtained from individuals who have been subjected first to a clinical examination.[12]

In the final paragraph of his editorial, Witmer wrote that it would be

> a mistake to suppose that this journal is devoted to a study of pathological conditions. There is no sharp line to be drawn between the pathological or normal on the one hand, and the normal on the other. . . . *The Psychological Clinic* is not a journal for the study of the *abnormal* child, but a journal for the study of the *individual* child.[13]

The November 1908 issue of *The Psychological Clinic* included an article by Witmer titled "The Treatment and Cure of a Case of Mental and Moral Deficiency."[14] Although certain expressions and terminologies in the case report are now somewhat dated (for example the term *moral deficiency* refers to what today would be called *behavioral problems* or *acting out behaviors*), the article nevertheless furnishes a good example of Witmer's clear and engaging style of writing. Largely devoid of psychological jargon and concentrating on actual behaviors, the article provides a lucid word picture of its subject, an 11-year-old boy. The theme of the report was that many cases of evident retardation and deviation in children could be alleviated and cured by careful and persistent individualized attention. This belief was illustrated by a problem child treated in the Hospital School.

Also in November, Witmer spoke at the Association of Colleges and Preparatory Schools in the Middle States and Maryland, meeting at Lancaster, PA, on the question of "Are We Educating the Rising Generation?"; this was published in the *Educational Review* in 1909.[15] In the article, Witmer generally decried the inadequate education being given to college students, although he applauded the increasing number of students attending college. He noted, in particular, that whereas when he had been an undergraduate, the average class included about 20 students, today it might contain 50, or even several hundred. It was impossible, he asserted, to give good (i.e., individualized) instructions under these circumstances. Witmer emphasized that the primary role of college instructors was to be good teachers and that scholarship in given fields should be considered as secondary.

Then in December of the same year, 1908, at the Annual Meeting of the American Psychological Association, in Baltimore, Witmer gave a paper on retardation. This was published, under the title "The Study and Treatment of Retardation: A Field of Applied Psychology," in the April 1909 *Psychological Bulletin.*[16] This article began with the words "No valid distinction can be made between a pure and an applied science."[17] It consisted primarily of a historical survey of Witmer's development of the clinical approach in psychology and, specifically, of his clinic. After paying tribute to the pioneering work of G. Stanley Hall, he emphasized the roles of both the clinical and statistical methods in the study of children and differentiated between two types of retardation: one in which a child failed to reach the normal level for a child of his or her age and one in which the child failed to develop to his or her own full capacity.

IN ADDITION TO WRITING the papers just summarized, plus all his other activities, Witmer found time, in late 1908 and early 1909, to write a long, three-part review and critique, which appeared in the last three issues of Volume 2 of *The Psychological Clinic.*[18] The review ostensibly concerned three publications: *Religion and Medicine*, by Elwood Worcester, Samuel McComb, and Isador Coriat; the first issue of the journal *Psychotherapy: A Course of Reading in Sound Psychology, Sound Medicine and Sound Religion*, and *Letters to a Neurologist*, by Witmer's friend Joseph Collins. Actually, it had a much broader scope and provided an opportunity for Witmer to condemn what he saw as a rising tide of antiscientism. His evaluation of the first two works, which supported the Emmanuel movement, was harshly negative, whereas that of Collins's book was—as might be expected—highly positive.

The spiritual and psychological movement termed *Emmanuelism*, prominent for a time early in the twentieth century, emphasized the role of the church in treating mental ailments through Christian psychotherapy, prayer, and occasionally hypnosis. The leader of the movement was Elwood Worcester, an Episcopal minister at the Emmanuel church in Boston. Emmanuelism espoused a close working relationship between the clergy and physicians.

The literature of the Emmanuel movement included extravagant claims of successful treatments, but Witmer considered the approach unscientific and basically fraudulent and attacked it vigorously. His ire, however, was not limited to the excesses of the Emmanuel movement. More generally, the article decried a widespread climate of opinion that uncritically accepted such systems of thought as Christian Science, spiritualism, and occultism, all of which Witmer considered the antithesis of science. In a like vein, he sharply criticized the psychotherapeutic practices of Münsterberg, who by this time had gained considerable attention for his claims of extensive cures of alcoholics through suggestion and hypnosis. Witmer assailed Münsterberg for not following ordinary scientific standards in evaluating his treatments. He referred to a recent article in which Münsterberg had written that "if I look back over the last years in which I often studied the effects of suggestion and hypnotism on habitual drinkers, I do not hesitate to say that it was, in most cases, an easy thing to cure the social drinker of the large cities, but very hard to break the lonely drinker of the temperance town."[19] Witmer's response was that "to the present time, the reports of cases presented by Professor Münsterberg do not warrant us in believing that he has cured any drunkard whatever."[20]

Having thus warmed up, Witmer then turned his attention to William James, whom he accused of having helped create, through his immense prestige and great personal charm, the kind of intellectual climate in which movements like Emmanuelism could flourish. Worcester, he pointed out, had quoted James in general support of his own particular orientation, as had John L. Nevius,[21] in his book espousing the reality of demons. Witmer's primary criticism of James was directed at the latter's interest in occult and transnormal phenomena, which he felt were unsupported and antiscientific. He quoted from an article in which James had written that "I find myself . . . suspecting that the thought-transference experiments, the vertical hallucinations, the crystal vision, yea, even the ghosts, are sorts of thing which with the years will tend to establish themselves."[22]

If Witmer had been wiser, more diplomatic, and less headstrong, he would have closed his critique of James at this point. Doubtless, most psychologists of the period shared his general view that James had gone overboard in his enthusiasm for psychic phenomena. Indeed, Cattell and James had some heated exchanges on this topic in the 1890s.[23] However, Witmer plunged ahead and assailed James's status as the most popular psychologist of the time:

> A philosopher–psychologist, temperamentally interested in mysticism, profession-
> ally engaged in philosophy, and temporarily assuming the role of a psychologist,
> Professor James represents today the survival of an academic tradition. . . . Gifted
> with a charming literary style, a keen sense for the dramatic in presentation, and
> a love of speculation without any positive determination to arrive at a solution,
> James has produced the most popular text book in psychology. This book is
> accepted by many as a standard work on the subject. As a matter of fact, it
> represents a transition between old and new psychology, and partakes more of the
> spirit and methods of the old than of the new.[24]

Witmer's basic evaluation of James was that he was neither an exper-imentalist nor a compiler and systematizer of experimental work done by others. Rather, in Witmer's view, James was essentially a litterateur, whose work was "characterized by a pronounced interest in psychological subjects."[25] Although Witmer was not the first to criticize James's psy-chological stance,[26] he did so at greater length and with more vehemence than others had, even verging into the personal, when he referred to James as "the spoiled child of American Psychology."[27]

Also, near the end of his review, Witmer had a few mildly negative criticisms of Harvard's philosopher Josiah Royce. It is clear that in the review, as well as in earlier comments, Witmer, at this stage in his life, saw himself as the guardian of scientific purity and rigor in psychology, especially applied psychology.

Münsterberg, after reading Witmer's review, immediately took um-
brage and wrote, or threatened to write, a protest to APA. He also called
the matter to the attention of James, who counseled against such a letter.
Later, James received a copy of the review directly from Witmer and
then wrote to Münsterberg as follows:

> Witmer has sent me a copy of the *corpus delicti*, and I find myself curiously
> unmoved. In fact he takes so much trouble over me, and goes at the job with
> such zest that I feel like "sicking him on", as they say to dogs. Perhaps the honor
> of so many pages devoted to one makes up for the dishonor of their content. It
> is really a great compliment to have anyone take so much trouble about one.
> . . . I think it undignified to take such an attack seriously. Its excessive dimensions
> (in my case at any rate), and the smallness and remoteness of the provocation,
> stamp it as simply eccentric. . . . Besides, since these temperamental antipathies
> exist—why isn't it healthy that they should express themselves? For my part, I
> feel rather glad than otherwise that psychology is so live a subject that psychol-
> ogists should "go for" each other in this way, and I think it all ought to happen
> *inside* of our Association.[28]

Despite James's counsel, Münsterberg evidently did not withdraw his
protest to APA, which—as fate would have it—was scheduled to hold
its next meeting the next December in Harvard's Emerson Hall, on the
invitation of Münsterberg. Before that meeting, rumor reached Witmer
that Münsterberg had written to APA, requesting, at least by implication,
that Witmer be expelled from the Association. Although the minutes of
APA's business session at the December meeting made no allusion to the
controversy,[29] evidently there was a brief public interchange.

In the "News and Comment" section of the January 1910 issue of
The Psychological Clinic, Witmer reported that at the business session, he
had requested that a copy of any correspondence between Münsterberg
and APA be made available to him.[30] Although the president, Charles
Judd of the University of Chicago, ruled Witmer's request out of order,
Münsterberg stated that he had indeed written a letter of protest, feeling
as he did that he could not invite to Emerson Hall an association that
included a member who by his criticisms had insulted men of the stature
of James and Royce.

In his response, in the last paragraph of the January "News and Comment" section, Witmer, referred to "Münsterberg's method of answering scientific criticism" in this way:

> The distinguished philosopher whose name adorns the building from which Professor Münsterberg sought to exclude his critic would be the first, were he alive, to appreciate the irony of the situation. No one stood more frankly for freedom of speech and thought than Emerson.[31]

Although Witmer, in his review, had attacked both Münsterberg and James, his criticism of James was undoubtedly more startling to other psychologists of the period. As Morris Viteles, who took his degree under Witmer in 1921 and knew him well, once remarked to me, concerning Witmer's review, "criticizing James was like criticizing God!"[32]

Substantively, and from the perspective of the rigorous experimental psychology of the period, Witmer's evaluation of James's work was not without merit. However, the injudicious nature of his personal comments, which went well beyond the accepted collegial norms, even in a period when bitter personal criticism was not unusual, tended to depreciate whatever value his review may have had. This whole episode demonstrates once again Witmer's tendency to believe strongly, even dogmatically, in certain causes and perspectives and to be willing to engage in controversy to defend and advance his positions. Indeed, one suspects that at some level of his personality, Witmer had come to savor controversy.

From this point on in his career, Witmer, while maintaining correct and friendly relations with the overall psychological establishment, increasingly tended to be independent of mainstream academic psychology and to follow his own star. The probability is that he felt that mainstream psychology had little to offer to the clinical orientation that he was developing.

IN MARCH 1909, the same month in which James wrote to Münsterberg, regarding the Witmer review, Witmer traveled to New York City to support Joseph Collins in his efforts to establish a center for the study and treatment of neurological disorders. Collins, who had become interested in neurology during his period in Europe while Witmer was at Leipzig, had in recent years shifted his practice almost entirely from general medical practice to neurology and nervous disorders. In 1908, he had published *Letters to a Neurologist*,[33] and in the same year, he had opened a private sanitarium in Brewster, NY. At this time, in 1909, he was attempting, with the collaboration of Joseph Fraenkel, also a physician, to establish a research-oriented hospital in New York City for neurological and mental disorders.[34]

To advance this plan, Collins invited a number of prominent local men to a dinner meeting at the Century Club on March 18. He also invited Witmer to come up from Philadelphia. At the meeting, Collins outlined his plans in some detail. Witmer, as an invited guest, spoke on the pedagogical service that the proposed institution would provide and pointed out the close relationships between abnormal states and the nervous system in youths.

The meeting was a success; Collins raised sufficient funds to get the project under way. In 1910, he sold his sanitarium at Brewster, and devoted himself full-time to the center, which was named the New York Neurological Institute. This medical center, in the years ahead, would make major contributions and eventually would become part of the Columbia–Presbyterian Medical Center.

THE AMERICAN ACADEMY OF POLITICAL AND SOCIAL SCIENCE held its Annual Meeting at the University of Pennsylvania on April 17–18, about a month after Witmer's return from New York City. Witmer had been invited to address the members, and he had decided to make his presentation, in part, in the form of a modified clinic. (The term *clinic* is used here in the sense of a teaching-demonstration session for the presentation and discussion of problem cases. Witmer had first tried this method of instruction, with some reluctance, in the first summer of his Hospital School, and had found it worked well.[35])

The meeting of the visiting group took place in College Hall, probably in the present room 200, one floor up from the Psychological Clinic. Witmer began by stating that his aim was to give the members a general idea of the work of the Psychological Clinic, though because of time limitations his presentation would necessarily be very superficial. After some preliminary remarks he invited a little girl to the front, where there was some appropriate furniture, along with several simple tests. The following excerpt from a later published account describes Witmer's interaction with the child (as is evident some of his words were directed to the little girl and some to the audience):

I am going to proceed this morning just as I would in an ordinary clinic.

This little girl, whom I know quite well, has consented to come here this morning and take one or two of these simple tests.

(Professor Witmer takes the form board, which is a shallow oblong tray of light oak, having depressions of various shapes in its surface, into which fit ten blocks of dark walnut shaped like the depressions,—a square, circle, triangle, star, cross, semi-circle, and so on. He removes the blocks from their places and throws them on the table.)

Q. I am going to give you a new name this morning; you are going to be called Gertrude. What is your name going to be this morning?

A. Gertrude.

Q. Now if I make a mistake and call you by any other name, don't you answer. Gertrude, will you put these blocks back again? Do it just as quickly as you can.

It is an extremely simple test, but a very valuable one for those on the border line between normality and abnormality. The fact that she uses her vision and hands co-ordinately and without hesitation is proof enough in my opinion that the child is of approximately normal intelligence. Now I am going to ask a few questions.

Q. What is that (showing Gertrude a doll)?

A. A doll.

Q. What is that (showing her a toy dog)?

A. That is a dog.

Q. Have you a dog yourself?

A. No.[36]

Witmer next briefly chatted with two other children, a girl referred to as Fannnie and a boy called R. S. All three children then left the room, and Witmer discussed each child for the assembled group. All three had difficult backgrounds and presented serious problems.[37] Although their brief appearances[38] were not adequate for any useful clinical inquiry, their appearances did serve to make Witmer's later remarks more meaningful.

Witmer then introduced and lauded Margaret Maguire and Helena Devereux, as well as Oliver Cornman and a number of other local officials concerned with the welfare of children. Maguire was now the supervising principal of the Wharton Combined School and Devereux was the teacher, under Maguire, of the class for special children. Maguire briefly reviewed some of the children in the special class. Maguire and Cornman are known to the reader, but Devereux is a new name in the present narrative. She was particularly interested in working with retarded children.

LATER IN THE SAME year, 1909, the Psychological Clinic achieved
enhanced recognition at the University of Pennsylvania. It was provided
with larger quarters and given additional financial support to provide for
a larger staff. Along with this recognition, the Clinic was made a special
administrative unit, with its director directly responsible to the Board of
Trustees, rather than to the college dean. This step, which placed the
Clinic on a par with certain other auxiliary units such as the library, was
an immensely important development, both financially and symbolically,
for the Clinic.[39]

Along with this development, Witmer, as the director of the Psychological Clinic, set up the organizational structure that in a general way
was to persist until his retirement in 1937 and for some years thereafter.
In addition to the director, the plan called for an assistant director; Arthur
Holmes, who had earned his doctorate under Witmer the year before,
was appointed to this post. There was also to be a social worker, who
would visit homes and schools, and a recorder. The first women to fill
these roles were Ann Campion and I. K. Schanche, respectively. In addition to Witmer and Holmes, clinical examinations were conducted by
Twitmyer and Clara Harrison Town, who had just received her doctorate.
Several physicians, including Samuel Ludlum, also filled this role. Finally,
clinical graduate students assisted in Clinic functions. The hours of the
Clinic were expanded, so that it was now open from 2:00 p.m. to 5:00
p.m. on weekdays and from 9:00 a.m. to 12:00 p.m. on Saturdays, with
about three new cases seen daily. Further, Witmer announced that a member of the Clinic staff would be available to travel anywhere in Pennsylvania to examine children, as requested by parents or teachers.

As an aspect of the systematic reorganization of the Clinic, and in
view of the expectation of an increase in the case load, a new system for
numbering successive cases was introduced. Beginning in April 1909,
new cases were assigned numbers beginning with Case 1, and continuing
in order thereafter (without the preceding zeroes). To the best of my
knowledge, this system continued througout the existence of the Clinic.[40]

The enlargement of the Clinic meant not only that it could handle
more cases but also that the training program for clinical psychologists
could be expanded.

LIKE MANY OTHER PSYCHOLOGISTS of the period, Witmer
had become interested in the concept of intelligence. One expression of

this interest was curiosity about the level of intelligence in infrahuman primates. One of Witmer's friends was William H. Furness III, the curator of the University of Pennsylvania's Museum of Science and Arts. Furness was also a famous explorer, being best known for his book *The Home Life of Borneo Head-Hunters*.[41] In a conversation with Furness in 1908, Witmer had expressed the belief that it should be possible to teach an ape to articulate at least a few elements of spoken language and indicated that he would like to undertake such an experiment. After the conversation, Furness, in February 1909, when in South Borneo, obtained an infant orangutan between 1 and 2 years old and brought it back to Philadelphia. It was kept at the Furness family estate at Wallingford, southwest of Philadelphia, where he and Witmer undertook to train the animal.[42] Meanwhile, in September 1909, Witmer attended a performance at Boston's Keith Theater, where the chief attraction was a chimpanzee named Peter. The animal performed a number of complex activities that led Witmer to believe that the chimpanzee's actions were not simply rote behaviors. Later, when the troupe featuring Peter came to Philadelphia, Witmer arranged for the chimpanzee to be tested (with its trainer present) at the Clinic. This occasion aroused excited interest in the local newspapers, with headlines such as "Chimpanzee Shows Signs of Rational Powers" and "Peter Close to the Educational Line."[43]

At the Clinic, Witmer gave Peter several tasks, including some of the same tests that he routinely administered to young children. A difference was that in Peter's case, the testing was carried out in a large room with over a hundred persons observing; it is doubtful, however, that the presence of this group bothered Peter, because he was used to performing before crowds. During the testing, Peter sat on a small, three-legged stool, 8 or 9 inches high, which itself was on a low kindergarten table. One task requested of Peter was to string beads. Witmer first demonstrated this with three beads, then asked Peter to do the same, which he was able to do. Other tasks included placing pins in a pegging board, opening a lock, using a hammer to drive nails, using a screwdriver, placing various shaped blocks in the proper spaces in a formboard, and copying the letter *W* on a blackboard. Peter's overall performance was good but not perfect (e.g., he did not succeed with the formboard).

Witmer was particularly interested in Peter's ability to articulate words. However, the only word that Peter was ever able to produce was *mama*. Efforts by Furness to teach the orangutan that he had brought back from

Borneo to speak were also essentially unsuccessful, although the animal did eventually manage the words *papa* and *cup*.[44]

Witmer published his work with Peter in 1909 under the rather grandiose title "A Monkey With a Mind."[45] Later, Furness procured several additional primates, including a chimpanzee named Mimi, who was then kept in the psychology laboratory at the University of Pennsylvania, under Witmer's observation. Unfortunately, Mimi later contracted pneumonia and was moved to Furness's place in the country. Although she recovered, she was never returned to Witmer's laboratory, and he never published data on her. He did, however, publish a brief additional article on a macaque monkey housed with Furness.[46] This publication emphasized the animal's curiosity and ability to learn from direct observation.

Witmer's brief excursion into the study of primates represents a fascinating sidelight in his career and illustrates the wide range of his intellectual curiosity. The idea of teaching apes to speak was discussed at length in Warden, Jenkins, and Warner's classic 1936 volume, which includes references to Witmer and Furness.[47] Witmer's prediction that within a few years, chimpanzees would be reared in childlike environments was first realized in the 1930s, when W. N. and L. A. Kellogg adopted the infant Gua into their home.[48] The dramatic breakthrough in a chimpanzee's use of language came in the 1960s, when R. Allen Gardner and Beatrix T. Gardner adopted the chimpanzee Washoe and reared her in a childlike environment in which American Sign Language (ASL) was used.[49] Washoe assimilated and used an extensive ASL vocabulary.

BY 1910, THE PSYCHOLOGICAL CLINIC had become a well-known institution and inquiries for its services were coming from as far away as California. At the same time, however, the Clinic was no longer the unique facility that it had once been, as other psychological clinics and related centers began to appear around the country. In addition, there were certain other relevant advances, concerned primarily with psychological assessment, during the century's first decade. Because all of these developments furnished the backdrop for the rest of Witmer's career, it is appropriate to review them here.

Such a review must begin with the publication in France, in 1895— one year prior to the founding of Witmer's Clinic—of "La Psychologie

Individuelle," by Alfred Binet and Victor Henri.[50] This article led the way to the seminal Binet–Simon intelligence scale, in 1905, which in turn spawned a number of later tests for measuring intelligence, particularly in children.

In the United States—the origin and development of clinical psychology were primarily an American story—William Krohn, in 1897, after receiving his doctorate in psychology from Yale, founded a laboratory for the study of mentally disturbed persons at the Eastern Hospital for the Insane at Kankakee, IL. Later, Krohn entered the Northwestern University Medical School, from which he graduated in 1905, and then went into the field of psychiatry.[51] In 1898, R. T. Wiley, a physician at the State Institution for the Feeble-Minded in Faribault, MN, undertook certain psychological testing, including measures of sensory acuity and memory, of children in the facility. This led to the establishment of a systematic research laboratory, of which Frederick Kuhlmann, a psychologist who had obtained his doctorate at Clark in 1903, was installed as director in 1910.[52]

In 1899 Shepherd I. Franz received his PhD, under Cattell, at Columbia University. While at Harvard and Dartmouth, he established a psychological laboratory at McLean Hospital in Waverly, MA. In 1906, Franz moved to Washington, DC, as psychologist at the Government Hospital for the Insane (now St. Elizabeth's Hospital) and was succeeded at McLean Hospital by F. Lyman Wells. In 1912, Franz published a comprehensive test manual[53]; the first such manual, however, had been published 2 years earlier by Guy M. Whipple, a Titchener graduate.[54]

Among Hall's students at Clark University two were to figure very prominently in the advance of clinical psychology, especially with respect to the measurement of intelligence. These were Henry H. Goddard, who received his doctorate in 1899, and Lewis M. Terman, who received the degree in 1905—directly, as it happened, from the hands of President Theodore Roosevelt, who was the commencement speaker. In 1906, Goddard became director of psychological research at the New Jersey Training School for Feeble-Minded Boys and Girls, at Vineland. In 1908, while on a tour of European institutions for the retarded, he was introduced to the Binet–Simon intelligence scale, and in 1910, he published his own translation of the 1908 Binet-Simon test.[55] Whereas Goddard was primarily interested in the use of intelligence tests in the classification of the intellectually subnormal, Terman focused on a broader perspective and in 1916 brought out the Stanford–Binet Test of Intelligence, which was to become the standard measure of intelligence for several decades—and indeed is still, in revised form, in wide use.[56]

Another rising young psychologist in this period was Edward L. Thorndike, at Teachers College, Columbia University. Thorndike was particularly interested in education and psychological measurement. In 1907, he had authored a bulletin, *The Elimination of Pupils from School*,[57] and this work was reviewed positively in the March 1908 issue of *The Psychological Clinic*, obviously by Witmer himself, although the author is not given.[58] Subsequently, Thorndike's publication was criticized harshly in the *Journal of Education*[59]; Witmer, reading that review, was greatly impressed by it, and in the May issue of *The Psychological Clinic*, he largely retracted his earlier positive comments about Thorndike's bulletin.[60] Thorndike, irked by these developments, sent letters defending his positions to both the *Journal of Education* and Witmer.[61] In his response, Witmer wrote to Thorndike, saying that "it appears Winship [author of the *Journal of Education* review] was wrong and *The Psychological Clinic* has been hasty in following up his criticism. I'll do all possible to straighten it out."[62] Then in the June issue of his journal, Witmer included a brief note referring to Thorndike's rejoinder and indicating that *The Psychological Clinic*, in its next issue, would present an analysis doing justice to Thorndike's "important contribution."[63] Witmer evidently had in mind an article by Leonard Ayres, which appeared in the subsequent (October 1908) issue.[64] Thus the matter ended, with Witmer having in effect apologized to Thorndike. However, that the April 1909 *The Psychological Clinic* carried a letter from Thorndike further clarifying his position.[65]

Early in the century, a number of university psychology clinics beyond Philadelphia, stimulated by and patterned after Witmer's Clinic, were established.[66] In 1908, Jacob D. Heilman, a Witmer 1908 graduate, took a position at the State Teachers College in Greeley, CO, and established a clinic there. In 1909, James B. Miner, psychology professor at the University of Minnesota, opened a mental development clinic. The year 1909 also saw the organization of clinical psychological facilities at Clark University and the University of Washington (later, in 1911, Stevenson Smith, a Witmer product, would become director of the Washington facility). About 1910, Carl Seashore, an 1895 Yale doctorate in psychology, inaugurated a clinic at the University of Iowa, and in 1913,

Reuel H. Sylvester, who graduated from Witmer's program in 1912, became its director. Although these instances are by no means inclusive, they do illustrate the growth of the idea of psychological clinics. None of the new clinics approached the University of Pennsylvania Clinic in size or range of services offered.

In Chicago, in 1909, William Healy, a psychiatrist, established a clinic for delinquent youth, called the Juvenile Psychopathic Institute, which was affiliated with the Chicago juvenile court.[67] While organizing his facility, Healy visited Witmer's Clinic and Goddard's research laboratory at Vineland, NJ. Grace Fernald, a psychologist who had obtained her PhD at the University of Chicago in 1907, was appointed as psychologist in the new institute. The next year, Fernald left her position to become director of the psychological laboratory at the Los Angeles State Normal School; she was replaced by Augusta Bronner, a Thorndike student who would earn her PhD in 1914, who later married Healy. The Juvenile Psychopathic Institute has sometimes been referred to as the first child guidance clinic, an attribution which hardly seems appropriate, for two reasons. First, the role of the institute was quite limited, focusing, as it did, primarily on delinquent youths brought before a court. Second, Witmer's Psychological Clinic, founded 13 years earlier, dealt with a much broader range of problem children, including those under the jurisdiction of courts. Although Healy functioned in many ways as a psychologist, it was in his role as a psychiatrist that he directed the Juvenile Psychopathic Clinic. This institution proved the model for later psychiatrist-headed facilities and thus contrasted with the psychologist-directed model provided by Witmer. Both, of course, are important in the history of mental hygiene.

Another physician who was active in evaluation and treatment during this early period was Hugo Münsterberg. Although as a psychologist he directed the Harvard laboratory, it was in his role as a physician that he carried on a psychotherapeutic practice, in which he relied primarily on suggestion and hypnosis. In a judgment probably directed at Witmer and his Clinic, Münsterberg wrote that "even the experimental psychologist is not prepared to enter into medical treatment; and a 'Psychological Clinic,' managed by a psychologist who is not a doctor of medicine is certainly not better than a church clinic."[68]

Finally, this was a period in which the theories of Sigmund Freud and Carl Jung were gaining considerable attention. In September 1909,

Freud and Jung, at the invitation of President Hall at Clark, delivered a series of lectures formally introducing their views to America. It is almost certain that Witmer did not attend, probably because, with his strong empiricist bent, he found their theories unattractive.[69]

THE APRIL 1909 ISSUE of *The Psychological Clinic* carried an editorial by Witmer titled "Orthogenics in the Public Schools."[70] The term *orthogenics* was proposed by Witmer to designate "the name of a science which concerns itself with the restoration of those who are retarded or degenerate to a condition where normal development becomes a possibility."[71] The editorial emphasized the role of the public schools in dealing therapeutically with retarded and difficult children and recommended the establishment of special classes and the training of teachers for special education. The issue included an article by Helena T. Devereux on her innovative work in a class for mentally retarded children.[72] Devereux had graduated from the Philadelphia Normal School in 1906, and later joined its faculty. (In 1912 she would resign her position there to establish a small private school for slow-learning children at Avalon, NJ.) Although Witmer himself was not a hands-on teacher in special education, he respected and encouraged those who were, and through his leadership and propagandistic efforts, he contributed in a major way to the development of the field. In a more personal sense, this interest reflected Witmer's growing commitment to the welfare of children.

Early in the twentieth century, during the period in which Witmer was beginning to grapple with broad social issues, a major theme in public discussion, particularly in psychology, concerned the respective roles in behavior of heredity and environment. The great issue was whether psychological traits, particularly intelligence but also moral characteristics such as honesty and criminality, were primarily hereditary or learned. The general weight of opinion strongly favored the hereditary assumption, with the specific implications that retarded and delinquent children were naturally, that is to say, inherently, that way, thus leading to the conclusion that nothing could be done to alleviate their conditions. This general societal position was carried further by the then popular doctrine of *eugenics*, which implied that feebleminded persons should not be permitted to reproduce.

This is part of the background cultural context of Witmer's early work, and indeed, it was a factor that would resonate throughout his career. Further, Witmer was a significant player in the heredity–environment controversy. Early in his clinical work, he had more or less taken for granted the prevailing hereditarian stance, and indeed, he was sensitive throughout his career to the role of hereditary influences on behavior. This interest was manifested, for example, in his emphasis on "racial, national, and individual inheritance factors in education" in a 1911 course description.[73] Nevertheless, by the time of the papers now to be reviewed, as a function of extensive accumulated clinical experience, he had come to an ardent, even passionate, environmentalistic position. This was at the time a distinctly unconventional attitude, and Witmer was one of the first to swim against the hereditarian tide.

In 1910, Witmer published an article titled "The Restoration of Children of the Slums."[74] He used the term *restoration*, and sometimes *conservation*, to refer to efforts to improve children to their maximal level. The theme of this article is articulated near its beginning:

> One does not expect figs to grow from thistles, and the slum child seems naturally destined by the force of heredity to grow into an inefficient adult. There are many reasons, however, for repudiating this belief in the potency of heredity. . . . The inefficient product of the slum is the result of the treatment received during infancy and childhood.[75]

The bulk of the article reports two Clinic cases in support of this conclusion. The first was a little girl of 7 who came from an impoverished home, who was in poor physical condition and somewhat retarded mentally and morally. Witmer arranged for proper medical and dental care and for her to stay for 2 months in a home for Jewish girls. During this period, the child manifested the "infantile instinct" of taking things that did not belong to her, which Witmer attributed to the lack of moral training, saying "I do not believe in the existence of criminal instincts."[76] The second child, referred to as *Fannie*, was

> the offspring of Russian Jewish parents, who with their seven children were crowded into two small rooms. The living room had one window, and contained a table, a few chairs, a stove, a lounge, dirty clothes piled in one corner, a barking cur and many flies. The table was covered with a piece of black oilcloth, and on this were usually to be found pieces of brown bread and glasses of tea. No meals were prepared and the family never sat down to table. Their diet consisted chiefly

of bread, tea, and sometimes fish. The bread was always on the table for the flies to crawl over, and for the children to eat when their hunger drove them to it.[77]

Fannie was failing the first grade, where she had already spent the previous 2 years. She was brought to the Clinic by a school nurse. She was discovered to have visual and auditory problems, but her most serious defects, in Witmer's opinion,

> were temperamental and lay in the emotional rather than the intellectual field. She did not seem to understand affection, showed at first no curiosity, no vanity, no generosity, no spirit of helpfulness, no domestic traits or interest in the house, and very little fondness for a doll.[78]

After Witmer arranged for Fannie to live in the Hospital School—this was in 1907—and later in a private home, her behavior and emotional outlook improved rapidly. Witmer wrote the following:

> If I were asked to state what had been most essential for this child's development, I believe I should say good food, a hygienic environment and a measure of happiness. . . . Certainly all of this child's defects flowed directly from the impoverished condition of her family."[79]

The concept of *retardation, feeblemindedness, or backwardness*—all of which terms were commonly used—was rather vague and ambiguous in this period. In another 1910 article, Witmer attempted a resolution of this problem.[80] After first reviewing the history of the notion of retardation, he developed his own conception. Retardation, he argued, is not a disease, nor is it necessarily the result of a defect in the brain. Rather, it is a mental status, a stage of mental development

> . . . We may, therefore, say that any child, the functions of whose brain are not developed up to the normal limit for his age, is suffering from retardation. . . . Retardation must be defined in terms of individual capacity for physical and mental development. . . . What may be retardation for one may not be retardation for another. Indeed, it may well happen that the child who stands at the head of his class in school may be more retarded than the child who is at the bottom of the class.[81]

Witmer's emphasis, in his conception of retardation, on the extent to which a person developed his or her capacities, as contrasted with some hypothetical organic definition of the condition, reflected his consistent and primary commitment to the worth of each individual.

In December 1910, Witmer described an 11-year-old girl, referred to as Mary, who had been brought to the clinic in October 1908 with the problem of incorrigibility.[82] She was described by the Children's Aid Society, which had been looking after her, as the most difficult child they had ever attempted to handle, with intense outbursts of aggression; in addition she was considered mentally deficient. Witmer arranged for Mary to be under the care of the Psychological Clinic and the Hospital School. As was his wont, he preferred to see the positive aspects of Mary's character, and he warned, using Mary as an example, of underestimating the capacities of a child. Writing metaphorically, he compared two children, the child as presented and the child who he hoped that person might become. "What is required of one who holds the fate of any troublesome child in his hands," he wrote, "is sufficient psychological insight to see the other child beneath the one who is apt to be uppermost."[83]

Very early in working with Mary, Witmer was impressed with her spontaneity and independence and determined that she was not feeble-minded. Her improvement was not immediate, but it was consistent and highly positive. In the article's last paragraph, Witmer wrote the following:

> The moral reconstruction of a child like Mary is in the nature of a work of art. The loving hands of many nurses, teachers, trainers, and social workers are acquiring today the skilful [sic] touch which is needed to mold the plastic human material into forms of beauty.[84]

The next year, 1911, saw another article by Witmer on the same general theme: "Criminals in the Making."[85] This was a carefully reasoned, yet at the same time highly passionate, examination of the etiology of criminal behavior, illustrated by the accounts of two severely delinquent boys who had come to the attention of the Clinic. Witmer ridiculed the kind of public comment that had been made with respect to one of the boys, George, to the effect that he had "manifested a criminal bent at an early age."[86] The boy, said Witmer, had indeed been handicapped from the start, but the handicap was from living in an unstable, injurious environment. George, he asserted, had never known a permanent home or adequate discipline, nor had the wellspring of love ever been tapped in the boy. Of the other boy, Witmer wrote that "I consider Harry the product of his environment—the very natural product of poor food, poor care, insufficient discipline, inadequate school facilities, and lack of expert assistance to guide the family in the art of controlling a difficult boy."[87]

Harry, in the month after he left the care of the Psychological Clinic, ran away from home and, stealing a ride on a freight train, fell under the wheels and was killed. George, at the time of the article, was in a state reform school and appeared to be doing well. "He may," wrote Witmer, "repeat the history of many men of eminence, influence, and respectability who were every whit as troublesome in their youth."[88] On the other hand, George might follow a criminal career. As to which course George would take, it was, asserted Witmer, actually the community that was on trial, and it would be the fault of society at large if George took the criminal road.

In these several articles, Witmer assumed the role of a social critic, and there was an evangelical fervor in his writing. There were two chief, albeit related, themes in the articles: first, the fundamental importance of children; second, the cause of environmentalism, as contrasted with a naive hereditarianism. This second commitment, however, although strong for that day, was not absolute:

> Feeblemindedness, insanity, moral degeneracy, these are doubtless in a certain proportion of the cases the direct result of an inherited factor. Nevertheless, mental and moral degeneracy are just as frequently the result of the environment. In the absence of the most painstaking investigation, accompanied by a determined effort at remedial treatment, it is usually impossible to decide, when confronted by an individual case, whether heredity or the environment has played the chief role. Who can improve a man's inheritance? And what man's environment can not be bettered? In place of the hopeless fatalism of those who constantly emphasize our impotence in the presence of the hereditary factor, we prefer the hopeful optimism of those who point out the destructive activity of the environment. To ascribe a condition to the environment, is a challenge to do something for its amelioration or cure; to ascribe it to heredity too often means that we fold our hands and do nothing.[89]

As the historian John O'Donnell commented on the passage above, which he also quoted: "This passage [illustrates] the ideological flavor of Witmer's vision with its typically progressive faith in the efficacy of the environment and the plasticity of the human being."[90]

Witmer's basic value was in the improvability of persons. With respect to children, Witmer's attitude was always positive, hopeful, and optimistic; he took their side and defended them, with something of a prophet's zeal, against the complaints and blamings of adults in authority. Thus, in pointing out that considerable time, perhaps months of careful observation, is required to diagnose a child fully, he wrote the following:

> I consider most reprehensible the celerity with which some physicians, not a few judges and probation officers, and most laymen, will reach a conclusion as to a child's moral normality or degeneracy after a brief inspection and a hasty review of mostly hearsay reports.[91]

Witmer did not limit his persuasive zeal to articles in professional journals. No doubt his opinions permeated into his classroom lectures, and he also expounded his views in various public lectures, interviews, and articles. In the spring of 1909, he wrote a brief piece for a local newspaper, which carried it with the headline "No Such Thing as Criminal Instincts, Says Psychologist," (the article concerned the case of a 9-year-old boy held for stealing).[92] Later the same year, a newspaper reporter covered a talk by Witmer with the headline "Penn Psychologist Defends 'Bad Boy' ";[93] in his remarks, Witmer asserted that many of the world's outstanding geniuses were "bad boys" in their youth, and he cautioned parents against overcontrolling their children. Later, in January 1910, before an audience of social workers, he took the school system to task for not providing better educational opportunity for intellectually superior children. With respect to the occurrence of feeblemindedness, he recommended that severely retarded persons should not be permitted to marry.[94] A similar sentiment, although with the emphasis on retraining and rehabilitation, was expressed in a talk he gave in Montreal, Canada, in December 1910.[95]

The modern reader, noting Witmer's progressive attitude on the deleterious effects of poor environmental conditions on child development, may be surprised to learn of his espousal, at this stage in his career, of a eugenic proposal. Indeed, his position does seem somewhat ambiguous and was perhaps undergoing development. In March 1911, he would support a bill in the Pennsylvania legislature to provide for the sterilization of severely retarded males.[96] It should be remembered that the eugenics movement, fed by a widespread hereditarianism, was rapidly gaining influence during this period, and clearly Witmer was not wholly immune to its influence. There is no doubt, however, as to his basic environmentalistic stance. His overall prosocial attitude is well represented by the penultimate sentence in an article summarized earlier: "To conserve the children of the next generation . . . we must begin by restoring their future parents, the children of this generation."[97]

9

Travels, Talks, and Tests

Witmer, by 1910, was one of the more prominent professors at the University of Pennsylvania. In February of that year, he took the train to Kansas City, MO, where he was to speak to the local alumni of the University of Pennsylvania and to deliver an address before that city's Knife and Fork Club. In his remarks to the alumni, Witmer reviewed developments at Penn during the preceding 20 years and emphasized the importance of universities as "the molders of states." He held that a "great future" of universities lay in the application of scientific remediation to prevent disease and retardation among children and asserted that this task could better be accomplished by state than by private universities.[1]

The *Kansas City Times* reported Witmer's views under the headline, "His Plan to Save Children: Dr. Witmer Would Establish Psychological Clinics," and quoted him directly:

In every large city there should be established a psychological clinic with a competent psychologist at its head to keep the children from being wasted. . . . I am taking as an example the model clinic, the one at the University of Pennsylvania, which was established in 1896. . . . The children must not be wasted. It should be the work of every city to seek out and encourage every agency which has for its purpose the assistance of unfortunate children. The city should see to it that the poor, as well as the rich, have the opportunity of treatment, because a majority of these cases exist among the poorer classes. For this reason, I am agitating in the universities and in the large cities for the establishment by these institutions of psychological clinics of criminology and laboratories for the study of the defective child.[2]

Even allowing for the probability that some of the phrases in this passage were not altogether correctly recorded (the last two lines do not quite ring as the way Witmer would have put it), the general meaning is clear enough. Witmer is speaking as a children's advocate, pleading—insisting—that society take heed to the needs of children, particularly poor children. This commitment to the optimization of each child's potential was not limited to a concern for the retarded and the deviant, but also included, in a preliminary way, a perspective that later was to become a major theme in his outlook, namely, an interest in gifted children. This concern was evidenced in an article by Ella Frances Lynch, "The Bright Child," which appeared in the October 1910 issue of *The Psychological Clinic*. Lynch quoted Witmer as saying that "the public schools are not giving the bright child a square deal. He is marking time, waiting for the lame duck to catch up."[3]

Although Witmer, in his more public persona, was active in advancing the cause of children's welfare, particularly the role of psychology in that cause, the central portion of his life continued to revolve around his professorial and direct clinical activities. In June, the then well-known author H. Addington Bruce had an article titled "Psychology and Daily Life" in the popular magazine *The Outlook*.[4] This article described the program at Penn in considerable detail. It included a portrait of Witmer and quoted him at length regarding the history of the Psychological Clinic.

Early in the next year (i.e., in 1911), in a respectful letter to Edgar F. Smith, the university provost, Witmer revealed that he had received an offer of a professorship in New York City with a higher salary than he was presently receiving.[5] He stated that he had declined this offer because of his loyalty to the University of Pennsylvania. This allegiance came, he said, because of his desire to make the university's psychology department the best in the country—a status that, indeed, it already held, in his judgment, except for its cramped quarters. Witmer made it clear, however, that his primary commitment was to his professional work in "practical psychology" and that he would keep himself open to moving if another institution should offer a greater opportunity "for the larger development of my work." The letter could thus be interpreted as something of a challenge, or a threat, for Pennsylvania to provide greater support for his program.

Specifically, Witmer took the occasion to request, first, that the trustees take the lead in developing a fund of $500,000 (a truly astounding sum in those days) for a building and equipment for the Psychological Laboratory and Clinic; second, that they look with favor on the development of 4-year and 2-year programs in psychology, or in psychology and sociology; third, that pending the construction and equipment of a suitable building, additional space within College Hall be assigned to psychology. The trustees, in their meetings on March 7 and April 11, discussed Witmer's proposals at length, and decided, first, that a letter should be written to him "assuring him of the great interest of the Board in his valuable work, and of the Board's appreciation of his services . . . [and of their desire] to aid him in any way which might be feasible"; second, that the question of expanded programs be referred to the Academic Council; and third, that the departments already in the space requested by Witmer in College Hall could not be moved at this time.[6]

Although Witmer's immediate, and perhaps overly ambitious, requests were thus not fulfilled, they can perhaps be seen as part of an ongoing campaign for expansion of Clinic facilities, and it is notable that in the subsequent years, the Clinic would grow considerably, both in personnel and space, though it was never to leave College Hall.

The Witmers (Fifi and Lightner) lived in central Philadelphia, at 2426 Spruce. The couple had no children. Fifi helped Lightner in the publication of the *Psychological Clinic* and, from time to time, wrote book reviews for the journal. These included reviews of *How Two Hundred Children Live and Learn*, by Rudolph R. Reeder[7]; *The Care of the Child*, by Mrs. Burton Chance[8]; *Open-Air Schools*, by Leonard P. Ayres[9]; *The Dawn of Character*, by Edith E. Reade Mumford[10]; *The World of Dreams*, by Havelock Ellis[11]; and *Changing America*, by Edward Ross.[12] Her reviews were signed ERW—Emma Repplier Witmer. Fifi's aunt, the famous author Agnes Repplier, also lived in Philadelphia. Agnes was continuing her high output of beautiful essays. The estimable Miss Repplier had known Walt Whitman and Henry James, among others of the upper literati, and a few years later was to dine with President Theodore

Roosevelt. She adored Fifi, and liked Lightner, and undoubtedly added a certain esprit to their lives. The Witmers themselves were modestly into Philadelphia society. Lightner was a member of the University and Contemporary clubs, and the City Troop, which was as much a social as a military organization.[13] These affiliations, along with Fifi's family connections, gave them an entrée into the city's social circles, and they were listed in Philadelphia's *Social Register*.

In 1911, or perhaps a year or so before, the Witmers purchased a summer place in Chester, Nova Scotia, Canada, on the Atlantic shore. They gave their place the name Flotsam. It was a modest but attractive two-story home with a frontage of windows. Beginning in 1911, and possibly before, the Witmers, along with staff from the Rose Valley School, would take the children to their place in Nova Scotia during the summers. Witmer even arranged for a schoolhouse, so that classes could continue. There were horses, a carriage, and parties on the beach.[14]

WITMER DID NOT SPEND the entirety of each summer at their Nova Scotia place; during many years, he organized and directed a 6-week special class for deviant children. These were held on the Penn campus and were basically experimental and demonstrative sessions designed to develop improved methods for helping problem children. In addition to directly benefiting the children who participated, these sessions, which were always put on by the Psychological Clinic, were of great benefit to the Clinic staff, participating special education teachers, clinical students, and, of course, to Witmer himself. In addition to the regular Clinic staff, additional teaching personnel, sometimes very extensive, were brought in for these sessions.

The first such special class, focusing on mentally defective children, was carried out in 1897 and was essentially repeated in 1898. The next such session, similar in its aims, was in 1908. There was no summer class in 1909, but in 1910, a more ambitious session, centered on troublesome adolescent boys, was organized by Witmer, with Arthur Holmes, the assistant director of the Psychological Clinic, in immediate charge. The primary aim of this session was to examine juvenile delinquent boys in some detail, to understand them better and to evaluate methods of treatment in a preliminary way. The group included youngsters who had been considered unmanageable, had stolen, or had been truant from school. The results, given the brevity of the treatment, could only be suggestive, but all of the boys stayed throughout the session, and follow-ups indicated that at least some of them benefited noticeably.[15]

The most intense and impressive of the special summer classes was the one carried out with 18 backward children in 1911, which Witmer conceptualized as an educational experiment. This session was described in considerable detail in a book published by Witmer, including chapters by himself and other key staff and over 40 photographs taken by Twit-myer.[16] For this class, several teachers experienced in working with backward children were brought down from New York. A special and somewhat unique aspect of this class was its emphasis on the children's diets. Witmer had come to suspect that many cases of mental backwardness might be due to poor diets.[17] Accordingly, he selected a dietary specialist from the Russell Sage Foundation to head this part of the program. She arranged enriched lunches for the children and advised the parents on proper home diets. All in all, the 1911 special session was an expensive procedure, but Witmer was able to obtain private support to make it possible.[18] As in all of the special summer sessions for selected children, the days were made up of class work, counseling, activities such as manual training, outdoor recreation, and visits to educational centers such as city museums. All children were given both medical and psychological examinations, and the overall staff was large enough to provide individual attention for each child.

The 1912 special summer class comprised 11 bright children from the local school district, selected on the basis of Binet scores. Little information is available on this or subsequent classes, but they appear to have been scheduled on a fairly regular basis.[19]

It is clear that Witmer saw these special sessions for deviant children in a very positive way. Such brief intensive efforts constituted, in effect, a third major therapeutic approach that he employed in clinical work with children, the other two being the Psychological Clinic and his residential school.

WITMER TOOK A LEAVE from the university for the spring semester of 1912 and sailed for Europe.[20] His purpose was to study pedagogical methods for working with exceptional children in England and on the continent, particularly the newer methods of Maria Montessori, in Italy.

Montessori was becoming known in informed circles for her innovative work with children. She was born in 1870, so she was about Witmer's age. In 1894, she became the first woman to receive a medical degree from the University of Rome, and thereafter, she became interested in working with mentally defective children. Early in the century, she developed an unusual and effective method for reaching and teaching such children. Later, she extended her system to normal children. The central motif of her system was to foster the child's independence and initiative in the learning process. When in Rome, Witmer visited Montessori's Casa dei Bambini and observed "little children three to seven years old, independently and resolutely setting about and executing fairly difficult tasks."[21] He was very favorably impressed by Montessori's approach and published a laudatory article, commenting that "with Montessori, I believe we know very little concerning the aptitudes of the child, and that we tend to circumscribe too narrowly the possible limits of a child's development."[22] His enthusiasm for Montessori, however, was not unqualified. Later, he developed his own method of "diagnostic education."[23]

THE YEAR 1912 ALSO included the publication of an important book, *The Conservation of the Child*, by Arthur Holmes.[24] The book's subtitle, "A Manual of Clinical Psychology Presenting the Examination and Treatment of Backward Children," accurately describes its content. The volume opened with a review of professional and societal concerns with backward children. The nature, functions, and operation of the Psychological Clinic were then described in some detail. Systems for the classification, or diagnosis, of Clinic cases were next examined, and the nature and uses of available mental tests were surveyed. The next topic covered was moral deviancy (delinquency), and the book closed with a chapter on the implications of the Clinic for a broader society.

This book is of notable historical importance for two main reasons: First, it was the first book-length treatment of the emerging field of clinical psychology; and second, it provides an excellent picture of the functioning of the Psychological Clinic around 1912.[25]

Holmes, who was a man of considerable homespun charm and forthrightness, often spoke, like Witmer, at various community or professional meetings. On one occasion, he admonished a group of mothers not to nag growing boys, but to permit them to develop their independence[26]; on another, he advised an audience of female teachers to deal understandingly with the instinct of love as it may appear among their pupils, maintaining that the better teachers were those who themselves were or had been in love.[27] His remarks were delivered with a touch of humor spiced with relevant anecdotes.

The Psychological Clinic was by this time a large operation. Physically, the Clinic proper, not counting offices, student quarters, and storage areas, occupied three rooms on the lower floor of College Hall; there was a reception room, an examination room, and a room for private conferences with children, parents, or others. The reception room included a variety of colorful toys to interest children, and a wide range of test materials was available for the examiners. The provision was provided for children in the examining room to leave without going through the reception room.

The Clinic's operation included two highly innovative features that were on the cutting edge of technical progress in 1912. First, and most novel, was the role of the recorder. The duties of this staff member were described in the following way by Holmes:

> Connected with the staff there is also a recorder, who is an expert stenographer, and who takes accurate notes of the examinations of each child, records them in a prescribed form and files them in a regular systematic way, ready for examination at any time by students and others interested in scientific research upon problems connected with children.[28]

The inclusion of the position of recorder, with its role analogous to the function of audiotape recording in modern clinics, was a fascinating aspect of the original Clinic. The second auxiliary feature was the inclusion of a complete photographic laboratory, including a dark room, which made it possible to maintain a picture file of children, as appropriate. There is at least some similarity between this facility in the Psychological Clinic and the current trend to use the video camera.

In 1912, Holmes left the University of Pennsylvania to become dean of the faculty at Pennsylvania State College.[29] He was succeeded as assistant director of the Psychological Clinic by Francis N. Maxfield, who had obtained his doctorate under Witmer in the same year, 1912. Maxfield was destined to be second in command at the Clinic until 1918.[30] The heart and soul of the Psychological Clinic was, of course, in the cases that came under its purview. The capsule summaries presented below, selected more or less randomly from the microfilmed records, provide a general picture of the Clinic's ongoing activity in the period under review.[31] In each instance, the first number is the case number assigned on the initial contact, and the second number indicates the year the case was opened. Psychologists primarily responsible for each case, when available, are indicated by the codes LW (Witmer), AH (Holmes), FM (Maxfield), and ET (Twitmyer). Of course, many cases involved assessment or intervention by several staff members or graduate students, and in some instances, a social worker was the primary contact person. Most cases were evaluated by a physician one or more times. Some records were brief, with the subject seen only once, whereas others comprised many contacts, in some instances going on for years. Although not specifically indicated below, all child cases involved contacts (frequently many contacts) with parents and with school and relevant municipal authorities.

285, 1910. Boy, age 13. Brought to hospital by mother, referred to clinic. Backward, excitable, uncontrollable fits of laughter and crying, in constant trouble. LW.

301, 1910. Boy, age 14. Brought by stepmother on physician's referral. Incorrigible, dishonest, conduct problem at home, school, at work. Extensive social service follow-up to 1918.

318, 1910. Man, age 30. Had swimming accident 6 years earlier, with consequent partial paralysis, memory loss, other cognitive, emotional disturbances. LW.

330, 1910. Girl, age 8. Brought by parents on physician's referral. Backward, nervous. Extensive testing, diagnosed low-grade imbecile; recommended for institutional care. AH, LW.

359, 1910. Boy, age 16. Brought by father on physician's referral. Backward, diagnosed middle- or low-grade imbecile. Recommended for Elwyn. LW.

468, 1911. Boy, age 13. Referred by school. Reported backward since head injury age 9. Difficult to manage, truancy. Problems attributed to home conditions. AH.

484, 1911. Boy, age 8. Physician referral. Moral delinquency, uncontrollable temper outbursts. Intelligence above average. Detailed follow-up to 1913. AH.

531, 1911. Girl, age 16. Without voice past 6 months. No discernible organic dysfunction; diagnosed hysteria, aphonia, hypnotherapy suggested. Left Clinic, treatment continued elsewhere. Follow-up 1914, voice regained. ET.

944, 1913. Girl, age 14, African American. Parents unknown, reared in church school. Had been raped. Diagnosed high grade imbecile, capable of improvement. Recommended to home for girls. FM. (Girl died in hospital in 1915; illness not stated.)

1037, 1913. Man, age 22. Examined at House of Correction, request by Juvenile Protective Association. Poor physical status, mental status better than physical condition would suggest. FM.

1116, 1913. Boy, age 8. Referred for backwardness in school, propensity for stealing. Diagnosed not mentally defective. Counsel given for dealing with undesirable behavior. FM.

1129, 1913. Man, age 21. Had developed nervous symptoms and withdrawn from college in first year. Referring physician suggested possible incipient dementia praecox, but this was discounted. FM.

1248, 1914. Girl, age 13. Referred by University Hospital because of nervousness and hyperactivity. Diagnosed developmentally normal. Recommended private country school, examination for hyperthyroidism. LW.

1405, 1914. Girl, age 3. Referred to see if mental problems likely to arise due to insanity of parents. Diagnosed normal, developmentally advanced. Recommended for Montessori class. LW.

1701, 1915. Boy, age 15. Referred for extreme nervousness, fear of ghosts. No diagnosis given, but possibility of fixed phobia discounted. FM.

1896, 1915. Girl, age 6. Referred by physician because of general retardation, inability to speak. Diagnosed Mongolian idiocy. Custodial care recommended. LW.

1911, 1915. Girl, age 9. Referred by social worker because of peculiar behavior. Diagnosed high grade imbecility associated with epilepsy, possibility of dementia praecox. LW.

WITMER SPENT THE SUMMER of 1913 lecturing in the West.[32] First, he traveled to Missoula, where he gave four lectures on clinical psychology at the University of Montana. These lectures were followed by a 4-week course of lectures and practical demonstrations in connection with the backward classes in the Missoula schools. This course was given by Carolyn E. Morrison, who was identified as the "clinical psychologist for the public schools of Hibbing, Minnesota." Morrison had received her training in the Summer School at the University of Pennsylvania; although referred to as a *clinical psychologist*, Morrison could more properly be termed a *school psychologist*.

From Missoula, Witmer went to Greeley, to lecture at the State Teacher's College. He presented 10 lectures at this institution, 5 in the mornings and 5 in the afternoons. The morning lectures were on problems of growth and retardation. These were part of a general course on modern education organized by the college, and other speakers included G. Stanley Hall, the president of Clark University, and David Starr Jordan, the president of Stanford. Witmer's afternoon lectures dealt with the clinical method in psychology and its application to the study of various types of children. These lectures were followed by presentations by J. D. Heilman, a regular faculty member at the college. Heilman had received his doctorate under Witmer in 1908. Probably, it was he who arranged for Witmer to go to Greeley.

Witmer's final lecture stop was at the University of California in Berkeley. Presumably, he made the trip there by train, a direct line going from Chicago, through Greeley, and on to Berkeley, Oakland, and San Francisco. At Berkeley, Witmer lectured from July 14 to August 1. During these 3 weeks he offered two courses: Clinical Psychology in the morning and Growth and Retardation in the afternoon.

I NOW BRIEFLY REVIEW several papers by Witmer. There was a growing interest during this period of American history in the situations of many children who, for one reason or another, were unable to participate successfully in regular school classes and for whom special educational opportunities were needed. P. P. Claxton, the U.S. commissioner of education, asked James H. Van Sickle, Witmer, and Leonard P. Ayres to examine the problem, and they prepared a report titled "Provision for Exceptional Children in Public Schools."[33] This report, published in 1911, focused on the training of retarded children, although it covered also the education of gifted children. As the first detailed survey of its kind, the report was highly influential in the further national development of special education. Subsequently, the U.S. commissioner of education asked Witmer to prepare a report of the progress made in this area during the 1912–1913 year.[34] To collect relevant information, Witmer mailed questionnaires to 935 city, state, and territorial school superintendents around the country, and his report was based primarily on replies to these inquiries. In general, the responses indicated some improvement in provisions for the education of exceptional children over the 1911 data; however, the questionnaire return rate was only 35%.

In a 1913 article in *The Psychological Clinic*, Witmer elaborated a distinction between "mentally defective children" and "children with mental defects."[35] He stated that people differ among themselves on all sorts of abilities and traits, including various characteristics that could, at least in certain circumstances, be considered as defects: "There is no so-called normal person who does not possess some defects along with his assets."[36] In particular, Witmer conceived that individuals naturally vary among themselves in terms of verbal, mathematical, and musical aptitudes. Only children who have so many and such severe defects as to seriously interfere with adequate development should be considered mentally defective. He asserted that "no Binet–Simon tests, nor any other tests"[37] can determine who is feebleminded; rather, he maintained, feeblemindedness should be defined in terms of social considerations, of the capacity of a child to adequately adjust in society. He therefore proposed substituting *socially defective* for the more common *mentally defective.*[38]

AT WITMER'S ROSE VALLEY SCHOOL[39] there were, in the period under review in this chapter, two new teachers who would gain considerable distinction in the years to come. These were Gertrude Stewart, who later, with Witmer's help, would found the famous Stewart School at Swarthmore, and Elizabeth O'Connor, who later would become the manager, and eventually the operator (after Witmer's death), of the larger Witmer School at Devon. Stewart was educated at the University of Pennsylvania, Fordham University, and Columbia University. O'Connor received her education at Drexel University and the University of Pennsylvania.[40]

The Rose Valley School, as observed earlier, was located in the countryside southwest of Philadelphia. The school was housed in a large former home. In addition to the living quarters and schoolroom, the residence included a large, comfortable room with bookcases and a huge fireplace, referred to as the "music room." There was an entrance foyer, with a large grandfather clock, and, of course, a kitchen and dining room. Outside, there were spacious, grass-covered grounds for play and a family collie named Senator. A gaslight was mounted on a post that stood outside the entrance. Witmer's intent was to provide a homelike, rather than an institutional, atmosphere for the children. The school had four or five staff in any given period and up to 10 students.[41]

THIS SECTION DESCRIBES THE development of two psychological tests by Witmer and his students. These were the Witmer Formboard and the Witmer Cylinders. (The present review, to be relatively comprehensive, will include some data published during the 1920s.) Both tests, especially the former one, were used extensively in the Psychological Clinic and, to some extent, elsewhere, particularly during the second and third decades of the century. These tests are very important in understanding Witmer's career and his clinical philosophy. He was, after all, trained in objective science, and these tests reflect the carryover of this attitude to clinical work. Although some observers have supposed that Witmer gave up his scientific attitude when he switched to clinical practice, this clearly was not the case.

Witmer's interests in psychological testing went back to his early days as a student of James McKeen Cattell and later to his service on an APA committee to review test procedures. At first, he had enthusiastically associated himself with the sensorimotor approach, as pioneered by Galton and Cattell, but by 1904, he had become disillusioned with this approach.

When Witmer began his clinical work, there was, of course, a paucity of any test procedures that could be useful in clinical evaluations. In the early decades of the clinical psychological movement, formboards of one sort or another (and there were quite a number of different ones in use) constituted the major objective type of clinical assessment tool. Nor was this confidence totally misplaced. The following statement, by Henry Goddard in 1912, is representative of the feelings of clinicians of that period: "We have in our laboratory no other test that shows us so much about a child's condition in so short a time as this formboard."[42]

The idea of formboards arose in connection with Jean Itard's attempts to train Victor, the Wild Boy of Aveyron. Itard pasted three pieces of brightly colored cardboard—a red circle, a blue triangle, and a black square—on a board 2 feet square and indicated that Victor should place other, similar pieces of cardboard in the appropriate places. In succeeding days, Victor was given other, more complex form-placement problems to solve.[43] Edouard Seguin, who took over the training of Victor from Itard, constructed, from this beginning, a number of formboards and introduced them to the United States when he came to America. Seguin's formboards were constructed of wood, with indentations of various shapes into which similarly shaped blocks of wood could be placed.

Further advances in the development of a systematic formboard test were made by Henry Goddard, at the Vineland Training School. Goddard's formboard was revised slightly by Twitmyer at the Psychological Clinic, and this formboard was widely employed at the Clinic.[44] It was this instrument that Witmer used in 1909 when he sought to evaluate the performance of Peter, the chimpanzee. As early as 1911, he described the method as a procedure which "very quickly gives the experimenter a general idea of the child's powers of recognition, discrimination, memory and coordination."[45] At this time, Witmer and others used the formboard technique primarily as a rough measure of intelligence, useful in helping distinguish between normal and feebleminded children.

In 1913, Reuel H. Sylvester, a Witmer student, published his doctoral thesis on the formboard test, as this was then used in the Clinic.[46] Sylvester's project, which involved the testing of 605 children in backward classes and 500 children in regular classes in the Philadelphia Public School System, was the first large-scale study anywhere on formboard testing. Subsequently, Witmer made certain alterations in the formboard standardized by Sylvester, and this modification, which came to be widely used, was known as the Witmer Formboard. In this final arrangement, the board was 1 foot square and divided into two compartments, with the smaller one (which in testing is placed farthest from the subject) compressing a space where 11 cutout pieces of wood (e.g., a circle, a star, and an oval) could be laid, and the larger one including indentations into which each of the pieces could be snugly placed. Each piece could be filled into one, and only one, of the recesses.[47] The task of the subject was to place the 11 blocks into the appropriate recesses as rapidly as possible. Typically, three trials were given, and several different scoring methods were devised.

Herman Young, a student under Witmer, carried out, in 1916, a large-scale normative study of the Witmer Formboard, based on 2,849 children and 221 adults.[48] His report, published in *The Psychological Clinic*, became the standard reference for clinicians using the test. Young called attention, as others had before him, to a strong relationship between performance and age. Later in the same year, Young, who was by now the psychologist at the juvenile court in Cincinnati, published a second paper on the Witmer Formboard.[49] This article was a discussion of the interpretative inferences that could be derived from a child's performance. Young identified such influences on performance as vitality, attention, and imagination and proposed a series of rating scales to be completed in evaluating a child's performance.

In the same volume of his journal in which Young's articles appeared, Witmer published a brief piece called "A Formboard Demonstration."[50] This brief article reported, in detail, the procedures and statements made by Witmer as he administered the Formboard to a 7-year-old boy before his Mental Analysis class. The session was recorded (presumably in shorthand) by the Clinic recorder.

Children, of course, did not always succeed in solving the Formboard. In 1918, Adam Kephart, another University of Pennsylvania student, examined, with a number of brief case reports, the nature and interpretation of children's failures with the Formboard and concluded that the underlying problem was an inadequacy of attention.[51] Young's work had carried the norms down only to the 6-year level, but in 1918, Gladys Ide, observing that many children brought to the Clinic were younger than 6, published a careful study on applications of the test to 2-, 3-, 4-, and 5-year-olds.[52] She found that in general, the test was of limited use for children under 4. Then, in 1923, the Youngs—Herman and his wife Mary Hoover Young (both Witmer students)—published a reanalysis of earlier research records, focusing on completion time for the first trial (of the three usually given).[53] A child's first trial on the Formboard was now considered especially important because it reflected the child's ability to solve a new problem, being in this sense in accord with Witmer's developing conception of intelligence (this is described in chaps. 10 and 11).

How, in retrospect, is the Witmer Formboard test to be judged? The test has, of course, long been succeeded by more sophisticated instruments, but the Witmer test can properly be seen as a useful step in the long story of assessment.[54] Of the various early formboards that were once widely used, Witmer's was probably the best. The respected scholar Grace Kent, looking backward in a 1950 survey of methods of child assessment, concluded that "among the various formboards which stem from Seguin, the Witmer board is the most convenient in respect to size and is by far the best standardized"[55] and, further, "on the whole . . . this is the best edition of the Seguin board the writer has seen."[56]

An obvious limitation of the Formboard was its emphasis on visual-motor skills, to the exclusion of the verbal domain. Another limitation was that although age gradations could be made up into the mid-teens on the basis of performance time, solving the test as such did not present any real problem to most children beyond the age of 6. Witmer therefore felt the need for a more complex test. As it happened, he had earlier adopted into the Clinic some free-play materials, conceived by Montessori, which involved the child's placing a number of cylinders into matching recesses. In the spring of 1915, stimulated by the Montessori materials, he undertook to construct a device, following a similar idea, that would constitute a practicable psychological test. The result was the Witmer Cylinders test: this consisted of a circular form ($10^3/_8$ inches in diameter and $2^1/_2$ inches high) made of metal, with an inner recess (7 inches in diameter) and with 18 holes (cylinders) of various diameters and depths, distributed around the rim; within the center recess were placed 18 circular wooden blocks, of differing diameters and lengths. The subject was asked to place these blocks in the appropriate cylinders, and times were recorded for three successive trials.

The major publications on the Witmer Cylinders were two by Franklin C. Paschal in 1918,[57,58] both based on his doctoral research at the University of Pennsylvania. Paschal opened his dissertation with these words:

> The differential diagnosis of the psychological clinic requires a variety of "behavior" tests, tests which give the child something to do, which place in his hands an article that to him is a thing to play with, in order that his actions may be observed,—that we may, so to speak, see his mind in action.[59]

In standardizing the Witmer Cylinders and developing normative data, Paschal tested 1,722 schoolchildren and 508 adults. Astonishingly for that early period, Paschal provided three kinds of what later would be called *validity data* (he referred to them as *relations between performance and proficiency*). First, he produced convincing evidence that test performance was related to pedagogical age, with children in higher school grades doing better than children in lower grades. Second, he compared several groups of adults, showing that their relative performances were as predicted (e.g., that college men scored better than a group of prisoners). Third, he found positive correlations between test performances and proficiency of students in shop classes, as rated by their instructors.

In a 1916 paper, Mary Hoover Young, addressing the question of the relation between Witmer's Formboard and his Cylinders, found an inter-test correlation of .47 for men (n = 55), but only .07 for women (n =

57), suggesting that the two tasks tended to be similar for men but different for women.[60] Then, in 1918 Ide, in the same study reported above, administered the Cylinders test to 368 five-year-old children and 20 four-year-olds and concluded that it was too complex for most children under 5 and very difficult for most children of 5.

In the broad historical current that led to contemporary assessment technology, Witmer's role cannot be accorded a major place. Nevertheless, his systematic work in test development, viewed against the standards of the time, was solid and creative. Unlike the case with most other tests devised in the period, Witmer's tests had the distinction of having been constructed in an actual treatment setting, for use in that setting. Although his tests were designed to yield meaningful scores, Witmer was actually somewhat suspicious of statistical norms and always emphasized to his students the importance of carefully observing how the child performs the task rather than depending primarily on test scores.

THE YEAR 1914 BROUGHT forth a new and important development in the structure of the Psychological Clinic. This was the establishment, by Twitmyer, of a satellite clinic—to be known as the Corrective Speech Clinic—for the diagnosis and treatment of speech defects. So far as can be determined, this was the first clinic of its type in the nation, although of course there had been earlier workers in the area, including Twitmyer's wife, Mary Marvin, who had been one of Witmer's earliest collaborators and whose special expertise was in teaching deaf persons to speak. Although functionally independent, the Corrective Speech Clinic, which was open for new cases twice weekly, was an integral part of the overall Psychological Clinic, and cases were numbered in the same sequence as other Clinic cases. Twitmyer's general approach, in working with persons with speech disorders, was based on the view that habitual disturbances in breathing constituted a major etiological factor. Treatment methods were thus designed to establish improved habits of breathing.

The Speech Clinic soon became a flourishing part of the larger Clinic, and Twitmyer, in the years ahead, would become known as a leading pioneer and authority in the treatment of speech disorders.

10

The War Era

In mid-1914, war broke out among the great powers in Europe. The major antagonists were, on one side, Germany, Austria-Hungary, and Turkey, referred to as the *Central Powers*, and on the other side, France, Great Britain, Belgium, Italy, and Russia, referred to as the *Allies*. Although the United States was not militarily involved in the war at its outset, it was, almost immediately, culturally, psychologically, and economically affected, because of its close ties with Europe. As the war progressed into 1915, American opinion was somewhat diverse; most people favored neutrality, but with an emotional preference for the Allied cause, in part because of revulsion over the German invasion of Belgium: Witmer was in this group. Some few, however, including, among figures noted earlier in this narrative, Hugo Münsterberg—who, despite his long residence in America, had remained a German at heart—spoke out in moral support of the Central Powers.

The president of the United States at this time was Woodrow Wilson. He was well-known to Philadelphians; he had graduated from nearby Princeton and had received his doctorate from Johns Hopkins. After that, he had taught at Bryn Mawr and then returned to Princeton as professor of political economy and, later, as its president. In 1910, he was elected governor of New Jersey and, 2 years later, as U.S. president.

Politically, he was considered a strong progressive, as was Witmer. When the war came, Wilson urged a strictly neutral role for the United States.

EXCEPT IN THE SENSE of his being a concerned citizen, Witmer's routine was not affected by the war in Europe. During the 1913–1914 academic year, as part of the university's series of free public lectures, Witmer spoke on "The Exceptional Child at Home and in School."[1] This was published by the University of Pennsylvania in 1915 and was reprinted with a slightly different title, in *School and Society*.[2] The article, although not a major one in the perspective of Witmer's entire corpus, included a brief account of the interest that people had shown in fee-bleminded persons, emphasized the importance of adequate training for teachers of exceptional children, and summarized the work of his Clinic.

Witmer's article "Clinical Records," published in *The Psychological Clinic*, was, in contrast, a major contribution.[3] More than any other paper, perhaps, it revealed the basic philosophy of his clinical approach. At this point—1915—Witmer, in his latter forties, was probably at the height of his powers, and the article merits a close look. It begins in this way:

> When asked for specimens of the record blanks which are used by the Psychological Clinic, my invariable answer is that we have none. I am often asked for a list of the tests which we employ at the Psychological Clinic. I do not furnish such lists, because I am in doubt whether there is a single test which I can recommend to be employed with every case which comes to the Clinic for examination. . . . My very early experience with cases at the Psychological Clinic revealed the necessity for keeping the examination in a fluid state. I acquired a fear of the formalism of a blank, especially a blank filled in by some more or less adequately trained assistant. Experience also led me to believe in the inefficacy of the quantified result of a test, as for example the Binet test. If someone reports to me that a fifteen-year-old child has a Binet age of twelve, I do not consider this fact as having by itself diagnostic value. It is an interesting statement, which however I would not risk making anything of, until I had further examined the child. I do not know of any single test on which I can rely for diagnostic purposes.[4]

Witmer described the clinical aims of the Psychological Clinic in the following way:

> We have always held before us as an object of our work, the primary necessity of doing something for the child, and for those who are responsible for his welfare.

Let us keep in mind the distinctive purpose of the Psychological Clinic. It is not, in my opinion, to study feebleminded or otherwise defective children. There are already experts in this field. . . . I am interested in the child who has a handicap, preferably a removable handicap. I believe that the clinical psychologist in conducting his examination must proceed directly to the work in hand. I want to know who brings or sends the child to the Clinic. Why is he brought? What do his parents or teachers complain of? I then proceed to find out whether the complaint is justified. . . . Now one question, now another, will serve to make the situation clear, and give me material for a prognosis and the recommendation of treatment. Frequently when I find a proximate course I do not search with great diligence for a more remote cause.[5]

These quotations make clear Witmer's underlying clinical commitments as a child clinical psychologist—to help the child and those responsible for his or her welfare. His clinical approach had a distinctly modern ring in several respects: first, in his skepticism concerning the utility of tests as final arbiters of intellectual status; second, in his insistence in obtaining case information from a variety of sources; and third, in his lack of interest in the remote, distal causes of a child's behavior problems when an understanding of the more immediate, proximal causes was sufficient to be helpful.[6]

The Psychological Clinic, Witmer reported, was now seeing fewer feebleminded children, to give greater attention to children who were more susceptible to being helped. Another new trend was that the Clinic was beginning to provide vocational guidance to selected cases. The article concluded with a summary of Clinic activities, based on a detailed analysis of 40 cases. This sample was obtained by taking every 25th case from case Numbers 300 through 1300 and covered a 3½-year period. The data showed, among other things, that a total of 224 test procedures had been administered to the 40 cases.

A major article by Witmer in the spring of 1915 concerned the relation of intelligence to efficiency.[7] This contribution can be described as a theoretical article, with a strong admixture of editorial-like comments. It was written during the early stages of what Witmer referred to as "the current European war," and references to that conflict appear throughout the article. The concepts of *efficiency* and *intelligence* were then prominent in the mainstream of ideas, in both the general culture and professional psychological thought. Witmer's interest in intelligence went back to his earliest experience with children and was also manifested in his brief work with chimpanzees. His article examined the nature of intelligence and efficiency, as well as several related terms, including *competency*. He emphasized the importance of distinguishing among intelligence, reason, and understanding. There was a tendency, he felt, for some writers to reify the notion of intelligence as a central teleological concept in the same manner in which terms like *psyche* or *mind* had formerly been used.

Intelligence, Witmer proposed, should be defined as the ability of a person to solve what for him or her is a new problem. An important distinction, he held, should be made between intelligence level and performance level, with the latter being influenced by a number of factors, such as education and culture, in addition to intelligence. With respect to performance level, two *growth scales* could in principle be conceived: the *species scale* and the *age scale*. The first of these referred to performance differences in, for example, humans, chimpanzees, and horses, whereas the second referred to performance differences in humans in the sense that children typically perform at a higher level than infants. Witmer considered the Binet test a performance measure and asserted that "a ten year old feebleminded child who has a 'mental age' of six years is not at all like a normal child of six."[8] Two *sex scales* of performance could also, in principle, be posited. These scales concerned "the manly man and the womanly woman" and "effeminate men and masculine women." Witmer added that "exactly what is meant by these terms, and whether performances have a sex quality or not, I confess I do not know."[9] Next, he suggested two *culture scales* of performance: one referring to a person's general level of civilization and the other to his or her educational level. He then proposed a pair of dimensions concerning persons' deviations from normality. The first of these was the *deficiency scale*, encompassing feebleminded though normal individuals. Although Witmer granted that this variable was clearly related to intelligence, the criterion he had in mind was a social one, that is, the inability of feebleminded persons to manage themselves adequately in society. The second culture scale was the *insanity scale*. Here, too, Witmer proposed a social criterion: "The insane are placed in institutions not because they have insane ideas—for many persons whom we call normal have insane ideas—but because their performances render them dangerous to themselves or a menace to society."[10]

In further elaboration of his view of intelligence, Witmer proposed two separate dimensions to this concept: first, the *invention scale*, and, second, the *resource scale.* The *invention* aspect refers to the degree of originality involved in the solution to a new problem, and the *resourcefulness* aspect gauges the breadth of resources in which the inventiveness is relevant. To illuminate this perspective, Witmer identified Aristotle, Plato, da Vinci, and Goethe as geniuses of the first rank because they excelled in both inventiveness and resourcefulness.

The article included several interesting personal references. One was to Münsterberg, whom Witmer now disliked. In recent years, Münsterberg had labored fervently to turn American public opinion to the support of the German nationalist position. Witmer quoted these words from Münsterberg: "The southern peoples are children of the moment; the Teutonic live in the things which lie beyond the world, in the infinite and the ineffable" and added, "No wonder we think of Harvard's department of psychology as virtually an 'outpost of Kultur' and only incidentally a psychological laboratory."[11] The article also included brief mentions of Wundt and James. Referring to Wundt, Witmer commented that "he has employed many resources and shown the highest proficiency, but seldom in his work do we see the invention which leaps up to us from every page of William James."[12] In view of Witmer's earlier criticisms of James, this is high praise, indeed, and indicates that Witmer had reconsidered his earlier evaluation of James.

During the years 1916 and 1917, Witmer published five articles, all in *The Psychological Clinic.* Three of these consisted essentially of transcripts of lectures that he had given to classes and must be considered minor contributions. Of these three, "A Formboard Demonstration" has already been noted in these pages. The other two concerned a case diagnosed as congenital aphasia and feeblemindedness,[13] and a study of two feebleminded girls.[14] The fourth of the articles just noted, titled "A Fettered Mind," was a case report of a 7-year-old girl who had been considered hopelessly backward, but who under concerted training showed remarkable improvement.[15]

The fifth paper was an address that Witmer had delivered before the American Philosophical Society in Philadelphia on April 15, 1917,[16] and published under a slightly different title.[17] In the talk and publication, Witmer described his approach to the treatment of retarded children; he considered his method—which he referred to as diagnostic education —to be a modern follow-up of the foundations laid earlier by Jacob

Pereira and Edouard Seguin. He laid particular stress on his concept of *analytical diagnosis*, by which he meant

> a continuing diagnosis, to be made not only at the time of the first examination
> of a child, but through a more or less prolonged period of educational treatment,
> so that every step is determined or prescribed as the result of known factors
> measured, so far as may be, and assigned relative values in the course of the
> educational treatment to be prescribed.[18]

It is evident that Witmer meant by analytical diagnosis, not primarily the attachment of psychopathological labels to a child, but rather the *process* of an ongoing evaluation and reevaluation of the child's capabilities and potentialities as treatment or education proceeds (the process of analytic diagnosis is discussed further in chapter 11).

A S T H E M O N T H S P A S S E D, the war in Europe increased in breadth and intensity. Along with this increment, there was a parallel rise, among Americans, in the level of anxiety about the war. There were a number of reasons for this increase, including disruptions in commerce and travel, concern for relatives in Europe, and—most pressing of all—the fear that the United States would eventually be drawn into the conflict.

The major factor contributing to immediate American unease about the war was the danger to shipping across the Atlantic and the fear of loss of American lives. The Germans had undertaken a blockade of Great Britain and warned that ships violating this warning would be subject to attack. The warning was enforced by German submarines patrolling the seas. On May 7, 1915, the British liner *Lusitania*, returning from New York to Liverpool, England, with nearly 2,000 civilian passengers, was sunk by a German U-boat; 1,198 persons, including 128 Americans, were drowned.

Indignation among U.S. citizens, and anger against Germany, was intense, and for awhile it appeared that war would be declared against Germany. Although this drastic step was avoided, at least for the time being, the incident brought about a sea change in attitudes toward the war.

Despite these highly charged concerns, which reached deep into the American consciousness, everyday life went on much as before; individuals went about their daily tasks, and institutions made their plans and decisions. At the University of Pennsylvania the Board of Trustees was scheduled to meet on June 14. One of the items on the agenda was the matter of a young assistant professor of economics, Scott Nearing.

Scott Nearing, 32, was a brilliant young man of abundant energy and strong convictions. In 1905, he had received a BS and, in 1909, a PhD from the Wharton School of the University of Pennsylvania. He had become an instructor in the Wharton School in 1905 and was appointed assistant professor in 1914. He was respected by his colleagues and supported by his department. In some respects, however, Nearing's political and economic views were believed to be decidedly at odds with those held by members of the Board of Trustees, and rumors had reached members of the university faculty, including Witmer, that the trustees might take some action against Nearing.

Here is some relevant background to help set the occasion: This era in America was a period of rapid and unregulated industrial expansion and profiteering, a concomitant of which was widespread abuse in child labor practices in mines, mills, and factories. Heated discussions of these practices and of the ethics of big business entered the political arena and, inevitably, the themes of economic theory. Several faculty in the Wharton School took decidedly liberal positions. Prominent among these was Nearing. For several years, there had been rumblings that the university trustees, most of whom were politically conservative, with ties to important business interests, were disturbed by what they saw as the seepage of dangerous radical ideas into the Wharton School and might take some sort of action. In 1915, at their June 15 meeting, they decided to do so. The decision was to dismiss Nearing from the faculty.

THE NEWS OF NEARING'S dismissal spread rapidly around the campus, and the next morning Professor Simon Patten (head of the Department of Economics, Nearing's department), while walking to the University Club for breakfast, met Witmer. "Is it true what I read in the morning paper," Witmer asked, "that Nearing was fired yesterday?"

Patten indicated that it was, and Witmer exploded: "I don't give a damn for Nearing. He and I disagree in almost everything, but this is my fight. If they do that to him they can do it to any of us. It's time to act."[19]

The issue, as Witmer and many—probably most—other faculty saw it, was essentially one of academic freedom. Nearing had been summarily fired without a hearing, against the express recommendation of his department and the dean of his college. Further, the action was taken at the final meeting of the trustees in the 1914–1915 academic year, much too late for Nearing to seek another position before the forthcoming academic year. Legally, the board was within its rights, yet there was no precedent in its actions in earlier years for its flaunting the recommendations of the faculty and administration.

The trustees steadfastly refused to explain their action, referring all questions to the provost, Edgar F. Smith. Smith, for his part, and undoubtedly feeling in a very difficult position, was also not forthcoming. The widespread opinion, however, was that the board's action was a direct manifestation of its members' desires to get rid of a professor whose views they found abhorrent and, more basically, of their wishes and intentions to assert complete control over faculty views and recommendations.

Witmer swung into action. First, he wrote a brief article, which was published in two Philadelphia newspapers, the *Public Ledger* and the *North American*, on June 20. The following are excerpts from that article:

> Under the circumstances, a clear statement of the reason for this unusual action was to have been expected. The Board of Trustees, however, assigns no motives for its action. In effect it throws down the gage to the faculty, which recommended Professor Nearing's appointment, and opens a battle here for academic freedom, which has been fought at so many other universities in our own and other times. . . . I hold no brief for Professor Nearing. I respect his honesty, his courage and his social sympathies; but I do not agree with all of his economic views, nor do I approve [of] some of the methods which he employs in placing his views before the public. Nevertheless, as a member of the faculty, I would consider differences in opinion and method as immaterial, and, if called upon, I should recommend the appointment of men with whom I disagreed even more than with Professor Nearing. . . . The conflict which this action of the Board of Trustees has unhappily forced upon the University of Pennsylvania is a part of the universal struggle of democracy against autocracy. An essential feature of the democratic form of government, whether in state or in university, is tolerance of opinion. The distinguishing characteristic of an autocracy is intolerance. Other common characteristics are secrecy, fear of public opinion, unenlightenment and aggressive self-assertion.[20]

The Nearing case aroused great interest, not only in Philadelphia, but nationally. For the most part, newspapers took stands regretting the action of the board, and supporting Nearing. Although numerous faculty members, as well as students, inveighed vehemently against the trustees' action, the acknowledged leader to the opposition was Witmer.[21] As Nearing later put it, Witmer "canceled his vacation plans, spent the summer at his desk, went exhaustively into the evidence, and produced a book which R. W. Huebsch published. It was titled *The Nearing Case*, with the subtitle, *The Limitations of Academic Freedom at the University of Pennsylvania by Act of the Board of Trustees.*[22]

The book comprised two sorts of material: first, certain background data, consisting chiefly of relevant newspaper reports, as assembled and organized by Witmer; and second, extended commentaries, arguments, and charges by Witmer himself, most of which had previously been published in the *Philadelphia Public Ledger* and the *North American*. For the most part, his remarks were measured and courteous, and he did not question the board's good intentions and devotion to the University. His arguments, however, were blunt and unrelenting, like an attorney's brief. As Raymond Fowler later put it, "Witmer's book made Nearing's dismissal, and academic freedom, an international issue." [23]

Despite the widespread outcry against the dismissal of Nearing, the trustees did not back down, and their action stood. What, then, were the consequences of Witmer's campaign?

So far as Nearing's position was concerned, the effort was a failure. In a broader sense, however, it was highly influential. At the University of Pennsylvania, no further faculty were dismissed, and a wiser policy of faculty involvement in decisions concerning faculty members was developed. Even more salient was the role the whole controversy played in the further development of the concept of academic freedom in American universities generally. As it happened, the American Association of University Professors (AAUP) at its January 1915 meeting—about 6 months before the Nearing affair—had decided to examine the whole problem of academic freedom. It was somewhat of an embarrassment to the University of Pennsylvania that the Nearing case, which had received adverse national publicity, provided such a handy example of the need for more enlightened guidelines on academic freedom. In part on the basis of the Penn case, at its December 1915 meeting, the AAUP came out with a more detailed policy on academic freedom.[24]

And what of Nearing? What happened to him? This is indeed a fascinating story, and since Nearing does not again appear in these pages, except peripherally, the story may be told here. From the University of Pennsylvania, Nearing went to the University of Toledo. In 1917, he was fired from there for agitating against American participation in the world war. In the same year, he joined the Socialist Party, and the next year, he ran, unsuccessfully, for Congress. In 1927, he joined the Communist Party but, in 1930, was expelled from that organization for being too independent. During this whole period—and thereafter—Nearing was busy writing radical books and tracts. In 1932, he and Helen Knothe purchased a farm in Vermont and later moved to a farm in Maine. In his later period, Nearing became a well-known proponent of the simple, rural life and was greatly honored by the newer, environmentally conscious generation. In 1972, he completed his best known book, the autobiographical *Making of a Radical*, which included a chapter on his ordeal at the University of Pennsylvania some 57 years earlier.[25]

In April 1973, there came about something of a belated reversal at the University of Pennsylvania. In a dinner at the faculty club President Martin Meyerson presented Nearing with a citation reading,

> In recognition of a singular career begun as a member of the Faculty of the Wharton School, and for adhering to the belief that to seek out and to teach the truth is life's highest aim, the Trustees have designated Scott Nearing honorary Emeritus Professor of Economics.[26]

In 1976, I wrote to Nearing, then 93, at his home in Maine, pointing out that I was writing a biography of Witmer and seeking any relevant reminiscences that Nearing might have. Here is the bulk of Nearing's reply:

> Dr. Witmer was in Psychology. I in Economics. So our academic paths seldom crossed.
>
> After the war began in 1914 I saw him frequently at the Faculty Club. In the Allied and Central Powers Line-up he and I were sharply opposed: he for helping the Allies, I against USA participation in the war.
>
> After my dismissal in June 1915 Witmer took up my case, despite our disagreements, because "if the Trustees can fire you, they can do the same thing to me." This is covered by *The Nearing Case*, which he wrote.[27]

Seven years later, at the age of 100, on August 24, 1983, Scott Nearing died.[28]

FOR MANY YEARS, the Department of Psychology at Penn had been the largest producer of trained clinical psychologists. Indeed, this had been the case since the origins of the profession. Further, the Penn department, in the period under review, was the only program anywhere to offer what would later come to be accepted as the full panoply of clinical psychological training, that is, basic courses in scientific psychology, a variety of clinical courses specifically designed to prepare the graduate for direct practice, and an extensive supervised clinical experience, all organized within a standard doctoral program. Most programs emphasized experimental rather than applied psychology, and this was the case until after World War II, when a number of clinical programs were established rather quickly.[29]

This is, of course, not to say that there were no early clinical psychologists other than those trained by Witmer. There were, of course, a number of such professionals—the names of Augusta Bronner, Henry Goddard, Lewis Terman, and J. E. W. Wallin come to mind. These were individuals who by relevant education and self-initiated experience gained expertise in the field. Other psychologists, such as Leta Hollingworth and Robert Yerkes, had some experience of a clinical nature. Some individuals, after obtaining a degree in experimental psychology, switched to clinical, although without the benefit of formal training or extensive experience. An example would be George Ordahl, a 1908 graduate under Hall at Clark University. In 1909, Ordahl took a faculty position at the Nevada State University in Reno. In 1914, after considering the possibility of spending some time at Witmer's Clinic, he instead spent a year at several state mental institutions and then took a clinical position at the Sonoma State Home for the Feebleminded in California.[30]

These various instances do not alter the conception of Penn as the first and, for a long time, the only university offering full-fledged training in clinical psychology.[31] Although this program naturally went through a period of development, by 1915, it had largely reached its final form.[32] It is of interest, therefore, to examine the program in some detail. First, the core clinical faculty. This consisted of Professors Witmer and Twitmyer (the latter having been promoted in 1914), Assistant Professor Maxfield, and Instructor David Mitchell. In addition, there were various relevant nonfaculty positions in the Clinic.[33]

Relevant courses included, at the basic level, Intelligence and Efficiency, Abnormal Psychology, Growth and Retardation, Child Psychology, Adolescence, The Exceptional Child, and the Training and Treatment of Exceptional Children; and at the advanced level, the Psychological Clinic (two successive courses, A and B), Orthogenics, Orthogenic Methods (two courses, A and B), Social Factors of Juvenile Efficiency, Clinical Tests and Measurements, and Clinical Field Work. The course offerings varied somewhat from year to year, as is true of contemporary departments, and the exact topics covered in the advanced courses, which were often in seminar formats, tended to reflect the instructors' interests. As evident from the course listings, the program emphasis was on child clinical psychology.

All graduate students, including those in the clinical area, were required to complete certain work in basic psychology; this involved, among other things, work on reaction times using the Hipp chronoscope and dissection of the human brain. It is not clear how many graduate students were enrolled; an educated guess would be from 8 to 12 doctoral candidates in clinical psychology at any given time and fewer in general or experimental psychology, with perhaps 10 to 15 in MA programs. Many classes also admitted graduate students from other university programs, such as education and religion. At least two fellowships, and several assistantships and teaching opportunities, were available for student support, but these did not cover expenses for all students. Certain profession-relevant jobs were available in the community from time to time, and in any event, academic expenses, speaking relatively, were much lower than now.

Gertha Williams arrived at the University of Pennsylvania in the summer of 1914. She had earned her BA and had done some additional work in psychology at Mount Holyoke, and after becoming interested in some of Witmer's publications and learning more about the program at Penn, she decided to go there: "I didn't want to just teach psychology," she recalled. "I wanted to be able to use it. And this offered that possibility and I never regretted it." [34]

Williams had a fellowship that paid her way, although she also did some other clinical work for pay. She saw children in the Clinic (for credit, not for pay) mostly under Maxfield. Like other students, she struggled with the Hipp chronoscope, doing work on reaction time; Twitmyer was in charge of this. She remembered a seminar with Witmer and also a course with Ludlum, a psychiatrist. While she was there, one of the other graduate students (presumably H. H. Young) was developing norms for Witmer's Formboard Test. The Clinic also used the Binet scale—but not the translation made by Goddard, used by most; rather, they used a translation from the French made by Clara Harrison Towne. Williams remembered that on one occasion the chimpanzee that Witmer had studied several years earlier returned to the department and visited some classes.

She recalled that Witmer did a lot of private work. One current case of his that the students learned about was a child whom others had diagnosed as feebleminded. Witmer discovered that the child's problem was emotional, and eventually the boy was able to learn to read well. Another of Witmer's cases that the students all knew about was his first case: This "was one thing you always prepared for—for your orals. You knew you would be asked about it." Williams, while there, had the opportunity to meet Margaret Maguire, now a school principal, who in a sense had started it all. It was Williams's impression, when at Penn, that APA "tried to look down on anything 'applied'," but that Witmer was immune to this because he was a Wundt PhD.

It is evident that Williams greatly enjoyed her years at Penn. Her dissertation, in 1917, was on "The Restoration of Children: A Clinical Study." After receiving her doctorate, she took a position at Wayne University. Later, she became an authority on projective techniques and, after her retirement from Wayne University in 1954 at the age of 70, carried on a private practice in Detroit, MI.

In the summer of 1916, Frances Holsopple, a young graduate student in psychology at Columbia, enrolled for the summer session at Penn. She had become intrigued with the idea of becoming a clinical psychologist, and her mentor, Leta Hollingworth, recommended that she go to Penn for the summer to see if the clinical profession was for her. Holsopple was very impressed with the scene at Penn and decided to stay; she received her PhD in 1919. Many years later, in 1977, she reminisced about her years at the University of Pennsylvania[35]:

The atmosphere at Pennsylvania was very different from Teachers' College. I spent the first summer working with the teachers' courses, going through a new book by Lewis Terman.[36] . . . I worked with other graduate students to prepare, assist and report the cases seen in Witmer's Clinic. . . . We read undergraduate papers . . . cleaned up after frog and brain dissections, took histories and prepared subjects for the Saturday clinics and sat in as substitute therapists as the faculty one by one went off for army work. . . . In between we held consulting jobs of our own in schools and helped with the journal, *The Psychological Clinic.*

Clinic subjects were brought from schools, private physicians, the University Hospital clinics and parents of all classes. Many adults were seen by E. B. Twitmyer in speech therapy which was practically the same method as the type of short therapy I saw later in Healy's clinic. Witmer had many students from the staffs of the social agencies and the Philadelphia School of Social Work. Because of these connections, I was allowed to become a field worker for the Philadelphia Commission on Protective Work for Girls.[37]

Holsopple vividly remembered dissecting the human brain and using the Hipp chronoscope. She recalled that Samuel Fernberger and Morris Viteles, other graduate students, were working on the ancestors of the lie detector, but she herself was more interested in people's reactions to the new Jung and Rosanoff word lists.

Holsopple was particularly impressed with Witmer's Saturday morning clinic course:

This was held on the stage of a 250 seat amphitheater with a small group of junior or kindergarten furniture, low screens and some carefully selected toys. . . . Sometimes Witmer asked an assistant to test while he commented, but he was likely to suddenly say "Why don't you take Billy out for popcorn now?" when he wanted to discuss fine diagnostic points. He was always careful never to talk over the head of a subject, and he conducted very good interviews with parents. This was a little disconcerting to an assistant who was trying to demonstrate perfect testing procedures, but everyone was happy and relaxed. . . . The real preparation for observation of behavior was in Witmer's Analytical Diagnosis, which he was then formulating. He continually elaborated this. . . . In other words, you were supposed to have a framework of personality theory ready to focus on the clinical problem rather than attempting to work from completed test scores. It was certainly far more abstract, coherent and logical than I was able to appreciate then.

Witmer loved controversy. He was carrying on a violent one with the Philadelphia Board of Education when I knew him; on one occasion he gave an interview to the *Public Ledger* . . . in which he said that the average age of the Phila. School Board was 78; the children were being brought up by their great-grandfathers.

After close association with Goddard and Hall for some years, he withdrew from the American Psychological Assoc. and would have nothing to do with it, or with assisting his PhD's to enter it, in my day. His quarrel with Goddard was over Goddard's generalizations over the Kallikak family. It was "oversimplified," he said, to discuss sterilization as a policy before more diagnostic work was possible.[38]

Holsopple received her PhD in 1919, with a dissertation on socially delinquent behavior in girls and women, possibly the first study on this theme.[39] In 1921, she took a position in Rochester, NY, as director of the Department of Child Study in the Society for the Prevention of Cruelty to Children. Later, she was affiliated with the University of Rochester. After a brilliant career in pediatric clinical psychology, she retired in 1967. Her death occurred in 1979.

IN NOVEMBER 1916, President Wilson was elected to a second term. Relations between the United States and Germany had continued to deteriorate, and there was widespread concern as to how long America could stay out of the war. An early casualty of the break between the two countries was Hugo Münsterberg. On December 17, 1916, while lecturing to a class at Radcliffe, he died suddenly, stricken by a cerebral hemorrhage. He was 53. Münsterberg had long worked vigorously to bring about a rapprochement between the two nations. Because of widespread anti-German feeling, the normal eulogies that would have followed for a man of his eminence did not take place. However, a memorial written by his German friend William Stern, which appeared in a German journal, was reprinted, in English translation, in America, in the new *Journal of Applied Psychology*, edited by Hall.[40]

In Germany itself, the scientific community, including Wilhelm Wundt, to the disappointment of his American admirers, staunchly supported the position of its Fatherland.

On February 3, 1917, Wilson severed diplomatic ties with Germany, and on April 6, following the loss of American lives in the sinking of three merchant ships, the United States declared war on Germany. With amazing speed, the entire resources of the nation were shifted to a wartime stance.

Although organized support in America for the German side was essentially nonexistent, there was a small but vocal minority that continued to argue, even at the risk of being accused of being unpatriotic, in favor of neutrality. One of these was Scott Nearing. At Columbia, James McKeen Cattell, with the war on, found himself in serious trouble with President Butler, with whom he had long been at odds. On August 23, 1917, Cattell wrote letters to three congressmen, on university stationery, urging them to vote against a bill sanctioning the use of American conscripts on European battlefields. When Butler and the Columbia trustees learned about this, they were incensed and saw Cattell's action as an opportunity to fire him. Protected as they were by the strong public repugnance for anything that could remotely be perceived as disloyalty, they succeeded in doing so.[41]

Most psychologists of the period were supportive of America's participation in the war. As it happened, the Society of Experimental Psychologists was meeting at Harvard on April 6, 1917, the very day that Congress declared war against the Central Powers. The members immediately turned their attention to identifying ways in which psychologists might contribute to the war effort.[42] In the weeks immediately ahead, organized psychology, led by Robert Yerkes, the APA president, proposed that a military testing program should be developed to assess the intelligence of each army recruit. This would be useful, they proposed, in weeding out individuals too low in intelligence to serve usefully, and to help in the assignment of all soldiers. A committee, headed by Yerkes, was set up to undertake the development of appropriate test instruments.[43] Later, the U.S. Army, after some hesitation, adopted the idea of general intelligence testing, and the committee came up with a group test, called the *Army Alpha*, and a test for illiterate persons, called the *Army Beta*. In all, more than 1.75 million soldiers would be tested.[44] The magnitude of the assessment program forcefully brought the idea of psychological testing, especially intelligence testing, to the attention of the American people, and in this sense, the program contributed indirectly to the historical development of clinical psychology.

Witmer was not involved in the army testing program. He was, however, involved in the war in a different way. The *Philadelphia Public Ledger*, in its December 12, 1917, issue, carried a story with the headline, "Dr. Witmer Leaves For Italy Service: Noted U. of P. Psychologist Assigned to Important Duties in Connection With Red Cross."[45]

The article explained that Witmer had obtained an extended leave from the University of Pennsylvania and, it was understood, would be engaged "in social service investigations in the areas disorganized and sometimes left destitute immediately behind the European battle lines." The work of the Red Cross, of which Witmer would be a part, would focus on rehabilitation of persons left homeless by the ravages of war. Witmer's rank in Italy was major, and his duty was deputy commissioner of the American Red Cross. Work with the Red Cross probably appealed more to his humanitarian impulses than actual military service would have; in any event, he was too old for such service. Further, the Red Cross stint provided him with the feeling that he was contributing per-sonally to a cause that he considered important and undoubtedly reso-nated also with his adventurous nature.[46]

In a fascinating aside to all of this, Witmer's close friend, Joseph Collins, the New York neurologist, also went to Italy with the Red Cross in latter 1917, in his case as a major in the U.S. Army Medical Reserve Corps, assigned to duty as medical director of the American Red Cross in Italy.[47] It would be too much of a coincidence to assume that Witmer's and Collins's roles were not planned and coordinated. It is even con-ceivable that they shared the same quarters on a ship on the way over; if so, this would have been a reprise of their first meeting some 26 years earlier.

BY THE LATTER PART of the second decade of the century, the profession of clinical psychology, although still very limited in the num-ber of its practitioners and not altogether clear on its mission, was be-ginning to achieve some degree of identity. Along with this increased prominence, there had been certain criticisms. As early as 1913, R. H. Sylvester, a Witmer graduate then teaching at the University of Iowa, had written an article defending clinical psychology against such com-plaints as that it tended to overemphasize diagnosis as opposed to treat-ment (he saw some justification in this criticism) and that it was in-truding into medical areas (he rejected this point).[48]

Over the years, a particularly difficult problem—one that faces all professions sooner or later—namely, the question of professional stan-dards, had come to the fore. On this matter, J. E. Wallace Wallin as-sumed some degree of leadership.[49] As early as 1911, according to his later reminiscences, he had discussed with some of his clinical colleagues the need for establishing appropriate standards of training and compe-tency.[50] At the 1916 convention of the American Psychological Associ-ation, held in New York City, it was decided to invite a number of clinicians to discuss the issue at the next APA convention.[51]

This roundtable discussion took place on December 28, 1917, in a room at the Carnegie Institute of Technology, where the 26th Annual Convention of the American Psychological Association was held. Although quite a number of psychologists had been invited, only seven showed up. These, in addition to Wallin, were Leta Hollingworth, Francis Maxfield, James Miner, David Mitchell, Rudolf Pintner, and Clara Schmitt.[52] Of those invited but not attending, some evidently avoided the meeting because of scruples about lending their support to a suspected schismatic movement. This, indeed, is what the occasion proved to be about. Thus, it was decided that the aims of the clinicians could best be met by their having their own separate organization. Accordingly, the American Association of Clinical Psychologists (AACP) was declared established, with Wallin as chairman and Hollingworth as secretary on a pro tem basis. In accord with the decision of the founding group, Wallin subsequently appointed a committee, consisting of Hollingworth, Mitchell, and Maxfield (as chairman) to draw up a proposed constitution for the fledgling organization, to be presented for discussion at the next APA convention, that is, in December of 1918.[53]

Witmer, on the occasion of the founding meeting of the AACP, was in Italy, or at least on his way there. However, two of his former students, Francis Maxfield (PhD 1912) and David Mitchell (PhD 1913), played central roles in the new clinical movement. After the organizational meeting of the AACP, a number of other psychologists, including Bronner, Fernald, Healy, Kuhlmann, Terman, Wells, and Yerkes, joined the association. The April 1918 issue of *The Psychological Clinic* carried a brief report on the new organization, possibly written by Witmer from Italy, or (more likely) by Francis Maxfield, who, as noted above, was a leader in the AACP and who, in Witmer's absence, was head of the Psychological Clinic. The report stated that the AACP included 45 members, identified as all doctorates in psychology engaged in the practice of clinical psychology.[54]

On November 11, 1918, an armistice was signed between the Central and Allied powers, and the war ended, with the Allies victorious. Before this outcome, in June of 1918, Witmer, after a stopover in London, had returned to Philadelphia—presumably because he was no longer needed in Italy. His early return may also have been prompted in part by the feeling that he might be needed at the Psychological Clinic, because Maxfield had accepted a position as professor of clinical psychology at Ohio State University. There was also a personal matter that may have influenced Witmer's return. His sister, Evelyn, afflicted with a condition described as nervous prostration, had taken leave from her work in chemical bacteriology and was scheduled to retire in June.

In December 1918, the APA held its annual convention in Baltimore. This was the occasion at which the Maxfield committee was to make its report on the putative formation of the American Association of Clinical Psychologists (AACP). Wallin had arranged for a symposium on The Field of Clinical Psychology as an Applied Science, with Arnold Gesell, Henry Goddard, and himself as speakers, to precede the committee report and attendant discussion. After numerous requests, Wallin reversed this order, with the result that the pro and con discussion about the AACP took so long that the symposium could not be held. Some members strongly favored the projected clinical organization, others were equally firm in opposition, fearing the detrimental effects of a splinter movement within APA. Under these circumstances, it was decided to defer final action on the new organization until the next APA convention, to be held in Cambridge in December 1919.[55]

The result of the 1919 convention was that a compromise was worked out between those wanting to set up an alternative organization to APA and those wishing to stay within the umbrella of the older, established association. The compromise was that there would not be a separate organization of clinical psychologists but instead a clinical section would be formed within APA. This section was destined to play the leading role in the organized structure of clinical psychology for many years to come.[56]

So far as can be determined, Witmer had no part in the movement among clinical psychologists to establish some kind of separate organizational structure,[57] although he may have discussed the matter with his former students Maxfield and Mitchell, as well as others, after his return from Italy. It is not known whether he attended the 1918 and 1919 APA conventions, where the question of the AACP was discussed and resolved, but in any event, it is evident that he was not a factor in the birth of organized clinical psychology. This is not to imply that he was unsympathetic to such organized expansion. Rather, the reasons for his on-the-sidelines approach must be sought elsewhere.

First, it is probable that he did not see organizational affiliations as all that important. Witmer himself was primarily dedicated to direct clinical practice, didactic work with students, and social causes; he had never, after his first few postdoctoral years, been an organization man.[58]

Indeed, he was too confrontational, too outspoken, and too undiplo-matic to succeed, or to feel at ease, in a major organizational role. There was also another important factor, which can be summarized by the phrase "generational shift." A new generation of clinical psychologists, more energetic and more ambitious for their calling, was coming to the fore and henceforth would take the lead in professional development.

IN MARCH 1919, a large 288-page issue of *The Psychological Clinic*, comprising Issues 5–9 of Volume 12, was published. This issue amounted, in effect, to a small book and, indeed, was titled *Reference Book in Clinical Psychology and for Diagnostic Teaching*.[59] Although Witmer evidently intended the publication to serve as a resource for clinical students at the University of Pennsylvania, it actually differed little in substance from earlier issues of the journal. The book included 22 articles, most by graduates or current students at Penn.

Witmer himself contributed four articles, none of them particularly memorable. The first of these, "Performance and Success: An Outline of Psychology for Diagnostic Testing and Teaching" consisted largely of a kind of psychological thesaurus, in which numerous technical terms, many of them idiosyncratic to Witmer's own usage, were defined and elaborated.[60] These included *attention, excitability, emotion, discernability,* and *judgment.* One gets the feeling, in reading the article, that these terms and their meanings had come to seem very important to Witmer. It can be doubted, however, that the array of abstruse definitions was of much use to Witmer's students, except in the sense of their becoming alert to the complexity of the human organism and of their gaining some familiarity with Witmer's technical terminology. Witmer's second article was a brief piece on elementary education, in which he argued for a clinical perspective in elementary schools.[61] His third article was adapted from a luncheon address he had given at the Engineer's Club of Philadelphia on December 3, 1918.[62] This was a lighthearted, some-what humorous talk, as would be suitable for the occasion. It focused on the psychology of efficiency, a theme of widespread interest in that era, but has no particular historical significance. The fourth piece by Witmer in the special issue was a 1 1/2-page report on a microcephalic boy.[63] (Although the author is not given, it was undoubtedly by Witmer, since it is stated that the report is from a clinical lecture.)

The April 1919 issue of the *Ladies Home Journal*, one of the most popular general magazines of the day, carried an article by Witmer titled "What I Did With Don."[64] This article was later reprinted, with an extended introductory footnote, in *The Psychological Clinic* for May 15, 1920.[65] The article, written in a snappy, popular style, details how Witmer undertook the treatment, or training, of a little boy who was first brought to him at the age of 2 years and 7 months. The boy was extremely backward and highly unstable emotionally.

It was difficult to obtain Don's attention, and at times—as when put on the floor and made to walk—he would burst into paroxysms of rage. One of the things that seemed to soothe him was to cling to some small object, such as a card, in his hands, and when this was forcibly removed, he would tear at his ears and mouth until they bled. Witmer saw the boy's expression of rage in a positive light, because they indicated an inner strength. However, if left alone, Donald was easy to care for: He would sit or lie in bed for hours indifferent to his surroundings. He also had a fondness for music.

The child was placed in a residential school under Witmer's control —presumably, this was Witmer's school at Rose Valley. Although the school's staff was involved in the training, Witmer himself played a central role.

> I try to approach the problem of educating a child like Donald without any preferred theory. More than twenty years of experience has [*sic*] led me to see that there is some good in most theories. A few are only for the scrap heap. One guiding principle, however, has stood the test of time and use: "The first task of teacher and parent is to gain and hold the child's attention by giving him something he *can* do, and after that, something he *can't* do"—this in general is my method.[66]

Donald was able to learn much more rapidly than had been anticipated, and after a few months, he went with the Witmers for a month's vacation in their cottage in Nova Scotia. After returning, he continued to improve—the article reports his progress in some detail—and eventually was able to do satisfactory work in the first grade.

By this time, Witmer had arrived at what he considered an adequate understanding of Donald's case. Human beings, he suggested, are driven by two great motive forces: fear and desire. Donald's problem, Witmer concluded, was that he was motivated primarily by fear. Thus, he was fearful of all animals, of a doll, and of a spinning top and was afraid to look down a well. It appeared, indeed, that he was frightened by anything new; for example, it took 2 months to convince him to take a ride in a little pony cart that Witmer kept at the school, but once he had gotten over this hurdle, he could not get enough of driving the pony.

Witmer's article in the *Ladies Home Journal* brought him considerable national publicity. Today, Don would probably be considered autistic, a clinical problem still not well understood.

11

New Directions

The American people, with the war and its sacrifices behind them, were relieved, ecstatic, and eager to move on with their lives. After the immediate postwar adjustments and with the dawn of the new decade, the nation moved into a new era. The 1920s were vibrant, exciting, and marked by striking new developments and cross-currents in the national psyche. This was the decade of Prohibition: the Eighteenth Amendment, which went into effect January 16, 1920, forbade the manufacture and sale of alcoholic beverages, with the consequent evils of bootlegging and gang wars. The Nineteenth Amendment to the Constitution, passed in 1920, guaranteed women the right to vote and to hold national office. Along with their new political rights, women opted for greater freedom in clothing and hairstyles. Another mark of the 1920s was the beginning of America's love affair with the automobile.

Politically, the dominant national mood of the 1920s was a deep conservatism—Witmer once remarked that in some parts of the country, it would be illegal to read certain parts of the Constitution—as reflected in the administrations of Harding, Coolidge, and Hoover. Witmer himself was what was then termed *progressive*: He was critical of ultraconservatives and admired Robert La Follette, the progressive senator from Wisconsin who ran for president in 1924, and he had defended Eugene

Debs, the imprisoned labor leader. Among other periodicals, he read *The New Masses* and H. L. Mencken's *American Mercury*. Economically, the decade, until the beginning of the Great Depression in 1929, was in a period of unparalleled prosperity. Witmer's salary in the 1920s was about $8,000, quite munificent for that day, and he invested any excess funds in government bonds.

In mainstream experimental psychology, the period was marked by the prominence of *behaviorism*, as developed and espoused by John B. Watson.[1] This was true even though Watson himself lost his position at Johns Hopkins, as the result of the furor associated with his divorce in 1921, and never reentered academia. He continued to write, however, and his popular book *Psychological Care of Infant and Child*, published in 1928, governed the child-rearing practices of a generation or so of parents, much as Benjamin Spock's works were to do in a later time.[2] In applied psychology, Freudian theory, although controversial, was increasingly influential; the dominant theme in clinical psychology, however, was the intelligence testing movement, powered especially by the results of the World War I's army testing program, as interpreted by Yerkes and others, and by tests such as the Stanford–Binet, as standardized by Terman, the influence of which extended beyond the clinic and laboratory and into the popular culture.

THE AMERICAN PHILOSOPHICAL SOCIETY had scheduled its Philadelphia Meetings for April 1920 with Witmer as one of the participants. In February, Titchener wrote to Witmer recommending that he support Hall for membership; in his reply, Witmer agreed to do so and said that he would do all he could to further the nomination. He added that he thought they should also recommend Thorndike. Witmer noted that the size of the psychology department at Penn could not compare with that of Titchener's at Cornell but stated that it had about 250 first-year students. In closing, he invited Titchener to stay at his home if he, Titchener, would be coming to the spring meetings.[3]

The University of Pennsylvania Department of Psychology, including the laboratory and the Clinic, was at this time administratively under the dean of the College, A. H. Quinn, with whom Witmer had certain disagreements—a circumstance not uncommon between deans and department heads, then as now. Witmer appealed to the board of trustees, asking that certain budgetary and personnel requests, presumably the ones that Quinn had denied, be approved and requesting that the Department of Psychology be transferred to the School of Education. Although Witmer had always been interested in education, this particular request was probably due to his desire to have greater control over his department. In any event, the trustees, at their June 14, 1920, meetings, rejected Witmer's proposals and requested that in any future communications, he "avoid acrimonious criticism and personal antagonisms."[4]

While this outcome was undoubtedly disappointing to Witmer, a happy conclusion to another goal was just at hand. For some time, he had been seeking a larger and more conveniently located facility for his private school. Such a place was now available. On June 23, 1920, he and Emma signed the papers to purchase a 7-acre estate at Devon, a village on the Main Line some 10 miles west of Philadelphia. The property was a beautiful, well-landscaped expanse in a lovely area. The main building, set atop a sloping grassy hill fronting on the Lincoln Highway[5] (later Highway 30), was an imposing three-story stone and concrete structure, with attached two-story wings and a large, open front porch. The main part of the building dated back to colonial days, and it was said that the place had been a stopping place for George Washington on his way from the battle of Brandywine (the site of the battle was about 25 miles southwest of Philadelphia) to Valley Forge, a few miles to the north of Devon. The structure, including, in all, 25 rooms and 5 baths, was large enough to furnish adequate living quarters for the resident children and staff, plus gracious areas for the Witmers. In addition, there were several smaller structures on the property. Lightner and Emma paid $45,000, a very considerable sum, for the Devon property. This consisted of $30,000 down, plus a $15,000 mortgage.[6]

In addition to the suitability of the property, there was probably another reason for the Witmer's choosing the Devon location. This was the fact that a few years before, in 1918, Helena Devereux had moved her growing school for retarded children to Devon. Witmer had been a supporter of Devereux since 1909[7] and, according to one report,[8] served as a sponsor for her school at Devon.

The Witmer School, as it would be called, began its services in the succeeding year, 1921. In the same year, on the last day of November, Lightner's father, David Lightner Witmer, who for many years had operated a wholesale pharmaceutical firm, died. He was 80.

WITMER HAD BEGUN HIS career with a deep concern for children with limited capacities; now, in the latter stages of his career, he developed a strong complementary interest in children with superior endowments. Although this interest was not entirely new with him—it had been manifested in print as early as 1910[9]—the emphasis was new and revealed Witmer's continuing curiosity and openness to new ideas. During the 1920s numerous superior children were brought to the Psychological Clinic, both for child guidance and for research.

In November 1919, at a meeting of educators in Harrisburg, PA, Witmer had spoken on the identification and training of very bright children, and his remarks were published in *The Psychological Clinic.*[10] "The bright child", he stated, is one "who is very much alive, and a fair measure of his liveliness is given by the relative speed of his thinking, doing, reacting and moving."[11] The bright child not only is highly intelligent, by which Witmer meant the ability to solve new problems, but also is high in intellect, that is, in the amount of accumulated knowledge. Such a child is also efficient mentally, in the sense of being able to utilize his or her intelligence effectively.

The student who was most fully captured by Witmer's interest in superior children was Alice M. Jones (later Rockwell). In 1922, she began the collection, under Witmer's supervision, of systematic data on superior children, and in 1923, she published detailed studies of four children who had scored very highly on Terman's revision of the Binet test.[12] Two of these children, both girls, had, as it happened, equal IQs of 181, and Jones was at pains to emphasize how utterly different the girls were in other respects, thus illustrating that although IQ measures may have considerable utility, they are highly inadequate assays of overall mentality. This point had long been stressed by Witmer. One of the other children, a boy of 24 months, was extremely advanced, obtaining an IQ score of 195.8. He was the first 2-year-old ever to complete the Witmer Formboard at the Psychological Clinic and showed a number of other signs of highly precocious development.

In the fall of 1923, Witmer, as quoted in a local newspaper,[13] indicated that the Psychological Clinic was conducting an investigation of children in the upper 1% of the population. About 200 such children were being examined, he was reported to have said, and it was planned to follow them through school and life to see if their promise would be realized. While these informal remarks may have been somewhat extravagant (ei-

ther as stated by Witmer or as reported by the newspaper) with respect
to what had been and might be accomplished, a great deal of progress
in the study of superior—or, to use a later term, *gifted*—children was
in fact being made. In 1925, Jones reported a large, highly informative
study of 120 superior children, collected through the facilities of the
Psychological Clinic.[14] This study, for its time, was a highly sophisticated
investigation and can still be read with profit. Although the quantitative
criterion for selection of cases was IQ as measured on the Terman scale,
the intent being to include children in the upper 1% of the distribution
on IQ, the test battery also included the Witmer Formboard and Witmer
Cylinders, as well as a variety of other procedures. In addition, Jones,
in accord with Witmer's emphasis on analytic aspects of behavior,
gave major attention to qualitative data. These were gathered primarily
through structured interviews with each child on the basis of which
Jones completed a number of rating scales devised by Witmer and his
students.

Jones's study, inspired and guided by Witmer, was one of the first
large-sample investigations to focus on gifted children. Jones was
concerned, in her investigation, with the economic, educational, and
cultural characteristics of the children's parents, and their likely effects
on the measured IQs of the children, and strove to take account of
indications of mental superiority not encompassed within the concept
of the IQ.

IN 1923, THE UNIVERSITY funded an enlargement in the Psychological Clinic. The main purpose of this additional funding was to
support a special Vocational Guidance Clinic, as a part of the overall
Psychological Clinic. The chief expense involved was the support of a
full-time faculty member, Morris Viteles, with the academic rank of
instructor. Viteles was to head the new facility, but several additional
staff persons, as well as the purchase of some new test equipment, were
also involved.[15]

Witmer had long been interested in vocational guidance; indeed, his
concern with his first problem student, when he taught at Rugby Academy in 1889, had been in part a matter of vocational counseling. Further, many of the adolescent and adult cases seen in the Clinic in earlier
years necessarily involved vocational counseling. Also, the idea of voca-

tional guidance was hardly novel. What was new was the establishment
of an organized center to meet this function. As Viteles later wrote, the
Vocational Guidance Clinic, "so far as I know, was the first center for
teaching, research, and service associated with a university, specifically
devoted to the appreciation of tests and clinical methods for purposes
of vocational guidance."[16]

The Vocational Guidance Clinic was the second special clinic under
the broader umbrella of the Psychological Clinic, the other being Twitmyer's Speech Clinic. Although the Vocational Guidance Clinic offered
its services to college students and other adults, it also emphasized the
role of vocational counseling in the elementary and secondary levels. The
new facility was a success from the beginning and tended to be copied
in other institutions.

Morris Viteles was born in Russia of middle-class Jewish parents.
Eventually, his family moved to Philadelphia, where he graduated from
the public schools and then the University of Pennsylvania. He entered
Witmer's doctoral program, which he completed in 1921. He was the
earliest of the Witmer graduates whom I got to know personally in the
course of gathering material on Witmer. What follows is an early experience with Witmer recalled by Viteles[17]:

In the 1919–1920 academic year, Viteles took a course in vocational
guidance, a new and exciting field, with Professor Arthur Jones in the
College of Education. In the spring, there was to be an important national meeting on vocational guidance in Atlantic City, and Jones invited
Viteles to give a talk at this gathering. After some initial concern by
Witmer and Twitmyer as to whether he was sufficiently advanced to
represent the department adequately, Viteles presented his talk, which
was extremely well received. He was surprised to find that Witmer was
in the audience. Witmer complimented him and took him out to lunch
at an elaborate, sumptuous restaurant.

Viteles's dissertation, on competency tests for streetcar employees, was
printed as the ninth and last of Witmer's monograph series.[18] It presaged
Viteles's later work on industrial psychology; more than anyone else Viteles deserves to be considered the founder of industrial-organizational
psychology.[19] He was probably Witmer's most famous student, and he
considered Witmer the most important influence on his career.[20] He
spent his entire career at Penn, until his retirement in 1968.

ANOTHER NEW VENTURE sponsored by Witmer in the 1920s focused on the relations between behavior and body chemistry. For many years, Witmer had been attracted to this general area, and he had always presented anatomical and physiological material in his classes. Further, from the very beginnings of the Clinic, he had emphasized the important connections between bodily dysfunctions and behavioral problems. This new direction, if viewed in the context of his overall life story, was therefore not altogether surprising. It was new, however, in its specific emphasis on biochemical factors and on the development of empirical research. Twitmyer, through his concerns with the etiology of speech disorders, had also become interested in physiological variables. Witmer's medical associate Samuel Ludlum, who in addition to psychiatry, was also knowledgeable in endocrinology, was also supportive of the new direction.

In 1920, Witmer and Twitmyer arranged for the collaboration of Henry Starr, then an instructor in physiological chemistry at the University of Pennsylvania Medical School, in the development of research on bodily chemistry and behavior. Starr, while continuing his affiliation with the Medical School, also undertook graduate work in psychology, where he met another clinical student, Anna Spiesman. The two were married in 1921; he received his doctorate in 1922, and she received hers in 1923. In 1924 Witmer and Twitmyer established the Psychobiochemical Laboratory as a division of the Psychological Clinic and arranged for the appointment of Starr as an instructor in psychology. This new division of the Clinic differed from the two earlier auxiliary units in that it was primarily devoted to research rather than to clinical service. In the spring of 1925, Starr offered a course, with an enrollment of 30 graduate students, on Metabolism and Behavior.[21]

Witmer's role in the biochemical research was primarily one of ideas, encouragement, and administration; also, it was he who coined the term *psychobiochemical.* Twitmyer probably had somewhat more of a hands-on role, since some of the research carried out concerned the pH values of saliva in stammerers. However, Starr was the major figure in the research and published several relevant papers.[22] In 1928, the Starrs moved from Penn to Rutgers, where Henry became chairman of the department of psychology and director of the Psychology and Mental Health Clinic and Anna became its assistant director.[23] Max Trumper, a 1928 Witmer graduate with a background in biochemistry, directed the laboratory until his departure in 1930, to take a position at Jefferson Medical College.

Although the behavioral–biochemical research at Penn was not the first in this area, it was the first to be carried out from the perspective of clinical psychology. Witmer's commitment to the approach is revealed in the closing words of a talk—titled "Clinical Psychology: Its Origin and Future"— he gave before the Section on Clinical Psychology of APA on December 31, 1924:[24]

> Young men and women—would you dedicate yourselves to original research in a field of science most likely to be distinguished above all others for discoveries of importance during the latter half of this century? Make ready, then in the laboratory of physiological chemistry for work in clinical psychology and diagnostic orthogenics.[25]

FOR MANY YEARS, Witmer and Fifi had maintained their residence at 24th and Spruce in Philadelphia, and they continued to do so. However, with the opening of the Witmer School at Devon, with its elegant, comfortable quarters, Witmer spent many nights there, so that in effect he had two homes: a country home and a city home. Fifi, however, whose health was somewhat delicate (she was particularly susceptible to attacks of migraine), spent much of her time in their Philadelphia home. Their Devon estate was very close to the Devon rail station, and it was easy for Witmer to commute to the campus, roughly a 40-minute trip. He came in to his office almost every school day. Neither Lightner nor Fifi ever learned to drive a car but depended on trains, taxis, and public transportation, which fortunately were very good in that area, for getting about.

Although both Lightner and Fifi liked and valued children, they had no children of their own, so that it was possible for them to have fairly independent living patterns. One of the things that they did together—although also sometimes one without the other or with friends—was to vacation in periods during the summers at Flotsam, their cottage in Nova Scotia. However, since opening the Witmer School in Devon, they had discontinued the practice of routinely taking children with them to Nova Scotia.

Witmer liked the out-of-doors and mountain climbing, and some of his favorite vacation spots, in addition to the Colorado Rockies were Jasper, Banff, and Glacier National Parks. It was not an uncommon summer occurrence for Fifi to head for Flotsam with friends and Lightner to take a train to the West. Both of them liked the New Mexico area, especially Taos, and there were occasional weekends in New York City or Atlantic City. Although they were welcome in the prominent social circles in Philadelphia, they entertained infrequently, probably because Lightner was so wedded to his work. Lightner was known as a very private person, but among his close friends, in addition to Collins, were Twitmyer, Stotesbury, and Ludlum.

In 1924, Evelyn Witmer's mental status worsened, and she was admitted to the State Mental Hospital at Norristown, PA, located some 15 miles north of Philadelphia. This was a sad and tragic development for Evelyn and her career, especially in view of the social stigma associated with mental illness in that period. It was also, in a different way, a time of crisis and stress for Lightner, who, as her eldest brother, must have felt the primary concern and responsibility for her welfare.

WITMER IS REMEMBERED primarily for his contributions to the practice and profession of clinical psychology and to its cousin, school psychology, rather than as a major psychological theorist. He was not uninterested in theoretical issues, however, when these impinged on clinical work or on the general theme of individual differences, and in the 1920s, he published several papers of a theoretical–conceptual nature. Theory construction was not Witmer's forte, and his papers in this genre were not highly sophisticated. Nevertheless, they are a part of his record, are quite interesting, and had some limited influence. Further, some of his ideas, even though framed loosely, were ahead of their time and were prescient of later developments in personality theory and clinical psychology. For the most part, his theoretical papers were quite discursive and even at times chatty. They relied, for their arguments, primarily on Witmer's accumulated clinical wisdom rather than on systematic empirical data and can better be described as critical essays, or informal discussions, on key issues than as rigorous theoretical presentations. At no point did he propose hypotheses that could be tested to determine the viability of some proposition; rather his purpose was to present what nowadays would be termed conceptual analyses of key concepts and terms. This process can, of course, be a worthy scientific contribution.

In clinical psychology as a whole, the 1920s were, preeminently, a period focused on the concept of intelligence.[26] Indeed, this was so con-spicuously true that it might have seemed that clinical psychologists were in danger of becoming mere intelligence testers. Witmer, while he re-spected the most widely used measure of IQ—Terman's (1916) Stanford–Binet test—and instituted its use in his Clinic, felt strongly that the prevailing conception of intelligence was wrong, that measures of IQ were overgeneralized, and that numerous other variables needed to be evaluated to describe the psychological makeups of persons ade-quately.

In two articles in 1922, he elaborated his earlier conception of intel-ligence, first set forth in 1915.[27] The first of these two, "Intelligence—A Definition," appeared in *The Psychological Clinic* for May–June,[28] and the second and longer article, "What Is Intelligence and Who Has It?" was published the following month in the *Scientific Monthly*.[29]

Intelligence, as conceived by Witmer (and as noted earlier),[30] is the ability of a person to solve what for him or her is a new problem. Problems vary in the degree to which they present new difficulties, and the degree of originality implicit in a successful solution is conceived to be a function of the number of novel elements involved in the perfor-mance. *Specialized intelligence* is the ability to solve new problems in a particular area, and *general intelligence* reflects intelligence over a broader area in which new problems occur. Witmer believed that the level of intelligence was determined by congenital factors, including but not lim-ited to inherited characteristics, and that it could not be increased by training.

The assessment of intelligence is difficult; "no one," Witmer wrote, "has ever devised an intelligence test that tests intelligence and nothing else."[31] He was disdainful of the usual interpretation of the intelligence quotient and emphasized "that the results of so-called intelligence tests have significance, only when analyzed and interpreted in relation to a particular set of antecedent conditions and attending circumstances."[32] His Formboard (which presented a new problem for a child taking it for the first time) was, he felt, an adequate measure of intelligence for up to about the age of 4 years.

The *Scientific Monthly* article, although it encompassed most of the material in the earlier paper, also explored some of the cultural, social, and human implications of *intelligence*, defined as the ability to solve new problems. Most of the recurrent problems of everyday living, Witmer pointed out, were solved long ago by our ancestors and were passed on to us without requiring the exercise of much intelligence. "Education," he wrote, "is the device of civilization to help us from encountering new problems. The method employed is showing the pupil how to solve problems instead of letting him solve them for himself."[33]

Since the exercise of intelligence, as conceived by Witmer, necessarily involves what for the individual is a new solution, it follows that intelligence is closely related to originality. Witmer developed this theme at length, showing the relation of novelty to art and invention and suggesting that to the beholder, novelty might inspire appreciation, but if too novel would arouse distaste. Novel productions (Witmer used Whitman's *Leaves of Grass* as an example) are often shocking at first and only later appreciated.[34] Progress in civilization necessarily involves change, and "the social order of tomorrow is the inventions of the few whose intelligence operates at a high intellectual level."[35]

As far as can be determined, Witmer's view of intelligence had no effect on mainstream theorizing about the concept. Why was this the case? One obvious reason is that it was not framed in such a way as to lead to empirical research. Witmer's conception was stated as a definition of intelligence and, thus, could neither be proved nor disproved. Further, he never developed an adequate measuring instrument, beyond the 4-year level, for his notion of intelligence, and when his student Alice Jones undertook to study children of superior intelligence, as described earlier, she was forced to use the Stanford–Binet.

Looking back, from the perspective of the 1990s, Witmer's views on intelligence fare considerably better. Thus, Robert Sternberg and William Salter, summarizing modern theory, conceive that intelligence is expressed in adaptive, goal-oriented behaviors[36]; this view is not particularly different from Witmer's identification of problem-solving activity as manifesting the existence of intelligence. Further, Witmer's conception is at least suggestive of R. B. Cattell's modern notion of *fluid intelligence*.[37] Witmer's criticisms of the concept of IQ are essentially congruent with later opinion concerning the limitations of IQ tests. In his own period, however, Witmer's virulent critiques of such tests, which in his view imposed "IQ's with a soothsayer's finality upon the ignorant and undiscerning,"[38] undoubtedly contributed to his gradual loss of status among the rising generation of clinical psychologists, who saw him as out of touch with the newer trends.

WITMER'S VIEW OF INTELLIGENCE was embedded in a broader, more inclusive conceptualization of behavior. The articles most crucial to this broader conceptualization were "The Analytical Diagnosis" (1922)[39] and "Psychological Diagnosis and the Psychonomic Orientation of Analytic Science: An Epitome" (1925),[40] along with the earlier (1919) article, "Performance and Success: An Outline of Psychology for Diagnostic Testing and Teaching."[41] These articles, unfortunately, are not easy to follow; their meaning, hampered as they were by Witmer's penchant for coining new terms, is extremely obscure and enigmatic at points.[42]

Witmer defined psychology as a science of behavior, with thoughts as well as actions included in the realm of behavior.[43] His overall aim was to develop a theoretical system to underlie clinical psychology, that is, a psychology of the individual child or adult. For this reason, he laid particular emphasis on individual differences, and this explains his efforts to construct a system of meaningful individual differences variables, as is discussed below. In espousing an idiographic approach, Witmer was thus on a different road than that of the major theorists of the period — Thorndike, Watson, McDougall, and Woodworth—all of whom were primarily nomothetic theorists.[44]

The most meaningful unit of ongoing behavior for Witmer was a *performance*. A particular performance is a sequence of behavior marked by a beginning, intermediary components, and an ending, for example, a child walking up a stairway or solving a problem. Performances, which can be either successful or unsuccessful, can be subdivided into smaller units termed *operations*, defined as motions that produce effects. Examples of operations would be the repetitive steps as a child climbs the stairs or the four elementary arithmetic procedures.

The central individual differences concept in Witmer's system was *competency*, defined as the aggregate of abilities necessary to achieve success in a given endeavor. Thus, a person's reading competence would be the combination of the numerous abilities required for reading, a skill that involves many different operations. In general, a specific competency is the ability to bring into existence some product, which can be either an object or a mental resultant. More broadly, the notion of a kind of overall competency was employed by Witmer to designate what many others meant by general intelligence; the two concepts were not the same, however, because the idea of competency involved motivation, specific talents, and intellect (acquired knowledge), as well as intelligence. Witmer was the first theorist to give primary importance to competence (or competency) as contrasted with intelligence, a position later developed, albeit somewhat differently, by David McClelland, Norman Sundberg, and, in particular, Robert White.[45]

Another central concept for Witmer was *analytical diagnosis* (discussed briefly in chapter 10). Not only was this the theme of a 1922 article,[46] but it also was the topic of a paper he delivered at the 1924 Western Psychological Association Meetings at Stanford, under the title "The Analytical vs. the General Diagnosis in Clinical Psychology."[47] Actually, the first article, bearing the title "The Analytical Diagnosis" was a three-page contribution by Witmer's student H. J. Humpstone in the May 1919 *The Psychological Clinic*,[48] and even before that, Witmer was working on the approach, as reported earlier in Holsopple's memoirs. Although never delineated as clearly as one would like, the general position espoused by Witmer under the phrase *analytical diagnosis* is clear enough. What he was opposed to was the practice of describing, that is, diagnosing, clinical cases by a label or a few test scores, however precise, and what he argued for was a more individualized approach based on a careful analysis of the child's personal characteristics and behaviors. There were two problems in implementing this orientation, although Witmer never put it as baldly as this. The first was what dimensions or variables the child should be evaluated on; and second, how the subject was to be assigned values on each of the relevant variables.

The answer arrived at for the second question was that the examining clinician should rate the child on each behavior or trait judged pertinent from the list provided and, in so doing, should use whatever relevant data, including but not limited to test data, are available. With respect to the first question, the list of characteristics and abilities to be considered, these were to be determined by Witmer and his associates on the basis of clinical experience. The first article in the sequence, that by Humpstone, begins in this way: "In arriving at a final diagnosis in a clinical examination the examiner should be able to state the specific defects and abilities of the individual and give some estimate of their extent"[49] and lists 22 separate capacities, several with subdivisions, that are to be rated on 5-point scales. Witmer, in his 1922 article, commented that "common sense and the purpose at hand determine how many categories it will be desirable to employ for the purpose of analytical diagnosis."[50]

A good example of Witmer's analytical approach in action is in Alice Jones's case study of a 9-year-old girl,[51] published in the pages immediately following Witmer's 1922 article. Jones's article reports the actual ratings assigned to the child on the Analytic Diagnosis Form, which includes spaces for rating 51 psychological characteristics. Jones's ratings were based on a clinical examination plus $2^{1}/_{2}$ months of diagnostic teaching, so that she knew the child well. Among the scales rated were competency (divided into ability and efficiency), coordination, initiative, excitability, motivation, trainability, intelligence, and confidence; these will suffice to give an idea of the nature of the traits rated. Application of the rating system is described in greater detail in Jones's 1925 article,[52] reviewed earlier in this chapter.

Witmer's attempt to develop a multiscale procedure for evaluating relevant behavioral and personality characteristics of the clinical subject, although primitive by modern standards and never satisfactorily completed, was nevertheless a highly innovative step. It was the first systematic approach of its kind for use in the clinical setting. Witmer's basic goal—to develop a workable quantitative system for describing individuality—is one that modern personologists find frustratingly difficult.

Perhaps dismayed by the complexity of a rating system based primarily on direct clinical experience, Witmer appears to have decided, in the early 1920s, that a more fundamental system of relevant dimensions could be derived on rational considerations. He came to the conclusion—on what basis it is not clear—that there were six fundamental psychological dimensions, or categories, as he preferred to call them, that affected a person's performance competency. He first presented this conception in his 1922 article noted above and elaborated it in a 1925 article, from which the following is taken:

> The universal room in which we live is a world of three dimensions defined by six oppositions of direction, and referred to a system of rectangular co-ordinates, because human thought is a form of three coherent forms, called "dimensions", defined by reference to six coherent but contrasting forms, which are the "criteria" of six universal categories of behavior.[53]

This quotation, although lifted out of context, nevertheless illustrates the extreme ambiguity of portions of Witmer's theoretical writings. Nevertheless, it is possible, by careful examination of his writings, to identify the six basic categories, or factors, that he saw as influencing performance: (a) motivation; (b) will, or determination; (c) discernment, or discrimination; (d) intelligence—the capacity to solve new problems; (e) intellect—accumulated knowledge; and (f) efficiency of mental operations.[54]

From combinations of these six basic categories, Witmer derived a list of "thirty-six analytic categories at the first level of specification,"[55] and although these 36 were not clearly enumerated, it is evident that they are similar to those referred to in Jones's (1922) article as part of Witmer's system for analytical diagnosis. It thus seems likely that Witmer developed his list of the characteristics to be rated in the clinical setting and his notion of basic mental categories more or less at the same time. According to Viteles, who was fairly close to Witmer during the 1920s, Witmer was constantly changing and revising his terminology, making it difficult for others to follow. One person with whom he discussed his category model was Francis Irwin, then a graduate student in experimental psychology. This was not because Irwin liked Witmer's system, however, because in fact Irwin was severely critical of it, feeling that it was essentially playing with words, without any empirical support.[56] Presumably, Witmer appreciated Irwin's candor as well as his judgment. Some of Witmer's own students and close associates, however, found his system of categories a meaningful and useful way to conceptualize mental functions.[57]

In December of 1926 the American Psychological Association held its Annual Convention at the University of Pennsylvania. At 2:00 p.m. on Tuesday the 28th, Witmer presented a paper, "Preterficient Nature—A Psychonomic Orientation."[58] Although a copy of his remarks did not survive, it is clear from the abstract that his focus was on his conception of six basic categories.

At the time, one of the students at Penn was Irvin T. Shultz. Many years later, in 1967, Shultz recalled Witmer's presentation in College Hall at the 1926 APA meeting. Witmer had earlier constructed a cardboard cube, or die, with each of its six sides—each about a foot square—printed with words indicative of a basic category, for use as a visual aid in class lectures, and he used this in his 1926 APA talk. After the talk, Thorndike, who was presiding, is reported to have remarked wryly that he was there to hear a lecture on psychology but it seemed that all he heard was some philosophy.[59] Witmer's goal, to identify and delineate the basic components of the human mental apparatus, was commendable and something that he shared with savants ranging from the ancient Stoic philosophers through Carl Jung up to contemporary personality and cognitive theorists. His approach, however, was rather simplistic and consisted essentially of listing mental functions that he considered important in successful behavior.

WITMER'S 1925 ARTICLE (discussed above), although primarily theoretical, also included, in its last three pages, material of a more personal, autobiographical nature.[60] In fact, this part of the article reads almost like preliminary valedictory remarks by Witmer to many of his professional colleagues, and indeed, this may, in a sense, have been just what it was. An introductory note states that the article was read, in part, before the Section on Clinical Psychology at the December 1924 APA Meetings in Washington, and it is plausible to assume that these autobiographical portions were included.

In these remarks, Witmer indicated that his "method of thought" was based on "personal experience, research, and reflection" and stated that he was "not aware of any large indebtedness to the current literature of psychology." He acknowledged his indebtedness to his teachers, Francis Jackson, George Fullerton, Edmund James, John McMaster, J. McKeen Cattell, Wilhelm Wundt, and Weir Mitchell, to his colleagues Edwin Cope, John Ryder, and Simon Patten, to his friend to whom he owed most, Joseph Collins, to his wife Emma, and to "not a few, both men and women, without whose intelligence and co-operation my life's work would have been vain endeavor—of whom, in justice and with grateful emotion, I name my first assistant in the Department of Psychology at the University of Pennsylvania—Edwin B. Twitmyer."

He then briefly traced the history of the Psychological Clinic, paying tribute to Oliver Cornman, George Twitmyer, and Mary Marvin. He also listed a large number of individuals who, although not themselves clinical psychologists, had nevertheless contributed to the eventual development of clinical psychology, including—but not limited to— Shakespeare, Rousseau, Pestalozzi, Seguin, Janet, Hall, Freud, Wundt, Walt Whitman, William James, Henry James, and Adolf Meyer.

He pointed out that in 1907, when he inaugurated the journal *The*

Psychological Clinic, there was only one psychological clinic in existence, his own, whereas since then so many had been established that "it would consume much time and patience to discover and name them all." Then he added—rather plaintively, one suspects—this sentence: "Thus, it appears, I have received from my professional contemporaries that most sincere tribute—imitation, often enough without acknowledgment." [61]

The article ends with the plea, quoted earlier in this chapter, for increased study of the biochemical aspects of behavior.

12

Slowing Down

This chapter carries the biographical narrative through 1930. In addition, the chapter reviews, from a descriptive and nonchronological stance, the major facets of Witmer's professional career. Such a cross-sectional approach, which could not have been undertaken earlier, when his career was in flux, will provide an overall picture of Witmer's major emphases. The areas to be covered are the Psychological Clinic, Witmer's clinical approach, the Witmer School, and school psychology.

In 1926, the Psychological Clinic was 30 years old, and the occasion was marked by a dinner given in Witmer's honor by the Department of Psychology. Twitmyer served as toastmaster, and many former students of Witmer were guests. The event was held on December 30, at the Hotel Pennsylvania. There were a number of congratulatory addresses, and in his response, Witmer attributed his success to two things: first, his choice of assistants who could do something better than he could and, second, setting them to do it.[1]

The overall organization of the Clinic staff had not changed appreciably over the years.[2] The staff had grown somewhat larger, and there were now several consultants from the community. Also, dating back to 1919, a Clinic teacher was now on the staff. Her function was primarily diagnostic rather than direct remedial work.

Although Witmer was less active than earlier, he remained deeply involved in the clinical, as well as in the administrative, side of the Clinic. In the morning, he would arrive by train from his place at Devon. Many years later, Helen Backus (later Graber), who was his secretary during the 1920s, reminisced in this way:

> I remember so well Dr. Witmer on winter mornings, striding down the hall to the Psychological Clinic, in a salt and pepper tweed overcoat, collar turned up, gray felt hat turned down in front, his head lowered, chin almost down into the collar, unsmiling and his small but piercing very blue eyes taking in the scene over his pince-nez. He wasn't tall—probably about five foot, eight, or thereabouts, and I would judge about 140 pounds. His hair was silver, and his appearance and weight seemed not to change during the eight years I was at the Clinic. . . . His suits were usually gray or navy blue and he wore good looking Brooks Brothers vests—usually gray background with thin stripes or plaids of pale yellow and blue.[3]

Witmer, as Clinic director, ran a tight ship. He was a demanding taskmaster, and although the day-to-day operations of the Clinic were more or less routinized and under the management of the Clinic's executive officer and while interactions in the Clinic were typically informal, Witmer was clearly in charge. He was generally pleasant and supportive, but he could be scathing in his criticism when things did not go to suit him. The students were generally in awe of him and felt more at ease with Twitmyer and Viteles. They always addressed faculty members with the prefix Dr.; among themselves, they referred to Witmer as "L. W."

Witmer was a man of changeable moods, and Graber further described his work-a-day disposition as follows:

> Dr. Witmer could stir up a storm when he came to the Clinic. . . . When people wanted permission for something, or had to break a bit of unpleasant news, they would always ask, "What kind of mood is he in today?" At other times, he would break into a wide smile and sit down and chat on many subjects. He was a versatile conversationalist. I never knew him to tell a joke, but he had an appreciation of wit and enjoyed good conversation—never small talk.[4]

Graber was a great admirer of Witmer; she had a good relationship with him and came to know him well. She recalled that although he was frequently irritable, and sometimes unreasonable, "he was never petty."[5] She remembered him, in particular, as a cultured and well-read man. He respected the work of George Santayana, and among the novelists, he liked Henry James, Edith Wharton, George Meridith, Katherine Mansfield, Joseph Conrad, Upton Sinclair (he admired Sinclair's fight for social justice), and Sinclair Lewis. A passionate lover of poetry, Witmer was especially fond of Whitman and Poe. He also admired Eugene O'Neill. Graber remembered that he often quoted from *Leaves of Grass* and, on occasion, from Milton, Wordsworth, Browning, and Lowell. Witmer appreciated good music, but once remarked that he couldn't bring himself to listen to the music of *Madame Butterfly* because of the inevitability of tragedy. He was also a lover of the visual arts, and one of his friends was Paul Cret, the architect.[6]

Graber had many opportunities to observe Witmer at work. She remembered one occasion when a mother and father contradicted each other constantly while Witmer was interviewing them about their child's problem. After they left, Graber said, "Isn't that awful the way they are forever quarreling?" Witmer responded, "That's a happy couple; they thrive on their mutual irritability."[7]

Another, later secretary to Witmer was Olive Norman (later Logan). She felt, in looking back on her years with Witmer, that what he was intent on doing by his peremptory handling of situations was to raise the level of a person's performance. After making this very plain to a graduate student one day, she recalled, "Dr. Witmer turned to me and said, 'I guess they think I'm pretty rough,' but he broke into a broad smile when I said, 'But you're soft underneath.'"[8]

Most of the clinical staff and students who worked under Witmer greatly respected and admired him and had a real, if somewhat distant, affection for him. In some cases, they almost idolized him, notwithstanding—perhaps in part because of—his sometimes brusque exterior. In particular, they considered him a superb clinician and tended to model their styles after him. Years later, many former students remembered with gratitude his emphasis on careful observation in the clinical setting and his admonition against premature case formulations. Generally speaking, his students and staff considered him a great man, one of historical dimensions, and considered it a privilege to serve under him, as if this gave them too some degree of historical significance.

Although often aloof and distant, Witmer was at pains to see that the students were well trained, provided them with opportunities to publish, helped them find positions, and followed their careers. Many of his students were women. Early in his career, he had manifested an attitude toward professional women that while typical of men for its time, could not be termed enlightened. His attitude had changed by the 1920s. Witmer was now a strong supporter of women's rights and privileges; he believed that they should hold jobs and receive salaries equal to those of men. He was on the lookout for good women candidates for training.[9]

Witmer was famous, over several generations of students, for a certain idiosyncrasy, the memory of which his alumni fondly cherished years later. This was his concern about room temperature.[10] Graber recalled an incident in the Clinic when he called the staff idiots and fools because they'd let the temperature get up to 73.[11] In his classroom Witmer was insistent that the temperature be 68 or 69.[12] His teaching assistant was assigned the task of guaranteeing that this was the case—by adjusting the thermostat and the windows as appropriate. At least two enterprising students, at different times, gained lasting eminence among their colleagues by artificially bringing the temperature gauge to the proper level, when necessary, either by holding a lighted match under it or by blowing on it, before Witmer entered the classroom. Several alumni independently reported this anecdote to me, always with a quiet chuckle. People often enjoy recounting the foibles of famous persons they admire.

IN THE SPRING OF 1927, there was a large meeting of educators at the university, and two of the featured presenters were Witmer and Twitmyer. Witmer, according to a newspaper report, played down the role of intelligence and emphasized the importance of memory and ability in achieving success. "After all," he was reported to say, "thinking is merely condensed talk." He further gave it as his view that the brilliance of child prodigies is more a matter of remarkable memory ability than of superior intelligence. After Witmer's remarks, Twitmyer offered a clinic on methods for treating stammering and stuttering.[13]

Two months later, in June, Witmer marked his 60th birthday. In the following month, July, his mother passed away. She was 84. Then, in August, his friend Edward Titchener, at Cornell, died unexpectedly, at the age of 60.

Witmer himself was slowing down and was gradually reordering his priorities. Since almost the beginning of his faculty career, he had been head of the Department of Psychology; indeed, it was through the power that went with this position that he was able to develop the Psychological Clinic and the clinical emphasis of the department. Now he began to turn over to Twitmyer various administrative chores, although he remained the power behind the throne. Also, he cut back on his teaching; however, he continued his seminars and frequently gave guest lectures in psychology classes.[14] Further, except for a few brief pieces, to be noted later, he no longer published. All this is not to say, however, that his interest in clinical issues came to a halt, since publications from his students continued to appear.

THE PSYCHOLOGICAL CLINIC was located on the ground floor of College Hall, a major building in the center of the campus. There was a direct, rather imposing entrance to the Clinic from the lawn area on the east side of the building; this area included paths and trees, creating a typical bucolic campus landscape.

Immediately on entering the building, one would have found oneself in a large hallway, which served also as a waiting room, with chairs to the left and a desk to the right. To the right, there was a smaller hallway with five offices on the right and a large library on the left. The five offices served various staff purposes, including rooms for Witmer and his secretary. The area reached by the main hallway also included, on the left, a large laboratory area and a machine shop in which the various tests, such as the Witmer Formboards and the Witmer Cylinders, as well as various laboratory equipment, were constructed. Across the hall from these rooms was the library room noted above. The area also included a stairway up to the next floor. On this floor there were other Clinic offices, along with a seminar room and a large room for lectures, demonstrations, and meetings of various sorts.[15]

The Psychological Clinic continued, during the 1920s, to see large numbers of cases. Fernberger reported a total of 5,883 examinations (including reexaminations) during the years 1920–1921 through 1929–1930, for an average of 588 per year, or 49 per month.[16] Each examination typically required several hours of individual case contact, plus, in many instances, social service visits on follow-up. In addition to the Clinic's work with children, the two special clinics (for speech disorders and for vocational guidance) served numerous adults. However, the heads of these special clinics, Twitmyer and Viteles, also saw children with other problems. During the 1920s and 1930s, the description of the Psychological Clinic in the university catalogs regularly stated that "Normal children and adults applying for educational and vocational guidance now comprise the larger part of the clientele of the clinic."[17]

In this period, too, a greater variety of psychological tests, as developed elsewhere, were being used. However, in accord with Witmer's philosophy, the emphasis was on individual, as opposed to group, tests and on performance, as opposed to paper-and-pencil tests.[18]

The heavy Clinic workload, which had existed for many years, required extensive and systematic record keeping. On a day-to-day basis, individuals (children, parents, or other adults) were given appointments, either by telephone or letter. Persons due for repeat visits were given an appointment card. Three main classes of permanent records were maintained. The most important and extensive of these was, for each case, the clinical file, consisting of a manila folder containing, as appropriate, referral and interview data, test results, recommendations, consultations, social work input, correspondence, and any other relevant paperwork. These files were numbered consecutively, in the order in which cases were first seen. Many of the files were quite voluminous, and some included follow-up information gathered many years after the initial contact. It is from microfilms of these folders that selected case descriptions have been summarized in this book.

In addition to the case files, the Psychological Clinic, beginning on March 1, 1912, maintained what was termed the *Psychological Clinic Day Book*. These Day Books—there were numerous such booklets, each succeeding a filled-up one—were essentially logs in which the day's activities were recorded.[19] The entries were quite brief, noting the cases seen, by name, whether they were new or old cases, and typically a word or so indicative of the problem presented by each case. At first, the entries were in longhand, with several cases reported on each page; later, the day books were loose-leaf notebooks, with typed entries and somewhat more detail on diagnosis and recommendations. In the 1920s and thereafter, vocational guidance and speech cases were seen frequently; these were entered into the same numbering system as other Clinic cases.

The third major type of record kept by the Psychological Clinic was the alphabetical card file, housed in drawers in a cabinet in the main

Clinic office. It is not clear when this file was actually inaugurated, but all cases, including Case 0001 in 1896, were eventually represented in the card file. Each large index card included the subject's name and number, referral source, clinical problem, name (or initials) of examiner, descriptive diagnosis, disposition or recommendation, and follow-up data.[20]

The three sets of data were, in toto, comprehensive: Thus, the clinical folders were filed consecutively, by case numbers, and one could locate a case with a given number by turning to them; the Day Book entries were by date, so that a clinician could locate names seen on a particular day through this record; and the cards, organized alphabetically, made it possible to locate a child or adult seen, solely by name. In all instances, the case number was the primary identifying symbol, so that confidentiality could easily be maintained.

Sometime in the early 1920s (the exact date is not known, and the process was probably gradual),[21] there was established, under the general umbrella of the Psychological Clinic, what amounted to a third satellite clinic. The purpose of this facility was to serve adults, primarily college students, seeking educational guidance or presenting personality problems. It was under the direction of Robert A. Brotemarkle, a Witmer protégé who had received his PhD in 1923. Although in practice a part of the Psychological Clinic, this facility was administratively separate, and its case data were not entered in the Clinic records described above. The program was deemed very successful, and in 1926, Brotemarkle, who had become a member of the faculty, was appointed college personnel officer, without, however, any particular change in his Clinic and departmental duties.

OF ALL THE PROFESSIONAL roles that Witmer filled—including teacher, administrator, author, and child advocate—he was, most fundamentally, a practicing clinical psychologist. Ever since he saw his first case in 1896, he had, with only occasional respites, regularly seen new cases, evaluated them, made recommendations, and followed them up. Although his general philosophy of clinical practice and his clinical methodology have been highlighted throughout this volume, a few additional observations will not be amiss.

Witmer identified himself as a clinical psychologist; it was a central part of his self-image. While he was deeply interested in the training of teachers and in special education, his interest in these areas was not as an educator as such, but rather as a clinical psychologist concerned with the welfare of children. His primary commitment as a clinician was to be helpful; he wanted to make a positive difference in each child he saw, and although he realized that the treatment methods available left much to be desired, his attitude was that it was better to do what he could than to wait for more adequate methods. His *therapeutic goal* (to use a modern phrase) was to help each child be all that he or she could be. He believed, as the central *value* of his approach, that each child should be permitted, encouraged, and helped to develop that child's particular talents and abilities to the fullest, regardless of whether the child was retarded, gifted, troubled, or delinquent. His attitude toward tests, as summarized by Louttit, was to use them "if they were indicated, but not to be bound by them . . . [and] to keep always in mind that understanding of the child was the goal, not accumulation of data concerning him."[22]

Witmer was wary of therapeutic theory and did not himself attempt to frame any broad treatment guidelines that could be called *theory*. In his day, Freud had developed a theory of therapy, but Freud's approach did not appeal to Witmer and, in any event, was hardly applicable to children.[23] At the beginning of Witmer's career, hypnosis and suggestibility had a considerable vogue as therapeutic methods, and he had interested himself in these, but again, these were not suitable with children. A major psychotherapeutic alternative to Freud would not exist until Carl Rogers's work in the 1940s, and Rogers's work, too, was with adults.[24]

Possibly modeling himself after physicians and lawyers, Witmer saw himself as a *psychological expert* (he actually used this term before settling on *clinical psychologist*), who by his advice and decisions would help create conditions favorable to a child's development. His expertise, as he saw it, was based on study, research, and experience. His primary method of treatment was to manipulate the child's environment, both at home and at school, and, if necessary, her or his total environment in a residence under his control. Changes in behavior were to be brought about by acceptance, praise, and strict behavioral rules. Witmer was a strong believer in the importance of developing positive habits in children.[25]

Witmer's clinical approach, disseminated widely through his students, no doubt had some influence on later orientations in clinical psychology, but in an indirect rather than direct sense. It cannot be said that his orientation is the ancestor of any major contemporary therapeutic approach; however, simply as a way of characterizing it, it can be said that Witmer's clinical style was closer to modern behavioral methods, with a strong touch of humanism, than to any other contemporary approach.

It is proper to consider Witmer primarily a child clinical psychologist, but only if one broadens the term to include the adolescent years: A sizable proportion of the cases he saw—perhaps as many as a third—were in the teen years. And, of course, he worked extensively with parents, although not—so far as is known—in the modern psychotherapeutic sense. Occasionally, other adults sought and received his services.[26] Thus, although he worked primarily with children, his overall perspective was broader than this.

The place of research in Witmer's clinical perspective should be emphasized. First, there were the case studies. These were based on extensive data and were conspicuous for clear delineation of character, with a minimum of jargon. Then there were the experimental summer workshops and classes, designed specifically for research purposes. *The Psychological Clinic* regularly reported Witmer-inspired clinical research. Most of these studies concerned assessment, and Witmer never progressed to the point of setting up controlled studies to evaluate given types of treatment; indeed, this would be difficult to do even today with his kind of clientele. A limitation in Witmer's research orientation was his distaste for statistics, a stance that followed from his strong idiographic position.

Witmer did not pioneer the treatment of seriously disturbed individuals by clinical psychologists, although some of his students, in particular Clara Harrison Towne, did some work in this area. Witmer's view, as expressed in 1908, was that for the present, the treatment of mental disease should be left to the "physician and neurologist." Looking to the future, however, he predicted that eventually psychology would develop greatly improved methods of treatment, and "psychological experts" would be associated "with institutions for the insane and with public school systems."[27]

FROM THE HISTORICAL PERSPECTIVE, the Witmer School looms as much less important than the Psychological Clinic. From the personal and biographical perspective, however, the Witmer School at Devon was a core part of Witmer's psychological reality, particularly in his latter years. Not only was the school a major focus of his professional interests and commitments but it was also his second, and increasingly primary, home: He spent many nights there, without returning to his Philadelphia home. (Fifi, who was not suited to such a vigorous life, stayed more frequently in Philadelphia.) The Witmers' personal quarters at the school were quite comfortable, without being elaborate. Lightner's office was located on the second floor.

The term *school*, although not inaccurate, was in some respects something of a euphemism. The institution, to be sure, did provide academic instruction, frequently on a one-on-one basis, to the children and young adolescents living there, but the facility was also the children's home. More significantly, however, the facility functioned as a residential treatment center for retarded and disturbed children. Despite its diverse functions, the facility was always known as the Witmer School, and the children living there were called *students*. Today such an institution might also be termed a *school*, or it might be given some even less descriptive label, such as the Witmer Center.

In addition to the school's main building, which served as the residence for the students and staff, there was a somewhat smaller, but still spacious, two-story building which included rooms for examinations, classes, and consultations with parents: This was called the School House. Another building served as a gymnasium. The grounds were spacious and were marked by trees, a brook, paths, and various outdoor facilities, such as a playground and a stable. Witmer himself loved to ride; he rode almost daily.[28] There was also a pony and cart for the younger children. In the 1920s, there was very little traffic on the main road that the school faced, and on the south side of the road, there was a vacant meadow with a pond. This area was evidently open to the use of school personnel, because one of my informants,[29] who was on the staff during the early period, recalled taking a group of children across the road and letting them wade in the pond. Near the rear border of the school and accessible through the school grounds was the Devon railway station, and it is here that Witmer would catch a train for a station near the campus (trains, in those days, ran every hour or more often). He would then walk to his office.

Elizabeth O'Connor, a single woman who had been a teacher at Witmer's Rose Valley facility, served as manager of the Witmer School.[30] She was immensely popular among the students and staff, and she and Witmer always got along well. In addition to her other duties, she did some teaching. The professional staff consisted of three and often four teachers, plus various consultants. Clinical students from the University of Pennsylvania were sometimes involved in school activities. Also, Witmer's secretary at the university came out one day each week, typically on Fridays, to handle correspondence and maintain the necessary financial and tax records. The support staff of the school included the gardener, his wife, who was the cook, and one or more maids. The school's teachers were required to have expertise in working with problem children and were expected to nurture close, caring relationships with them.

As head both of the university's Psychological Clinic and the Witmer School at Devon, Witmer found it convenient and useful to shuffle personnel back and forth to some extent. Thus, a person might occupy a clinical position at the university for a period, then work at the school, and vice versa. Although typically members of the professional staff came with prior experience or training in working with retarded or disturbed children, this was not always the case. Genevieve McDermott Murphy recalled that after receiving her BA in education in 1923, a friend mentioned that Witmer needed a teacher at Devon for the summer. She applied for the position, was interviewed by Witmer, and was fascinated by him. At the conclusion of the interview, he said "You'll do."[31] McDermott later worked at the Clinic, earned her MA under Witmer, and eventually became the Clinic's executive officer, responsible for coordinating daily activities.

It is believed that there were always at least 4 to 6 youngsters in residence, and typically more, up to a maximum of 15; perhaps an average of 10 or 12 would be a fair estimate. Their ages ranged from 5 years to 15 years and occasionally higher. Both genders were represented. It is difficult to know the average length of stay at the school; some of the children resided there for years, and probably only a few were there for less than a year. There was also some degree of transferring of students to and from other institutions, in particular the Stewart School (more on this below). Most of the children at the school over the years were mildly to moderately retarded, occasionally severely so. Some of the students were able to become independent away from the school, and at least 2 eventually completed college. A few of the children were afflicted with what would now be called Down's syndrome. Some of the cases, however, were not mentally retarded but rather had emotional problems or moral (in modern terms, behavioral) problems. In addition, Witmer sometimes had several intellectually superior children at the school. And, of course, even a generally retarded child might show areas of brilliance. For example, one boy had an incredible memory for dates. When Helen Ford (later Joyce), a teacher at the school in the 1940s, was attempting, many years later (1983), to remember her exact period at the school, this person, with whom she corresponded regularly after both left the school, was able to give her both the dates and days of the week of her arrival and her departure.[32]

Where did the children come from? The school had no special public or private grants and was supported entirely by charges to parents. Although a limited number of children from poorer families were admitted without charge, the bulk of the students came from affluent families, sometimes from great distances. Occasionally, Witmer discreetly advertised the school's services. The school, which operated on a year round basis, was not a profit-making institution, and the income just barely met expenses.[33]

As far as can be determined, the children and their parents felt very positive about the Witmer School. I had access to personal reminiscences prepared some years later by two former students at the Witmer School.[34] Both wrote well, and both were clearly pleased with their periods at the school. One of them stated that when at the school, she kept a diary and studied a number of subjects, including French and Spanish. She also mentioned bicycling, stamp collecting, and horseback riding. She listened to opera broadcasts and the Hit Parade show on the radio, and she noted a number of short trips on which the students were taken, such as to the Planetarium and the Museum of Natural History.

As owner and director of the school, Witmer set high standards of behavior, decorum, and performance, and he expected others to conform. The air of authority and dominance that had long characterized his persona and his way of dealing with people assured that his ways were largely accepted as a matter of course. Witmer knew each child and his or her parents well, and he was characteristically gentle and reassuring—although he could also be curt and matter-of-fact, but not demeaning—with parents. With the professional staff, he was demanding but supportive, and although he could be brusque and controlling with them, he could also be understanding and accepting of human frailty. As an example of the former, there was an incident in which he yelled at a teacher and she walked out; then later, he telephoned her at home and apologized. As an example of the latter, on one occasion, his then secretary at the Clinic, Olive Norman (later Logan), was taking a train to Devon for weekly duty as private secretary when she realized that she had forgotten to bring with her a paper that he had expressly asked her not to forget. She feared she would be fired, but when she confessed her error, Witmer looked at her with surprise, then smiled and said, "You have intermittent amnesia," and that was the end of the matter.[35]

Gertrude Stewart, one of the teachers at the Witmer School, was a longtime friend of Elizabeth O'Connor and had been associated with Witmer for many years, first, as a very young woman, at his Hospital School and then at his Rose Valley School. In 1913, Witmer had asked her to take a young girl, who would neither walk nor talk, to the Neurological Institute in New York to see Joseph Collins, the neurologist. Stewart stayed there to work for a period but later rejoined Witmer. In 1927, with Witmer's assistance, she founded a school of her own, the Stewart School for Retarded Children, at Swarthmore.[36] This school maintained an outstanding reputation until its closure in 1972, after Stewart's death in 1970. It was succeeded by the Gertrude A. Stewart Foundation.

Witmer was also involved, at least indirectly, in the Devereux School, which was also located in Devon and which now continues as the Devereaux Foundation.[37]

WITMER'S PIONEERING contributions to the field of school psychology have long been recognized.[38] Whereas he specifically and formally established clinical psychology, his relation to the origins of school psychology is one of seminal influence, rather than of a founding. Indeed, it cannot be said that school psychology had a founder; instead, it slowly emerged to fill perceived educational needs in public schools, and it was not for many years after Witmer's early work that school psychology became a recognized profession.

A few words at this point on professional subdisciplines. There

are, in applied psychology, several related and overlapping fields, including clinical psychology, school psychology, counseling psychology,
industrial–organizational psychology, and neuropsychology. The last four
of these are, in a very real sense, later offshoots or branchings from the
first. Witmer essentially founded the first area and helped pioneer the
second; his influence was much less significant, though not absent, in
the last three. He considered himself a clinical psychologist but showed
no interest in fine professional distinctions. Clinical psychology and
school psychology use similar methods, and it would be inappropriate
to conceive a too strict distinction between them. Nevertheless, they are
separate specialties, and it is of interest to point out Witmer's major
contributions to the development of school psychology.

First, Witmer helped make school psychology possible. This statement
is true in the sense that school psychology consists essentially of the
application, in the school context, of what Witmer referred to as "the
clinical method,"[39] and it was Witmer who first developed this method
and made it available to schools.

Second, Witmer demonstrated clearly that his clinical approach could
readily be adapted to the school situation and that it would be helpful
in working with problem children. Many of Witmer's earliest cases were
schoolchildren brought to the Psychological Clinic, and in a few instances, he himself went to a public school to carry out clinical evaluations. In addition, Witmer served, in what amounted to a consulting
school psychologist role, at the Pennsylvania Training School for Feeble-
minded Children at Elwyn, the Haddonfield Training School, and Mary
Marvin's Home School. Finally, Witmer obviously served as a school
psychologist in his own schools, at Rose Valley and Devon.

Once it began to be evident, in the Philadelphia Public Schools System, that problem children could be helped by referring them to the
Psychological Clinic at the University of Pennsylvania, it was only a short
step for the system to employ its own psychologists, to work directly in
the schools. This process took some years and was probably more or less
repeated in other cities, as it became apparent that psychologists in the
schools could provide a valuable service.[40] This interpretation does not
assert that modern school psychology arose solely out of the sequence
just noted; almost certainly, the profession had multiple origins in different times and places.[41] It seems probable, however, that the sequence

indicated, or something much like it, was importantly involved in the origins of school psychology in the United States.

There were four important features in Witmer's clinical practice that carried over into the initial nature of school psychology. These included, first, a commitment to dealing with each child as a unique individual rather than as a member of a particular group; second, an emphasis on the strengths and positive features in a child's makeup, as well as an awareness of problem areas; third, an emphasis on treatment to help the child when possible, rather than limiting services to psychological evaluations; and fourth, a dedication to helping each child achieve his or her maximum potential.

Witmer was not involved in any efforts to systematize or professionalize school psychology, and it was not until 1945, in the reorganization of APA, that school psychology achieved a national organization, in APA's Division 16, School Psychology.[42] Witmer's graduate program did not specifically train students for work as school psychologists, even though a number of his MA-level clinical students took psychology positions in schools.[43] A related area in which Witmer took a strong interest was special education. Although he cannot be considered a pioneer in this area (its beginnings significantly predate his work) it was an area that he strongly championed and urged on educational systems.[44]

FEBRUARY 21, 1928, was the date of the 102nd Annual Alumni Dinner of the University College Department, held at the Penn Athletic Club. In addition to alumni and university officials, there were four honored guests, all university professors with long periods of service, at the affair. One of these four was Witmer, who had served 36 years on the faculty. The evening was generally filled with fellowship and mirth as those assembled reminisced about the old days. In this spirit, each of the three professors other than Witmer responded to toasts to them with humorous recollections and praises for the College. Then came Witmer's turn.

His remarks were jarringly different, as he took the occasion to offer a serious and highly negative critique of the College. His remarks at first startled and then captured the rapt attention of the audience. Had the alumni and the members of the press who were present been more familiar with Witmer's characteristic outspoken style, they would have been less surprised by the tone of his remarks. He began by lavishly praising the College of his own student days: In those days, he claimed, intellectual distinction was the soul of the College, and there were giants on the faculty—men such as Weir Mitchell, J. McKeen Cattell, and William Pepper (the provost in that earlier era). Then came the jarring part: The current College, Witmer asserted, was a mere factory, for which efficiency had been substituted for intellectual distinction and inspiration.

He objected in particular to the huge classes: "How can we achieve real intellect in education when we are compelled to lecture to students by the hundreds?"[45] Another criticism was that virtually the only contacts the current students had was with underpaid laboratory assistants and readers, rather than with distinguished professors.

Although Witmer closed on a positive note, predicting that the tide would turn and that the old, more scholarly conditions of education would return, the bulk of his remarks were caustic and critical. He was followed by Josiah H. Penniman, the university provost, who had long known Witmer—indeed, they had been undergraduates in the same period class at Penn. Penniman insisted that the university still had an outstanding faculty, with many distinguished members. He agreed with Witmer, however, that current classes were too large and expressed the hope that it would be possible to return to the days of smaller classes.

SOME CHANGES WERE BEING MADE in the publication of *The Psychological Clinic.* In 1928, beginning with the combined September–October issue (Vol. 17, Nos. 4–5), Witmer, who hitherto had been the sole editor, brought Miles Murphy on board in a new position, that of managing editor. Then, in 1930, in the March issue (Vol. 19, No. 1), Viteles joined the staff as associate editor. Witmer remained as editor, at least titularly so.

Viteles was introduced earlier, but Miles Murphy is new in these pages. Witmer's junior by 33 years, Murphy earned his doctorate under Witmer in 1927. He was an outstanding student, and a positive chemistry developed between him and Witmer. Murphy was appointed as instructor in the Department of Psychology in 1925; after graduation, he joined the department and became an assistant professor in 1929. While working in the Psychology Clinic, Murphy met Genevieve McDermott, the executive officer of the Clinic. In 1931, the two were married.[46]

The lead article in the November–December 1928 issue of *The Psychological Clinic* narrated the training and psychological development of a 4-year-old boy referred to as *George*. Although the case study is quite interesting, the most fascinating thing about it is that its authors were Emma Repplier Witmer and Lightner Witmer.[47] This is the only paper that Witmer ever published with his wife, although she had frequently appeared in the pages of *The Psychological Clinic* as the author of book reviews. The article describes an earlier, rather than a current, case; George is described as having entered Witmer's school in 1918 and is followed, in the article, to 1923. This dating raises a question as to when the article was actually written. Its primary author, most likely, was Emma; it will be recalled that she had experience as a writer before her marriage. The beautifully written article details the limited capacities of George on entering the Witmer School, as well as the extent to which he improved under careful training and nurturance.[48]

Mary E. Ambler was a prominent teacher at the Witmer School. She had studied under Witmer at the university and had become a good friend of both Witmers, especially Fifi. In the January–February 1929 issue of *The Psychological Clinic*, Ambler coauthored an interesting case study with Lightner.[49] The article concerned a 5-year-old boy who had been diagnosed as a low-grade imbecile by a psychiatrist and whose mother entered him into the Witmer School as a day student. He stayed there a year, and his backward condition improved rapidly, so that he was able to enter the public schools at his chronological age level. The case description dramatically demonstrated that each backward child has a unique personality.

Later in the year, the lead article in the same journal was a brief case report by Witmer and Arthur Phillips.[50] Phillips was a Clinic teacher, who later became its executive officer. The report, which concerned the mental and behavioral evaluation of a 9-year-old boy, is not of particular substantive interest, and its relevance here is that was the last case report of which Witmer was the author or coauthor.

WITMER'S CONTINUING INTEREST in the scientific side of psychology was reflected in two news reports, one in 1929[51] and one in

1930.[52] The first of these concerned Witmer's views on genetics and criminality. He was quoted as describing the nature of chromosomes and mutation in some detail and as holding that there was a strong hereditary component in criminal behavior but that environmental factors were also important.

The second report, evidently based on an interview, indicated that Witmer was developing a "new behavioristic approach to the study of social behavior, particularly of small children," to be known as "experimental sociology." The aim of the method was to provide for the objective assessment of overt behaviors in varying situations of social interaction. Witmer observed that the presently available data on social behavior consisted largely of case histories and diaries and that although these could be very illuminating, they lacked the requisites for rigorous statistical analysis. For this reason, it was necessary, he asserted, to delineate units of social behavior that could be objectively identified; it would thus be possible to follow a given child over a period of time and record his or her overt behavior in a systematic way. Current efforts at the Clinic, Witmer stated, were directed toward the development of specific techniques that would make such objective social research possible.

In this endeavor, the plan was to "control the observer" rather than the situation; this, of course, was the purpose of precisely defining the behaviors to be recorded. The social situation, in contrast, was to be left free to vary. Accordingly, Witmer was quoted as saying that "we are using a relatively 'uncontrolled' social environment, the nursery school, as a laboratory for developing our techniques." Specifically, it was reported that the research was being carried out on two groups of about 20 children each, one varying in age from 18 to 32 months and the other varying from 33 to 48 months.[53]

If Witmer's concern with the objective measurement of overt behaviors can be considered an attempt at objectivity, then a special concept that he developed in the same period reflected a more humanistic orientation. This was his concept of *surpassionism*. This term, coined by Witmer, designated the posited tendency of persons to achieve beyond their expectations, to surpass themselves, to put it figuratively. Although Witmer never delineated the concept clearly in print, he did publish two brief pieces on it. The first of these was a three-page pamphlet, privately printed in 1927, and titled "The Breviary of Proficiency and Progress in Surpassing Venture,"[54] and the second was a one-page article, in the May 1930 issue of *The Psychological Clinic*, titled "Psychonomic Personeering" (the word *personeering*, another of Witmer's coinages, was presumably derived, by analogy, from *engineering*).[55] Both pieces were written in a highly obscure and idiosyncratic terminology, which contrasts markedly with the clarity of Witmer's comments on the observation of children's overt behavior. It seems probable that the writing was abstruse because the concepts were abstruse and were not fully developed in his own mind.[56]

Some of Witmer's students and associates were strongly attracted to the idea of surpassionism, and the following summary owes a great deal to their input: Individual human beings are inherently motivated to gain proficiency, to progress, and to become superior in the development of their particular capacities; this implies, as a goal, going beyond—that is, surpassing—mere competence and excellence toward a full realization of one's potentialities. As Viteles once remarked, this general theme ran through all of Witmer's work, in the sense of helping children live up to their full potential.[57] Viteles also observed that the notion of surpassionism was suggestive of the later theme of *self-actualization*, as developed and popularized by Abraham Maslow,[58] Carl Rogers,[59] and others in the 1940s and 1950s. The concept of surpassionism also appears to have had something in common with Adler's[60] idea of *striving for perfection*, as suggested in these thoughts on motivation expressed by Witmer in a lecture: "What is our aim? What do we struggle for? We struggle for perfection. We struggle to perfect our behavior to do better and better."[61]

To convey the meaning of *surpassionism*, Witmer often resorted to poetry, as in the following brief selection from Whitman's "Passage to India":[62]

Sail forth—steer for the deep waters only,
Reckless, O soul, exploring, I with them, and thou with me,
For we are bound where mariner has not yet dared to go,
And we will risk the ship, ourselves and all.

O my brave soul!
O farther farther sail!
O daring joy, but safe! are they not all the sons of God?
O farther, farther, farther sail!

13

Later Career and Retirement

The year 1931 marked the 35th anniversary of the founding of the Psychological Clinic. The anniversary was celebrated at the University of Pennsylvania by a special convocation of the College faculty at 4:00 p.m., Friday, December 11, convened to mark the Clinic's anniversary and to honor its founder.[1] The convocation was held in the same large classroom in College Hall in which Witmer had frequently taught and in which meetings of APA and other professional societies had sometimes been held. The highlight of the convocation was the presentation to Witmer of a commemorative volume, prepared especially by Witmer's associates and former students, to mark the anniversary. Witmer, on the occasion, was about 6 months shy of his 65th birthday.

Most of Witmer's colleagues and students, and many of his former students, were in attendance. Paul Musser, the College dean, presided. He first called on Professor Robert Brotemarkle, the editor of the commemorative book, and Brotemarkle expressed the pleasure of all the contributors in honoring their former teacher and present colleague. Twitmyer, as department chairman and assistant director of the Psychological Clinic, then extended the felicitations of the department and the Clinic to Witmer and recalled memories going back some 40 years as a student and faculty colleague. The major commemorative address of tribute was delivered by Josiah Penniman, the university provost. Penniman lauded Witmer and extolled his work. Thomas Gates, president of the university, then presented Witmer with a leatherbound copy of the commemorative volume, *Clinical Psychology: Studies in Honor of Lightner Witmer. To Commemorate the Thirty-Fifth Anniversary of the Founding of the First Psychological Clinic.*[2]

Witmer, in accepting the volume and the tributes, paid special tribute to Twitmyer, Viteles, Brotemarkle, and others. He was clearly deeply moved by the accolades, and in his reminiscences, he noted the contrast between the current widespread acceptance of clinical psychology and the way his "new psychology" was viewed when he first proposed it 35 years ago. Figuratively pointing a triumphant finger at the bygone professors who had rejected his perspective, he commented that "they laughed, all of them. They thought my ideas unworthy of notice," and then he added jokingly that "a certain Columbia University professor said that 'Witmer's new psychology is just too new for me.'"[3] It is evident that Witmer was proud of his role in the origin and development of clinical psychology, and it can also be inferred, from these and other, earlier remarks, that he felt that he had never been given proper credit for his contributions. For this reason, the 35th anniversary affair must have been an occasion of great satisfaction for him.

The Philadelphia newspapers gave considerable coverage to the celebratory events, with pictures and headlines, among others, reading "Penn Will Honor Dr. Witmer on 35th 'Birthday' of Clinic He Founded For Psychology"[4] and "Dean of Modern Psychology Has Last Laugh at Scoffers," with the latter article referring to Witmer as "silver-haired" and as a "small, dapper person."[5]

The main feature of the commemorative book was 25 chapters by former doctoral students of Witmer. These were preceded by historical chapters by Collins and Fernberger[6] and followed by reprints of three of Witmer's earlier papers. Anna McKeag was the earliest doctorate represented (1900) and Dallas Buzby (1930) the most recent. The list included David Mitchell (1913), the first clinical psychologist in full-time private practice, who affectionately referred to Witmer as "our chief."[7] The volume is of historical importance not only because of its biographical significance in framing Witmer's life story but also because it amounted, with its wide range of topics covered, to a compendium of areas addressed by the growing profession and because it was, so far as can be determined, the first book to bear the title *Clinical Psychology*.[8]

DURING THE SUMMER SESSION of 1930, Witmer, with the assistance of Miles Murphy, C. L. Altmaier, and Arthur Phillips, conducted a special clinic from 10:00 a.m. to 12:00 p.m. on Monday, Tuesday, and Wednesday mornings. In all, 72 cases were examined during these sessions, and 6 cases of dyslexia were identified and treatments recommended. The program was summarized by Arthur Phillips,[9] then executive officer of the Psychological Clinic. When Phillips left in 1931 to take a clinical position at the State Industrial School at Huntington, PA, Witmer brought in Mildred Loring Sylvester to be the Clinic's executive officer. Sylvester, an extremely able woman, took on an increasingly large role in the operation of the Clinic as Witmer cut back on his own responsibilities. He was, of course, still clearly in charge, but he came in only 2 or 3 days a week, and for the most part, the cases that he saw had already been tested and had a preliminary workup performed. Sylvester was the first "non-Penn" person to occupy such a responsible position in the Clinic. She had obtained her PhD at Johns Hopkins in 1916 and later had a variety of experiences, including teaching at the University of Minnesota. Sylvester and Witmer liked each other and got on well. She admired his versatility and originality and was impressed by his clinical acumen. She was destined to stay at the Clinic well beyond Witmer's retirement several years later.[10]

On March 12, 1932, Witmer, assisted by Miles Murphy, presented a clinical demonstration of five superior children at the annual Schoolmen's Week at the University of Pennsylvania. These cases were reported by Sylvester; she included, in the article, several observations by Witmer.[11] These comments—which in affect constituted Witmer's last technical publication—were similar to those he had made earlier concerning the nature and measurement of intelligence.[12] Also in 1932, there was a modest change in the services of the Psychological Clinic. In that year, the division of the Clinic that Brotemarkle had been heading for some years was made more formal, under the designation Personnel Clinic.[13] The functions of this special Clinic, which was open 1 day each week, was to examine and counsel young adults seeking educational guidance or who presented personality problems. Men were seen by Brotemarkle and women by Sylvester; some graduate students were also involved.

DESPITE THE IMPORTANCE of the satellite clinics—in speech correction, vocational and industrial guidance, and adult counseling— the main focus of the Psychological Clinic, and of clinical training, continued to be clinical work with children. Witmer, until his retirement later in the decade, maintained a strong interest in this function. While less active than before, he continued to offer his seminar, to engage in direct practice, and to supervise clinical students. Four students of that period remembered, a half-century later, what it was like.

Wendell R. Carlson entered the program at Penn in 1930.[14] He participated in Witmer's seminar, which, he recalled, was "mostly on his philosophy and some of his theoretical positions relating to psychology and its clinical applications. He was a fascinating and stimulating teacher." Kinsley R. Smith remembered Witmer's attempt to develop his system of personality development: "I don't believe even the best graduate students understood it (I didn't)."[15]

Jay L. Otis worked in the Psychological Clinic for 2 years.[16] He recalled that after he had done the psychometric workup for Witmer on a case, "Witmer relied on his own observations and he was uncanny in his diagnosis." Otis's "attitude toward Witmer was one of considerable fear and respect. . . . I was impressed with his system of personality even though he was changing it so often that I was never sure of the latest version. His punch line was that man is the only species that sincerely attempts to surpass his best performance. He competes with himself." In Otis's eyes, Witmer was the stereotype of the "true German Professor—Herr Professor and HEAD."

John R. Martin worked at the Clinic and assisted in Witmer's Saturday morning clinics.[17] He was, according to his own memories, perhaps somewhat unusual in that he was never in awe of Witmer and always felt comfortable in his presence. He recalled one instance in which he questioned Witmer's diagnosis of a child, ("apparently not the thing to do") whom he, Martin, had tested and carefully observed. Witmer listened, reviewed the entire case and changed his diagnosis. Here is how Martin remembered Witmer:

a mild-mannered man. . . . There was no mistaking the fact that here was an exceptional mind. . . . He was deeply interested in the welfare of each case and he taught me to synthesize the various aspects of the findings. . . . He taught me, not by lecture, but by observation to take a total clinical view. His insights were terrific . . . although he insisted on the tests he considered them merely as a contribution to the total picture. . . . Witmer . . . was a man strong of ego and profound self confidence that, I suspect, never caused him to be concerned about or give a damn for what others thought of him. I can't imagine Witmer being boastful or small.

The 1930s, especially the earlier portion, was the time of the Great Depression throughout America. It was the policy at Penn that "no one was 'awarded' a degree until he got a job: Penn did not like to have unemployed PhDs."[18] The department, with Twitmyer as chairman, did manage to add two new faculty persons during this period: Malcolm G. Preston and Yale S. Nathanson, both Penn PhDs.[19]

WITMER'S JOURNAL, *The Psychological Clinic*, had been the major voice of clinical psychology since the origin of the profession. Its tenure came to an end, however, in 1935, when the last issue appeared. There was no notice in the issue that it was the final one, and there is reason to believe that Witmer assumed, or at least hoped, that the journal would continue in one form or another. What turned out to be the last issue was dated January–June, 1935, Volume 23, Nos. 1–2. It comprised 140 pages and consisted, in its entirety, of the "Report of Committee of Clinical Section of American Psychological Association."[20] The identification with APA was a tacit recognition that *The Psychological Clinic* was the appropriate organ for clinical affairs. The report was divided into two parts: I. The Definition of Clinical Psychology and Standards of Training for Clinical Psychologists and II. Guide to Psychological Clinics in the United States.

The committee responsible for preparing the report comprised Andrew Brown, chairman (Institute for Juvenile Research, Chicago); Robert Brotemarkle (University of Pennsylvania); Maude Merrill (Stanford University); and Clara Harrison Town (Children's Aid Society, Buffalo). Two of these (Brotemarkle and Town) were Witmer graduates. The report was a highly detailed, carefully prepared document, with a degree of sophistication comparable to modern surveys. Part I, which was quite brief, defined clinical psychology and stated, among other requirements, that clinical psychologists should possess a doctoral degree in psychology, something hardly new. It also stated that there were about 800 psychologists currently engaged in work that they would consider clinical: Obviously, clinical psychology as a profession had come of age. This conclusion is further supported by the data in Part II, which summarized 87 existing psychological clinics, plus 56 other facilities offering psychological services.

The Psychological Clinic had been the major publication outlet for Witmer and his students, but it would be a gross error to consider it as primarily a house organ. Its "News and Comments" section actually included very little about the Psychological Clinic or Department of Psychology but was typically devoted to national and international news concerning professional appointments, meetings and conventions, position openings, new clinical agencies, new journals, and the like and amounted, in effect, to a kind of professional bulletin board.

Substantive articles formed the journal's main content. Although most of these were written by current or former members of the Clinic staff, particularly in the early years, the journal also accommodated many authors having no connection with Witmer's Clinic or program. Some of these authors were quite prominent, for example, Edgar Doll, William Healy, Clark Hull, Adolph Meyer, Carl Murchison, Edward Strong, Lewis Terman, Edward Thorndike, and Wallace Wallin. Most of the articles focused on child clinical psychology, and many of these were also relevant to the fields of school psychology and special education. Not all papers were of this type, however; many of them, particularly in the later years, concerned various adult-level topics.

Many of the articles in the journal were case studies, and a good number of these were written by advanced graduate students or recent graduates in the Penn clinical program. Following Witmer's guidelines, these tended to be written in a narrative, easily readable style, with a minimum of jargon. Another large segment of articles concerned psychological tests and their applications. While many of these focused on Witmer's tests—the Formboard and the Cylinders—other instruments, in particular the Binet series, were also extensively represented. For example, Terman, primary author of the Stanford–Binet, had a number of articles in *The Psychological Clinic,* including one, in 1911, in which the entire issue was devoted to the Binet tests.[21] A number of other psychological tests were also represented in the journal.

The quality of the articles in *The Psychological Clinic* varied greatly, from the outstanding to the commonplace. This characteristic was probably due in part to a paucity, at times, of sufficient submissions of high quality to fill the pages of the journal. Actually, it is amazing that over its long period of issue, the articles were as solid as they were, given the small size of the profession, especially early in the century.

A special feature of *The Psychological Clinic* was its book reviews. Most of the major books in the clinical and developmental areas, as well as many works in related fields, were reviewed over the years. For example, *The Psychology of Dementia Praecox*, by C. G. Jung, was reviewed by Clara Harrison Town,[22] and *Purposive Behavior in Animals and Men*, by Edward C. Tolman, was reviewed by Francis Irwin.[23] Occasionally, the journal published special issues designed around a central theme. One such instance was noted above; others included "The Psychology of Vocational Interests," 1930, 19, No. 2; "The Psychology of the Interview," 1930, 19, No. 4; and "The Measurement of Vocational Aptitudes," 1930, 19, No. 7. There were very few articles concerning clinical psychology as a profession. Thus, little was included concerning the efforts by psychologists around the country to develop professional standards, to delineate the scope of the profession, to form professional associations, and the like.[24] This stance, which reflected Witmer's primary commitment to hands-on clinical practice and his lack of interest in broad organizational issues, was in marked contrast to the contents of the new *Journal of Consulting Psychology*, which would be established in 1937 and which gave central attention to professional issues and developments.

It is impossible, at this temporal distance, to know precisely why *The Psychological Clinic* came to the end of its days. The most likely explanation is personal: Witmer had been the guiding spirit of the journal since its inception; in the latter 1920s, as his career wound down, he began turning the conduct of the journal over to Viteles and Murphy, but these men probably did not have the deep kind of commitment that he had had and elected not to continue its publication. Whatever the reasons for suspending publication of the *The Psychological Clinic*, a decline in quality was not one of them, because the last several issues maintained notably high standards.

At the time of the journal's demise, Witmer had been its editor for

28 years. During this extended period, the journal had been the primary unifying agent for a small but growing profession. The nature of the field, however, was gradually changing, as younger members of the profession moved to center stage.

AS THE NUMBER OF CLINICAL PSYCHOLOGISTS in the nation increased and as the roles of members of the profession became more fully delineated, there was a renewed impetus toward a more effective professional organization. Although Witmer himself—as well as other prominent clinically oriented members of his generation, such as Terman, Goddard, and Wallin—did not figure centrally in the developing movement, nevertheless, a brief account of the movement is important to the present narrative. During the 1920s, the primary role of the Clinical Section was to provide opportunities at the annual APA conventions for members to present papers. Witmer's 1924 address, described earlier, was given under such auspices.[25] By the end of the decade, many clinical psychologists felt the need for more aggressive representation than that provided by APA's Clinical Section, and as a result, various state professional organizations began to appear. As early as 1921, the New York State Association of Consulting Psychologists was organized, under the leadership of David Mitchell, a 1913 Witmer doctorate.[26] In 1930, various state organizations formed a national coalition under the name of the Association of Consulting Psychologists (ACP).[27]

Although Witmer did not play a central role in advancing the organizational development of clinical psychology, he was not totally out of the loop. In March 1934, interested Pennsylvania psychologists met together at the Harrisburger Hotel in Harrisburg, the state capital, and organized themselves into the Pennsylvania Association of Clinical Psychologists (PACP). Witmer was elected president of the association, and Twitmyer was chosen as a member of the Executive Committee. Witmer served two terms, 1935–1936 and 1936–1937, as president and was a member of the Executive Committee during the next year.[28] Although these positions may have been in part honorary, it is clear that he played an active role in the association.

In 1935, the mimeographed newsletter of the ACP was succeeded by a small but regular publication called the *Consulting Psychologist*. The officers of the association and the journal's editor, Johnnie P. Symonds, decided to mark the 40th anniversary of the founding of the Psychological Clinic with special material in their journal, and this appeared in the March 1936 issue. The issue opened with a brief tribute[29] by the incoming ACP president, Gertrude Hildreth,[30] to both Witmer and Terman, the former for his founding of the first psychological clinic in 1896 and the latter for the 20th anniversary of his 1916 revision of the Binet scales. This was followed by a full-page portrait of Witmer,[31] a brief biography of Witmer,[32] an article titled "The Present Organization of the Psychological Clinic at the University of Pennsylvania," by Sylvester,[33] and "Cases Examined During the Past Twenty-Five Years at the Psychological Clinic of the University of Pennsylvania," by Murphy.[34] Witmer had been asked to contribute an article but elected not to do so, and Sylvester's article was prepared on his behalf.

Sylvester reported that during the 40 years since its founding, until March 1936, the Psychological Clinic had examined 12,798 cases, including about 750 annually during the past 5 years; that the Clinic typically had a waiting list of approximately 200 cases; and that the Speech Clinic provided speech training to about 125 persons each year. Murphy's article examined the kinds of cases seen at the Clinic during the preceding 25 years. It is clear, from these articles, that the Psychological Clinic was a large operation and remained so as Witmer approached retirement.

The *Consulting Psychologist* was succeeded in 1937 by a larger, more formal, bimonthly publication, with the same editor, retitled the *Journal of Consulting Psychology*. Then, later in the same year, its parent organization, the ACP, ceased to exist as such and helped form a new, larger American Association of Applied Psychology (AAAP). The Clinical Section of the APA was then dissolved and its members urged to join the AAAP. The overall result of all this shifting about was that there were now two major psychological organizations: APA and AAAP.[35]

While the existence of the AAAP appealed to many clinical psychologists, there was also some feeling of isolation from the larger body of psychologists. It was not long, therefore, before efforts were started to bring the two organizations together. These moves were delayed by WW II, but in 1945 the two groups merged under the banner of the APA. The interests of clinical psychologists were represented in the new Division 12 (originally titled "Division of Clinical and Abnormal Psychology," but changed, in 1955, to "Division of Clinical Psychology"). The first post-war APA convention, in which the new organization was fully represented, took place at the University of Pennsylvania in 1946.

IN THE SPRING OF 1937 Witmer retired from the University of Pennsylvania. This was 45 years after his appointment to the university faculty, and 53 years after his first affiliation, as a college freshman, with the institution. The university marked the occasion by awarding Witmer an honorary degree of *doctoris in scientia* at the annual commencement exercises, held at 10:00 a.m., on Wednesday, June 9. In presenting the degree, university president Thomas S. Gates lauded Witmer's contributions to education and to the understanding of underprivileged children.[36]

Nineteen days after the commencement exercises, Witmer marked his 70th birthday. This decade milestone, along with the prior commencement honor, undoubtedly stimulated in him—as they would in any retiring longtime professor—some degree of self-reassessment and new self-identification. In Witmer's case, however, his professional future was already well set and consisted of a commitment to his school at Devon. After receiving his ScD, he prepared and distributed an attractive, illustrated brochure, or small booklet, of eight letter-size pages, describing and advertising the Witmer School. The following selections are from this booklet:

Planned for not more than fifteen boarding pupils, my residence School has some distinct advantages over larger schools which tend to become institutional. A limited number of children can be treated as a family unit and when the child is ready to return to his own family, he takes his place naturally in a small intimate group. . . . The school buildings top a sloping hill in the midst of spacious grounds. Back and front are the children's playing fields through which wind roads and paths for horseback rider and bicyclist. At the foot of the hill is the brook and the willows under which the children picnic on summer days. . . . From time to time I have had a limited number of day pupils also, whom I have accepted for varying periods of time. Recently, I enlarged my school buildings and can now accept up to ten day pupils as well as those children who may be under observation for briefer periods. . . . With many children entrusted to my care I have had considerable success. Two were recently graduated from a college of the first rank in academic standing; one, a boy who was brought to me at the age of three years and remained six years before I felt sure he would pass through high school and college among boys of more than average ability. A larger number, after leaving my School, did well in college preparatory schools and later on married and took their place in society. . . . I get the best results with children of from five to ten years of age, but at any age up to fifteen rapid progress may usually be predicted, especially for children who have only speech or other language difficulties. . . . To achieve this result I secure as members of my professional staff college graduates skilled in education and especially equipped to arrive at a sound understanding of a child's personal character and to employ the methods best suited to each child's personality.[37]

During the ensuing years, Witmer continued to operate his school at Devon and to make his home there. After he retired, he had taken all his books, papers, and personal items to his home, which became his professional as well as his personal headquarters. At the university, Twitmyer took over as head of the Psychological Clinic.

Sometime in the mid-1930s, probably in 1937, Witmer offered *The Psychological Clinic*, along with its extensive subscription list and free of debt, to the AAAP. The only restriction was that the association would continue to publish the journal under its own title, so as to maintain its continuing identity. The Board of Editors of the AAAP, which, incidentally, included Brotemarkle and Viteles, considered the matter at its meeting in 1938, and again in 1939, but no action was taken— possibly because it was felt that the association's new outlet, the *Journal of Consulting Psychology*, was all that could be supported. The hiatus in the publication of *The Psychological Clinic* therefore became permanent.[38]

Although the *Journal of Consulting Psychology* (later the *Journal of Consulting and Clinical Psychology*) was not in any formal sense the heir of Witmer's journal, it was, in a looser sense, the clear successor to that publication. In 1982, Sol L. Garfield, then editor of the *Journal of Consulting and Clinical Psychology*, published in that journal, on my suggestion, an editorial commemorating the 75th anniversary of the inauguration of *The Psychological Clinic*. In it, Garfield commented that "perhaps there is continuity between JCCP and Witmer's journal as important journals in the history of clinical psychology. However, although we strive to maintain high standards for JCCP, we cannot match the subscription price of *The Psychological Clinic*."[39]

On May 6, 1938, Witmer delivered an address at the annual meeting of the New Jersey Association of Psychologists, held at Rutgers University.[40] This was probably his last invited public presentation.

M A R I O N   B R A U N G A R D was a graduate student under Witmer and then a social worker in the Psychological Clinic in the latter 1920s. She left in 1931 to take a position with the Philadelphia Municipal Court, at which time she married Kenneth Graham, a chemical engineer of some standing. She continued, however, to take Witmer's seminar and so often quoted Witmer to her husband that he would jokingly say of some issue, "What does God think about this?"

It developed that on one occasion—this was probably about 1937—Kenneth came home and said, "Well, the engineers club has got him—God is speaking at the club, and I think you'd like to go. He's talking on 'personeering.'"

So the Grahams went to the meeting. There was a dinner, with Witmer the speaker. Afterward, Marion introduced her husband to Witmer, and the two men began to talk. Presently, Witmer said he would like to continue the conversation but unfortunately had to catch a train for Devon, to which Kenneth said, "Come on, we'll drive you out." So they did; it was about 25 miles, quite a distance in the cars of those days, especially at night. Witmer invited them in (it was quiet because everyone was asleep) and offered them wine. During the brief conversation, Marion complimented Witmer on the way he had some interior renovation, including frescoes, done.

"That's a beautiful job," she said.

"Well," Witmer said, "I'll tell you how I did it. . . . I got some good Italian workmen. They're the best workmen . . . and I told them exactly what I wanted done. I'd come down every so often . . . and I'd look around and I'd find something and I'd raise hell with them!" [to make sure they did it right]. And Marion, momentarily forgetting herself and the formal way she'd always addressed Witmer, said, "I know what you mean—the same method that you used with us when you'd come storming into the Clinic."

There was a momentary pause, and then Witmer remembered that he was the host and that she was not a student, and he threw back his head and laughed.

Sometime later, Marion had a formal letter from the Witmers inviting her and Kenneth to dinner at the School on New Year's Day. The invitation, Marion supposed, was in repayment for their having driven him home. She was all atwitter because she, as was true of most of her associates, had never seen Mrs. Witmer.

The dinner, which was served at midday, as was the custom, and preceded by aperitifs, was splendid and elegantly served. Witmer was the true charming host: Instead of talking psychology, he drew Kenneth out, found out what his interests were, and manifested some knowledge of his own in engineering. Mrs. Witmer was equally gracious, asking, among other things, about the Grahams' daughter. The entire occasion, including the conversation after dinner, was, as Marion remembered it, fully delightful and interesting, much like sophisticated drawing room comedy. She was very impressed by Mrs. Witmer and observed that the Witmers were relaxed together and kidded each other a bit, like a happily married couple. Most memorable of all, for Marion, was the experience of a softer, more personable image of Witmer than the characteristically businesslike, in-charge man that she had known at the Clinic.[41]

Despite Marion Graham's pleasant interlude, the Witmers in fact were growing apart. A date cannot be provided for this interpersonal change, perhaps it was in the late 1930s and probably was a gradual process, but the result was that Lightner and Fifi came to adopt somewhat different lifestyles. Their eventual relationship can be described as a partial but amicable separation. Lightner continued to live at his school in Devon, and Fifi, along with Mary Ambler, who had become a very close friend, moved to an apartment in the Overbrook area of west Philadelphia. Ambler, who was called M. A. by her friends, had been a teacher at the Witmer School. She gave up this position, however, after she and Fifi took an apartment together.

Although the Witmers had grown apart in their latter years, they remained on good terms and continued to see quite a bit of each other, even as they led largely separate lives. This kind of arrangement was unusual in that period, but both Lightner and Fifi were highly independent characters, and the new relationship appears to have been satisfying to both of them. Lightner was deeply engrossed in his school, and he saw living there, amidst his staff and students, as his home. Fifi, whose health was somewhat delicate, sought a quieter living space. Lightner sometimes took the train to Overbrook to see Fifi, and more frequently, she went to Devon to see Lightner. Several informants mentioned that she typically came on Sundays. Presumably, she also traveled by commuter train, although at least on some occasions, she arrived in a chauffeured car. She was a highly sophisticated, cultured woman, who maintained an elegant lifestyle at Overbrook. Her chief interest was in writing;

it will be recalled that she had some publications even before her marriage and had frequently written book reviews for *The Psychological Clinic*. It is known that in 1931, she published an article in *Harper's Magazine*,[42] and in 1938, a short piece of hers, on Pavlova, the ballerina, appeared in a Santa Fe newspaper.[43]

AS THE YEARS PASSED, some of Witmer's closest associates and relatives departed the scene. In 1942, his brother Ferree, a physician practicing in New York, died. In 1943, his closest professional associate and longtime friend, Edwin B. Twitmyer, passed away.[44] In the next year, 1944, Witmer's old mentor, James McKeen Cattell, died. Witmer's sister, Evelyn, died in 1945.

Witmer, during the 1940s, continued to operate his school at Devon, although most details were left to O'Connor. In 1947, Helen Ford (later Joyce), the niece of Gertrude Stewart, applied for a position at the Witmer School:

> One day [my Aunt] confronted me with the suggestion that I go to work for Dr. Witmer at his school in Devon so that I might learn what it was like to have a real "boss." [Upon arriving at Devon for a job interview, Joyce and her Aunt were] ushered into a very formal and traditionally furnished living room where Dr. Witmer joined us. He was a very little man with white hair and spectacles. His eyes were dark and piercing, and he had an aura of strength and importance about him that immediately commanded respect. I found him formidable but not forbidding. He was very cordial and kindly and had a most winning smile. The interview was short and I can't recall what was said but there seemed to be no question about my being acceptable. I was to teach four teenage students. . . .
>
> To be honest, I had very little to do with Dr. Witmer himself. He occasionally visited my classroom which was in the school house, a building set apart from the main residence, but at such times he no more than bade me time of day. . . . My students were very much in awe of the doctor and would speak in hushed tones, "Here he comes!" leading me to believe that no one wanted to cross him in any way! I found this same attitude in all who worked for him. I can't say I ever saw him angry, nor did I want to![45]

Despite his age, Witmer's powers of reminiscence remained acute. In 1948, Edwin G. Boring, the nation's preeminent historian of psychology, wrote to a number of senior psychologists asking each one who that person considered to have been his most influential teacher. Boring was

interested in tracing the professional genealogy of America's most prominent psychologists. In his response, Witmer identified Cattell as the
person to whom he owed most, with Fullerton as next most influential.
His two-page letter, which was very helpful in preparing the present
volume, was a cogent and well-written typed summary of his early period
as a student at Penn and Leipzig. Its last sentence, except for closing,
was "I have here at Devon a lot of material which I hope to make
sufficiently interesting to publish some day."[46] Unfortunately, he never
did.

On June 11, 1950, Joseph Collins, Witmer's oldest and perhaps closest
personal friend, died in New York City. The careers of Witmer and
Collins were in many ways parallel. Both went to Europe in 1889 for
advanced study, Witmer in psychology and Collins in neurology, and
both had distinguished and innovative careers. In addition to his professional career, including publication of numerous technical and popular
books, Collins also enjoyed wide success in a second area, that of literary
criticism. In this domain, he published review articles in the *New York
Times*, the *New York Herald*, and other quality publications, and among
his friends were such major figures as Henry James, James Joyce, Van
Wyck Brooks, and Edna Ferber. Later in the same year, on December
15, Agnes Repplier, the distinguished essayist and aunt of Emma Witmer, passed away, at the age of 95.

Sometime in the early 1950s, Mildred Sylvester, who had been living
in Florida, paid Witmer a visit at Devon. He was now quite elderly. She
found him to be "his same gracious self but failing badly. . . . He sat in
his big comfortable chair [but] was unable to rise."[47]

L I G H T N E R W I T M E R died on July 19, 1956, in the hospital at Bryn
Mawr, of heart failure. He was 89. In his will, Witmer left the name of
the school, the right to operate the school, and all the equipment at the
school to Elizabeth O'Connor. The property of the school itself, plus all
the rest of his estate, he left to Fifi.

Among the many letters of condolence received by Fifi was one from
Provost Jonathan E. Rhodes, extending the University of Pennsylvania's
"deep sympathy" and acknowledging "once again the important contributions to our civilization which Professor Witmer has made." Another
letter was from Ivan N. Mensh, secretary of the APA Division of Clinical

Psychology, expressing the sympathy of the 1,500 members of the division and referring to the great contributions made by Witmer. One former student, Charlotte Grave, recalled that she had been one of the students assigned to see that the temperature was just right in Witmer's lecture room!

Miles Murphy, although much younger, had come to be one of Witmer's closest friends. In the course of his warm letter of condolence to Mrs. Witmer, he made the following remarks:

> Dr. Witmer was a character and a personality, as incapable of being reproduced as of being repressed. . . . Dr. Witmer was always very gracious and very kind to me. Over a period of many years we spent many hours together. . . . He was withal a warm-hearted person, and I shall always remember him with esteem, affection, and gratitude.[48]

Witmer's death came 60 years after he had established the first psychological clinic and 19 years after his retirement. He was the last surviving charter member of APA. By the time of his death, the field that he founded had grown to become one of the larger and most respected of society's helping professions.[49]

14

Epilogue: The Significance of Witmer's Lifework

This final chapter examines, interprets, and evaluates the contributions of Witmer to psychology and to society. First, some brief comments on Witmer as a person. He was, most strikingly, a unique, highly complex, and dramatically etched individual, with both positive features and limiting characteristics writ large. Intellectually brilliant, hardworking, deeply principled, and personally courageous, he lacked the diplomatic skills that might have made it easier for him to achieve his ends. Yet, he was a man of considerable presence and tended to dominate any group of which he was a part. In his relations with his staff, Witmer was typically businesslike, open, and straightforward; he was not one to play devious, behind-the-scenes games; however, he could on occasion be brusque and autocratic. He was very demanding of his students and staff and was sometimes abrupt with them, but he gave them strong support; and they, for their part, respected him, admired him, and were inspired by him.

Witmer was known as a very private person, and although he could be a charming conversationalist and had a good sense of humor, he typically had little small talk, and some of his associates considered him aloof and remote. In his interests, he was something of a Renaissance man—with strong attachments to the arts, music, and literature, especially poetry, and, at the same time, enthusiasms for rugged outdoor activities such as horseback riding and mountaineering.

Intrapersonally, Witmer was self-assured and self-sufficient. He had a profound sense of mission and of doing things that he deemed important and in need of being done, and he was not easily deterred from his goals. Although he was not himself religious, he had a missionary's zeal, and it is perhaps no accident that many of his protégés were, or had been, ministers. He was supremely self-guided and was inclined to follow his own star.

At least from his undergraduate days, Witmer was known as a strong-willed, plain-spoken person, and as he matured, these traits ripened into an aggressive, single-minded pursuit of goals he deemed important. Although such a trait does not easily make for casual camaraderie, it is safe to say that without it Witmer would never have founded and carried through the full development of the Psychological Clinic. This revolutionary accomplishment, both because of its novelty and because of the continuous support it required, depended for its success on the efforts of an inspirational and forceful leader.

Over his long career, Witmer's interests and intellectual commitments went through considerable change. He began his professional career as an enthusiastic experimental psychologist in the new scientific pattern, and he established a sound beginning in this area. Gradually, his interests turned to making scientific psychology practical and useful in an everyday sense. At first, he tried also to maintain his experimental credentials, and he always maintained allegiance to the experimental paradigm. However, as his interests in the clinical area increased, Witmer found it necessary—although he never acknowledged this in so many words—to relax his scientific rigor in order to carry out his clinical commitments. Associated with this development, there was a concomitant change in Witmer's basic research orientation. Early in his career, he had adopted a generally nomothetic approach (i.e., an approach concerned with general laws of behavior) as espoused by Wundt, Titchener, and other prominent theorists. This approach, however, was tempered in Witmer's mind by the individual differences model championed by Cattell, and gradually this model became central for Witmer as well. Later, even this conception seemed inadequate, as his focus shifted—in line with a more humanistic valuation of persons—to an emphasis on the study of individuals as such.

Looking at Witmer's life as a whole, one would have to say that he was, first and foremost, a hands-on practicing clinical psychologist. This was the role that gave his life its central meaning and coherence. It was what he did, who he was. But associated with this, and in a sense underlying it, was his conviction that scientific psychology could be, and should be, of practical benefit to humankind.

IT IS INTERESTING to speculate about the factors that may have made Witmer the kind of man he was. Because there is a profound absence of detailed information about his parents, his early experiences, his relations with his siblings, and the like, such an analysis must necessarily be highly tentative and conjectural. But this having been said, a few provisional thoughts may be put forth.

His superior intelligence and consistently good health must be attributed primarily to the genes of his ancestors. It seems clear that his paternal forbears were highly able people; there are fewer data on his mother's side. His parents were evidently strongly upwardly mobile, and they instilled in their children a passion for excellence and achievement. According to several informants, Witmer, as an adult, was not a churchgoer and was probably agnostic, but he came from an Episcopal background and went to an Episcopal prep school, and it is not unlikely that an early religious climate may have influenced him toward a career of service. Another, less speculative, factor is that the school he attended, the Episcopal Academy, not only was very challenging academically but also had a tradition of preparing young men for positions of importance.

A factor that may have contributed to Witmer's characteristic assurance and domineering attitude may have been the fact that he was first-born; some theorists have suggested such a relationship. Conceivably, Witmer's modest stature may also have played a role in determining his domineering attitude toward others; the idea here would be that Witmer's commanding mien was in some sense a compensation for a suppressed feeling of physical inferiority. This aspect of Witmer's character may also have been influenced, or at least reinforced, by his experiences as a student at Leipzig, where the imperious role of the professor was taken for granted. Further, note that Cattell, who, perhaps more than anyone else Witmer modeled himself after, was an extremely outspoken and commanding figure.

Before he turned to psychology, Witmer considered a career in the law, and he probably would have followed this had Cattell not arrived on the scene. Indeed, Witmer's professorial tenure, with its causes and controversies, had a certain lawyer-like quality. After obtaining his AB, Witmer taught for 2 years at a secondary school. This experience made a lasting impression on him and appears to have been a major source of his lifelong interest in education. His early interest in children may have come in part from his courses in pedagogy in Leipzig and from the influence on him of the child study movement that was sweeping the country. For an explanation of his more intense concern with the welfare of children—a theme that centered his career—it is necessary to look further. An obvious answer, in part, is that he and Fifi had no children of their own. Although his interest in working with children had appeared before their marriage, it did not become truly central until later. It is certainly legitimate to suggest that the lack of being a parent in a personal sense may have contributed to Witmer's concern with children in a broader sense.

There were also various academic and scientific influences on Witmer's career. Of these, the influence of James McKeen Cattell was the most profound. Witmer also gave an important place in this category to George Fullerton, the Penn philosophy professor in Witmer's undergraduate days.[1] Another important influence dating from Witmer's college period was that of Edmund James, who taught political science. And Wilhelm Wundt, of course, was a major influence in Witmer's scientific development. Other men who either by example or by close association had some meaningful influence on Witmer's career and clinical perspective include Joseph Collins, G. Stanley Hall, Seymour Ludlum, Weir Mitchell, and Herbert Stotesbury.[2]

THERE WERE FORMAL EVENTS marking his establishment of the Psychological Clinic to celebrate its 30th, 35th, 40th, and 50th anniversaries, and his contributions were given various other acknowledgments. R. S. Woodworth, one of the leading psychologists in the first half of the century, is reported to have included Witmer, along with Hall, James, Cattell, and Thorndike, as one of the important pioneers of his period.[3] Louttit, in 1936 and 1939,[4] and Murphy, in 1949,[5] emphasized Witmer's priority and significance in the history of clinical psychology.

Despite these and other early recognitions of Witmer's work, there was a general tendency, until fairly recently, to underappreciate the significance of his overall contributions. There were several reasons for this. Judgments of one's status and importance in a science or profession are made primarily by one's colleagues. In Witmer's case, there were two relevant groups: the experimentalists and the clinicians. Many experimentalists, by the 1920s, had come to consider Witmer unforgivably loose, and—perhaps more important—as being an applied, rather than a pure, scientist. There was, however, something ironic in this evaluation of Witmer as having insufficiently rigorous scientific standards, since he himself had not too many years before been a champion of scientific purity: first, in his attempt, in 1896, to raise the standards for membership in the APA, and then later in his criticisms of Münsterberg and James for what he perceived as his scientific laxity. Furthermore, he had been instrumental, under the leadership of Titchener, in founding what later became the Society of Experimental Psychologists.

Witmer's image also suffered in the views of clinical psychologists, but for different reasons. Although they honored him as their founder and paid him discreet homage, they considered him—during the 1920s and 1930s—as quite out-of-date. There were two main reasons for this. The first was the IQ testing movement, which was at its height during that period. Witmer was out of sympathy with this movement, not only with what he considered an overemphasis on, and misinterpretation of, the concept of IQ, but even more with the growing tendency to essentially equate clinical psychology with assessment.

The second prominent clinical trend of the period that Witmer found unappealing, which to many made him seem behind the times, was the emphasis on psychodynamic psychology, particularly on the views of Freud. Freudian theory, although controversial, nevertheless became quite influential after being introduced into the United States at G. Stanley Hall's 1909 conference at Clark University. It was largely Healy's adoption of a Freudian perspective that conferred prestige on his center. Robert Watson, in an influential obituary of Witmer, pointed to Witmer's lack of interest in dynamic psychology, along with his failing to ally himself with analytically oriented psychiatrists, as the lacks in Witmer's work that limited his influence.[6]

As it turned out, Witmer's reservations on both the issues just discussed were later largely adopted by many mainstream clinical psychologists. Thus, by the 1950s and 1960s, Freud's influence in psychology had declined considerably, and similarly, the measurement of IQs no longer held the central place in clinical practice that had formerly been the case.

By the end of World War II, Witmer had long been retired. Now, however, there was another trend that made his brand of clinical psychology seem old-fashioned. This was the new emphasis on adult clinical psychology, especially psychotherapy with adults. Until this point, clinical psychologists, except for a few practitioners such as David Mitchell, had focused almost exclusively on children and adolescents; now, it seemed, this was largely forgotten, and for awhile, it appeared that clinical psychology would be essentially defined in terms of working with adults. Today, fortunately, the situation is more balanced: It is recognized that the profession is very broad and that both child and adult emphases are legitimate areas. As Witmer expressed it in 1907, "Whether the subject be a child or an adult, the examination and treatment may be conducted and their results expressed in the terms of the clinical method."[7]

A number of other factors also contributed to the decline of interest in Witmer and his career. After his early experimental period, he published relatively little in the mainstream psychological journals; most of his articles were in his own journal, which had a limited circulation among the major names of the period. This fact was not negated by the circumstance that there was no other journal, before Witmer's retirement, in which most of his papers, and those of his students, would have been appropriate.[8] Another factor was the nature of much of Witmer's written corpus. Many of his articles, or those he sponsored, were case studies, and while these were well written and relevant in their day, they have not worn well.[9] Most, although not all, of his theoretical articles were sufficiently obscure to be difficult to follow in his own day, much less for readers in a later era. There is, however, an opposite side to this coin. Viteles suggested that one of the reasons that Witmer was not more widely appreciated was that some of his ideas were ahead of his time.[10] This category, for example, might include Witmer's efforts to devise systematic rating scales to capture human individuality, his adumbration of the humanistic conception later termed self-actualization, his early concern with proper diets for children, and his early emphasis on the biochemical determinants of behavior.

History is written by historians, and the past eventually comes to be seen as historians portray it. There are two reasons why Witmer, at least until recently, has been sparingly represented in psychological histories. First, most histories, following the pattern of Boring's classic work, emphasize the growth of experimental psychology and see clinical psychology as highly peripheral.[11] Beyond this, historians, when they write about a figure from the past, tend to focus on that person's books and positions on theoretical issues. They are less inclined to review the individual's contributions to an important field, or area of psychology. In Witmer's case, he wrote very little on major theoretical issues, and he left no books outlining his systematic positions, although on several occasions he indicated a desire to do so.

In recent years, Witmer's lifework and its significance have received increased attention from a number of authors, including Garfield,[12] Reisman,[13] Goldenberg,[14] O'Donnell,[15] Bernstein and Nietzel,[16] and Korchin.[17] Reisman's balanced work is the major history of clinical psychology and includes considerable material on Witmer, and O'Donnell's article critically examines Witmer's influence on the development of clinical psychology. I myself have contributed several articles on Witmer.[18] Witmer's contributions to school psychology have been the subject of articles by Fagan[19] and French.[20] The *American Psychologist* March 1996 issue included a special section marking the 100th anniversary of the Psychological Clinic.[21]

WITMER'S HISTORICAL SIGNIFICANCE derives from his invention and early development of clinical psychology, his pioneering contributions to school psychology and special education, and his public efforts to provoke society into improving the welfare of its children.

Of these several respects, the one for which Witmer is best known, and the one in which his role was unique, is the first: the founding of clinical psychology, in particular, the establishment, in 1896, of the first psychological clinic. This latter step was based on Witmer's most creative conception, the idea that scientific psychology, just newly emerged from philosophy, could be of direct, practical human benefit. This was a greater insight than it may at first seem: All new ideas, once their implementation becomes commonplace, appear to have been obvious, but such a view is a misconception. In seeing the potential of psychology earlier than others had, Witmer deserves the credit of priority.

Witmer's major contributions to the origins and development of clinical psychology, in addition to founding the first psychological clinic, may be reiterated briefly: coining the name *clinical psychology* and providing its first description; establishing and editing the first journal in the new area; developing the first systematic doctoral program for clinical psychologists; and training many of the first generation of clinical psychologists, who took positions around the country, and in so doing spread the word about clinical psychology, and helped it take root.

Further, Witmer set several important patterns, at the very beginning of the profession, that have lasted to the present day. Perhaps the most basic of these was his delineation and implementation of clinical psychology as a specialized, doctoral-level profession, related to medicine and education, but independent of both. Another important initial pattern was Witmer's emphasis on treatment. There is a long history of interest in psychological assessment, even predating Galton, but Witmer was the first psychologist to emphasize treatment as well as assessment, and to integrate the two functions. He also stressed the importance of research and made it clear from the outset that clinical psychology was to be a science-based profession. Although the persistence and development of these patterns over the years is due to the activities of later generations of clinical psychologists, it was Witmer who initially set them in place.

As a clinical psychologist and professor Witmer did not restrict himself to the consulting office or the classroom. Throughout his career he was an active and strident—sometimes perhaps overly strident, or at least impolitic—participant in the broader community. His role was as an advocate for the rights and welfare of children, and he effectively used his platform as a psychologist to advance these causes.

It is conceivable that if Witmer had not founded clinical psychology someone else would have, since the profession, once established, filled a clear need in society. Indeed, if this need had not existed, Witmer's vision would have died aborning. It does not follow, however, that someone else would have seen and answered that need. Certainly no other name of a psychologist in the early period comes to mind as a person who plausibly could have carried through the innovations made by Witmer.[22] Even if eventually some more-or-less equivalent profession would have developed, it might have been quite different—possibly less research oriented and less independent of medicine and education, and probably with a different name—than clinical psychology as we know it today, which derives from the directions set by Witmer.

The most direct effect of Witmer's innovative work was seen in the spread of psychological clinics (most of them modeled after Witmer's) and university courses in clinical psychology across the country. The indirect effect of his work was, in the long run, perhaps more profound: thus Witmer's work altered, or helped alter, the public perception of psychologists, so that psychologists were increasingly seen as constituting, or including, a helping profession.

Witmer's contributions to school psychology and special education are on a par with his importance in clinical psychology. His contributions in these areas are, however, less singular; indeed, the field of special education was well established before Witmer's interest, and, although he was the preeminent pioneer in school psychology, he did not actually found the field. Clinical and school psychology are closely related professions, however, and Witmer's contributions to each of these fields were also, in effect, contributions to the other.

To say that Witmer was the founder, or father, of clinical psychology is not to depreciate the contributions of other important pioneers, such as Augusta Bronner, Sheldon Franz, Henry Goddard, Leta Hollingworth, Arthur Holmes, Francis Maxfield, Lewis Terman, J. E. W. Wallin, Frederic Wells, and Guy Whipple, as well as others who contributed in significant ways to the early development of the profession. Further, it is important, in acknowledging Witmer's prime role in the origins of clinical psychology, to acknowledge also the significant parts played by his colleagues, associates, and students. First in such a listing must be Edwin Twitmyer, who was Witmer's close associate for 35 years. Not only was Twitmyer eminent in his own right, but he also served as a balance to Witmer's more impetuous and domineering nature. Other important working associates of Witmer included Arthur Holmes, Francis Maxfield, Morris Viteles, Michael Murphy, and Mildred Sylvester. Then, too, there were the two women, Margaret Maguire and Mary Marvin, whose help and inspiration were so crucial early in his career.

Finally, there were Witmer's students. There were over 40 doctoral graduates, plus numerous MA-level students, in his program over the years. (The contributions of many—but by no means all—of these students, including Holmes, Maxfield, Viteles, and Murphy from the names just given, have been highlighted throughout this volume.) It is important to acknowledge their significant roles in the early history of clinical psychology.[23]

While all of the individuals just listed or alluded to were important in the early history of clinical psychology, it was Witmer who set the philosophical basis for the new discipline, and although contemporary clinical psychology is much broader, and much more advanced, than it was in Witmer's day, the field is still based on the fundamental vision that he espoused: an independent, forward-looking, helping profession, grounded on scientific principles and committed to public service.

NOTES

Data obtained from the Archives of the University of Pennsylvania are acknowledged by the letters AUP. Similarly, information provided by the Archives of the History of American Psychology is indicated by the letters AHAP. Other sources are indicated by name. See also the Sources and Acknowledgments section.

PREFACE

1. McReynolds, 1987, 1996a, 1996b, 1996c, 1996d.

CHAPTER 1. EARLY LIFE

1. This date—June 28, 1867—is the date given in most sources, including Witmer's numerous entries in volumes of *Who's Who in America*, various University of Pennsylvania biographical summaries, alumni records, and obituaries, and is also the date provided by Witmer himself, in his own handwriting, in a form completed for the University of Pennsylvania Alumni Society shortly after the Spanish-American War, AUP. However, it is not the date on Witmer's birth certificate that I obtained in 1979, this being June 27, 1867. Since birth certificates were not employed in the earlier period, I infer that this date was obtained from the official registry of births. It seems likely that Witmer himself—and presumably his parents, from whom he must have learned his birthday—considered the date of birth to be June 28. The simplest, though uncertain, explanation is that the official data entry was for some reason in error.
2. For additional information on the Philadelphia of Witmer's period, see N. Burt, 1963; S. Burt, 1945; and A. Repplier, 1898. Repplier's niece, Emma Repplier, was Witmer's wife.
3. The genealogical data in this section are primarily based on material from the Lancaster Mennonite Conference Historical Society, Lancaster, PA, generously provided to me in 1978 by Lois Ann Zook, Society librarian. Other helpful information was furnished in 1979 by Joseph L. Davis, West Laurel Hill Cemetery, Bala-Cynwyd, PA, in 1979 by Robert Waller of Temple University, and in 1980 by Peter P. Kuch, Laurel Hill Cemetery, Philadelphia.

4. Melvin J. Horst, owner of the Folk Craft Museum at Witmer, kindly furnished me (1978) with considerable information on the history of the town of Witmer. It was originally known as Mount Sidney, then as West Enterprise. Christian Witmer, probably in the 1860s, built a warehouse alongside the railroad tracks in the village and persuaded the railroad company to establish a flag station there, which was designated Witmer. Later, the village assumed this name.

5. There is some uncertainty about Witmer's original given name, perhaps due to the fact that early recorded vital statistics were not always precise. The dates given here are from the document completed by Witmer himself in his application for a name change, a copy of which was obtained for me by Robert Waller through the offices of John Walter, Philadelphia attorney, in 1979. My copy of Witmer's birth certificate, also obtained in 1979 (See Note 1) lists his name as Lightner Witmer Jr., but this evidently took account of the change engineered by Witmer. Witmer's reason for officially changing his name is not known, but most likely it was simply that he wished to achieve a congruence, for matters of convenience, between his legal name and the name by which he was known. On November 27, 1917, he requested the change in name; 2 weeks later, on December 12, 1917, he left for service with the American Red Cross in Italy. It seems likely, then, that the timing of his application for an official name change was somehow related to his imminent foreign service. Note that in the official document requesting the name change, Witmer gave his birth date as June 27, 1867; probably, he used this date to be congruent with the data in his birth registry (See Note 1).

6. From data kindly provided me in 1983 by Nancy L. Weinstock, then rare book librarian, of the Philadelphia College of Pharmacy and Science (this has been the name of the institution since 1921).

7. Obituary clipping from unidentified newspaper, dated December 1, 1921. AUP. The obituary is not entirely accurate, in that the firm was a retail pharmacy until 1895.

8. Collins, 1931, p. 4. In some documents the spelling of Lightner's mother's name is Catherine.

9. The birth certificate reads "Albert Witmer." His full given name, however, was Albert Elam Ferree, and he evidently went by the name of Ferree Witmer. In those days, birth data were sometimes less precise than today. I do not know the origins of the name Ferree; however, records in the Lancaster Mennonite Historical Conference Historical Society indicate that in the late 1700s or early 1800s, Benjamin Witmer, brother of the David Witmer who married Jane Lightner (i.e., Albert Ferree's great grandfather), married Ann Ferree, so the name Ferree, as well as Elam, was in the family tradition.

10. My 1987 article (McReynolds, 1987) did not refer to Paul DeLancey Witmer, because only later did I learn that Lightner had *two* brothers. The clue was a letter in which he referred to "my brothers." The birth certificate for Albert Ferree indicates that his parents resided at 1514 North 8th Street, and the same is true for the birth certificate of Paul DeLancey, whereas the address given on Lilly

Evelyn's birth certificate is 1541 North 8th Street. It seems probable that two numbers were inadvertently reversed on the latter entry and that 1514 North 8th is correct for all three of the children. I am indebted to Millicent Berghaus for relevant information on Paul Witmer. The 1900 census report, also provided by Berghaus, makes it clear that the Witmer family was as described here.

11.   This anecdote was passed on to me by Marion Graham, who was a social worker on the staff of Witmer's Psychological Clinic in the late 1920s. She had heard the story directly from Witmer.

12.   Much later, Witmer met and became friendly with Bell (reminiscences of Mildred Sylvester), probably as a result of Bell's work on training teachers of the deaf.

13.   The Witmer's home was now given as 1814 Franklin. This address is different from any of those reported when the children were born, although in the same part of the city. Evidently the Witmers moved fairly often, possibly as their circumstances improved.

14.   This narrative was passed on to me by Mildred Sylvester in 1974, based on information she obtained during the 1930s. She did not specifically recall hearing it from Witmer but assumed that she must have.

15.   Related to me by Marian Braumgard Graham, to whom Witmer recounted it during an informal chat after a seminar.

16.   C. Latham, Jr. (personal communication, July 1981).

17.   Collins, 1931, p. 4.

18.   For a detailed treatment of the origins and early development of scientific psychology, see standard histories of psychology, for example, Boring (1950), Hergenhahn (1997), and Klein (1970).

19.   Weber, 1905/1846.

20.   Fechner, 1860/1966.

21.   Fechner, 1876.

22.   Until 1896, Princeton University was officially the College of New Jersey.

CHAPTER 2. COLLEGE YEARS

1.   More specifically, the College faculty comprised the faculties of arts, science, finance and economy, biology, and music. *University of Pennsylvania Catalog*, 1884–1885, p. 13. AUP.

2.   *University of Pennsylvania Catalog*, 1884–1885, pp. 14–15. AUP.

3.   The Philadelphia area also has, among its grander ornaments, the Benjamin Franklin Parkway, the Franklin Institute, and the Benjamin Franklin Bridge; also, the University's stadium is called Franklin Field. Underneath the seats of this structure, at the north end, is housed the University Archives, which were invaluable in the preparation of this biography.

4.   For more information on the early history of the University of Pennsylvania, see N. Burt (1963); S. Burt (1945); Dowlin (1940); and, in particular, Cheyney (1940/1977).

5.   Cheyney, 1940/1977, p. 297.

6. Ibid., p. 297.

7. *University of Pennsylvania Catalog*, 1884–1885, p. 19. AUP.

8. Ibid., pp. 45–46 and 48 for data on enrollments. In the figures in the text I have allowed for one prospective student who died prior to enrollment. Data on Witmer's courses from academic records of Witmer. AUP.

9. Letter, L. Witmer to E. G. Boring, March 18, 1948, courtesy of the Harvard University Archives. This letter, as is true of all letters and documents by Witmer referred to in this book, is used with the generous permission of the legatees of Witmer's estate (see Sources and Acknowledgments).

10. This interpretation is based on Witmer's statements in the letter cited in Note 9.

11. It is not clear whether Witmer took these courses in his senior or graduate years (see text referenced by Note 13, Chap. 3).

12. Lotze, 1886/1881.

13. Letter, L. Witmer to E. G. Boring, March 18, 1948 (see Note 9).

14. Biographical items concerning University of Pennsylvania alumni, AUP.

15. Penniman, in Brotemarkle 1931, p. viii. Penniman, who later was the University's provost, was two years behind Witmer.

16. I have no information on where Lightner's youngest brother, Paul, obtained his secondary education (it was not at the Episcopal Academy). Presumably, this took place in the latter 1890s, because in 1905, he graduated from the Philadelphia College of Pharmacy.

17. From materials provided in 1983 by Nancy L. Weinstock, rare book librarian, Philadelphia College of Pharmacy of Science. In the completed college forms, Ferree is referred to as "Albert Elam Ferree Witmer." Elam Witmer was Ferree's (and Lightner's) grandfather, who died in 1886. The forms indicate that Ferree had worked for 4 years in the pharmaceutical firm of D. L. Witmer and Brother.

18. The material on Friends' Central School is based primarily on a letter, dated May 17, 1983, kindly sent to me by Clayton L. Farraday, of the Friends' Central School faculty, and from which the brief quote is taken.

19. My information on the Rugby Academy for Boys was provided by the Historical Society of Pennsylvania, through the courtesy of Antoinette Adam, research assistant at the academy (1983). There is some ambiguity about when Witmer completed his teaching at the Rugby Academy. Collins (1931, p. 4) stated that Witmer taught there 2 years, but Witmer, in his *Who's Who* entries, gives the inclusive dates as 1888–1891. A probable resolution is that he taught a full load for 2 years, 1888–1890, and had a minor affiliation with the school at the beginning of the 1890–1891 academic year. Certainly, he could not have had a full-fledged position during 1891, because, as the text will indicate, he was an assistant in the psychology department at the University of Pennsylvania during the 1890–1891 year and left early in 1891 for Germany.

20. This is my studied conclusion, although the available documentation is ambiguous. Collins (1931) in his brief biography of Witmer, wrote that after obtaining his bachelor of arts degree, Witmer "believed himself destined for the legal profession, and while teaching English and History in Rugby Academy, in Philadel-

phia, which he did for two years, he studied in the Law School of the University for a year, long enough be convinced that law was not to be his career" (p. 4). Witmer himself, in his letter to Boring (see Note 9), stated that "after my graduation from the College department where I took in my last two years the Wharton School courses in Finance and Political Economy, I entered the Law School and at the same time entered for graduate work at the University of Pennsylvania with Political Science as a major under Edwin [*sic*] James. . . ." These statements appear to make it clear that Witmer was in the law school during the 1888– 1889 academic year. However, the University records for the law school (department) do not list him among either the matriculated or special students for 1888–1889, although they do show him as a matriculate in the philosophy department for 1889–1890. Although this apparent discrepancy may be due to faulty memory on the part of Collins and Witmer, another resolution seems more likely. The 1888–1889 *University of Pennsylvania Catalog* states, regarding the Department of Law, that each law professor had the option of issuing tickets, for a fee set by himself, to students to attend his classes. Perhaps Witmer arranged to do this, without the formality of actually enrolling in the law school. AUP.

21.   In this period of the university's development, all aspirants for the PhD degree enrolled in the Department of Philosophy, regardless of the field in which they proposed to study.

22.   Letter, L. Witmer to E. G. Boring, March 18, 1948 (see Note 9).

23.   L. Witmer, 1907b.

24.   L. Witmer (1907b) felt that the boy's defect could have been alleviated if adequate attention had been provided in his early years. Witmer conjectured that the problem was possibly due to a head injury suffered in the second year of the boy's life. It would be inappropriate to think of this unnamed boy as Witmer's first case, because at that time, Witmer did not conceive of himself as a psychologist and was not yet educated in that discipline. It is conceivable, however, that the psychology courses Witmer was taking at Penn in 1889 may have stimulated his interest in the boy's problem (the reverse is also possible). In 1894–1895, when he was teaching at Penn, Witmer had the young man in class. The student's verbal skills were still deficient, but he completed his AB degree and later graduated from one of the university's professional departments.

25.   See McReynolds, 1981, pp. 2–14. The six papers referred to (p. 6) included two on *psychometrics*, a term that, in large part due to the early influence of Galton, has come to signify psychological measurement in the individual differences sense, although the word has a longer history. For further information on Galton, see Diamond (1980), Fancher (1996), and Forrest (1974).

26.   The dichotomy described here is essentially the same as that identified and discussed by Lee J. Cronbach in his 1957 APA presidential address. Cronbach refers to the two approaches as *experimental psychology* and *correlational psychology*. In the former the psychologist manipulates variables to see what the consequences are; in the latter approach the researcher intercorrelates variables, typically among different individuals, to determine the relationships among the variables. A related,

but somewhat different distinction is that between the nomothetic and idiographic orientations; the former emphasizes the search for laws of behavior, whereas the latter, which grows out of individual differences in psychology, focuses on the uniquenessess of particular individuals (e.g., this book is an idiographic study of Lightner Witmer).

27. W. James (1879). His answer was No, we are not automata; we have free will. He had long been tormented with the problem of free will, for personal as well as for philosophical reasons.

28. My account of the Cattell family, as well as much of the material on James McKeen Cattell that follows, is heavily dependent on the excellent biographical treatments by Sokal (1972, 1981); see also Sokal (1982).

29. Littman, 1979, p. 49.

30. Blumenthal, 1980, p. 36. The trek of Americans to the German-speaking countries largely stopped after World War I, except in limited areas, such as persons going to study with Freud. For a detailed survey of the role of German universities in the higher education of Americans in the last century, see Sokal (1981, pp. 1–6).

31. As Sokal (1972) noted, it has been part of the accepted understanding—Sokal called it a "mythology"—that Cattell, with his forceful personality, simply appointed himself as Wundt's assistant (e.g., Boring, 1950, p. 324). Although this account may have some truth to it, since it derives from Wundt's own memoirs published in 1920, it is notable that Cattell's letters home and his journal at the time "make it clear that he was 'offered' the assistantship" (Sokal, 1972, p. 218). The traditional account seems incongruent with the good relationship that existed between Cattell and Wundt. It is possible that Wundt's later account was intended more as a metaphorical tribute to Cattell's enterprise than as a literal report, but the full truth cannot now be known with certainty.

32. Galton's primary contribution to statistical analysis was the origination of the concept of *co-relation*, a procedure developed further by his follower Karl Pearson. Correlational analysis, in the form of the Pearson product moment correlation coefficient and its variants, has been the foundation stone of the psychology of individual differences.

33. Although Cattell's father was instrumental in Pepper's original interest in the younger man, it was Fullerton—according to Witmer (see Note 9)—who was primarily responsible for Cattell's appointment as professor.

34. Cattell (1930, p. 119) considered his appointment as professor of psychology to be the first anywhere, and this has sometimes been accepted by historians (R. I. Watson, 1978, p. 409), but it is true only in a limited sense (Sokal, 1972, p. 362). Thus, G. Stanley Hall had been appointed professor of psychology and pedagogy at John Hopkins in 1884, and Joseph Jastrow had been appointed professor of experimental and comparative psychology at the University of Wisconsin in 1888. James's appointment as professor of psychology at Harvard was in 1889, although later than that of Cattell. Cattell's rise from PhD in 1886 to lecturer at Penn and Cambridge to professor in 1889 was meteoric, but not undeserved, and not as atypical then as it would be today.

CHAPTER 3. PHILADELPHIA AND LEIPZIG

1. It is quite possible that Witmer knew Cattell, or at least knew about him, even before the fall term of 1889, because Cattell, as noted in chap. 2, gave a series of lectures at the University of Pennsylvania in the spring of 1888. Witmer at the time was a graduating senior and may well have attended some or all of the lectures. In the spring semester of 1890, Cattell taught Experimental Psychology (advanced course); of the nine students, five were graduate students (Sokal, 1972, p. 385). Presumably, Witmer was one of these five.

2. Letter, L. Witmer to E. G. Boring, March 18, 1948 (see Note 9, chap. 2).

3. *University of Pennsylvania Catalog*, 1890–1891, p. 27. AUP.

4. Collins, 1931, p. 5.

5. Ferree's address is taken from an 1889 document of the Philadelphia College of Pharmacy, provided me by Nancy L. Weinstock (see Note 6, chap. 1); Lightner's is from the *University of Pennsylvania Catalog*, 1889–1890, p. 115. AUP.

6. Described in *Alumni Register*, undated, but probably 1897, p. 6, AUP. Among the subscribers were Charles C. Harrison, Dr. William Pepper, Wiliam C. Cattell, and Dr. S. Weir Mitchell. Pepper was the university provost, Harrison was destined to be the next provost, Mitchell was a famous Philadelphia specialist in nervous disorders, and W. C. Cattell was James McKeen's father. For a more detailed treatment of Cattell's new laboratory, see Sokal, 1972, pp. 368–376. In dollar values of that day, the amounts dedicated to the new psychological laboratory were considerable and support the inference that the facilities established by Cattell, which were shortly to be inherited by Witmer, were outstanding.

7. The fact that the psychology program was located in Biological Hall was significant, as Cheyney (1940/1977, pp. 353–354) observed, in pointing out that the new psychology was to be considered a branch of science rather than of philosophy.

8. Letter, L. Witmer to E. G. Boring, March 18, 1948 (see Note 9, chap. 2).

9. J. M. Cattell, 1890.

10. The tests, adapted from those developed by Galton, concerned dynamometer pressure, rate of movement, pressure causing pain, least noticeable differences in weight, reaction time for sound, time for naming colors, bisection of a 50-cm line, judgment of 10 s in time, and number of letters remembered on one hearing.

11. L. Witmer, 1915c, p. 548. AUP.

12. The arrangement whereby Witmer went to Leipzig to study with Wundt is described in Witmer's letter to Boring (see Note 8, chap. 2). He states there that his salary as assistant was raised to $1,200, but this clearly refers to the entire 18 months (thus, $800 per year). One of my informants (Genevieve McDermott Murphy) was of the opinion that Witmer's parents also contributed to his expenses in Europe. For further information on Cattell's move to Columbia see Sokal, 1972, pp. 459–462.

13. This list of graduate courses was in a document sent to the University of Leipzig by E. Otis Kendall, the vice provost of the University of Pennsylvania, March 20,

1891, to certify the graduate work Witmer had completed at Penn. The enclosures to Leipzig also included a signed copy of Witmer's AB degree. Copies of these documents were kindly provided to me by G. Schwendler (1986) of the Archives of the University of Leipzig. It is possible that some of the courses were taken before Witmer switched to psychology (i.e., in the 1888–1889 academic year). Note that Witmer did not receive an MA degree at Penn, as some authors have incorrectly stated.

14. This date is based on a letter statement in Witmer's handwriting, as follows: "1889 Entered Dept. of Philosophy/Left as student Feb. 1891" (form titled "Military and Navy Record of the Graduates, Matriculates and Undergraduates of the University of Pennsylvania who served in the Spanish–American War," as completed by Lightner Witmer). AUP.

15. Collins, 1931, p. 3.

16. Judd, 1921, p. 175. Judd's comments are in accord with the experience of Cattell, who stated in a letter to his parents that "Wundt asked me things I was sure to know and then to make it plausible a couple of questions that no one but a German professor of psychology could possibly know. During the rest of the examination he was even more nervous than the candidate" (as quoted in Sokal, 1972, pp. 235–236).

17. Bringmann, Balance, & Evans, 1975, p. 294. This outstanding article provides a good overview of Wundt's life and accomplishments. The most detailed treatment, in a work including numerous illustrations, is in Meischner and Eschler (1979).

18. For summaries of Wundt's theoretical system and methodological orientation, see Blumenthal (1979, 1980) and Humphrey (1968).

19. The information that follows concerning Witmer's period at the University of Leipzig is based largely on data generously furnished me, in 1986, by G. Schwendler of the Archives of the Karl Marx University (originally, and now again, the University of Leipzig).

20. Letter, L. Witmer to E. G. Boring, March 18, 1948 (see Note 9, chap. 2).

21. Ibid.

22. Ibid. The materials were unfortunately destroyed along with his other papers after Witmer's death.

23. L. Witmer (1894g). The two articles were published together and also separately under the same title in the same year (Leipzig: Wilhelm Engelmann). I express my indebtedness, in preparing the review of Witmer's dissertation, to Klaus Ludwig and Ingrid Moore, for extensive translations of relevant technical portions.

24. L. Witmer, 1894g, p. 209. Külpe went to Würzburg, Germany, in 1894, where he became famous in connection with the school of "imageless thought." I have been unable to further identify Mitgliedern.

25. L. Witmer, 1894g, p. 110.

26. L. Witmer, 1894a.

27. L. Witmer, 1894g, pp. 105–117.

28. Witmer reported his data in terms of the ratios between a standard of 1 and longer comparison stimuli of varying lengths. The average obtained ratio was 1:1.63, which translates into a proportion of .6135.

29. L. Witmer, 1894g, p. 254.
30. L. Witmer, 1894g, p. 257. Although Witmer's dissertation was not, as such, a study of individual differences in aesthetic preference, its strong emphasis on variations among persons not only tells something about Witmer's thinking at this stage but also suggests, as indicated in the text regarding Fechner, that research involving sensitivity to individual differences was not altogether prohibited in Wundt's laboratory, as generally thought.
31. Ibid, p. 126.
32. Woodworth (1938, pp. 384–391), summarized the literature on the aesthetics of simple forms, including the early work of both Fechner and Witmer. There have been a number of more recent studies on the aesthetic values of forms with varying productions, including, among the most recent instances, Boselie (1992) and Davis and Jahnke (1991). See also chapter 4, this volume, regarding the dissertation by Miller (1893).
33. Letter, L. Witmer to E. G. Boring, March 18, 1948 (see Note 9, chap. 2).
34. Ibid. I learned here that funds for Witmer came from the Seybert fund.
35. Cheyney, 1940/1977, p. 319, and Sokal, 1972, pp. 271–272. It is probable that part of Cattell's salary, at least initially, was also paid out of the Seybert fund.
36. Collins, 1931, p. 9. The account here is inferential in that Collins does not specifically state that it was during this particular period in Europe that he and Witmer visited the Louvre and Uffizi. The two men were both in Europe during the latter part, and at the close, of World War I; however, it seems unlikely that they visited the museums during that unsettled time. They may also have been in Europe together on some other occasion for which I have no record.
37. Alumni Records for W. R. Newbold. AUP.
38. Steffens, 1931, pp. 150–151.
39. Steffens's book, (1931, pp. 132–133) includes a reminiscence to the effect that he and several other students, in looking over some of the remaining data of an American who had previously studied with Wundt, discovered that he had been guilty of fudging his data. There has been considerable speculation as to whether this accusation was valid and, if so, the identity of the errant scholar. Witmer, who did not personally vouch for Steffens's indictment, later (see Note 8, chap. 2) stated that he thought Steffens had Titchener's investigation in mind, or possibly Angell's. For a discussion and evaluation of the matter, see Raphelson (1967). My inclination is to be skeptical of Steffens's conclusions and to suspect that given his naïveté in the field, he may have misinterpreted the data. Another plausible explanation of the apparent alteration of data is that suggested by Solomon Diamont (cited in Sokal et al., 1976, p. 61). Cattell reported that while at Leipzig, he discovered at one point that Wundt's chronoscope was giving erroneous readings and that data based on these readings had to be corrected. Perhaps Steffens happened on these data and jumped to the conclusion that Cattell had fudged his data. (Steffens seems to have had an oversensitivity to the possibility of cheating; see Steffens, 1931, pp. 132–133.)
40. Eckener's results are summarized in Woodworth (1938, p. 699).

41. Interview with Marion Graham, May 30, 1979. Eckener died in Germany in 1954, 2 years before Witmer's death.
42. L. Witmer (1892).

CHAPTER 4. PROFESSIONAL BEGINNINGS

1. The matter of who actually attended the organizational meeting is a matter of some historical curiosity (see Dennis & Boring, 1952; Fernberger, 1943; Hilgard, 1987, pp. 738–740).
2. All of these except Baldwin and Ladd have been identified earlier. Baldwin, who had spent a year with Wundt but took his doctorate under McCosh at Princeton, was professor of psychology at the University of Toronto but would return to Princeton in 1893. Ladd, a senior member of the discipline, was professor of mental philosophy at Yale. At the time of the meeting, Hall was located at Clark, Fullerton at Penn, Jastrow at Wisconsin, James at Harvard, and Cattell at Columbia.
3. Sokal, 1973. Included in Sokal are reports of the preliminary meeting in Worcester, MA, in 1892, the first annual meeting in Philadelphia in 1892, and the second annual meeting in New York in 1893.
4. Dennis and Boring (1952), evidently assuming that Witmer was in Philadelphia during the meeting, incorrectly attributed his absence to his not being a "joiner" (p. 96). Later, this characterization would be true; however, Witmer was active in the American Psychological Association during its early years.
5. In 1897, James's title was changed back to professor of philosophy.
6. W. James, 1890.
7. James exemplified the role of a naturalist examining human experience, rather than that of the systematic, rigorous scientist (see in this connection, W. James, 1901, p. 388, and L. Witmer, 1908–1909, p. 295). Hilgard (1987) refers to James as the "preeminent psychologizer" (p. 50) among psychologists.
8. James may also have been favorably influenced by the fact that Münsterberg, like himself, held an MD degree. Münsterberg's disagreement with Wundt concerned the nature of voluntary action. In opposition to Wundt, Münsterberg maintained that in such activity, there is no representation in consciousness of the will to action, but only of associated kinesthetic sensations.
9. Frank Angell, who will not appear again in these pages, is not to be confused with James Rowland Angell, a cousin, who, after heading the University of Chicago's Department of Psychology, became interim president of that university, and later president of Yale. Frank Angell was primarily interested in psychophysics as pioneered at Leipzig.
10. Boring, 1950, p. 347.
11. *University of Pennsylvania Catalog,* 1892–1893, p. 21. AUP.
12. Ibid., pp. 151, 180. Presumably, Witmer had forwarded the catalog entries to the university by mail while still in Germany.
13. Ibid., p. 21.

14. This inference is based on the following statement, from the University of Pennsylvania's *Alumni Register* (updated, but apparently sometime in 1897), "In 1892, at the beginning of the college year, the work in Psychology was resumed under his [Witmer's] direction" (p. 7). AUP. This statement also implies that Fullerton (or others) had not kept the laboratory active during Witmer's period in Germany.

15. Information concerning the first APA meeting is taken from Sokal, 1973.

16. G. S. Hall, 1894.

17. J. M. Cattell, 1894.

18. Jastrow, 1894.

19. Münsterberg, 1894.

20. Information concerning Jastrow's activity at the Columbia Exposition is based on Blumenthal (1991), Hilgard (1987), and Jastrow (1894).

21. L. Witmer, 1894f.

22. L. Witmer, 1894f, pp. 6–7.

23. Witmer, 1894.

24. This section, including the letters of Witmer to Wundt, is based on data received in 1987 from the Wundt files at the Karl Marx University (formerly University of Leipzig) in Leipzig. I am grateful to Prof. Dr. sc. G. Schwendler, then the director of the archives, for her help. Note that Witmer's letters were typed (typewriters were then a very new contraption and were not yet widely used). The letters were written in German (English translations given here were by Ingrid Moore).

25. Münsterberg, 1894.

26. Ibid., p. 11.

27. The Witmer–Münsterberg letters from which I quote are the property of the Rare Books and Manuscript Division of the Boston Public Library and are used here by courtesy of the Trustees of the Boston Public Library.

28. W. James to Charles Eliot, February 21, 1895, courtesy of the Harvard University Archives.

29. Faculty salaries, 1893–1894 academic year. Fullerton, at $3,750, was the highest paid faculty member. AUP.

30. From the James McKeen Cattell collection in the Library of Congress. Only the last page of the letter is preserved, and this does not include the date. I refer to the letter at this point in my narrative because this seems a logical point for it, but this is purely a matter of judgment.

31. *University of Pennsylvania Catalog*, 1893–1894, pp. 104, 198. AUP.

32. *University of Pennsylvania Catalog*, 1894–1895, p. 32.

33. Ibid., pp. 63, 175.

34. *University of Pennsylvania Catalog*, 1895–1896, p. 200.

35. L. Witmer, 1914a, p. 28. George Twitmyer, a pioneer in the application of psychological principles in schools, was awarded a PhD by Lafayette College in 1903. He died in 1914. (See also G. W. Twitmyer, 1907.)

36. Mach, 1886.

37. Miller, born in 1868, was only a year younger than Witmer. Although a physician,

he did not practice medicine but devoted himself to biochemical research in the University of Pennsylvania Medical School. Among other responsibilities, he served as a member of the Board of Directors of the Pennsylvania School for Feebleminded at Elwyn. He died in 1940.

38. In this book, I generally use the term currently standard for doctoral research (i.e., *dissertation* rather than *thesis*, the term earlier in use).

39. Miller, 1893. In the dissertation, which was never published, Miller expressed "my indebtedness to Dr. Lightner Witmer, of the University of Pennsylvania, for a number of valuable suggestions in regard to the method of conducting these experiments" (pp. 38–39). He also thanked Fullerton and others for making subjects available. Although Witmer was not formally listed as Miller's research supervisor, it is evident that this was the case: Not only was Miller's study an extension of Witmer's own research but further Witmer was the only faculty member knowledgeable in experimental aesthetics.

40. Witmer's colleague William Newbold, however, was seriously interested in abnormal psychological states. In a paper at the Third Annual Meeting of the American Psychological Association, 1894, later printed in the *Psychological Review* (Newbold, 1895), he described "phantasms of the glass," that is, hallucinatory scenes that may spontaneously appear to some individuals when they concentrate on a glass ball.

41. The program of the first meeting of the American Psychological Association, 1892, included one paper on pain; the second annual meting included two, and the third annual meeting included six such papers. In addition, there was a book by Marshall (1894) and an important article by Strong (1895). Both Wundt and James were also interested in the psychology of pleasure and pain.

42. L. Witmer, 1894d.

43. L. Witmer, 1894e. Witmer's paper, so far as I can discern, had no long-term effects, although it was reviewed favorably by the young Harvard philosopher George Santayana (1894).

44. Marshall, 1894.

45. J. M. Cattell, 1896a. This address consisted of an optimistic review of the current state of American psychology.

46. L. Witmer, 1896d.

47. Cornman, 1896.

48. Farrand, 1896. In this project, a battery of tests, of the type developed by Galton and Cattell, were being administered to undergraduates at Columbia on entrance and at the end of their sophomore and senior years. (For later reports on this study, see J. M. Cattell & Farrand, 1896, and Wissler, 1901.)

49. Sanford, 1896, p. 122. The *Psychological Review*, a brand new journal, was established in 1894 by Cattell and Baldwin as an alternative journal to the *American Journal of Psychology*, which had been founded by Hall in 1887.

50. L. Witmer, 1894c.

51. The invention and construction of precise instrumentation constitute an interesting chapter in the early history of psychology (see Sokal et al., 1976; for detailed

information on the Hipp chronoscope, see Hilgard, 1987, p. 81, and Zschuppe, 1984).

52. L. Witmer, 1895. (Systematic tests of statistical significance were not yet available.)

53. Data on Ferree Witmer presented here are abstracted from alumni records, AUP, and information from the Library and Archival Services of the American Medical Association, courtesy of Micaela Sullivan.

54. Data on Evelyn Witmer are abstracted from alumni office records, AUP, and from information provided by the Office of Personnel Management, U.S. government.

55. Peter P. Kuch, Laurel Hill Cemetery, personal communication, January 9, 1980.

56. This inference is based on information provided by Nancy L. Weinstock, of the Philadelphia College of Pharmacy and Science (February 23, 1983), stating that David Witmer was a retail pharmacist until 1895, and information contained in his obituary (unidentified newspaper clipping, dated December 1, 1921, AUP) that he had been in the wholesale pharmaceutical business for many years.

57. Collins, 1931, p. 9. Although it is not clear precisely what period Collins was referring to in this account, we may safely assume that it covers a rather long period of time. As Collins noted, he and Witmer, over a long period of years, frequently took their vacations together. No doubt some of these excursions, although by no means all, included the period of the 1890s. It was in this decade that the bicycle attained its standard form and rapidly became immensely popular. Witmer's love of the outdoors, especially of mountains, is supported by other evidence and was one of his lifelong passions.

CHAPTER 5. THE FIRST PSYCHOLOGICAL CLINIC

1. L. Witmer, 1905. Witmer also continued to direct dissertation research in experimental areas in which he was expert.

2. See Note 33, chap. 4.

3. Johann Heinrich Pestalozzi (1746–1827), an innovative educational reformer in Switzerland. Friedrich Froebel, (1782–1852), in Germany, was the founder of the kindergarten movement. Johann Friedrich Herbart (1776–1841) was a prominent German pedagogist and psychologist.

4. Commager, 1950, p. 41.

5. Morgan, 1971, p. 120.

6. Commager, 1950, p. 43.

7. Camfield, 1973.

8. L. Witmer, 1896b. At the time Witmer was writing this paper the terms *applied psychology* and *clinical psychology* had not yet come into use.

9. L. Witmer, 1897c.

10. For other instances of the focus on the practical in the period under review, see Hyde (1892), Krohn (1894), and Taylor (1898). Further, the theme is still relevant (see Sternberg & Wagner, 1986).

11. Darwin, 1877.

12. Preyer, 1888.

13. Moore, 1896. Moore's article credited the indirect influence of Preyer and Wundt in her study, but did not acknowledge the help of any University of Pennsylvania faculty member. This fact, however, was not unusual in that period, because it was important that the student's research be seen as independent. Fullerton approved the dissertation for the university, but this does not necessarily mean that he supervised it, although he may have. Moore did not follow her graduation with a professional career. She and her husband had three children, a boy and two girls. In 1901, she published an article on the comparative observations of the development of movements in a boy (as already reported in her 1896 article) and a girl (presumably one of her later children). In 1931, Dorothy Keen Hallowell, a Witmer 1928 graduate and a specialist in preschool children, noted (p. 57) the importance of Moore's (1896) dissertation. Moore was the second woman to receive a PhD in psychology in America. The first was Margaret Floy Washburn, who was Titchener's first PhD in 1894; two other women, Mary Whiton Calkins and Christine Ladd-Franklin, had completed their doctoral work earlier but were not awarded the degree.

14. For an excellent review of studies on baby diaries see Wallace, Franklin, & Keegan, 1994. This review includes Moore (1896), but not Moore (1901).

15. For more detailed information on the child study movement, see D. Ross (1972, pp. 279–308) and Zenderland (1988).

16. This course is described in the 1895–1896 *University of Pennsylvania Catalog*, (p. 184), AUP, as a 2-year course titled Psychology, with the first year serving as an introduction and the second year focusing on mental development. Because each part was for a full year but earned only 2 hours credit, the courses probably met weekly. It should be remembered that Witmer also offered, beginning in 1894–1895, a Seminar for the Study of Child-Psychology in the regular department offerings and that this course was for teachers and others with opportunities for observing children. To enroll in this latter course, which probably included some of Witmer's doctoral students, teachers would have to have been college graduates. What most likely happened is that Witmer, in 1894, organized his child psychology seminar because of his intrinsic interest and then added the special class for teachers without undergraduate degrees in 1895–1896 (Cheyney, 1940/1977, p. 401). Whatever the reason, the special course, probably given on Saturdays, proved very popular. Thus, we find reference, in the Report of the Provost for 1897, to "the growing popularity of Dr. Brumbaugh's work in Pedagogy and Dr. Witmer's in Experimental Psychology among the teachers of the city. Twenty-three special students have taken Dr. Brumbaugh's work this year as against 9 last year, and 17 have taken Dr. Witmer's as against 6 last year" (p. 88). AUP.

17. *University of Pennsylvania Catalog*, 1895–1896, p. 184.

18. L. Witmer, 1896c. (It is from the note on the first page of this publication that I know of Witmer's February presentation.)

19. Cheyney, 1940, p. 354. From Cheyney's description, I inferred that Maguire was a student in Witmer's course for teachers. L. Witmer (1907b) himself wrote that

Maguire "was at that time a student of psychology at the University of Pennsylvania" (p. 3). These statements are not mutually exclusive, because teachers in the special courses organized for them were students at the university, although not in the regular courses. However, I have been unable to find documentary evidence that Margaret T. Maguire was actually enrolled during the year in question. Neither the *Catalog* for 1894–1895 nor that for 1895–1896 lists a Margaret T. Maguire, although a Margaret Tilden Maguire is listed as having attended courses in philosophy in 1897–1900 and the College Courses for Teachers program in 1902–1903, 1903–1904, and 1914–1915. I do not see these several discrepancies as being of major concern. Perhaps Maguire was an unenrolled student (auditor) or perhaps the remaining records are incomplete. AUP.

20. L. Witmer, 1907b, p. 4.
21. Ibid., p. 4.
22. Breuer and Freud, 1895.
23. See Note 19.
24. Witmer 1907b, p. 3. The school referred to by Witmer was quite possibly the Wharton Combined School; in 1909 Witmer (1909b) identified Maguire as Principal of this school in a meeting in which she actively participated (described in Chapter 8).
25. From an article by Laura Laedlein in an unidentified newspaper. The article was titled, "Tribute to a Seeker: Dr. Lightner Witmer Is Honored as Founder of Clinical Psychology" (December 6, 1931). AUP.
26. Witmer, 1907b, p. 4.
27. Fernberger, 1931, p. 13. L. Witmer (1907b), in reconstructing the early history of the Clinic, did not mention this summer 1896 course. However, it is probable that Fernberger obtained his information directly from Witmer.
28. L. Witmer, 1896c. *The Citizen*, in which this article appeared, was published by the American Society for the Extension of University Teaching.
29. L. Witmer, 1896a. I am indebted to Donald K. Routh for calling my attention to this article.
30. L. Witmer, 1896b, p. 462.
31. Ibid., p. 463.
32. Ibid., p. 463.
33. Ibid., p. 463.
34. Ibid., p. 464.
35. L. Witmer, 1920b. The possibility that this case (of a boy referred to as *Don*) may have been autistic was first noted by Rimland (1964, p. 6).
36. Fullerton, 1897. The address was essentially a philosophical analysis designed to support a rational science approach to the study of the self. The concept of self was highly topical in psychology then, as it is today. Fullerton's interest in the self does not appear to have been inspired by W. James's (1890) well-known chapter on the self; rather, both treatments were probably reflections of the same Zeitgeist.
37. L. Witmer, 1897c. That the paper was given on the 29th rather than the 30th is an inference on my part. We know from the proceedings that papers were given

only on the mornings of the 29th and the 30th and that all papers on the morning
of the 30th were philosophical in character. In all, 21 papers were presented, of
which the last 10 listed were clearly philosophical in character. Assuming that the
afternoon of the 30th was given over to the addresses of the president and the
business meeting, it follows that Witmer's presentation, which is the 7th listed,
was almost certainly given on the morning of the 29th. Assuming further that
from 8 to 11 papers were presented on the morning session of that day, it also
follows that 20–25 minutes were allotted for each paper.

38. L. Witmer, 1907b.
39. L. Witmer, 1897c, p. 116.
40. L. Witmer, 1897c, p. 117.
41. See, e.g., Brotemarkle (1947, pp. 2–3); Sexton (1965, p. 409); Reisman (1991,
     p. 39).
42. Collins, 1931, p. 5.
43. I am wary of any interpretation that attributes an alleged unresponsiveness of
     Witmer's audience to a feeling that psychology should remain a pure science and
     not engage in practical applications. Witmer, after all, was just 5 years out of
     Wundt's laboratory and had excellent experimental credentials; thus, it is difficult
     to read his proposal as in any sense an attack on the scientific approach. Further,
     his emphasis on the practical was in accord with the spirit of the times, as observed
     earlier. Also, the disharmony that was later to arise between the clinical and ex-
     perimental wings of psychology was at this time several decades in the future.
44. For further details on the preserved case files of the Psychological Clinic see Levine
     and Wishner (1977). The files cover the full life of the Clinic, 1896–1961, and
     include 22,000 case records. I am deeply grateful to my good friend, the late
     Julius Wishner of the University of Pennsylvania, for entrusting to me microfilms
     of the Clinic records. The microfilms are now in the collections of the Archives
     of the History of American Psychology at the University of Akron, Akron, Ohio.
     I also thank John Popplestone, Director of the Akron Archives, for providing me
     with certain materials from the microfilms. For additional information on the
     overall records of the Psychological Clinic see Chapter 12, this volume.
45. It is only by inference that I state that the notes are by Witmer, because they are
     not signed. However, there seems no doubt that they are his, although some of
     the records do contain longhand materials from other persons. One certainly gets
     the impression, in looking over Witmer's early longhand notes, that they were
     made quickly and solely for his own use, and without any thought of their having
     historical value. It should be emphasized that the surviving records for 1896 can-
     not be assumed to include all of the data that Witmer gathered at the time.
46. Earlier this date was incorrectly, and inexplicably, given as November 26, 1896
     (McReynolds, 1987, p. 853).
47. Case 0018 was apparently seen in 1898, and Case 0019 in 1911.
48. Brief summary of 1896 case records (except for Cases 0001 and 0023, discussed
     in the text): Case 0002—3-year-old boy, referred from Day Nursery, evidently
     concerning possibility of retardation. Conclusion: "no evidence to suggest imbe-

cility." Case 0003—boy, speech problem, possibility of nasopharyngeal obstruc-
tion, referred to a Dr. Packard for examination. Case 0004—boy, 9, referred by
a nurse, history of nervous trouble, chorea, referred to a Dr. Ludlow. Case 0005
—boy, 10, speech problem, referral and Witmer's role unclear, student of Miss
M [Marvin?]. Case 0006—boy, 9, screams in class, active, restless, poor school
performance. Case 0007—girl, problem unclear. Case 0008—boy, history of
convulsions or spasms, nervous prostration, chorea, nightmares. Case 0009—boy,
backward, restless, referred to physician. Case 0010—girl, 13, nervous manner,
stammers, chorea. Case 0011—boy, 6, problem unclear. Case 0012—boy, defective speller. Case 0013—boy, 12, stutters. Case 0014—girl, 7, referred from Day
Nursery, restless, hard to teach, tonsils large, recommended be sent to throat
specialist. Case 0015—girl, referred from public school, concern over mental
level, no recommendation stated. Case 0016—boy, 3½, does not speak, very
active, appears deaf but specialists have found no defects. Had been diagnosed
hydrocephalic, but head now appears normal. Also had earlier been labeled "feebleminded." No recommendations. Case 0017—girl, 12, has strabismus. Case
0018—evidently misfiled, probably first seen 1898. Case 0019—evidently misfiled, first seen 1911. Case 0020—boy, problem unclear, evidently referred by
physician. Case 0021—girl, 5, referred from Day Nursery, problem not clear,
recommended referral to throat specialist for removal of adenoids. Case 0022—
no data. Case 0024—no data. Case 0025—no data. Case 0026—boy, 9, 3 years
in 3rd grade, can't tell time, seems underdeveloped.

49. L. Witmer, 1907a.

50. *Dyslexia* is the most widely used term for the disorder that I am referring to and
has been for many years. The term is highly appropriate in that it means, literally,
poor or inadequate (*dys*) use of words (*lexia*). Other terminology is, however,
sometimes used. For example, the latest edition of the *Diagnostic and Statistical
Manual of Mental Disorders* (American Psychiatric Association, 1994) prefers—I
think unwisely—the term *reading disorder*. The underlying nature and etiology of
dyslexia are still poorly understood, although it is generally considered to be due
in some manner to congenital factors. Professor Paul Hollingsworth, reading specialist at the College of Education, University of Nevada, Reno, (1983), at my
request, read Witmer's 1907 case report and gave me his independent opinion,
which was that Charles's primary affliction was most likely developmental dyslexia,
with ocular imbalance being an additional difficulty.

51. The following is the complete text of Ide's note: "GGI at a lecture heard Witmer
refer to his first case as one of a bad speller. He further described the case as that
of a boy brought to the Clinic by his teacher because he could not spell although
he had reached the fifth grade. The teacher found him a good student in history
and geography, which seemed odd inasmuch as the child was not able to read
without spelling the words letter by letter. It was developed that the older sister
was reading the history and geography lessons aloud to the boy and in that way
he had been able to maintain himself in his class although unable to read the
lessons for himself. Careful examination at the Clinic brought out the fact that

the boy had weak eye muscles, and that he was able to focus but momentarily upon a word, so that in order to get the entire word, he had to spell the word, letter by letter as he was able to focus upon the separate letters. As soon as he had transferred his eyes from one letter to the next, the first one became two, and the whole word was so confused that he could not grasp it at once. Glasses and later an operation changed the sight a great deal, and careful teaching at the Clinic brought the boy to such a stage in six months that he was able to read books by himself for pleasure."

52. Lewis, 1897.

53. Harmon, 1897.

54. Other evidence of continuing research on reaction time in Witmer's laboratory is provided by a brief article in 1895 in the *Psychological Review*. Its author, R. Meade Bache, was a prominent Philadelphian and a descendant of Benjamin Franklin; he had been a student at the University of Pennsylvania in 1846–1847 and had spent his career in the U.S. Coast and Geodetic Survey. In his article, Bache attempted to show the intellectual superiority of Caucasians over Indians and African Americans on the basis of reaction times from small samples of subjects (10 in each group). The relevance of the study, inferior even by the standards of the day, is that Bache stated that he had obtained his data from Witmer, who, he stated, had collected them at his request. I think it likely that in fact Witmer, rather than collecting data specifically at Bache's request, made available to him certain requested data already collected, possibly from the Lewis study. Notably, Bache's conclusions were not in accord with the more extensive data in Lewis's study.

55. Neither Lewis's nor Harmon's study was ever published, so far as I have been able to learn, and they are known only through abstracts in the Proceedings of the Fifth Annual Meeting of the American Psychological Association, 1896 (1897), published in *Psychological Review*. Also, to the best of my knowledge, the broad-scale study envisaged by Harmon was never completed.

56. Proceedings of the Fifth Annual Meeting of the American Psychological Association, 1896 (1897), pp. 132–138.

57. It will be recalled that Witmer had presented a paper on the patellar reflex at the 1895 APA meeting.

58. Proceedings of the Fifth Annual Meeting of the American Psychological Association, 1896 (1897), pp. 108–110.

59. Quoted from Goodwin, 1985, p. 386.

60. Goodwin, 1985, p. 386.

61. Mason, 1896.

62. L. Witmer, 1897e. Mason responded to Witmer in an 1897 article.

63. This instructor was probably Mary E. Marvin.

CHAPTER 6. AT THE TURN OF THE CENTURY

1. This description is based on shared reminiscences of persons who knew Witmer and on photographs. All informants who mentioned Witmer's stature described

him as "short," with retrospective estimates ranging from 5 feet 4 inches to 5 feet 8 inches. Helen Backus Graber, who knew Witmer well, judged his weight as about 140 pounds; she specifically stated that his eyes were blue, though one informant remembered his eyes as "dark." Several informants described his gaze as "piercing."

2. I am indebted to Lucy Fisher West and Caroline Rittenhouse, Byrn Mawr Archivists, for furnishing me (in 1983 and 1990, respectively) with relevant information on Witmer's period there.
3. *University of Pennsylvania Catalog*, 1896–1897, p. 165. AUP.
4. *University of Pennsylvania Catalog*, 1896–1897, p. 182. AUP.
5. *University of Pennsylvania Catalog*, 1897–1898, pp. 206–207. AUP. From this point forward I will no longer routinely report the courses for which Witmer was responsible.
6. *University of Pennsylvania Catalog*, 1897–1898, p. 207. AUP.
7. Alumni Register, University of Pennsylvania, March 1897, p. 7.
8. Ibid., p. 7. AUP.
9. A. F. Witmer, 1897. Ferree Witmer, who had obtained his MD degree in 1893, co-taught a course with Lightner, under the category of Courses for Teachers, in each of the 1898–1899 and 1899–1900 years.
10. Witmer, 1907b, p. 5. Note the role of Mary E. Marvin.
11. Cheyney, 1940, p. 354. The policy of no fees would be maintained throughout the long history of Witmer's Clinic. Cheyney was a graduate of the University of Pennsylvania, a few years ahead of Witmer, and was later on the faculty. He undoubtedly knew Witmer well.
12. Technically, psychology was not a separate department at this time. Rather psychology was part of the Department of Philosophy, which included philosophy, ethics, psychology, and pedagogy. For 1897–1898, William Newbold, whose interest in psychology was discussed earlier, served as chairman of the department. Witmer filled this role for 1898–1899. Fullerton was the senior man in the department, with the rank of professor. AUP.
13. This institution was founded in 1850 to provide an opportunity for women to become physicians. It is now the Medical College of Pennsylvania. I thank Sandra L. Chaff, its director of archives for providing me with information on the school's history in 1978.
14. L. Witmer, 1897d.
15. Ibid., p. 906.
16. Ibid., p. 913.
17. Ibid., p. 917.
18. Ibid., p. 917.
19. L. Witmer, 1897a, 1897b.
20. I am indebted to George W. Corner, Executive Officer of the American Philosophical Society (1976) for information on Witmer's election to the Society. Although elected in 1897, Witmer did not become a member until he signed the roll book on October 21, 1898. The delay may have been due to his service in

the Spanish-American War; he was not formally discharged from the Army until November 1898. AUP.

21. Collins, 1931, p. 9.
22. Data concerning Witmer's military service are abstracted from a military record of University of Pennsylvania alumni form completed in longhand by Witmer (n.d.) and from the Minutes of the University of Pennsylvania Board of Trustees, dated July 12, 1898, p. 547. AUP.
23. N. Burt, 1963, p. 274.
24. N. Burt, 1963, p. 275.
25. I am indebted to Sergeant John Gallagher (first name not available) of the City Troop (1979) for information concerning Witmer's induction into the organization. Witmer attained the rank of corporal in 1905 and of sergeant in 1907. He became inactive in 1909 and received honorary status in 1926. Several informants told me, in the course of my research, how proud Witmer was to be a member of the City Troop.
26. *University of Pennsylvania Catalog*, 1898–1899, p. 172. AUP.
27. Cornman, 1896, 1902.
28. "Dr. O. P. Cornman Dies at Age of 64," September 7, 1930, *Philadelphia Inquirer*. AUP.
29. McKeag, 1902 (see also McKeag, 1931).
30. Data on McKeag were generously furnished me by Jean N. Berry, Wellesley College Archives, February 15, 1991.
31. *University of Pennsylvania Catalog*, 1898–1899, p. 172.
32. E. B. Twitmyer, 1902 (see also Irwin, 1943).
33. Although firm documentary evidence that Witmer supervised Twitmyer's research is lacking, it seems evident that in fact he did, because the study was in an area in which he, Witmer, had done research, because he was the only faculty member knowledgeable in this area, and because he was cited by Twitmyer (see also Coon, 1982).
34. Lombard, 1887. This was the lead article in the first issue of the *American Journal of Psychology*.
35. W. James, 1890, Vol. 2, p. 380.
36. Cited by W. James, 1890, Vol. 2, p. 380.
37. On Pavlov, see Anokhin, 1968.
38. E. B. Twitmyer, 1905.
39. Coon, 1982.
40. Dallenbach, 1959.
41. *Pittsburgh (PA) News*, April 22, 1898, AUP.
42. *Philadelphia Inquirer*, November 2, 1898, AUP.
43. *West Chester (PA) Republican*, February 4, 1899, AUP.
44. *Philadelphia Inquirer*, February 16, 1900, AUP.
45. Indications of this interest at the academic level are provided by the granting of the Seybert fund at the University of Pennsylvania (see chap. 3) and, in the same era, the grant by Thomas Welton Stanford, the brother of Stanford's founder, to that university's psychology department, for studying paranormal phenomena.

46. Witmer's earlier career had been touched twice by the psychical movement: First, his period in Germany was financed in part by the Seybert fund and, second, before leaving Germany, he had taken the occasion to visit Baron Carl DuPrel, a European leader of the spiritualistic movement.

47. Allen, 1967, p. 285. James's interest in spiritualism and mysticism generally is well documented (see, e.g., Allen, 1967, especially pp. 281–285). This particular bent in James's wide-ranging interests was probably due in part to the influence of his father, Henry James, Senior, who had been greatly influenced by the Swedish mystic Emanuel Swedenborg. William James was instrumental in helping found the American Society for Psychical Research.

48. *Philadelphia Inquirer*, February 16, 1900, p. not available. AUP.

49. Letter, L. Witmer to H. Münsterberg, May 28, 1900. Witmer, writing as a member of its Executive Committee, extended the invitation on behalf of the Contemporary Club. It is not known whether anything came of Witmer's offer.

50. *Norristown (PA) Herald*, August 23, 1900. AUP.

51. *Philadelphia North American*, November 16, 1900. AUP.

52. Letter, L. Witmer to J. M. Cattell, May 24, 1901, from the Cattell papers in the Library of Congress. The collection includes 37 letters from Witmer to Cattell during the period of 1894 through 1909, and one in 1931, plus one letter from Cattell to Witmer in 1931.

53. L. Witmer, 1902a. The book, published by Ginn and Company, was hardcover and included 251 pages of text, plus introductory material.

54. L. Witmer, 1902a, pp. iii–iv.

55. Titchener, 1901, 1905.

56. Letter, L. Witmer to J. M. Cattell, April 13, 1902 (see Note 52).

57. I am grateful to Janet D. McCarthy, of Silver Burdett and Ginn, publishers, for this information (1991).

58. Based on my interview with Frank Irwin (June 1, 1979), who obtained a BA at Pennsylvania in 1926. Leonard Carmichael, a later, highly eminent developmental psychologist, wrote, in Witmer's obituary (1957), "Even today [Witmer's] really remarkable volume is of value to students of psychology because it contains many illustrations demonstrating sensory and perceptual psychology in an ingenuous way that has never been surpassed."

59. Cornman, 1902.

60. McKeag, 1902.

61. Urban, 1908.

62. Letter, L. Witmer to J. M. Cattell, September 6, 1897 (see Note 52).

63. Letters of L. Witmer to J. M. Cattell, July 2, 8, 1902 (see Note 52).

64. Wissler, 1901.

65. I thank Marie C. Boltz, Special Collections, Lehigh University, for providing me (in 1991) materials from the relevant Lehigh catalogs. My description of Witmer's period at Lehigh is also based on data from a Witmer to Cattell letter dated January 29, 1904, from the Library of Congress Cattell collection, and on Witmer's later *Who's Who* entries.

66. Cases 0031 and 0055.
67. I am indebted to Michael A. Ermilio, archivist, Philadelphia College of Pharmacy and Science, for information (1993) on Paul DeLancey Witmer. Like his father and his brother Ferree before him, Paul wrote a required essay, titled "The Differentiation of Hyoscyamis Niger, Atropa Belladonna and Datura Stramonium."
68. Scripture, 1895.
69. Letter, L. Witmer to E. B. Titchener, January 20, 1904. Excerpts from the Witmer to Titchener letters used in this biography are from the Edward Bradford Titchener papers in the Cornell University Library and are used with permission of the Division of Rare and Manuscript Collections of that Library.
70. Letter, L. Witmer to E. B. Titchener, January 25, 1904.
71. Letter, L. Witmer to E. B. Titchener, March 21, 1904.
72. Letter, L. Witmer to E. B. Titchener, March 31, 1904.
73. For detailed accounts of the origins of the Society of Experimentalists, see Boring (1938, 1967) and Goodwin (1985).
74. For abstracts of Witmer's papers, as well as of the other papers presented at the April get-together, see "Meeting of Experimental Psychologists at Cornell University," *Journal of Philosophy, 1,* 238–240. Witmer's papers, to the best of my knowledge, were never published: Of course, the meeting was deliberately informal and was not geared to the presentation of completed studies.
75. Information on the background of Emma Repplier and on her marriage to Witmer is abstracted from a number of sources, including newspaper articles from AUP, correspondence (1976) with Sidney Repplier, and conversations with Carolyn and John Walters (1976). I am indebted to Joan G. Rammel, director of alumni activities, for providing me with information (1981) on Agnes Irwin School and on Emma Repplier's period there; this included Joanne Loewe Neel's (1969) history of the school.
76. E. Repplier, 1900.
77. I am indebted to Whitfield J. Bell, Jr., Executive Officer, American Philosophical Society, for furnishing me (April 12, 1983) with information concerning Emma Repplier's work at the Society Library. Emma's work on the Benjamin Franklin papers was later published as the Appendix (E. R. Witmer, 1908) to a work edited by I. M. Hayes.
78. E. Repplier, 1906a.
79. E. Repplier, 1906b.
80. Interview with Helen Graber, May 26, 1979. Graber was Witmer's secretary during the 1920s and picked the story up from Witmer himself. It is conceivable that she did not remember the name of the hotel precisely.

CHAPTER 7. A NEW PROFESSION: CLINICAL PSYCHOLOGY

1. W. James, 1905.
2. Proceedings of the Thirteenth Annual Meeting of the American Psychological Association, 1904 (1905), p. 37.

3. E. B. Twitmyer, 1905.

4. Münsterberg, 1905.

5. L. Witmer, 1905.

6. This is not to say that Witmer gave up all interest in experimental psychology after this study. As one indication of his continuing interest in that area, he had his students (at least up to the time of World War I) carry out exercises on the Hipp chronoscope.

7. Another possible explanation for the decline in cases seen during the 1897–1906 period is that Witmer to some degree may have lost interest in clinical work, having not yet arrived at the certainty of mind which he was to attain later, that the clinical area was his true calling.

8. Fernberger, 1931, p. 13. Samuel W. Fernberger received his PhD from the University of Pennsylvania in 1912, with a dissertation under Witmer on psychophysics. After a period at Clark, he returned to Penn, where he spent the rest of his career. He was a renowned experimental psychologist.

9. A certain degree of arbitrary judgment was required in compiling the listing of cases by year, because it was not always clear from the records, particularly around the ending or beginning of a year, to which year a given case belonged and also because some of the cases appeared to have been incorrectly numbered. For example, Case 0041 would appear, by file number, to have been seen in 1897, yet the preserved data labeled Case 0041 actually comprises two cases dated 1905; and Case 0090, although including data beginning January 24, 1903, was filed with 1905 cases. As observed in Chapter 5, it is probable that the numbers were assigned to early cases some years after the cases were originally seen, thus leading to certain inaccuracies. According to Dorothy Lynn (personal communication, August 8, 1992), Julius Wishner's secretary when the files were microfilmed, the records were filmed in exactly the order in which they were filed, with the case numbers already assigned.

10. Witmer, himself the brother of two physicians, had excellent relations with the medical fraternity, as evidenced by the frequency with which they referred cases to him. He had the strong support of Weir Mitchell, probably the best known physician in America specializing in nervous disorders, and William Pepper, a graduate of the University of Pennsylvania Medical School and university provost (then its highest officer), when Witmer began his work, as well as with other physicians to whom he referred cases. This general support was important, perhaps essential, in making it possible for Witmer to function smoothly in areas, especially diagnostic practices, previously within the sole purview of physicians.

11. See for example, Mulford, 1897.

12. Terman, 1914, chap. XII. As observed by Levine and Wishner (1977), concern in the Clinic with problems possible due to enlarged adenoids dropped around 1915. It later disappeared, and a review article by Gladys Lowe (1923) in *The Psychological Clinic* indicated essentially no empirical support for the practice.

13. Although I was aware of these school-based cases from examination of the case microfilms loaned to me in 1976 by Julius Wishner, I was made more aware of

their historic significance by an article by Fagan (1988), who had independently identified the four cases.

14. Seymour DeWitt Ludlum, a close friend of Witmer, obtained his MD from Johns Hopkins in 1902. In 1912, he established the Gladwyne Colony, near Philadelphia, for mental patients and, in 1914, he became professor of psychiatry at the University of Pennsylvania. He had a distinguished career in neuropathology and died in 1956.

15. Witmer saw this young man, an instructor in a local school for boys, on March 20, 21, and 22, 1907 (the case records, labeled 0091, were misfiled with 1905 records). Witmer also advised the man to take a vacation in Atlantic City, but was not optimistic that this would be helpful. It is not stated how the case was resolved; presumably the young man returned to his physician for further treatment. Another early adult case (Case 0083) is of interest in that it involved Witmer's close friend Joseph Collins, who was practicing neurology in New York. In a letter dated December 27, 1904, Collins informed Witmer of a woman patient whom he had diagnosed as one of hysteria manifested in dissociation and a dual personality. Collins included a workup on the woman and suggested that Witmer, sometime when he was in New York, might wish to interview her. It is not clear whether this ever occurred, although it probably did, because Witmer was interested in the case.

16. This judgment is based in part on the internal contents of the manuscript, but more particularly on its existence in the Case 0090 data. The documents in this case range from January 24, 1903 to May 13, 1905 (plus a later followup query), and the manuscript immediately follows a document dated February 26, 1904. (These data reflect my own inspection of the relevant microfilms, and followup review by Sheila Ochsenhirt, AHAP.)

17. L. Witmer, 1904. The document is evidently an unedited and incomplete draft (it ends abruptly just before a planned case description).

18. This is the first recorded instance of Witmer's use of the term *clinical psychology*, as distinct from the expression *psychological clinic*.

19. I am indebted to Marvin Rosen for generously providing me with extensive information on the Elwyn Institutes. He wrote that Witmer "may have been associated with the school before 1906 but I cannot document that" (June 14, 1983). My own conclusion that Witmer's affiliation went back to 1896, at least in an informal way, is based on Witmer's biographical data in *Who's Who* (e.g., 1934–1935). Further, L. Witmer (1907b), in explaining his relevant background for the founding of the journal, *The Psychological Clinic*, wrote that, "my own preparation for the [clinical] work has been facilitated through my connection as consulting psychologist with the Pennsylvania Training School for Feeble-minded Children at Elwyn, and a similar connection with the Haddonfield Training School and Miss Marvin's Home School in West Philadelphia" (p. 6).

20. I thank Delores M. Barker (1992) for detailed information on the Bancroft School and its history.

21. Herbert Stotesbury, PhD, was a member of the prominent Stotesbury family in

Philadelphia. After some work at the University of Pennsylvania, he completed his education at the University of Heidelberg and Cambridge University. He taught at Temple University and the University of Pennsylvania and later served as clinical psychology consultant and teacher at the Institute of Nervous and Mental Diseases in Philadelphia (a part of the Pennsylvania Hospital, which goes back to 1751; Benjamin Franklin was cofounder) and with the Human Research Corporation in Philadelphia.

22. Later published in *The Psychological Clinic*, (L. Witmer, 1907c).
23. *Old Penn Weekly Review*, January 1907, p. 2. AUP.
24. Ibid., p. 2.
25. Letter, L. Witmer to Mrs. J. Lewis Crozer, January 12, 1907. AUP.
26. Intrauniversity memoranda, AUP. It should perhaps be noted that up until this time, and for many years into the future, the provost was the University's highest ranking official (i.e., instead of a president).
27. Letter, L. Witmer to J. M. Cattell, March 1, 1907. Cattell Papers, Library of Congress. The number 10,000 copies was possibly meant figuratively.
28. L. Witmer, 1907b, pp. 5–6.
29. Town, 1907. Town at the time was resident psychologist at Friend's Asylum for the Insane, Frankford, Ontario, Canada.
30. Huntington, 1907. Huntington had earlier (Huntington, 1905) given a paper (introduced by Witmer) on the beneficial effects of removal of enlarged adenoids in children.
31. L. Witmer, 1907f.
32. L. Witmer, 1907b.
33. Ibid., p. 1.
34. Ibid., p. 7.
35. L. Witmer, 1904.
36. L. Witmer, 1907b, p. 8.
37. Ibid., p. 9.
38. Butler, 1983. See also Butler, 1985. It could, however, be argued that the term *clinical psychology* is essentially a variant of *psychological clinic*, introduced by Witmer in his 1896 paper before APA. As noted above, Witmer's first recorded use of the phrase *clinical psychology* was in his 1904 unpublished prospectus.
39. Prévost, 1969, p. 119.
40. Prévost is to be commended for this bit of historical sleuthing. He states that three volumes (incomplete) of the *Revue de Psychologie Clinique et Thérapeutique* are to be found in the Bibliothèque Nationale. Notably, Maurice Reuchlin, in his *Histoire de la Psychologie* (1967), highlighted the role of Witmer in the ongoing clinical psychology.
41. L. Witmer, 1907f.
42. Ibid., p. 25.
43. Ibid., p. 25.
44. Ibid., p. 25.
45. Ibid., p. 26. Hall was president of Clark University but also superintended the psychology program.

46. Ibid., p. 26.

47. Ibid., p. 27.

48. Ibid., p. 26.

49. Ibid., p. 26.

50. It is ironic, or at least confusing, that despite Witmer's implied criticism of Mün-
     sterberg's Harvard program for its lack of attention to child psychology, Mün-
     sterberg had evidently recently written to him concerning appropriate tests for
     children.

51. Letter, L. Witmer to H. Münsterberg, March 28, 1907 (see Note 27, chap. 4).

52. Münsterberg, 1898.

53. Ibid., p. 166.

54. Cattell, 1898a.

55. Hall, 1895; Münsterberg, 1895.

56. Bjork, 1983, chap. 3, gave a number of examples of Münsterberg's thin-skinned
     nature.

57. Baird, 1907, p. 383.

58. Letter, L. Witmer to H. Münsterberg, May 17, 1907 (see Note 4, chap. 4).

59. Fifth Annual Meeting of Experimental Psychologists (1908).

60. Witmer and Münsterberg had ample opportunity to interact over the years. Both
     were members of APA and the unnamed group of experimental psychologists, and
     both were on APA's governing council during 1905 and 1906. (Witmer was
     elected, in 1904, to a 3-year term but served only 2 years; presumably, he resigned
     after 2 years, although it is not clear why.)

61. H. Münsterberg, 1898, p. 163.

62. Münsterberg achieved outstanding stature in philosophy, being elected president
     of the American Philosophical Society in 1908 (he had been president of APA in
     1898). His orientation, toward German idealism, clashed with James's pragma-
     tism, for which Münsterberg had a general disdain. Over the years, James and
     Münsterberg, although mutually supportive, had grown increasingly distant
     (Bjork, 1983; Perry, 1935, Vol. 2, chap. 40). For biographies of Münsterberg, see
     Hale, 1980; M. Münsterberg, 1922; Moskowitz, 1977.

63. See, e.g., Hale, 1980; Moskowitz, 1977; Roback, 1964; Sahakian, 1975. Roback
     was a student of Münsterberg.

64. One matter on which Witmer and Münsterberg held similar opinions was that
     both vehemently rejected spiritualism. James was enraged (Hale, 1980, p. 110)
     when Münsterberg exposed a famous medium as fraudulent.

65. See *The Psychological Clinic*, 1907, *1*, inside front cover, opposite p. 69.

66. Münsterberg, 1906.

67. Ibid., p. 96. Items in the "News and Comment" section of *The Psychological Clinic*
     were never signed; hence, this citation is not listed in the Witmer Bibliography,
     although it was almost certainly by Witmer.

68. Letter, R. Yerkes to E. B. Titchener, in the Titchener papers collection, Cornell
     University Library, used with permission of the Division of Rare and Manuscript
     Collections, Cornell University Library, and of Roberta Yerkes Blanshard. Date

not clear, but by context I place it in 1908, with the meetings referred to being those of the experimental psychologists in 1907.

69. Letter, L. Witmer to E. B. Titchener, April 27, 1908, in Titchener papers, Cornell University Library, used with permission of the Division of Rare and Manuscript Collections, Cornell University Library.

CHAPTER 8. THE RESTORATION OF CHILDREN

1. L. Witmer, 1897c, p. 117.
2. Description of the Hospital School during the 1907 summer session is based on Witmer, 1907d, which provides considerable detail.
3. Witmer (1907d, p. 139–140) credited the "liberality" of Mrs. Crozer for making the Hospital School possible.
4. L. Witmer, 1908b, 1909b, 1909f.
5. L. Witmer, 1911a, pp. 9–10. Beginning in 1909, Witmer (1909f, p. 122) sometimes referred to the Hospital School as *The Orthogenic School* (he coined the term *orthogenics*—discussed later in this chapter—to refer to the science of normal development), and advertised it in several issues of *The Psychological Clinic* (e.g., 1909, 3, opposite p. 29).
6. Fernberger, 1931, p. 14. Fernberger states that the school for pay patients "continues to function" (i.e., in 1931). I have no confirmation of this surprising statement, and certainly the Hospital School as such did not persist; I take it that Fernberger is suggesting that the Clinic had the policy of occasionally placing problem children in selected pay-for-care homes, where they could be systematically observed. My impression is that Witmer's enthusiasm for the Hospital School waned after he established his own private school.
7. Roback (1964) stated that Witmer "In 1907 . . . founded the Witmer School for Psychological Diagnosis and Treatment of Mental Retardation and Deviation" (p. 231). I cannot account for this statement. Conceivably, the term may have been applied by Witmer to the school started in 1908, but I have no verification of this. Incidentally, Roback incorrectly refers (p. 232) to Helen Witmer as Lightner's daughter; actually, Lightner and Emma had no children.
8. L. Witmer, 1937, p. 5. Description of the Rose Valley School is based primarily on data generously provided by Marion Mack (1976) and Helen Joyce (1984), referring to the school building as it existed in 1911. On the basis of contextual factors, I conclude that that building probably was also the original school site, in 1908.
9. L. Witmer, 1908a, p. 1–4.
10. Ibid., p. 1.
11. Ibid., p. 3.
12. Ibid., p. 4.
13. Ibid., p. 4.
14. L. Witmer, 1908b.
15. L. Witmer, 1909a.

16. L. Witmer, 1909f.

17. Ibid., p. 121.

18. L. Witmer, 1908–1909. For another perspective on Worcester and the Emmanuel movement, see Reisman, 1991, p. 72.

19. Münsterberg, 1908, p. 440.

20. L. Witmer, 1908–1909, p. 241. Witmer was not alone in criticizing Münsterberg's exaggerated claims of therapeutic efficacy. Thus, Hale (1980) wrote that "Witmer . . . like others . . . found fault with Münsterberg's over-blown claims, his premature airing of laboratory results, and his self-advertising popularizations" (p. 110).

21. Nevius, 1894. See also W. James, 1895; and L. Witmer, 1908–1909, p. 288.

22. W. James, 1892, pp. 737–738.

23. W. James, 1896, and J. M. Cattell, 1896b; see also W. James, 1898, and J. M. Cattell, 1898a; and also J. M. Cattell, 1893; and W. James, 1909.

24. L. Witmer, 1908–1909, p. 291. The passage of time has shown that Witmer was wrong in his evaluation of James's (1890) book, *Principles of Psychology.* Today, over a hundred years after its publication, it remains a classic, perhaps *the* classic in psychology. In point of fact, the advance of science requires both the creative explorations represented by James and the hard-nosed empirical research recommended by Witmer. Other authors noting Witmer's criticism of James include Curti, 1980, p. 210; and B. Ross, 1991, p. 13.

25. L. Witmer, 1908–1909, p. 294.

26. See, e.g., Ladd, 1894.

27. L. Witmer, 1908–1909, p. 295. Witmer's critique of James was not wholly negative. Thus he wrote that "the art of William James resembles that of his brother, Henry, though the medium in which they give expression in their thought and feeling differs greatly. William James may be something better than a psychologist. . . . [He] belongs to the list of semi-scientific, semi-imaginative writers of whom Maeterlinck is one of the best examples. . . . James himself commends the natural history method, which he so conspicuously exemplifies," pp. 294–295.

28. Letter, W. James to H. Münsterberg, March 16, 1909. In H. James, 1920, Vol. 2, pp. 320–321.

29. Proceedings of the Eighteenth Annual Meeting of the American Psychological Association, 1909 (1910).

30. *The Psychological Clinic,* 1910, *3,* p. 248. In "News and Comment" section. Unsigned, but presumably written by Witmer.

31. Ibid., p. 248. After this indecorous episode, the failed friendship of Witmer and Münsterberg, so far as can be ascertained, faded into history. Perhaps, given the personalities of the two men, some sort of breach was inevitable. Yet in retrospect, it was unfortunate, because both made major contributions to the advance of psychology.

32. Interview with Morris Viteles, May 31, 1979.

33. Collins, 1908. This is the book that was reviewed in Witmer 1908–1909.

34. Material in the section on Collins and Witmer is abstracted from the *National*

Cyclopedia of Biography (1955), p. 418; and from information in the Joseph Collins Papers, Rare Book and Manuscript Library, Columbia University, made available through the courtesy of Bernard R. Crystal (1993).

35. Witmer 1907d, p. 141. In a typical clinic, which became a standard part of Witmer's approach with advanced students, and generally were given on Saturday mornings, several students would be brought before the class, and Witmer himself, or one or more of his students under his supervision, would administer selected tests to the children. Witmer would also interview the children and make edifying remarks to the class.

36. Witmer, 1909b, pp. 141–142. Presumably the recorder for the Psychological Clinic took down the interchange in shorthand.

37. The ages of the children were not given; however, they were evidently about the same age, and Fannie was in her third year in the first grade. Gertrude had earlier lived in a county poor-house, where she had been a menace to the other children; she was now in the Hospital School. Fannie was nearly deaf, and came from a deprived environment. R. S., a new case, was extremely backward in school.

38. Presentation of problem children (or adults) in a quasi-public setting, while commonplace in Witmer's day, would not be acceptable today.

39. Information in this section is based primarily on Fernberger (1931) and L. Witmer (1909e).

40. A detailed accounting of the Clinic records through the entire 22,000 plus cases is beyond the scope of this biography. It is important to note, however, that this new numbering procedure did not take systematic account of the earlier cases seen. It is difficult to determine precisely how many cases were seen with a 0 prefix, but it was apparently somewhat over 300 altogether. According to my notes the new Case 1 was dated April 29, 1909. My guess is that it may have been around this time that the decision was made to put the earlier cases into a more systematic order than had previously existed.

41. Furness, 1902.

42. Witmer, 1909c, p. 179; Furness, 1916. Evidently Furness did most of the training, although the original idea was Witmer's.

43. First headline, January 2, 1910, *Providence Journal*; second headline, date and newspaper not identified. AUP.

44. Furness, 1916.

45. L. Witmer, 1909c.

46. L. Witmer, 1910a.

47. Warden, Jenkins, and Warner, 1936.

48. Kellogg and Kellogg, 1933 (see also W. N. Kellogg, 1968).

49. Gardner, Gardner, and Van Cantfort, 1989.

50. Binet and Henri, 1895.

51. Reisman, 1991, p. 43.

52. Smith, 1914, pp. 144, 147.

53. Franz, 1912. Franz made major contributions on the localization of brain functions (see Boring, 1950; Hilgard, 1987).

54. Whipple, 1910.
55. Goddard, 1910.
56. Terman, 1916. For a biography of Terman, see Minton (1988).
57. Thorndike, 1907.
58. Review of E. L. Thorndike, "The elimination of pupils from school," *The Psychological Clinic, 2*, 23–24.
59. Winship, 1908.
60. Unsigned note, but clearly by L. Witmer, *The Psychological Clinic*, 1908, *2*, 87–88.
61. The brief disagreement between Witmer and Thorndike is elaborated in Jançich, 1968, p. 303.
62. Quoted in Jançich, 1968, p. 303.
63. Unsigned note, but clearly by L. Witmer, *The Psychological Clinic*, 1908, *2*, 119.
64. Ayres, 1908.
65. Thorndike, 1909.
66. Data in this paragraph are based primarily on Misiak and Sexton, 1966, pp. 200–204; Smith, 1914; and Wallin, 1914.
67. For further information on Healy and the Juvenile Psychopathic Institute, see Louttit, 1939, p. 366; Misiak and Sexton, 1966, pp. 203–204; Reisman, 1991, pp. 67–68; Snodgrass, 1984.
68. H. Münsterberg, 1909, p. 380.
69. Available records of attendance do not include Witmer, and although such records are incomplete, Saul Rosenzweig, the leading authority on the Clark meeting, indicated to me (personal communication, October 18, 1994) his belief that Witmer did not attend.
70. L. Witmer, 1909d. Witmer derived *orthogenics* from Greek words meaning *straight* in the sense of normal and *development*.
71. Ibid., p. 29.
72. Devereux, 1909. I am indebted to the Devereux Foundation for furnishing me (in 1981) with extensive information on its founder, history, and current status.
73. L. Witmer, 1911a, p. 260.
74. L. Witmer, 1910c.
75. Ibid., p. 266.
76. Ibid., p. 272.
77. Ibid., p. 272.
78. Ibid., p. 273.
79. Ibid., p. 276.
80. L. Witmer, 1910d.
81. Ibid., p. 127.
82. L. Witmer, 1910b.
83. Ibid., p. 198.
84. Ibid., p. 210.
85. L. Witmer, 1911b.

86. Ibid., p. 234.
87. Ibid., p. 229.
88. Ibid., p. 238.
89. Ibid., pp. 231–232.
90. O'Donnell, 1979, p. 8.
91. L. Witmer, 1910b, p. 199.
92. *The North American* (Philadelphia), May 1909 (date not identifiable). AUP. The boy described, under a different name, may have been the boy referred to as *George* in L. Witmer (1911b).
93. Preserved newspaper clipping, newspaper and date not identifiable. AUP.
94. *Philadelphia Ledger*, January 1, 1910. AUP.
95. Preserved newspaper clipping, December 7, 1910, dateline Montreal, headlined "Special Training for Feeble-Minded" (name of newspaper not identifiable). AUP.
96. *The Psychological Clinic*, 1911, 5, p. 26. In "News and Comment" section. Unsigned but presumably written by Witmer.
97. L. Witmer, 1910c, p. 280.

CHAPTER 9. TRAVELS, TALKS, AND TESTS

1. Witmer arrived in Kansas City, MO, on February 20, spoke to the alumni on the evening of the 21st, at the city's University Club, and spoke at a dinner of the Knife and Fork Club on the 22nd, at Coates House. Also on this trip he gave talks before the students of two high schools in Kansas City. These data are abstracted from newspaper clippings from the *Kansas City (MO) Times*, February 21 and 22, 1910, pp. not available. AUP. This trip, it may be noted, took place before his December 1910 trip to Montreal, as reported in the preceding chapter; that trip was summarized earlier in keeping with the context in which it was reviewed.
2. *Kansas City (MO) Times*, February 21, 1910. p. not available. AUP.
3. Lynch, 1910, p. 141.
4. Bruce, 1910.
5. Letter, L. Witmer to E. F. Smith, University of Pennsylvania provost, February 11, 1911. AUP. Witmer does not say what university in New York was seeking his services, but it may have been Columbia, where his old mentor, Cattell, was located. Also, Fullerton had moved to Columbia in 1904. In any event, Witmer did not leave Penn.
6. Minutes of the Board Trustees for March 7, 1911, p. 187, and April 4, 1911, p. 201. AUP. Academic administrative minutes are often somewhat cryptic, but I take these words pretty much at face value (i.e., that the trustees did appreciate Witmer but were wary of committing themselves to extravagant financial help). It is not clear precisely what academic program Witmer had in mind (e.g., what degree); in any event, nothing came of his suggestions for new programs.
7. E. R. Witmer, 1910c.
8. E. R. Witmer, 1910b.

9. E. R. Witmer, 1910a.

10. E. R. Witmer, 1911.

11. E. R. Witmer, 1912.

12. E. R. Witmer, 1914.

13. Witmer was also a member of a number of academic and scientific organizations, including APA, the American Association for the Advancement of Science, the American Philosophical Society, the National Educational Association, the National Society for the Scientific Study of Education, the Neurological Society of Philadelphia, and the American Institute of Criminal Law and Criminology (of which he was vice president), the American School Hygiene Association, and Sigma Xi (he was president of the University of Pennsylvania chapter). Untitled biographical sheet, 1910. AUP. Although Witmer was neither particularly interested nor skilled in organizational activities, these affiliations show that he was by no means isolated from professional colleagues.

14. My account is based primarily on snapshots (1911), some with data written on the backs, taken by Gertrude Stewart, a teacher at the Rose Valley School, and kindly given me by her niece, Helen Joyce; from references in several interviews and letters; and from legal data generously provided by John Walter. Over the years, Witmer added to the property, which eventually totaled over 16 acres. Summers at Flotsam were a salient aspect of the Witmers' lifestyle, and Fifi and her companion Mary Ambler went there for some years even after Lightner died.

15. The 1910 special summer class is described in Holmes (1910). A local newspaper headline read " 'Bad Boy' School Closes: Psychological Experts Get Results From Youngsters Considered Incorrigible." Name and date of newspaper not available. AUP.

16. L. Witmer, 1911c. The head teacher was Elizabeth E. Farrell, and the dietician was Louise S. Bryant.

17. As a newspaper of the time put it, "Prof. Witmer believes that many children who are considered as stupid . . . are merely underfed. . . . If the experiment proves successful and the children improve in their studies as the result of proper food training, Prof. Witmer will present the matter to the board of education of Philadelphia, which already has in a limited way begun the giving of noonday lunches to the children." From the *Springfield Republication* (*PA*), July 3, 1911. AUP.

18. I have been unable to firmly identify the generous donor. However, it was almost certainly Eliza Otto, whom Witmer generously thanked, on an opening page (L. Witmer, 1911c) for making the experiment possible, as well as the publication of the volume reporting the study.

19. That there was a 1912 class and that it enrolled bright children are revealed in Harley (1913). Harley did not indicate which translation of the Binet scale was administered, but it was almost certainly the one made by Witmer's graduate Clara Harrison Town, which was used in the Clinic at this time. Limited information on later sessions is provided in Fernberger (1931, pp. 33–34), who stated that after 1921, except for 4 years, Gladys G. Ide (a Witmer 1918 graduate) was in charge of the special summer classes.

20. Little documentary evidence is available concerning Witmer's leave, although it can be inferred from University records that he was on leave during the spring of 1912. AUP. (See also M. L. Sylvester, 1932, p. 114.)

21. L. Witmer, 1914b, p. 2. (See also Montessori, 1912/1964.)

22. L. Witmer, 1914b, p. 4.

23. L. Witmer, 1917a, p. 70.

24. Holmes, 1912. The book, profusely illustrated, contained 345 pages, included a Preface by Martin G. Brumbaugh (M. G. B.). Brumbaugh was the university's first professor of pedagogy (in 1895) and later held a variety of positions, including governor of Pennsylvania (see also chap. 1).

25. To be sure, there had been earlier books on psychopathology and on child development, and Guy M. Whipple's book on mental testing had come out in 1910, but there was no earlier book that could be considered as a work on the new profession of clinical psychology. Holmes appeared to prefer the terms *clinicist* and *psychoclinicist* to *clinical psychologist.*

26. *Perth Amboy News (NJ)*, June 13, 1916. AUP.

27. Talk given before Delaware County (IN) Teachers Institute; reported in newspaper (name and date not identifiable, but I infer 1910 or 1911) with the headline "Wants All School Teachers in Love," AUP. Holmes strongly inveighed against laws, then commonplace, that forbade school boards to employ married women as teachers in public schools.

28. Holmes, 1912, p. 44 (see also p. 90).

29. Holmes was a major player in the systematic development of the Psychological Clinic. He was born in 1872 and graduated from Hiram College before entering the University of Pennsylvania. In 1918 he left Pennsylvania State College to become president of Drake University in Iowa. In 1922, he returned to the University of Pennsylvania as professor of psychology. He was the author of a number of books in psychology and theology. He died in 1967 at the age of 95.

30. Maxfield was also a key figure in the history of the Psychological Clinic. He obtained his AB degree at Haverford College, west of Philadelphia, in 1897, and later was vice principal at Germantown Friends Schools. He received his PhD at Penn in 1912 and stayed at the Clinic until 1918, at which time he left to become director of special education for the state of Pennsylvania. In 1925, he became professor of clinical psychology at Ohio State University. He died in 1946.

31. I have read a great many of the case records—far more, running into the hundreds, than are referred to, even obliquely, in this volume—and this experience has left me with a deep feeling of respect and admiration for the dedication of the Psychological Clinic staff to the welfare of the children and parents with whom they worked. To read some of these now ancient case records, composed in the critical stages of a new profession, and to empathize, as best one can, with the anguish and fears of the parents and children involved, and with the commitments and concerns of Witmer and his associates, is a deeply moving experience.

32. The data in this section are taken from a newspaper article dated June 14, 1913, name of newspaper not clear. AUP.

33. Van Sickle, Witmer, and Ayres, 1911. Van Sickle was Superintendent of Schools at Springfield, MA, and Ayres was Associate Director, Department of Child Hygiene, Russell Sage Foundation.

34. L. Witmer, 1914c.

35. L. Witmer, 1913.

36. Ibid., p. 180.

37. Ibid., p. 181.

38. Ibid., p. 181.

39. Witmer's Rose Valley School has not been noted by any author but me (McReynolds, 1987, 1996a, 1996b, 1996c) probably because Witmer himself never referred to his private schools in his writings, except obliquely. Detailed information on the Rose Valley School is sparse (see chap. 8). It is definite that Witmer maintained a private school in the country from 1908 to 1921, when he moved its operation to Devon, and it is almost certain, though without firm documentary verification, that this school was at Rose Vally throughout the period. It is possible that he also had additional schools, at least for brief periods. Several informants suggested to me that they had heard that Witmer, at one time or another, in addition to his Rose Valley School, had schools at Atlantic City, NJ; Media, PA, and Philadelphia; however, I have been unable to confirm these reports. The Philadelphia school was probably the Hospital School, and the other two may have been temporary arrangements with schools operated by others.

40. Probably, there were also other new teachers in this period, but these two are the only ones known by name and the only two who later achieved some eminence. It is not known precisely when they joined the Rose Valley staff, but the text represents my best judgment, based on letters and materials received from Marion Mack, O'Connor's sister, and from Helen Joyce, Stewart's niece. O'Connor and Stewart were lifelong friends, having met when both, early in life, were working for the Curtis Publishing Company (*Saturday Evening Post*).

41. The description of the Rose Valley School is based on a number of snapshots taken by Stewart in 1916, made available to me by Helen Joyce, and by O'Connor, probably at an earlier date, made available by Marion Mack. Both Stewart and O'Connor were involved in trips with children to Nova Scotia as early as 1911.

42. Quoted by H. H. Young, 1916a, p. 149.

43. Itard, 1962, pp. 40–43.

44. For information on Goddard's formboard, including a diagram of its parts, see Whipple, 1914, pp. 298–305.

45. L. Witmer, 1911a, p. 249. The article includes a picture of the formboard, which is clearly that developed by Goddard.

46. R. H. Sylvester, 1913b.

47. I have a Witmer Formboard in my collection of earlier tests. It, along with most of the other instruments, was kindly given to me by Mildred Sylvester, the last executive secretary of the Clinic to serve under Witmer. The formboard is constructed of heavily varnished wood. For a picture of the instrument, see McReynolds (1996c) and the present volume.

48. H. H. Young, 1916b.
49. H. H. Young, 1916a.
50. L. Witmer, 1916b.
51. Kephart, 1918.
52. Ide, 1918.
53. H. H. Young and M. H. Young, 1923.
54. Successful applications of the Witmer Formboard depended largely on the examiner's expertise and observational skills. As Kent (1950) put it, "only a small part of what the examiner learns from the performance can be expressed in a score" (p. 83). One of Witmer's later associates, Genevieve Murphy, once remarked to me (in 1979) that although she had mastered later psychological tests, she felt she could learn more about a child with the Formboard than with other, more recent instruments.
55. Kent, 1950, p. 83. The Witmer Formboard was also described in Bronner, Healy, Lowe, and Shimberg (1929).
56. Kent 1950, p. 139.
57. Paschal, 1918b.
58. Paschal, 1918a. This article includes a picture of the test, as does Paschal (1918b) and McReynolds (1996c) and the present volume.
59. Paschal, 1918b, p. 5. The Witmer Cylinders Test is also described in Bronner et al. (1929). Both the Witmer Cylinders and the Witmer Formboard tests were built by John Roberts, machinist in the department shop.
60. M. H. Young, 1916.

CHAPTER 10. THE WAR ERA

1. L. Witmer, 1915c. This article included one interesting biographical revelation: The boy at Rugby Academy whose language deficiencies had so captivated Witmer when Witmer was a teacher there many years before, and whom Witmer had helped cope with this handicap, had eventually graduated from college, and even from medical school, and was now a practicing physician.
2. L. Witmer, 1915b.
3. L. Witmer, 1915a.
4. Ibid., pp. 1–2.
5. Ibid., p. 3.
6. Witmer's emphasis on current, rather than on long past, contributors to personal problems can be seen as in accord with modern behavioral approaches rather than with Freudian-oriented conceptions.
7. L. Witmer, 1915e.
8. Ibid., p. 73.
9. Ibid., p. 71.
10. Ibid., p. 73.
11. Ibid., p. 61.
12. Ibid., p. 80.

13. L. Witmer, 1916a.
14. L. Witmer, 1917d.
15. L. Witmer, 1917b.
16. L. Witmer, 1917c.
17. L. Witmer, 1917a.
18. L. Witmer, 1917a, p. 70.
19. As recalled by Nearing, 1972b, pp. 18–19.
20. L. Witmer, 1915d, pp. 15–16.
21. Cattell had for some time been a leader in advancing the concept of academic freedom and may have given Witmer some moral support, although no record of this exists. One of my informants was of the opinion that there had been some danger of Witmer losing his own position as a result of his agitation against the trustees.
22. L. Witmer, 1915d.
23. Fowler, 1978, p. 126.
24. General Report of the Committee on Academic Freedom and Academic Tenure (adopted January 1, 1916, signed by John Dewey, president, and Arthur Lovejoy, secretary). In Walter P. Metzger (1977; relevant pages not numbered). See also Hofstadter and Metzger, 1955, p. 479.
25. Nearing, 1972a.
26. The present account is based on Sherman, 1989, p. 15; *The New York Times*, April 29, 1973; and Minutes of the Board of Trustees, April 13, 1973, AUP.
27. Letter, S. Nearing to P. McReynolds, October 4, 1976. Permission to quote this letter is granted by the Good Life Center, Harborside, ME, and the Trust for Public Land, Boston, MA. My personal thanks to John Saltmarsh and Peter Forbes.
28. For additional information on Nearing see Saltmarsh, 1991, and Sherman, 1989.
29. The basic thrust of these new programs, which led to the standard-setting Boulder Conference in 1949, was that clinical psychologists should have appropriate doctoral level training plus extensive supervised experience. Although this plan may have seemed innovative, and even revolutionary, to some of the participants, it was actually the same basic model that Witmer had pioneered years before. Further, the same general plan had been strongly supported by members of the Clinical Section of APA in 1924 (L. Witmer, 1925c, p. 9 footnote). I am not suggesting that Witmer's training program ever reached the breadth and sophistication of contemporary programs, but it was probably more adequate, at least in child clinical psychology, than many programs established shortly after World War II.
30. McReynolds, 1988, pp. 75–76.
31. By the mid-1920s and 1930s, certain other universities were offering substantial clinical training, especially in assessment. Although this history has never been studied in detail, one thinks of Ohio State, with Maxfield, Goddard, and Rudolph Pinter on its faculty, and Stanford, with Terman, Maude Merrill, and Edward K. Strong. Perhaps the best source on early clinical programs is the final issue of *The Psychological Clinic* (*23*, 1935, January–June). It is probable, however, that none of the other prewar training programs were as broad as that at Penn.

32. Later changes were additions, not alterations, in philosophy. Thus, in the coming years, several faculty members and a number of courses would be added, and more emphasis would be put on experience with adult cases (primarily in the satellite clinics of Twitmyer, Viteles, and Brotemarkle).

33. Data are from *University of Pennsylvania Catalog* for 1914–1915 and 1915–1916. Mitchell obtained his PhD at Penn in 1913. For personnel in the Psychological Clinic in this period, see Fernberger (1931).

34. Data on Gertha Williams are based on an interview by John Popplestone, 1977, to whom I am grateful for the transcript. AHAP.

35. My thanks to Catherine Parsons Smith, daughter of Frances Holsopple Parsons, for making available to me her mother's memoir, plus other biographical information. Excerpts included with Smith's permission.

36. This was undoubtedly Terman's (1916) *The Measurement of Intelligence*, just published.

37. This position largely financed Holsopple's period at Penn.

38. I do not know why Witmer was irritated with APA at this point. His withdrawal must have been in terms of moral support, because he maintained his membership (personal communication, S. Pisano, APA Library, May 21, 1996). Goddard's (1913) book took a strongly hereditarian position. Despite Witmer's substantive disagreement with Goddard, he evidently maintained a cordial relationship with him. In a letter (October 28, 1916, AHAP), Witmer invited Goddard "to come and see us sometime when you are in Philadelphia."

39. Holsopple, 1919a. See also Holsopple (1918, 1919b). Holsopple is not among those listed as "Presented by" or "Accepted by Professor Witmer" (See Note 23, chap. 14). However, it is clear from her memoir that Holsopple considered Witmer her major professor.

40. Stern, 1917.

41. See Hofstadter and Metzger, 1955 (pp. 495–502). The authors decry the actions of Butler and the Columbia trustees, but they do not fully exonerate the behavior of Cattell, whom they describe as "brash, tactless and offensive" (p. 499). Despite his involuntary separation from academia, Cattell remained a major figure in psychology. He owned and edited the journal *Science*; in 1925, was elected president of the American Association for the Advancement of Science; and in 1929, was chosen as president of the International Congress of Psychology.

42. Titchener, who had maintained his British citizenship, did not participate in this effort (Boring, 1967, p. 323).

43. Although Yerkes is best known to later generations for his work in animal behavior, he was, at the time of the war, also known for his work in test construction (Yerkes, Bridges, & Hardwick, 1915).

44. For descriptions of the army testing program, see Carson (1993) and Samuelson (1977).

45. AUP.

46. Emma Witmer, in a tribute to the role of women left behind while their men were in Europe, contributed a poem, *The Woman's Part*, to a local literary journal

(E. R. Witmer, 1918); the first stanza read: 'Tis not too much to ask—/A gay farewell/To hold back tears,/And hide with laughter any trace/Of haunting fears.

47. *National Cyclopedia of American Biography*, 1955, pp. 418–419; Collins, 1919.

48. R. H. Sylvester, 1913a.

49. J. E. W. Wallin was a major figure in the early history of clinical psychology. He received his PhD (Yale) in 1901 in experimental psychology but, through a variety of experiences, became skilled in the clinical area. In 1912, he founded a Psychoeducational Clinic at the University of Pittsburgh. He published widely, including articles in *The Psychological Clinic*. His books include *The Mental Health of the School Child* (1914)—in which he pays tribute to Witmer, although he prefers *psycho-clinicist* to *clinical psychologist*—and *The Odyssey of a Psychologist* (1955).

50. Wallin, 1961, p. 257.

51. Ibid., p. 257.

52. Ibid., p. 257; Routh (1994, p. 13) lists the same 7 but also includes Guy M. Whipple.

53. Wallin, 1961, p. 257.

54. "News and Comment," *The Psychological Clinic*, 1918, *12*, p. 64. Routh (1994, p. 14) lists 46 members, based on data from the Library of Congress; this list does not include Witmer. However, the Arnold Gesell Papers, also in the Library of Congress, list 48 members, including Witmer (Fagan, 1986, Note 3, pp. 851 –852). I cannot explain the differences in these lists, but it seems probable that the lists were made at different times, and each may have been accurate at the time it was made.

55. Wallin, 1961, pp. 257–258.

56. Ibid., p. 258.

57. For a detailed treatment of the organizational history of clinical psychology, beginning with the AACP, see Routh (1994).

58. In the opinion of Morris Viteles, a Witmer graduate and colleague in the 1920s, Witmer never sought a position of national leadership. Wallin (1960) remembered Witmer as active "sporadically" in APA; Witmer, he recalled, was "often referred to as an 'extreme individualist' " (p. 290).

59. L. Witmer, 1919e.

60. L. Witmer, 1919c.

61. L. Witmer, 1919d.

62. L. Witmer, 1919b.

63. L. Witmer, 1919a.

64. L. Witmer, 1919g.

65. L. Witmer, 1920b.

66. Ibid., p. 101.

CHAPTER 11. NEW DIRECTIONS

1. Watsonian behaviorism, of course, was not the only major theory of the period. Other important theoretical conceptions were those of Wolfgang Kohler, William

McDougall, Edward L. Thorndike, and Robert S. Woodworth (cf. Heidbreder, *Seven Psychologies*, 1933). None of these had any major influence on Witmer.

2. J. B. Watson, 1928.

3. Based on letter, Witmer to Titchener, February 12, 1920, in the Titchener Collection, Cornell University Library. It is not known whether Titchener attended the meetings of the American Philosophical Society. The occasion that probably attracted him was a symposium, held on April 23, on "Psychology in War and Education." Witmer (1920a) gave the Introduction, and probably organized the event. Other speakers included Cattell, Yerkes, Raymond Dodge, James R. Angell, Beardsley Ruml, and Arthur J. Jones.

4. Minutes of the June 14, 1920, Meeting of the Board of Trustees, University of Pennsylvania. AUP. Witmer was also engaged during the spring of 1920, in a brief skirmish, in the columns of the *Philadelphia Public Ledger*, with W. W. Atterbury, a prominent alumnus. Atterbury charged that radicalism was being taught at the university. Witmer responded that if Atterbury would provide a list of radical faculty, then he would provide an equal list of reactionary alumni. This, apparently, was the end of the matter. *Philadelphia Public Ledger*, February 26, 1920. AUP.

5. The Lincoln Highway, begun in 1912 and completed in 1926, was the nation's first (and then famous) transcontinental highway (New York to San Francisco).

6. Information on the Witmer's new property, including a copy of the purchase papers, was kindly obtained for me by John Walter.

7. Witmer, 1909b, 1909d.

8. This possibility is suggested by a statement in the memoirs of Frances Holsopple, excerpts of which were quoted in Chapter 10. Holsopple, in a passage not quoted in Chapter 10, stated that "One of the products of the clinic was Dr. Helena Devereux . . . who founded the Devereux schools with Witmer's sponsorship" (actually, Devereux did not receive a doctoral degree). Adequate documentation of Witmer's role in Devereux's early work is lacking. She attended certain classes at Penn between 1915 and 1921, and may have taken work with Witmer, possibly in the summer of 1917. AUP. It is certainly plausible that Witmer, with his greater prestige, and given his positive feeling for her, may have facilitated her early work. The Devereux facility at Devon still exists, and has expanded to campuses around the nation, with national headquarters in Devon. I thank the Devereux Foundation for information on its history and current activities.

9. In Lynch, 1910.

10. L. Witmer, 1919f.

11. Ibid., p. 89.

12. Jones, 1923.

13. *Philadelphia Public Ledger*, November 11, 1923. On Witmer's plan to follow gifted children over the years, see M. I. R. Hall, 1934. Note that Terman, in 1921, inaugurated his classic longitudinal study of bright children. Rockwell (née Jones; 1931) integrated her own work with that of Terman.

14. Jones, 1925. See also Rockwell (1931) and M. I. R. Hall (1934). Hall, in 1934,

completed (for her dissertation at Penn) a 10-year followup on Jones's study. She
was able to contact 70 of the original 120 children, and found that, in general,
they were still achieving at a high level.

15. Information given here about the new Vocational Guidance Clinic is based primarily on Viteles (1967); personal discussions with Viteles; and a newspaper article, "U. of P. Enlarges Children's Clinic" (*Philadelphia Public Ledger*, November
11, 1923). It is conceivable that the additional funding was in part a result of
Witmer's appeals to the dean and trustees a few years earlier, as described earlier
in this chapter. Although this possibility is mere speculation, it is known that
Quinn had now been succeeded by a new dean. AUP.

16. Viteles, 1967, pp. 423–424. Viteles gives 1921, the year of his doctorate, as the
year of establishing the Vocational Guidance Clinic. However, 1923 is perhaps a
more meaningful date, since Viteles had spent the prior year on a fellowship in
Europe.

17. Interview with M. S. Viteles (May 31, 1979).

18. Viteles, 1922. A story (told me by Viteles) is relevant here. Witmer first proposed
to publish Viteles's research, then later, after looking at it, decided not to, on the
ground that it was not sufficiently well written. (Witmer was always urging his
students to write better, even to use a "novelistic" style.) Eventually, however,
presumably after Viteles had made some changes, Witmer did publish it. Years
later, when Viteles gave Witmer a copy of his *Industrial Psychology* (1932), Witmer
complimented him on his writing style.

19. For additional information on Viteles, see his (1967) *Autobiography*.

20. Despite their mutual regard, Viteles and Witmer were never close. Viteles never
visited the Witmer home until after the latter's retirement. He felt (personal interview, May 31, 1979) that Witmer was not personally close to any faculty
colleague except Twitmyer.

21. Information on the Psychobiochemical Laboratory is abstracted from Starr (1931)
and a news release dated June 21, 1925, and archival biographical data. AUP.

22. Starr, 1922, 1928 (for additional Starr references, see Starr, 1931).

23. Looking ahead, Henry died, prematurely, of Bright's disease, in 1935, at the age
of 42. Anna Spiesman Starr stayed at Rutgers, where she later became Clinic
Director and Professor. She had a long and highly distinguished career. A diplo-
mate in clinical psychology, she died in 1977.

24. L. Witmer, 1925b. According to its abstract (p. 129), Witmer pointed to autobiography, biography, and imaginative literature as precursors of the clinical
method; located its scientific antecedents in physiology and psychology; and highlighted the role of the Psychological Clinic.

25. L. Witmer, 1925c, p. 18. Witmer described this article as "Read in part" (p. 1)
at the December 1924 APA meeting; from its context I infer that the excerpt
quoted here came at the close of that talk (Witmer, 1925b), although this cannot
be objectively verified.

26. As noted earlier in this chapter, discussions of the concept of IQ reached the
public arena in the 1920s; it was highlighted by a debate in the press between

Terman and the commentator Walter Lippmann on the meaningfulness of the concept of IQ (cf. Hilgard, 1987, pp. 466–470).

27. L. Witmer, 1915e.

28. L. Witmer, 1922b.

29. L. Witmer, 1922c.

30. See chap. 10.

31. L. Witmer, 1922b, p. 65.

32. Ibid., p. 65.

33. L. Witmer, 1922c, p. 58.

34. Witmer's conception that some novelty is pleasant, whereas too much novelty is unpleasant, although not put in systematic theoretical terms, was an anticipation of later work relating quality of affect to degree of novelty in perception (e.g., Fiske & Maddi, 1961; McClelland, Atkinson, Clark, & Lowell, 1953).

35. L. Witmer, 1922c, p. 65.

36. Sternberg and Salter, 1982, p. 24.

37. R. B. Cattell, 1963.

38. L. Witmer, 1925c, p. 2.

39. L. Witmer, 1922a.

40. L. Witmer, 1925c.

41. L. Witmer, 1919c.

42. Witmer's difficult, tortured writing style in his theoretical papers is in sharp contrast to the clarity of his case reports, which are largely devoid of jargon and flow easily. My impression is that Witmer had numerous creative theoretical ideas, but that he tended to publish before he had fully articulated the ideas in his own mind.

43. L. Witmer, 1922a, p. 129; 1925c, p. 11.

44. Witmer's idiographic approach led to a deemphasis on statistics, as in his reference to "a statistical psychology, from which the collective characteristics of conventional groups may be discerned, but not the discriminated characteristics of individuals, which are the concern of clinical psychology, diagnostic education, and orthogenics" (1925c, p. 2).

45. McClelland, 1973; Sundberg, 1977; White, 1959.

46. L. Witmer, 1922a.

47. L. Witmer, 1925a.

48. Humpstone, 1919.

49. Ibid., p. 171.

50. L. Witmer, 1922a, p. 133.

51. Jones, 1922.

52. Jones, 1925, pp. 25–26, 58–59, 69–70.

53. L. Witmer, 1925c, p. 13.

54. This summary is based primarily on L. Witmer 1922a, 1925b, and 1932. I also had available H. E. Starr's class notes (AHAP) on the categories and a later class essay on Witmer's conception by a post-Witmer student, W. W. Wilkinson (from Mildred Sylvester).

55. L. Witmer, 1925c, p. 15.

56. Based on an interview with Francis Irwin, June 1, 1979. Irwin had begun his
     doctoral work at Penn in the clinical area, but before long, both he and Witmer
     agreed that he was not "cut out to be a clinician," and he switched to experi-
     mental. He received his PhD in 1931 and taught at Penn until his retirement in
     1974. He died in 1985. He had an outstanding career and was a nationally
     recognized motivation theorist (cf. Irwin, 1971). Although Irwin liked Witmer
     personally, he had a generally negative opinion of his clinical work, feeling that it
     was too intuitive and not sufficiently data based.

57. A number of informants in the clinical area who had taken degrees under Witmer
     or worked in the Psychological Clinic in the 1920s reminded me with real en-
     thusiasm of his system of categories. Unfortunately, none of them, over 50 years
     later, could reconstruct the fine details of the system.

58. L. Witmer, 1927b.

59. From *Reminiscences Concerning Psychology and Psychologists*, February 1963, by
     Irvin T. Schultz. AHAP. Shultz was more pleased with Woodworth's commentary,
     although its details are unknown. The six categories recalled by Shultz are slightly
     different from Witmer's published lists (his recollection included *talent* instead of
     discernment). Shultz's opinion of Witmer was highly positive, and he felt that
     posterity had not done justice to Witmer. Shultz received his PhD at Penn in
     1928.

60. L. Witmer, 1925c, pp. 16–18.

61. Ibid., p. 18.

CHAPTER 12. SLOWING DOWN

1. *The Pennsylvania Gazette*, University of Pennsylvania, January 7, 1927. AUP.

2. For more detailed information on the organization and staffing of the Psycholog-
    ical Clinic, see Fernberger (1931).

3. Letter from Helen Backus Graber, March 13, 1975. Her estimate of Witmer's
    height is probably a little high. His hair was prematurely gray, or silver.

4. Personal document, "Memories of LW," by Helen Graber, given to me in 1974.

5. Ibid.

6. Paul Cret, a professor of architecture at the University of Pennsylvania, is best
    known for his designs of the Valley Forge Memorial Arch near Philadelphia, the
    Folger Shakespeare Library in Washington, and the Federal Reserve Building in
    Washington.

7. Graber; see Note 4.

8. Letter from Olive Norman Logan (October 28, 1979), who was Witmer's secretary
    in the early 1930s.

9. These accounts are based primarily on the recollections of Genevieve McDermott
    Murphy in a letter to me August 7, 1980. In the memory of Graber (interview,
    May 25, 1979) Witmer was not prejudiced against women or against blacks.
    However, he "didn't like ultra-conservatives and couldn't stand the DAR." Graber

(see Note 4) stated that "he always said that progress is inevitable—whether the hand that carries the torch be yellow, white, or black."

10. Witmer was also a stickler about proper foods. At his school he insisted on fresh, natural foods, and was concerned, by the mid 1920s, about the dangers of additives in food products. The children at the school had the same diets that he did (Graber, see Note 3).

11. Graber. See Note 4.

12. M. Sylvester remembered Witmer saying that no worthwhile intellectual work could be done when the temperature was above 68 degrees (interview, September 1, 1974).

13. This account of the Schoolmen's Meeting is based on an article in the *Philadelphia Inquirer* for April 1, 1927, from which the brief quotation is taken. AUP.

14. It is not altogether clear why Witmer was cutting back on his obligations in the latter 1920s. No doubt advancing age with the consequent decrement in energy and drive had something to do with it, although his health, according to several informants, remained good. Perhaps he simply felt that he had already made such contributions as he had to offer and wished to take life easier.

15. This description is based on a detailed map of the Clinic in 1928, drawn from memory in 1979 by Helen Backus Graber. She pointed out that there were changes in the uses of rooms, as well as actual physical changes, from time to time, so that no map could represent the entire history of the Clinic. I am also grateful for a less detailed map, possibly for a later period, furnished me by Viteles.

16. Fernberger, 1931, p. 21, Table II. (This table includes considerable additional information.)

17. For details on the problems presented by children seen at the Clinic during the latter Witmer period, see M. Murphy (1930, 1936). Fernberger (1931, p. 25) indicated that for several years, while Jones was doing her work on gifted children, the Clinic concentrated on that group. This should not be taken to mean that retarded and delinquent children were not also seen.

18. Fernberger, 1931, p. 26. Group tests, especially in the assessment of intelligence, had by this time become very popular, but Witmer strongly eschewed these. He objected to paper-and-pencil tests because they revealed only the product and not actual performances.

19. The existence and nature of the Clinic Day Books have not previously been reported in the literature. I am deeply grateful to the staff of the Archives at the University of Pennsylvania, in particular Hamilton Elliott and Gail Pietrzyk, for their assistance in identifying the existence of these Day Books and in making them available for my inspection. The booklets still exist (they were not microfilmed), and to a historian, it is an emotionally moving experience to leaf through them. The first 10 books carry the Clinic clientele through 1934, ending with Case 11,665. There were various changes in the booklet formats during this period.

20. The existence and nature of these *control cards* (as they were called) have not previously been reported. I am indebted to the University of Pennsylvania Archives

for alerting me to the existence of these cards and to the Archives of the History of American Psychology for furnishing me with photocopies of numerous cards for study. The cards were microfilmed along with the case folders and appear at the end of the filmed case records. Not all of the cards included all the data indicated. In addition to the control cards, there was, for certain cases, a file of summary cards. Further details are beyond the scope of this biography.

21.   Fernberger, 1931, pp. 24–25.
22.   Louttit, 1939, p. 363.
23.   Witmer considered Freud "too much concerned with sex and the pathology of sex" and also overly "concerned with what is non-normal and pathogenic," to the exclusion of "what is normal and orthogenic" (L. Witmer, 1925c, p. 8).
24.   Rogers, 1942, 1951. Witmer was probably too directive, in any event, to have appreciated Rogers's nondirective approach; however, he would have resonated with Rogers's strong sense of worth in each client, especially with Rogers's concept of self-actualization.
25.   The comments here concern Witmer's approach in dealing with adjustment and behavioral problems of children. He also advocated what he termed "diagnostic education" for children with learning problems.
26.   Some examples of adult cases were given earlier. I learned of one friend of Witmer's who sought Witmer's counsel on a difficult marital problem. Witmer turned him down on the ground that he could not properly counsel a close friend.
27.   L. Witmer, 1908–1909, p. 220.
28.   He typically wore a riding habit on these occasions. Sometimes he was accompanied by Elizabeth O'Connor or Miles Murphy.
29.   Genevieve McDermott Murphy.
30.   It is not clear what O'Connor's title was, possibly it was principal, manager, or assistant director, or perhaps she had no title. According to her sister, Marion Mack (letter November 10, 1976), who refers to her as the school's manager, O'Connor was responsible for creating a homelike atmosphere in the school. Her "duties entailed meeting with visiting parents . . . shopping for the pupils with regard to their wardrobe requirements, etc. . . . also helped to plan their schedules of work, play and exercise programs and to take care of the multitude of details . . . also responsible for having a competent staff of domestic help."
31.   Letter from G. M. Murphy, May 30, 1979.
32.   Letter from Helen Ford Joyce, February 2, 1984.
33.   Letter from Helen Backus Graber, March 13, 1975. I gathered from several informants that Witmer was sometimes criticized for charging large fees for personal profit. According to Graber, who kept the financial records, such criticisms were unjustified. She recalled that the fees were $250 per month per child, except for a few at $500 for very wealthy parents. Some students were admitted without fee. In addition to the Clinic and the school, Witmer had a small private practice. His typical fee for evaluation of a child was $25.
34.   These letters were furnished to me by Helen Ford Joyce, on a not-for-identification-or-quotation basis.

35. Letter, Olive Norman Logan, October 28, 1979.

36. Material provided by Helen Ford Joyce.

37. See Note 8, chap. 11.

38. There is a rich literature on the history of school psychology. See Fagan (1986, 1988, 1990, 1992, 1996a, 1996b) and French (1984). French's otherwise excellent article includes one error (personal communication, October 3, 1996), based on inaccurate information that French had received. On page 982, it is stated that Witmer, in 1952, opposed the formation of a School Division in the Pennsylvania Psychological Association. Actually it was Carol Whitmer who opposed the move, Witmer having long since retired from organizational activities.

39. L. Witmer, 1907b, p. 9.

40. This interpretation lacks strong documentary evidence but is a plausible and probable reconstruction. A detailed history of school psychology in the Philadelphia schools has not been written but would be a useful project. See, in this connection, Anderson (1933).

41. Fagan (1996a), who has researched the origins of school psychology, concludes that except in North America the profession arose independently of Witmer's early work.

42. Since 1973, Division 16 has honored an outstanding school psychologist with the Lightner Witmer Award, presented at APA's annual convention.

43. Genevieve McDermott Murphy, who had worked at both the Psychological Clinic and the Witmer School, was a Philadelphian school psychologist from 1930 to 1963, and in conversations with her, I got the strong impression that there were, and had been, a number of such employees. Margaret Forrest worked at the Witmer School from 1930 to 1938 and later was a psychologist in the Philadelphia schools. Both of these women did advanced work under Witmer but neither completed the doctorate.

44. Oliver P. Cornman, an 1899 Witmer PhD, was an early leader in special education. Another was Gladys G. Ide, who received her doctorate at Penn in 1918; she later became director of special education in the Philadelphia Public School System (see Ide, 1931).

45. This quotation is from an article in the *Philadelphia Bulletin*, February 22, 1928, p. 10; the headline read "U. of P. Losing Soul, Witmer Declares." The headline in the *Philadelphia Inquirer* was equally bold: "Alumni Astounded at Charge of U of P. Mere 'Factory' " (February 22, 1928). The present account is based on clippings from these two newspapers and the *Philadelphia Ledger* and *Philadelphia Record*. AUP.

46. Data on Miles Murphy are from Genevieve McDermott Murphy and from AUP.

47. E. R. Witmer and L. Witmer, 1928.

48. The article states that the child was admitted to "Dr. Witmer's School of Observation and Diagnostic Teaching" on June 21, 1918 (p. 154). Presumably, this was the Rose Valley School, and possibly this was its official title at one time.

49. L. Witmer and Ambler, 1929.

50. L. Witmer and Phillips, 1929.

51. Newspaper article, *Philadelphia Inquirer*, July 28, 1929. AUP.

52. Newspaper article, *Philadelphia Inquirer*, November 19, 1930. AUP.

53. So far as I have been able to determine, reports of this research were never published, and the study may not have been completed.

54. L. Witmer, 1927a.

55. L. Witmer, 1930.

56. The text of the *Breviary* is highly enigmatic. It is conceivable that Witmer was becoming somewhat less able to frame his ideas clearly. Opposed to this possibility, however, is the fact that his business correspondence in this period, as well as later, was straightforward and clear. Informants, including Genevieve Murphy, Mildred Sylvester, and Morris Viteles, reported that they noted no decline in Witmer's mental powers. Margaret Forrest, who worked at the Witmer School 1930–1938, commented that "his writing was painful—cryptic, much rewriting, he was critical of his own sentences" (letter, July 28, 1976).

57. Interview with Morris Viteles, May 31, 1979.

58. Maslow, 1954.

59. Rogers, 1959.

60. Adler, 1956.

61. Graber, 1974 (see Note 4).

62. Untermeyer, 1949, p. 386. Helen Graber, at Witmer's request, typed a number of Witmer's favorite poems, some of which he had committed to memory. In 1974, she made these available to me.

CHAPTER 13. LATER CAREER AND RETIREMENT

1. Details are based largely on newspaper accounts in the *Philadelphia Inquirer*, *Philadelphia Ledger*, and *Philadelphia Record*, December 6, 1931. AUP.

2. Brotemarkle, 1931. The general price of the book was $3.50; however, 250 copies, autographed by Witmer, were priced at $5.00.

3. *Philadelphia Record*, December 12, 1931. AUP.

4. *Philadelphia Record*, December 12, 1931. AUP.

5. *Philadelphia Record*, December 12, 1931. AUP.

6. Collins, 1931; Fernberger, 1931.

7. Mitchell, 1931, p. 189. Mitchell is generally considered the first person identifying himself as a clinical psychologist in full-time private practice. Witmer had earlier a part-time private practice. Twitmyer also had a limited private practice.

8. However, there was an earlier book (1927) by Wallin with a very similar title, *Clinical and Abnormal Psychology*.

9. Phillips, 1930.

10. Sylvester was later appointed assistant professor. She collected and maintained numerous historical papers, tests, and other items relating to Witmer and to the Psychological Clinic and kindly donated these to me. During the latter years of Witmer's tenure, she took on an increasingly large load in the operation of the Clinic.

11. M. L. Sylvester, 1932.

12. L. Witmer, 1932. Witmer restated his conception of six important categories of performance, listed here as intelligence, intellect, discernment (discrimination), efficiency, motivation, and will.

13. Based on data provided by Sylvester.

14. Letter from Wendell R. Carlson, January 19, 1981. Carlson (PhD 1946) was a longtime friend and colleague of mine. It was he who put me on to the other three students quoted in this section. Carlson spent his career in the U.S. Public Health Service, the Veterans Administration, and the National Institute of Mental Health and as a consulting psychologist.

15. Letter from Kinsley R. Smith, August 4, 1981. Smith (PhD 1936) took his degree with Viteles and became a prominent industrial psychologist.

16. Letters from Jay L. Otis, October 7, 1982, and July 5, 1983. Otis (PhD 1936) also took his degree under Viteles; he taught at Case Western Reserve University.

17. Letters from John R. Martin, February 3, 1986, to W. R. Carlson and January 26, 1987, to me. Martin (PhD 1940) spent his career as a management consultant and established his own firm.

18. Letter from Jay L. Otis, October 7, 1982.

19. Nathanson was the junior author of a book with Twitmyer (1932).

20. Reports of Committee of Clinical Section of American Psychological Association, 1935.

21. Terman, 1911.

22. Town, 1909.

23. Irwin, 1932.

24. Exceptions to this generally were R. H. Sylvester (1913a) and Wallin (1930).

25. L. Witmer, 1925b.

26. Routh, 1994, pp. 27–28.

27. Ibid., p. 28.

28. The present account of Witmer's role in the PACP is based on, first, documentation kindly provided in 1986 by Zita Levin, past executive officer of the Pennsylvania Psychological Association; and second, a newspaper article in the *North Kensington (PA) Dispatch*, April 20, 1934. AUP. The PACP had its own printed newsletter, *Clinical Psychology*.

29. Hildreth, 1936.

30. Henry Starr had been elected ACP president for 1935–1936; however, he died in 1935 and was succeeded by Hildreth.

31. This portrait, possibly taken for this occasion, is the one that appeared later on the cover of the August 1992 issue of *American Psychologist*. The photographer was Elias Goldensky, who was also responsible for the portrait on the March 1996 issue of the *American Psychologist*, and which also appears on the cover of this book.

32. This was unsigned but was possibly written by Witmer. It included a long list of the organizations and learned societies of which Witmer was a member.

33. M. L. Sylvester, 1936.

34. M. Murphy, 1936.

35. Routh, 1994, p. 29.

36. Witmer was appointed Professor Emeritus on September 28, 1937. AUP.

37. L. Witmer, 1937.

38. Statements based on Symonds, 1946; see especially pp. 354, 356.

39. Garfield, 1982, p. 167. (The annual subscription price of *The Psychological Clinic*, at the time of its termination, was $3.00. This journal had a circulation of about 500.)

40. Reported in *Journal of Consulting Psychology*, 1938, *2*, p. 93.

41. The episode recounted here is based on a taped interview with Marion Braungard Graham, May 30, 1979.

42. E. R. Witmer, 1931.

43. E. R. Witmer, 1938.

44. Irwin, 1943.

45. Letter from Helen Ford Joyce, February 2, 1984.

46. Letter, L. Witmer to E. G. Boring, March 18, 1948 (see Note 8, chap. 2).

47. Letter from Mildred Loring Sylvester, December 12, 1974.

48. I am indebted to Carolyn and John Walter for copies of the letters noted. The quotation from the letter from Miles Murphy to Emma Witmer is reproduced with the kind permission of Scott Murphy, the son of Miles and Genevieve Murphy.

49. Some follow-up data: On October 3, 1958, Miles Murphy, died, suddenly, of a heart attack, at the conclusion of a classroom lecture. He was only 58. In 1957, Emma Witmer published a book-length biography of Agnes Repplier. Then, on March 31, 1972, Emma passed away at her home in Overbrook, at the age of 94. The last of the Witmer associates to die was Morris Viteles. His death came in 1996. He was 98.

CHAPTER 14. EPILOGUE: THE SIGNIFICANCE OF WITMER'S LIFE WORK

1. Letter, L. Witmer to E. G. Boring, March 18, 1948 (see Note 8, chap. 2).

2. This paragraph is limited to individuals whom Witmer knew personally. A larger number of persons influenced him indirectly. For information on European influences on Witmer, see Routh and del Barrio (1996).

3. Irvin T. Schultz, 1963. *Reminiscences Concerning Psychology and Psychologists*. Unpublished memoir, AHAP, pp. 9–10. Schultz, reporting a conversation with Woodworth, added this: "Woodworth replied that Witmer was rather nasty to the Harvard boys and got them down on him but that he, Woodworth, liked him."

4. Louttit, 1936, 1939.

5. G. Murphy, 1949.

6. R. I. Watson, 1957.

7. L. Witmer, 1907b, p. 9.

8. The *Journal of Abnormal Psychology* was founded in 1906, but it was devoted primarily to the nature of abnormal behavior in adults, rather than to assessment and treatment.

9. The language in Witmer's case studies now seems dated. In addition, his reports, as compared with contemporary examples, included fewer test data and, of course, fewer references to research studies and diagnostic categories, which, for the most part, were not available to Witmer. On the other hand, Witmer's case reports focused on history data and actual behaviors and were very readable.

10. Interview with M. S. Viteles, May 31, 1979.

11. Boring, 1950.

12. Garfield, 1965.

13. Reisman, 1991.

14. Goldenberg, 1973.

15. O'Donnell, 1979.

16. Bernstein and Nietzel, 1980.

17. Korchin, 1983.

18. McReynolds, 1987, 1996a, 1996b, 1996c.

19. Fagan, 1988, 1990, 1992, 1996a, 1996b.

20. French, 1984.

21. The issue included articles by Fagan (1996b), McReynolds (1996a), and Routh (1996), plus Witmer's 1907b paper.

22. Cattell wrote later (1937, pp. 2–3) that "in the middle of the nineties" he asked the president of Columbia "to let us establish a psychological clinic which would make tests and examinations for the poor without charge and be supported by fees from those who could afford them." The plan, however, was not approved and was never implemented. It seems probable that despite the word "clinic" what Cattell had in mind was something close to the Galtonian test battery he was then using.

23. It would be difficult to overestimate the importance of Witmer's students in forming the legacy that he left for future generations. Without their interest in, and their espousal of, his message, that message would have had little influence. In the course of this biography of Witmer, I have had occasion to mention many of these students. Unfortunately, it has also been necessary, for reasons of space, to omit notice of many of them, including some of the more prominent ones. In this final note, I attempt at least to list most of the PhDs graduated at Penn during Witmer's tenure who were profoundly influenced by him. This task, although pleasant, is not as easy as it might seem, because there is no obvious and available criterion by which to identify Witmer's students among all those who obtained their PhDs at Penn during Witmer's tenure.

    I can begin, however, by listing the 25 psychologists represented in the commemorative volume *Clinical Psychology: Studies in Honor of Lightner Witmer* (Brotemarkle, 1931). These 25 were clearly identified, both by themselves and indirectly by Witmer himself, as students of his. Listed in the order in which they received their degrees, they were Anna J. McKeag, Edwin B. Twitmyer, Robert

H. Gault, Jacob D. Heilman, Stevenson Smith, Clara H. Town, Francis N. Max-field, Reuel H. Sylvester, David Mitchell, Frank H. Reiter, Henry J. Humpstone, Gladys G. Ide, Franklyn C. Paschal, Karl G. Miller, Morris S. Viteles, Henry E. Starr, Robert A. Brotemarkle, Charlotte Easby Grave, Alice Jones Rockwell, Earl S. Rudisill, Miles S. Murphy, Anna E. Biddle, Dorothy K. Hallowell, Arthur Phillips, and Dallas E. Buzby.

There was not space in the 1931 volume to accommodate all of Witmer's students, not to mention those who graduated later. On the basis of their research areas, publications, and other data, I would suggest that the following students probably considered Witmer their primary mentor. Listed, in the order of their doctorates, they were Caspar W. Miller, Oliver P. Cornman, Arthur Holmes, James E. Bryan, Aaron M. Snyder, Norman Cameron, George B. A. Phillips, Samuel Fernberger, Eleanor Lattimore, Herman H. Young, Gertha Williams, Adam P. Kephart, Francis Q. Holsopple, Rebecca E. Leaming, Anna Spiesman Starr, Frederick W. Ninde, Mary Hoover Young, Mabel G. Kessler, Selinda McCaulley, Carl L. Altmaier, Marion E. R. Hall, and Thomas W. Richards.

The two lists just given are made up of 47 names, not an exorbitantly large number considering Witmer's long tenure at Penn, and in view also of the fact that for many years after he joined the faculty he was the only member with sufficient status and background to supervise doctoral students. Eventually Twitmyer, Fernberger, Viteles, and other faculty had their own students (e.g., Yale Nathanson, PhD 1930, worked with Twitmyer; and Jay Otis, PhD 1936, worked with Viteles). Although the lists of Witmer students given above are necessarily somewhat approximate, they clearly indicate Witmer's vital role in turning out a good share of the next generation of psychologists. Most of the graduates were in the clinical area, but several, including Krause (1908) and Fernberger (1921), were in experimental psychology. It is also true that several clinical students, including Francis Maxfield, Frank Reiter, and David Mitchell, did their research in the experimental area. Finally, although I have focussed here on PhD graduates at Penn during the Witmer years, it should be noted that Witmer's influence also extended to numerous MA level students.

Directory of Notes by Chapters

REFERENCES

ADLER, A. (1956). Edited by H. L. Ansbacher & R. R. Ansbacher. *The individual psychology of Alfred Adler: A systematic presentation of his writings.* New York: Harper & Row.

ALLEN, G. W. (1967). *William James: A biography.* New York: Viking Press.

American Psychiatric Association. (1994). *Diagnostic and statistical manual of mental disorders* (4th ed.). Washington, DC: Author.

ANDERSON, R. G. (1933). Concerning school psychologists. *The Psychological Clinic, 22,* 41–47.

ANOKHIN, P. K. (1968). Ivan P. Pavlov and psychology. In B. B. Wolman (Ed.), *Historical roots of contemporary psychology* (pp. 131–160). New York: Harper & Row.

AYRES, L. P. (1908). Some factors affecting grade distribution. *The Psychological Clinic, 2,* 121–133.

BACHE, R. M. (1895). Reaction time with reference to race. *Psychological Review, 2,* 475–486.

BAIRD, J. W. (1907). The proceedings of the Philadelphia Meeting of Experimental Psychologists. *American Journal of Psychology, 18,* 383–388.

BERNSTEIN, D. A., & NIETZEL, M. T. (1980). *Introduction to clinical psychology.* New York: McGraw-Hill.

BINET, A., & HENRI, V. (1895). La psychologie individuelle [The psychology of the individual]. *L'Année Psychologique, 2,* 411–465.

BJORK, D. W. (1983). *The compromised scientist: William James and the development of American psychology.* New York: Columbia University Press.

BLUMENTHAL, A. L. (1979). The founding father we never knew. *Contemporary Psychology, 24,* 547–550.

BLUMENTHAL, A. L. (1980). Wilhelm Wundt and early American psychology: A class of cultures. In R. W. Rieber & K. Salzinger (Eds.), *Psychology: Theoretical–historical perspective* (pp. 25–42). New York: Academic Press.

BLUMENTHAL, A. L. (1991). The intrepid Joseph Jastrow. In G. A. Kimble, M. Wertheimer, & C. L. White (Eds.), *Portraits of pioneers in psychology* (pp. 75–87). Washington, DC: American Psychological Association.

BORING, E. G. (1938). The Society of Experimental Psychologists. *American Journal of Psychology, 51,* 410–421.

BORING, E. G. (1950). *A history of experimental psychology* (2nd ed.). New York: Appleton-Century-Crofts.

BORING, E. G. (1967). Titchener's experimentalists. *Journal of the History of the Behavioral Sciences, 3,* 315–325.

BOSELIE, F. (1992). The golden section has no particular aesthetic attractivity! *Empirical Studies of the Arts, 10,* 1–18.

BREUER, J., & FREUD, S. (1895). *Studien Über Hysterie.* Leipzig, Germany: Deuticke.

BRINGMANN, W. G., BALANCE, W. D. G., & EVANS, R. B. (1975). William Wundt 1832–1920: A brief biographical sketch. *Journal of the History of the Behavioral Sciences, 11,* 287–297.

BRONNER, A. F., HEALY, W., LOWE, G. M., & SHIMBERG, M. E. (1929). *A manual of individual mental tests and testing.* Boston: Little, Brown.

BROTEMARKLE, R. A. (Ed.). (1931). *Clinical psychology: Studies in honor of Lightner Witmer.* Philadelphia: University of Pennsylvania Press.

BROTEMARKLE, R. A. (1947). Clinical psychology 1896–1946. *Journal of Consulting Psychology, 13,* 1–4.

BRUCE, H. A. (1910). Psychology and daily life. *The Outlook, 95,* 397–410.

BURT, N. (1963). *The perennial Philadelphians.* Boston: Little, Brown.

BURT, S. (1945). *Philadelphia, holy experiment.* New York: Doubleday.

BUTLER, R. A. (1983, August). *French contributions to the origin of clinical psychology.* Paper presented at the 91st Annual Convention of the American Psychological Association, Anaheim, CA.

BUTLER, R. A. (1985). Clinical psychology in Western Europe. *Dynamic Psychotherapy, 3,* 209–216.

CAMFIELD, T. M. (1973). The professionalization of American psychology. *Journal of the History of the Behavioral Sciences, 9,* 66–75.

CARSON, J. (1993). Army Alpha, army brass, and search for army intelligence. *Isis, 84,* 278–309.

CATTELL, J. M. (1890). Mental tests and measurements. *Mind, 15,* 373–381.

CATTELL, J. M. (1893). Esoteric psychology. *The Independent, 45,* 316–317.

CATTELL, J. M. (1894). Errors of observation in psychology and physics [Abstract]. *Proceedings of the American Psychological Association* (pp. 3–4). New York: Macmillan. (Reprinted in Sokal, 1973)

CATTELL, J. M. (1896a). Address of the president before the American Psychological Association. *Psychological Review, 3,* 134–148.

CATTELL, J. M. (1896b). Psychical research. *Psychological Review, 3,* 582–583.

CATTELL, J. M. (1898a). Professor Münsterberg on "The danger from experimental psychology." *Psychological Review, 5,* 411–413.

CATTELL, J. M. (1898b). [Untitled note]. *Science, 7,* 641–642.

CATTELL, J. M. (1930). Psychology in America. *Scientific Monthly, 30,* 114–126.

CATTELL, J. M., & FARRAND, L. (1896). Physical and mental measurements of the students of Columbia University. *Psychological Review, 3,* 618–648.

CATTELL, J. M. (1937). Retrospect: Psychology as a profession. *Journal of Consulting Psychology, 1,* 1–3.

CATTELL, R. B. (1963). Theory of fluid and crystallized intelligence. *Journal of Educational Psychology, 54,* 1–22.

CHEYNEY, E. P. (1940/1977). *History of the University of Pennsylvania.* Philadelphia: University of Pennsylvania Press.

COLLINS, J. (1908). *Letters to a neurologist.* New York: Wood.

COLLINS, J. (1919). *Italy re-visited: My Italian year 1917–18.* London: T. Fisher Unwin.

COLLINS, J. (1931). Lightner Witmer: A biographical sketch. In R. A. Brotemarkle (Ed.), *Clinical psychology: Studies in honor of Lightner Witmer* (p. 3–9). Philadelphia: University of Pennsylvania Press.

COMMAGER, H. S. (1950). *The American mind.* New Haven, CT: Yale University Press.

COON, D. J. (1982). Eponymy, obscurity, Twitmyer, and Pavlov. *Journal of the History of the Behavioral Sciences, 18,* 255–262.

CORNMAN, O. P. (1896). A experimental investigation of the processes of ideation [Abstract]. *Psychological Review, 3,* 126–127.

CORNMAN, O. P. (1902). Spelling in the elementary school: An experimental and statistical investigation [Monograph]. In L. Witmer (Ed.), *Experimental studies in psychology and pedagogy,* 1. Boston: Ginn.

CURTI, M. (1980). *Human nature in American thought.* Madison: University of Wisconsin Press.

DALLENBACH, K. M. (1959). Twitmyer and the conditioned response. *American Journal of Psychology, 72,* 628–633.

DARWIN, C. (1877). A biographical sketch of an infant. *Mind, 2,* 285–294.

DAVIS, S. T., & JAHNKE, J. C. (1991). Unity and the golden section: Rules for aesthetic choice? *American Journal of Psychology, 104,* 257–277.

DENNIS, W., & BORING, E. G. (1952). The founding of the APA. *American Psychologist, 7,* 95–97.

DEVEREUX, H. T. (1909). Report of a year's work on defectives in a public school. *The Psychological Clinic, 3,* 45–48.

DIAMOND, S. (1980). Francis Galton and American psychology. In R. W. Rieber & K. Salzinger (Eds.), *Psychology: Theoretical–historical perspectives* (pp. 43–55). New York: Academic Press.

DOWLIN, C. M. (Ed.). (1940). *The University of Pennsylvania today: Its buildings, departments, and work.* Philadelphia: University of Pennsylvania Press.

FAGAN, T. K. (1986). School psychology's dilemma: Reappraising solutions and directing attention to the future. *American Psychologist, 41,* 851–861.

FAGAN, T. K. (1988). Historical moments: Shedding more light on Witmer can be illuminating. *Communiqué, 17,* 23.

FAGAN, T. K. (1990). A brief history of school psychology in the United States. In A. Thomas & J. Grimes (Eds.), *Best practices in school psychology* (pp. 913–929). Washington, DC: National Association of School Psychologists.

FAGAN, T. K. (1992). Compulsory schooling, child study, clinical psychology, and special education: Origins of school psychology. *American Psychologist, 47,* 236–243.

FAGAN, T. K. (1996a). *Correlation without causation: Witmer's connection to international school psychology.* Paper presented at the 104th Annual Convention of the American Psychological Association, Toronto.

FAGAN, T. K. (1996b). Witmer's contributions to school psychological services. *American Psychologist, 51,* 241–243.

FANCHER, R. E. (1996). The measurement of mind: Francis Galton and the psychology of individual differences. In R. E. Fancher, *Pioneers of psychology* (3rd ed., pp. 216–245). New York: Norton.

FARRAND, L. (1896). Series of physical and mental tests on the students of Columbia College [Abstract]. *Psychological Review, 3,* 121–133.

FECHNER, G. T. (1876). *Vorschüle der Aesthetik* [Introduction to aesthetics]. Leipzig, Germany: Breitkopf & Härtel.

FECHNER, G. T. (1966). *Elements of psychophysics* (Ed. by D. H. Howes & E. G. Boring, trans. by H. E. Adler). New York: Holt, Rinehart & Winston. (Original work published 1860.)

FERNBERGER, S. W. (1931). The history of the psychological clinic. In R. A. Brotemarkle (Ed.), *Clinical psychology: Studies in honor of Lightner Witmer* (pp. 10–36). Philadelphia: University of Pennsylvania Press.

FERNBERGER, S. W. (1943). The American Psychological Association: 1892–1942. *Psychological Review, 50,* 33–60.

Fifth annual meeting of experimental psychologists. (1908). *American Journal of Psychology, 19,* 288.

FISKE, D. W., & MADDI, S. R. (1961). *Functions of varied experience.* Homewood, IL: Dorsey Press.

FORREST, D. W. (1974). *Francis Galton: The life and work of a Victorian genius.* New York: Taplinger.

FOWLER, R. (1978). Historical bits: Lightner Witmer and academic freedom. *Professional Psychology, 9,* 126.

FRANZ, S. I. (1912). *Handbook of mental examination methods.* New York: Journal of Nervous and Mental Disease.

FRENCH, J. L. (1984). On the conception, birth, and early development of school psychology: With special reference to Pennsylvania. *American Psychologist, 39,* 976–987.

FULLERTON, G. S. (1897). The "knower" in psychology. *Psychological Review, 4,* 1–26.

FURNESS, W. H. (1902). *The home-life of Borneo head-hunters.* Philadelphia: Lippincott.

FURNESS, W. H. (1916). Observations on the mentality of chimpanzees and orangutans. In *Proceedings of the American Philosophical Society* (pp. 281–290). Philadelphia: American Philosophical Society.

GARDNER, R. A., GARDNER, B. T., & VAN CANTFORT, T. E. (1989). *Teaching sign language to chimpanzees.* Albany: State University of New York Press.

GARFIELD, S. L. (1965). Historical introduction. In B. B. Wolman (Ed.), *Handbook of clinical psychology* (pp. 125–140). New York: McGraw-Hill.

GARFIELD, S. L. (1982). Editorial: The 75th anniversary of the first issue of *The Psychological Clinic. Journal of Consulting and Clinical Psychology, 50,* 167–170.

GODDARD, H. H. (1910). A measuring scale for intelligence. *The Training School, 6,* 146–155.

GODDARD, H. H. (1913). *The Kallikak family: A study in the heredity of feeble mindedness.* New York: Macmillan.

GOLDENBERG, H. (1973). *Contemporary clinical psychology.* Monterey, CA: Brooks/Cole.

GOODWIN, C. J. (1985). On the origin of Titchener's experimentalists. *Journal of the History of the Behavioral Sciences, 21,* 383–389.

HALE, M. J. (1980). *Human science and social order: Hugo Münsterberg and the origins of applied psychology.* Philadelphia: Temple University Press.

HALL, G. S. (1894). History and prospects of experimental psychology in America [Abstract]. *Proceedings of the American Psychological Association* (p. 3). New York: Macmillan. (Reprinted in Sokal, 1973)

HALL, G. S. (1895). Closing discussion. In L. Dunton, H. Münsterberg, W. T. Harris, & G. S. Hall (Eds.), *The old psychology and the new* (pp. 36–38). Boston: New England.

HALL, M. I. R. (1934). *Ten years after: A followup of one hundred and twenty superior children.* Unpublished doctoral dissertation, University of Pennsylvania, Philadelphia.

HALLOWELL, D. K. (1931). The pre-school child. In R. A. Brotemarkle (Ed.), *Clinical psychology: Studies in honor of Lightner Witmer* (pp. 56–69). Philadelphia: University of Philadelphia Press.

HARLEY, H. L. (1913). The physical status of the special class for bright children at the University of Pennsylvania, Summer Session of 1912. *The Psychological Clinic, 7,* 20–23.

HARMON, M. P. (1897). Psycho-physical tests on normal school and kindergarten pupils [Abstract; Introduction by L. Witmer]. *Psychological Review, 4,* 117–118.

HEIDBREDER, E. (1933). *Seven psychologies.* New York: Appleton-Century-Crofts.

HILGARD, E. R. (1987). *Psychology in America: A historical survey.* San Diego, CA: Harcourt Brace Jovanovich.

HILDRETH, G. (1936). Tribute [to Witmer and Terman]. *Consulting Psychologist, 2,* unnumbered introductory page.

HOFSTADTER, R., & METZGER, W. P. (1955). *The development of academic freedom in the United States.* New York: Columbia University Press.

HOLMES, A. (1910). An educational experiment with troublesome adolescent boys. *The Psychological Clinic, 4,* 155–178.

HOLMES, A. (1912). *The conservation of children: A manual of clinical psychology presenting the examination and treatment of backward children.* Philadelphia: Lippincott.

HOLSOPPLE, F. (1918). Clinic report XXIV. *The Psychological Clinic, 11,* 262.

HOLSOPPLE, F. (1919a). Diagnostic teaching. *The Psychological Clinic, 12,* 255–257.

HOLSOPPLE, F. Q. (1919b). *Social non-conformity: An analysis of four hundred and twenty cases of delinquent girls and women.* Unpublished doctoral dissertation, University of Pennsylvania, Philadelphia.

HUMPHREY, G. (1968). Wilhelm Wundt: The great master. In B. B. Wolman (Ed.), *Historical roots of contemporary psychology* (pp. 275–297). New York: Harper & Row.

HUMPSTONE, H. J. (1919). The analytical diagnosis. *The Psychological Clinic, 12,* 171–173.

HUNTINGTON, E. A. (1905). Mental and moral effects following the removal of adenoids [Abstract]. *Psychological Bulletin, 2,* 42.

HUNTINGTON, E. A. (1907). A juvenile delinquent. *The Psychological Clinic, 1,* 21–24.

HYDE, W. D. (1892). *Practical ethics.* New York: Holt.

IDE, G. G. (1918). The Witmer formboard and cylinders as tests for children two to six years of age. *The Psychological Clinic, 12,* 65–88.

IDE, G. G. (1931). Special education. In R. A. Brotemarkle (Ed.), *Clinical psychology: Studies in honor of Lightner Witmer* (pp. 91–102). Philadelphia: University of Pennsylvania Press.

IRWIN, F. W. (1932). Review of E. C. Tolman, *Purposive behavior in animals and men. The Psychological Clinic, 21,* 64–66.

IRWIN, F. W. (1943). Edwin Burket Twitmyer: 1873–1943. *American Journal of Psychology, 56,* 451–453.

IRWIN, F. W. (1971). *Intentional behavior and motivation.* Philadelphia: Lippincott.

ITARD, J.-M.-G. (1962). *The wild boy of Aveyron* (G. Humphrey & M. Humphrey, Trans.). New York: Appleton-Century-Crofts. (Original work published 1802)

JAMES, H. (Ed.). (1920). *The letters of William James* (Vols. 1–2). Boston: Atlantic Monthly Press.

JAMES W. (1879). Are we automata? *Mind, 4,* 1–22.

JAMES W. (1890). *Principles of psychology* (Vols. 1–2). New York: Holt.

JAMES, W. (1892). What psychical research has accomplished. *The Forum, 13,* 727–742.

JAMES, W. (1895). Review of J. L. Nevius, *Demon possession and allied themes. Psychological Review, 2,* 529–531.

JAMES, W. (1896). Psychical research. *Psychological Review, 3,* 649–652.

JAMES, W. (1898). Mrs. Piper, "the medium" [Letter to the editor]. *Science, 7,* 640–641.

JAMES, W. (1901). Frederic Myer's service to psychology. *Popular Science Monthly, 59,* 380–389.

JAMES, W. (1905). The experience of activity. *Psychological Bulletin, 2,* 39–40.

JAMES, W. (1909, October). The confidences of a "psychical researcher." *The American Magazine,* 580–589.

JASTROW, J. (1894). Experimental psychology at the World's Fair [Abstract]. *Proceedings of the American Psychological Association* (p. 8). New York: Macmillan. (Reprinted in Sokal, 1973)

JONÇICH, G. (1968). *The sane positivist: A biography of Edward L. Thorndike.* Middletown, CT: Wesleyan University Press.

JONES, A. M. (1922). Miss inconsistency. *The Psychological Clinic, 14,* 136–142.

JONES, A. M. (1923). The superior child. *The Psychological Clinic, 15,* 1–8.

JONES, A. M. (1925). An analytical study of one hundred twenty superior children. *The Psychological Clinic, 16,* 19–76.

JUDD, C. H. (1904). Meeting of experimental psychologists at Cornell University. *Journal of Philosophy, 1,* 238–240.

JUDD, C. H. (1921). In memory of Wilhelm Wundt. By his American Students. *Psychological Review, 28,* 153–180.

KELLOGG, W. N. (1968). Chimpanzees in experimental homes. *The Psychological Record, 18,* 489–498.

KELLOGG, W. N., & KELLOGG, L. A. (1933). *The ape and the child: A study of environmental influence on early behavior*. New York: McGraw-Hill.

KENT, G. H. (1950). *Mental tests in clinics for children*. New York: Van Nostrand.

KEPHART, A. P. (1918). Clinical studies of failures with the Witmer formboard. *The Psychological Clinic, 11*, 229–253.

KLEIN, D. B. (1970). *A history of scientific psychology*. New York: Basic Books.

KORCHIN, S. J. (1983). The history of clinical psychology: A personal view. In M. Hersen, A. E. Kazdin, & A. S. Bellack (Eds.), *The clinical psychology handbook* (pp. 5–19). New York: Pergamon Press.

KROHN, W. O. (1894). *Practical lessons in psychology*. Chicago: Werner.

LADD, G. T. (1894). Is psychology a science? *Psychological Review, 1*, 392–395.

LEVINE, M., & WISHNER, J. (1977). The case records of the Psychological Clinic at the University of Pennsylvania (1896–1961). *Journal of the History of the Behavioral Sciences, 13*, 59–66.

LEWIS, A. L. (1897). Comparison of the times of simple reactions and of free-arm movements in different classes of persons [Abstract; Introduction by L. Witmer]. *Psychological Review, 4*, 113–114.

LITTMAN, R. A. (1979). Social and experimental origins of experimental psychology. In Eliot Hearst (Ed.), *The first century of experimental psychology* (pp. 39–86). Hillsdale, NJ: Erlbaum.

LOMBARD, W. P. (1887). The variations of the normal knee-jerk, and their relation to the central nervous system. *American Journal of Psychology, 1*, 1–71.

LOTZE, R. H. (1886). *Outlines of psychology: Dictated portions of lectures of Herman Lotze* (3rd ed., G. T. Ladd, Trans.). Boston: Ginn. (Original work published 1881)

LOUTTIT, C. M. (1936). *Clinical psychology of exceptional children*. New York: Harper.

LOUTTIT, C. M. (1939). The nature of clinical psychology. *Psychological Bulletin, 36*, 361–389.

LOWE, G. M. (1923). Mental changes after removing adenoids and tonsils. *The Psychological Clinic, 15*, 92–100.

LYNCH, E. F. (1910). The bright child. *The Psychological Clinic, 4*, 141–144.

MACH, E. (1886). *Beiträge zur Analyse der Empfindungen* [Contribution to the analysis of sensations]. Jena, Germany: Fischer.

MARSHALL, H. R. (1894). *Pain, pleasure and aesthetics*. London: Macmillan.

MASLOW, A. (1954). *Motivation and personality*. New York: Harper.

MASON, R. O. (1896). Educational uses of hypnosis. *North American Review, 163*, 448–455.

MASON, R. O. (1897). Educational uses of hypnosis: A reply to Prof. Lightner Witmer's editorial in *Pediatrics*. *Pediatrics, 3*, 97–105.

McCLELLAND, D. C. (1973). Testing for competence rather than for "intelligence." *American Psychologist, 28*, 1–14.

McCLELLAND, D. C., ATKINSON, J. W., CLARK, R. A., & LOWELL, E. L. (1953). *The achievement motive*. New York: Appleton-Century-Crofts.

McKEAG, A. J. (1902). *The sensation of pain and the theory of the specific sense energies* [Monograph]. In L. Witmer (Ed.), *Experimental studies in psychology and pedagogy, 2*. Boston: Ginn.

McKEAG, A. J. (1931). The principles of education. In R. A. Brotemarkle (Ed.), *Clinical psychology: Studies in honor of Lightner Witmer* (pp. 202–216). Philadelphia: University of Pennsylvania Press.

McREYNOLDS, P. (1981). Introduction. In P. McReynolds (Ed.), *Advances in psychological assessment* (pp. 1–21). San Francisco: Jossey-Bass.

McREYNOLDS, P. (1987). Lightner Witmer: Little known founder of clinical psychology. *American Psychologist, 42,* 849–858.

McREYNOLDS, P. (1988). Psychology at the University of Nevada-Reno: A retrospective account. *Journal of the History of the Behavioral Sciences, 24,* 74–80.

McREYNOLDS, P. (1996a). Lightner Witmer: A centennial tribute. *American Psychologist, 51,* 237–240.

McREYNOLDS, P. (1996b). Lightner Witmer: Father of clinical psychology. In G. A. Kimble, C. A. Boneau, & M. Wertherimer (Eds.), *Portraits of pioneers in psychology* (Vol. 2, pp. 62–71). Washington, DC: American Psychological Association.

McREYNOLDS, P. (1996c). Lightner Witmer: The first clinical psychologist. In W. Bringmann, H. W. Lueck, R. Miller, & C. E. Early (Eds.), *A pictorial history of psychology* (pp. 465–470). Carol Stream, IL: Quintessence.

McREYNOLDS, P. (1996d, August). *The lasting influence of Lightner Witmer.* Paper presented at Annual Convention, American Psychological Association, Toronto, Canada.

MEISCHNER, W., & ESCHLER, E. (1979). *Wilhelm Wundt.* Leipzig, Germany: Urania-Verlag.

METZGER, W. P. (Ed.). (1977). *The American concept of academic freedom and information.* New York: Arno Press.

MILLER, C. W. (1893). *A statistical study in experimental aesthetics.* Unpublished doctoral dissertation, University of Pennsylvania, Philadelphia.

MINTON, H. L. (1988). *Lewis M. Terman: Pioneer in psychological testing.* New York: New York University Press.

MISIAK, H., & SEXTON, V. S. (1966). *History of psychology: An overview.* New York: Grune & Stratton.

MITCHELL, D. (1931). Private practice. In R. Brotemarkle (Ed.), *Clinical psychology: Studies in honor of Lightner Witmer* (pp. 177–190). Philadelphia: University of Pennsylvania Press.

MONTESSORI, M. (1964). *The Montessori method.* New York: Schocken. (Original work in English, published 1912; original work in Italian, published 1909)

MOORE, K. C. (1896). The mental development of a child. *Psychological Review: Monograph Supplement* (3).

MOORE, K. C. (1901). Comparative observations on the development of movements. *Pedagogical Seminary, 8,* 201–238.

MORGAN, H. W. (1971). *Unity and culture: The United States 1877–1900.* Allen Lane, London: The Penguin Press.

MOSKOWITZ, M. J. (1977). Hugo Münsterberg: A study in the history of applied psychology. *American Psychologist, 32,* 824–842.

MULFORD, H. J. (1897). The throat of the child. *Educational Review, 13,* 261–272.

MÜNSTERBERG, H. (1894). The problems of experimental psychology [Abstract]. *Proceedings of the American Psychological Association* (pp. 10–11). New York: Macmillan (Reprinted in Sokal, 1973)

MÜNSTERBERG, H. (1895). The new psychology. In L. Dunton, H. Münsterberg, W. T. Harris, & G. Stanley Hall (Eds.), *The old psychology and the new* (pp. 14–26). Boston: New England.

MÜNSTERBERG, H. (1898). The danger from experimental psychology. *Atlantic Monthly, 81,* 159–167.

MÜNSTERBERG, H. (1905). The order of tone sensations. *Psychological Bulletin, 2,* 46–47.

MÜNSTERBERG, H. (Ed.). (1906). *Harvard psychological studies 1906.* Boston: Houghton Mifflin.

MÜNSTERBERG, H. (1908). Prohibition and social psychology. *McClure's Magazine, 31,* 438–444.

MÜNSTERBERG, H. (1909). *Psychotherapy.* New York: Moffat, Yard.

MÜNSTERBERG, M. (1922). *Hugo Münsterberg: His life and work.* New York: Appleton.

MURPHY, G. (1949). *Historical introduction to modern psychology.* New York: Harcourt, Brace.

MURPHY, M. (1930). What do children come to the Psychological Clinic for? *The Psychological Clinic, 19,* 1–6.

MURPHY, M. (1936). Cases examined during the past twenty-five years at the Psychological Clinic of the University of Pennsylvania. *Consulting Psychologist, 2,* 5–8.

National Cyclopedia of American Biography. (1955). New York: White.

NEARING, S. (1972a). *The making of a radical.* New York: Harper & Row.

NEARING, S. (1972b). On being fired. *The Pennsylvania Gazette, 70,* 16–20.

NEEL, J. L. (1969). *Miss Irwin's of Philadelphia: A history of the Agnes Irwin School.* Wynnewood, PA: Livingston.

NEVIUS, J. L. (1894). *Demon possession and allied themes, being an inductive study of phenomena of our own times.* Chicago: Revell.

NEWBOLD, W. R. (1895). Experimental induction of automatic processes. *Psychological Review, 2,* 149–172.

O'DONNELL, J. M. (1979). The clinical psychology of Lightner Witmer: A case study of institutional innovation and intellectual change. *Journal of the History of the Behavioral Sciences, 15,* 3–17.

PASCHAL, F. C. (1918a). A report on the standardization of the Witmer Cylinder Test. *The Psychological Clinic, 12,* 54–59.

PASCHAL, F. C. (1918b). *The Witmer Cylinder Test.* Hershey, PA: Hershey Press.

PENNIMAN, J. H. (1931). Preface. In R. A. Brotemarkle (Ed.), *Clinical psychology: Studies in honor of Lightner Witmer* (pp. vii–x). Philadelphia: University of Pennsylvania Press.

PERRY, R. B. (1935). *The thought and character of William James* (Vols. 1–2). Boston: Little, Brown.

PHILLIPS, A. (1930). The clinical examination and diagnostic teaching of cases at the Psychological Clinic of the University of Pennsylvania. *The Psychological Clinic, 19,* 169–200.

PRÉVOST, C. (1969). A propos des origines de la psychologie clinique [On the origins of clinical psychology]. *Bulletin De Psychologie, 23,* 119–124.

PREYER, W. (1909). *The mind of the child* (2nd ed., Vols. 1–2; H. W. Brown, Trans.). New York: Appleton. (Original work published 1881)

Proceedings of the American Psychological Association [Included 1st and 2nd meetings, 1892 and 1893]. (1894). New York: Macmillan. (Reprinted in Sokal, 1973)

Proceedings of the Third Annual Meeting of the American Psychological Association, 1894. (1895). *Psychological Review, 2,* 348–362.

Proceedings of the Fourth Annual Meeting of the American Psychological Association, 1895. (1896). *Psychological Review, 3,* 121–133.

Proceedings of the Fifth Annual Meeting of the American Psychological Association, 1896. (1897). *Psychological Review, 4,* 107–141.

Proceedings of the Thirteenth Annual Meeting of the American Psychological Association, 1904. (1905). *Psychological Bulletin, 2,* 37–63.

Proceedings of the Eighteenth Annual Meeting of the American Psychological Association, 1909. (1910). *Psychological Bulletin, 7,* 37–64.

RAPHELSON, A. C. (1967). Lincoln Steffens at the Leipzig Psychological Institute, 1890–91. *Journal of the History of the Behavioral Sciences, 3,* 38–42.

REISMAN, J. M. (1991). A history of clinical psychology (2nd ed.). New York: Hemisphere.

REPPLIER, A. (1898). *Philadelphia, the place and the people.* New York: Macmillan.

REPPLIER, E. (1900). *Calendar of the correspondence relating to the American Revolution of Brigadier-General George Weedon, Hon. Richard Henry Lee, Arthur Lee, and Major-General Nathanial Greene.* Philadelphia: American Philosophical Society.

REUCHLIN, M. (1967). *Historie de la psychologie* [The history of psychology]. Paris: Presses Universitaires de France.

RIMLAND, B. (1964). *Infantile autism.* New York: Appleton-Century-Crofts.

ROBACK, A. A. (1964). *A history of American psychology* (Rev. ed.). New York: Collier Books.

ROCKWELL, A. J. (1931). The superior child. In R. A. Brotemarkle (Ed.), *Clinical psychology: Studies in honor of Lightner Witmer* (pp. 46–55). Philadelphia: University of Pennsylvania Press.

ROGERS, C. R. (1942). *Counseling and psychotherapy.* New York: Houghton Mifflin.

ROGERS, C. R. (1951). *Client-centered therapy.* New York: Houghton Mifflin.

ROGERS, C. (1959). A theory of therapy, personality, and interpersonal relationship, as developed in the client-centered framework. In S. Koch (Ed.), *Psychology: A study of a science* (Vol. 3): *Formulation of the person in the social context* (pp. 184–256). New York: McGraw-Hill.

ROSENZWEIG, S. (1944). *The historic expedition to America: Freud, Jung and Hall the king maker.* St Louis, MO: Rana House.

ROSS, B. (1991). William James: Spoiled child of American psychology. In G. A. Kimble, M. Wertheimer, & C. White (Eds.), *Portraits of pioneers in psychology* (pp. 13–25). Washington, DC: American Psychological Association.

ROSS, D. (1972). *G. Stanley Hall: The psychologist as prophet.* Chicago: University of Chicago Press.

ROUTH, D. K. (1994). *Clinical psychology since 1917: Science, practice, and organization.* New York: Plenum.

ROUTH, D. K. (1996). Lightner Witmer and the first 100 years of clinical psychology. *American Psychologist, 51,* 244–247.

ROUTH, D. K., & DEL BARRIO, V. (1996). European roots of the first psychology clinic in North America. *European Psychologist, 1,* 44–50.

SAHAKIAN, W. S. (1975). *History and systems of psychology.* New York: Halsted Press.

SALTMARSH, J. A., (1991). *Scott Nearing: An intellectual biography.* Philadelphia: Temple University Press.

SAMUELSON, F. (1977). World War I intelligence testing and the development of psychology. *Journal of the History of the Behavioral Sciences, 13,* 274–282.

SANFORD, E. C. (1896). Report of the Secretary and Treasurer of the APA. In Proceedings of the Fourth Annual Meeting of the American Psychological Association. *Psychological Review, 3,* 121–123.

SANTAYANA, G. (1894). Pleasure and pain. Review of L. Witmer's "The psychological analysis and physical basis of pleasure and pain" (1894). *Psychological Review, 1,* 544.

SCRIPTURE, E. W. (1895). *Thinking, feeling, doing.* New York: Flood & Vincent.

SEXTON, V. S. (1965). Clinical psychology: An historical survey. *Genetic Psychology Monographs, 72,* 401–434.

SHERMAN, S. (1989). *A Scott Nearing reader.* Mutucher, NJ: Scarecrow Press.

SMITH, T. L. (1914). The development of psychological clinics in the United States. *The Pedagogical Seminary, 21,* 143–153.

SNODGRASS, J. (1984). William Healy (1869–1963): Pioneer child psychiatrist and criminologist. *Journal of the History of the Behavioral Sciences, 20,* 332–339.

SOKAL, M. (1972). *The education and psychological career of James McKeen Cattell, 1860–1904.* Unpublished doctoral dissertation, Case Western Reserve University, Cleveland, OH.

SOKAL, M. M. (1973). APA's first publication: Proceedings of the American Psychological Association, 1892–1893. *American Psychologist, 28,* 277–292.

SOKAL, M. (Ed.). (1981). *An education in psychology: James McKeen Cattell's journal and letters from Germany and England, 1880–1888.* Cambridge, MA: MIT Press.

SOKAL, M. (1982). James McKeen Cattell and the failure of anthropometric mental testing, 1890–1901. In W. R. Woodward & M. G. Ash (Eds.), *The problematic science: Psychology in nineteenth-century thought* (pp. 322–345). New York: Praeger.

SOKAL, M., DAVIS, A. B., & MERZBACH, U. C. (1976). Laboratory instruments in the history of psychology. *Journal of the History of the Behavioral Sciences, 12,* 59–64.

STARR, H. E. (1922). The hydrogen ion concentration of the mixed saliva considered as an index of fatigue and of emotional excitation and applied to a study of the metabolic etiology of stammering. *American Journal of Psychology, 33,* 394–418.

STARR, H. E. (1928). Psychological concomitants of high aveolar carbon dioxide. *The Psychological Clinic, 17,* 1–12.

STARR, H. E. (1931). Psychobiochemistry. In R. A. Brotemarkle (Ed.), *Clinical psychology: Essays in honor of Lightner Witmer* (pp. 155–166). Philadelphia: University of Pennsylvania Press.

STEFFENS, L. (1931). *Autobiography*. New York: Harcourt, Brace.

STERN, W. (1917). Hugo Münsterberg: In memoriam. *Journal of Applied Psychology, 1,* 186–188.

STERNBERG, R. J., & SALTER, W. (1982). Conceptions of intelligence. In R. J. Sternberg (Ed.), *Handbook of human intelligence* (pp. 3–28). New York: Cambridge University Press.

STERNBERG, R. J., & WAGNER, R. K. (1986). *Practical intelligence*. Cambridge, England: Cambridge University Press.

STRONG, C. A. (1895). The psychology of pain. *Psychological Review, 2,* 329–347.

SUNDBERG, N. D. (1977). *Assessment of persons*. Englewood Cliffs, NJ: Prentice Hall.

SYLVESTER, M. L. (1932). A clinical demonstration of superior children. *The Psychological Clinic, 21,* 114–125.

SYLVESTER, M. L. (1936). The present organization of the Psychological Clinic at the University of Pennsylvania. *Consulting Psychologist, 2,* 2–5.

SYLVESTER, R. H. (1913a). Clinical psychology adversely criticized. *The Psychological Clinic, 7,* 182–188.

SYLVESTER, R. H. (1913b). *The form board test*. Princeton, NJ: Princeton University Press.

SYMONDS, J. P. (1946). Ten years of journalism in psychology. *Journal of Consulting Psychology, 10,* 335–374.

TAYLOR, J. S. (1898). Some practical aspects of interest. *Pedagogical Seminary, 5,* 497–511.

TERMAN, L. M. (1911). The Binet–Simon Scale for measuring intelligence: Impressions gained by the application upon four hundred non-selected children. *The Psychological Clinic, 5,* 199–206.

TERMAN, L. M. (1914). *The hygiene of the school child*. Boston: Houghton Mifflin.

TERMAN, L. M. (1916). *The measurement of intelligence*. Boston: Houghton Mifflin.

THORNDIKE, E. L. (1907). *The elimination of pupils from school* (Bulletin No. 4). Washington, DC: Department of the Interior, Bureau of Education.

THORNDIKE, E. L. (1909). The elimination of pupils from schools [Letter to the editor]. *The Psychological Clinic, 3,* 58–59.

TITCHENER, E. B. (1901, 1905). *Experimental psychology: A manual of laboratory practice* (2 Vols. in 4). New York: Macmillan.

TOWN, C. H. (1907). An infantile stammer ("baby-talk") in a boy of twelve years. *The Psychological Clinic, 1,* 10–20.

TOWN, C. H. (1909). Review of the C. G. Jung, *The psychology of dementia praecox*. *The Psychological Clinic, 3,* 141–145.

TWITMYER, E. B. (1902). *A study of the knee jerk*. Philadelphia: Winston.

TWITMYER, E. B. (1905). Knee-jerks without stimulation of the patellar tendon [Abstract]. *Psychological Bulletin, 2,* 43–44.

TWITMYER, G. W. (1907). Clinical studies of retarded children. *The Psychological Clinic, 2,* 97–103.

TWITMYER, E. B., & NATHANSON, Y. S. (1932). *Correction of defective speech: A complete manual of psycho-physical technique for the treatment and correction of defects of speech.* Philadelphia: Blakiston.

UNTERMEYER, L. (1949). *The poetry and prose of Walt Whitman.* New York: Simon & Schuster.

URBAN, F. M. (1908). *The application of statistical methods to the problem of psychophysics* [Monograph]. In L. Witmer (Ed.), *Experimental studies in psychology and pedagogy, 3.* Philadelphia: Psychological Clinic Press.

VITELES, M. S. (1922). Job specifications and diagnostic tests of job competency designed for the auditing division of a street railway company. In L. Witmer (Ed.), *Experimental Studies in Psychology and Pedagogy, 9.* Philadelphia: Psychological Clinic Press.

VITELES, M. S. (1932). *Industrial psychology.* New York: Norton.

VITELES, M. S. (1967). Autobiography. In E. G. Boring & G. Lindsey (Eds.), *A history of psychology in autobiography* (Vol. 5, pp. 417–449). New York: Appleton-Century-Crofts.

WALLACE, D. B., FRANKLIN, M. B., & KEEGAN, R. T. (1994). The observing eye: A century of baby diaries. *Human Development, 37,* 1–29.

WALLIN, J. E. W. (1914). *The mental health of the school child.* New Haven, CT: Yale University Press.

WALLIN, J. E. W. (1927). *Clinical and abnormal psychology.* Boston: Houghton Mifflin.

WALLIN, J. E. W. (1930). Must we continue to train clinical psychologists for second string jobs? *The Psychological Clinic, 18,* 242–245.

WALLIN, J. E. W. (1955). *The odyssey of a psychologist.* Wilmington, DE: Privately printed (widely available through most university libraries).

WALLIN, J. E. W. (1960). History of the struggles within the American Psychological Association to attain membership requirements, test standardization, certification of psychological practitioners, and professionalization. *Journal of General Psychology, 68,* 287–308.

WALLIN, J. E. W. (1961). A note on the origin of the APA Clinical Section. *American Psychologist, 16,* 256–258.

WARDEN, C. J., JENKINS, T. N., & WARNER, L. H. (1936). *Comparative psychology* (Vol. 3). New York: Ronald Press.

WATSON, J. B. (1928). *Psychological care of infant and child.* New York: Norton.

WATSON, R. I. (1957). Lightner Witmer: 1867–1956. *American Journal of Psychology, 69,* 680–682.

WATSON, R. I. (1978). *The great psychologists* (4th ed.). Philadelphia: Lippincott.

WEBER, E. H. (1846/1905). *Der Tastsinn und das Gemeingefühl* [The sense of touch and common sensibility]. Leipzig, Germany: Engelmann.

WHIPPLE, G. M. (1910). *Manual of mental and physical tests: Part I. Simpler processes.* Baltimore: Warwick & York.

WHIPPLE, G. M. (1914). *Manual of mental and physical tests. Part I. Simpler processes* (2nd ed.). Baltimore: Warwick & York.

WHITE, R. W. (1959). Motivation reconsidered: The concept of competence. *Psychological Review, 66,* 297–333.

WINSHIP, A. E. (1908). Thorndike's elimination by grades. *Journal of Education, 67,* 425–427.

WISSLER, C. (1901). The correlation of mental and physical tests. *Psychological Review: Monograph Supplement, 3,* (No. 6).

WITMER, A. F. (1897). Stigmata of degeneration in epilepsy. *Pediatrics, 4,* 295–299.

WITMER, E. R. (1906a). Franklin's trials as a benefactor. *Lippincott's Monthly Magazine, 77,* 63–70.

WITMER, E. R. (1906b). How many mutineers did Paul Jones kill? *The Independent, 60,* 832–834.

WITMER, E. R. (1908). Calendar of the papers of Benjamin Franklin in the library of the University of Pennsylvania. Appendix to I. M. Hayes (Ed.), *Calendar of the Papers of Benjamin Franklin in the Library of the American Philosophical Society.* Philadelphia: University of Pennsylvania Press.

WITMER, E. R. (1910a). Review of Leonard P. Ayres, *Open-air schools* (1910, New York: Doubleday). *The Psychological Clinic, 4,* 145–146.

WITMER, E. R. (1910b). Review of Mrs. Burton Chance, *The care of the child* (1910, Philadelphia: Penn). *The Psychological Clinic, 4,* 145–146.

WITMER, E. R. (1910c). Review of Rudolph R. Reeder, *How two hundred children live and learn* (1909, New York: Charities Publication Committee). *The Psychological Clinic, 3,* 281–283.

WITMER, E. R. (1911). Review of Edith E. Reade Mumford, *The dawn of character* (1910, London: Longmans, Green). *The Psychological Clinic, 4,* 277–279.

WITMER, E. R. (1912). Review of Havelock Ellis, *The field of dreams* (1911, New York: Houghton Mifflin). *The Psychological Clinic, 5,* 293–295.

WITMER, E. R. (1914). Review of Edward Ross, *Changing America* (1912, New York: Century). *The Psychological Clinic, 8,* 25–26.

WITMER, E. R. (1918 June). The woman's part (poem). *The Forge, 4.* Philadelphia.

WITMER, E. R. (1931). The messenger of evil. *Harper's Magazine, 163,* 632–636.

WITMER, E. R. (1938, September 18). Pavlova. *The New Mexico Sentinel,* p. 14.

WITMER, E. R. (1957). *Agnes Repplier: A memoir.* Philadelphia: Dorrance.

WOODWORTH, R. S. (1938). *Experimental psychology.* New York: Holt.

WUNDT, W. (1873–1874). *Grundzüge der Physiologischen Psychologie* [Fundamentals of physiological psychology]. Leipzig, Germany: Engelmann.

YERKES, R. M., BRIDGES, J. W., & HARDWICK, R. S. (1915). *A point scale for measuring mental ability.* Baltimore: Warnick & York.

YOUNG, M. H. (1916). Correlation of the Witmer Formboard and Cylinder Test. *The Psychological Clinic, 10,* 112–116.

YOUNG, H. H. (1916a). Physical and mental factors involved in the formboard test. *The Psychological Clinic, 10,* 149–167.

YOUNG, H. H. (1916b). The Witmer formboard. *The Psychological Clinic, 10,* 93–111.

YOUNG, H. H., & YOUNG, M. H. (1923). The Witmer formboard—First trial records. *The Psychological Clinic, 15,* 85–91.

ZENDERLAND, L. (1988). Education, evangelism, and the origins of clinical psychology: The child-study legacy. *Journal of the History of the Behavioral Sciences, 24,* 152–165.

ZSCHUPPE, V. (1984). Matthaus Hipp: In memoriam (Publication of Division 26, APA). In W. Bringmann (Ed.), *History of Psychology Newsletter* (Vol. 16, pp. 1–5). Mobile, AL: Department of Psychology, University of South Alabama.

BIBLIOGRAPHY OF WITMER'S PUBLICATIONS

Included in this listing are all of Witmer's known professional publications. The list also includes one incomplete and unpublished work (Witmer, 1904), which was evidently intended for eventual publication and is of historic importance. The list does not include numerous entries in the News and Comment sections of *The Psychological Clinic*, most of which were probably written by Witmer in his role as editor but were not published under his name. The more important of these are referred to in the text, with their sources indicated in the appropriate notes. Several rare or unique items have been deposited in the Archives of the History of American Psychology, and are identified here by the letters AHAP.

VAN SICKLE, J. H., WITMER, L., & AYRES, L. P. (1911). *Provision for exceptional children in public schools. Bulletin, 1911* (14, Whole No. 461). Washington, DC: U.S. Government Printing Office.

WITMER, E. R., & WITMER, L. (1928). Orthogenic cases—XIV—George: Mentally restored to normal but intellectually deficient. *The Psychological Clinic, 17,* 153–169.

WITMER, L. (1892). The aesthetic value of the mathematical proportions of simple figures:—A contribution to an experimental aesthetic [Abstract]. *Proceedings of the International Congress of Experimental Psychology,* 2nd Session, 70–73. London: Williams & Norgate.

WITMER, L. (1894a). Aesthetics of form [Abstract]. *Psychological Review, 1,* 205–208.

WITMER, L. (1894b). The chronoscopic measurement of simple reactions on all classes of persons. *Proceedings of the American Psychological Association* (pp. 6–7). New York: Macmillan. (Reprinted in Sokal, 1973)

WITMER, L. (1894c). The pendulum as a control-instrument for the Hipp chronoscope. *Psychological Review, 1,* 506–515.

WITMER, L. (1894d). Pleasure and pain from the psychologist's standpoint. *American Medico-Surgical Bulletin, 7,* 351–353.

WITMER, L. (1894e). The psychological analysis and physical basis of pleasure and pain. *Journal of Nervous and Mental Diseases, 19,* 209–228.

WITMER, L. (1894f). Some experiments upon the aesthetics of visual forms. *Proceedings of the American Psychological Association* (p. 6). New York: Macmillan. (Reprinted in Sokal, 1973)

WITMER, L. (1894g). Zur experimentellen Aesthetik ein facher räumlicher Formverhältnisse [On the experimental aesthetics of simple spatial relationships of form]. *Philosophische Studien, 9,* 96–144, 209–263.

WITMER, L. (1895). [Untitled] review of two papers by J. J. van Biervliet, "On the influence of pulse rapidity on reaction time to sound," and "On the influence of pulse rapidity on reaction times to light and touch." *Psychological Review, 2,* 426–428. (Originals published in *Philosophische Studien, 10,* 160ff; *11,* 125–135)

WITMER, L. (1896a). The common interests of child psychology and pediatrics. *Pediatrics, 2,* 390–395.

WITMER, L. (1896b). Practical work in psychology. *Pediatrics, 2,* 462–471.

WITMER, L. (1896c). The teaching of psychology to teachers. *The Citizen, 2,* 158–162. (Also issued as a separate pamphlet, AHAP)

WITMER, L. (1896d). Variations in the patellar reflex as an aid to the mental analysis [Title only]. *Psychological Review, 3,* 131.

WITMER, L. (1897a). Courses in psychology for normal schools: Part I. *Educational Review, 13,* 45–57.

WITMER, L. (1897b). Courses in psychology for normal schools: Part II. *Educational Review, 13,* 146–162.

WITMER, L. (1897c). The organization of practical work in psychology [Abstract]. *Psychological Review, 4,* 116–117.

WITMER, L. (1897d). Pain. In *Twentieth century practice of medicine* (Vol. 11, pp. 905–945. New York: Wood.

WITMER, L. (1897e). The use of hypnotism in education. *Pediatrics, 3,* 23–27.

WITMER, L. (1902a). *Analytical psychology: A practical manual for colleges and normal schools.* Boston: Ginn & Company.

WITMER, L. (1902–1922), Series Editor. *Experimental studies in psychology and pedagogy.* Authors and titles in this series were: 1. *Spelling in the elementary school,* by Oliver P. Corman (1902); 2. *The sensation of pain and the theory of the specific sense energies,* by Anna J. McKeag (1902); 3. *The application of statistical methods to the problems of psychophysics,* by F. M. Urban (1908); 4. *Two experimental studies of the insane,* by Clara H. Town (1909); 5. *A clinical study of retarded children,* by Jacob D. Heilman (1910); 6. *Retardation in the Reading public schools,* by Aaron M. Snyder (1911); 7. *Some aspects of the memory span test. A study in associability,* by H. J. Humpstone (1917); 8. *The competency of fifty college students: A diagnostic study,* by Karl G. Miller (1922); and 9. *Job specifications and diagnostic tests of job competency designed for the auditing division of a street railway company,* by Morris Viteles (1922). The publisher for the first two monographs was Ginn & Company (Boston); for 3–7, the Psychological Clinic Press (Philadelphia); and for 8 and 9, not given but very likely Psychological Clinic Press.

WITMER, L. (1904). [1904 clinical perspective] Unpublished manuscript originally filed with Psychological Clinic records. AHAP.

WITMER, L. (1905). Some experiments on lifted weights looking toward a restatement of the psycho-physical problem [Abstract]. *The Psychological Bulletin, 2,* 45–46.

WITMER, L. (1907a). A case of chronic bad spelling—amnesia visualis verbalis, due to arrest of post-natal development. *The Psychological Clinic, 1,* 53–64.

WITMER, L. (1907b). Clinical psychology. *The Psychological Clinic, 1,* 1–9. (Reprinted in *Clinical psychology: Studies in honor of Lightner Witmer,* pp. 341–352, by R. A. Brotemarkle, Ed., 1931, Philadelphia: University of Pennsylvania Press; and in the *American Psychologist,* 1996, *51,* 248–251)

WITMER, L. (1907c). The fifteen months' training of a feeble-minded child. *The Psychological Clinic, 1,* 69–80.

WITMER, L. (1907d). The hospital school. *The Psychological Clinic, 1,* 138–146.

WITMER, L. (1907e). Retardation through neglect in children of the rich. *The Psychological Clinic, 1,* 157–174.

WITMER, L. (1907f). University courses in psychology. *The Psychological Clinic, 1,* 25–35.

WITMER, L. (Ed.). (1907–1935). *The Psychological Clinic* (Vols. 1–23). (volumes do not match years)

WITMER, L. (1908a). Retrospect and prospect: An editorial. *The Psychological Clinic, 2,* 1–4.

WITMER, L. (1908b). The treatment and cure of a case of mental and moral deficiency. *The Psychological Clinic, 2,* 153–179.

WITMER, L. (1908–1909). Mental healing and the Emmanuel movement. *The Psychological Clinic, 2,* 212–223, 239–250, 282–300. (Also published as a separate, unnumbered monograph, AHAP)

WITMER, L. (1909a). Are we educating the rising generation? *Educational Review, 37,* 456–467.

WITMER, L. (1909b). The clinical study and treatment of normal and abnormal development. *Annals of the American Academy of Political and Social Science, 34,* 141–162.

WITMER, L. (1909c). A monkey with a mind. *The Psychological Clinic, 3,* 179–205.

WITMER, L. (1909d). Orthogenics in the public schools. *The Psychological Clinic, 3,* 29–33.

WITMER, L. (1909e). The Psychological Clinic: The university's work for defective and backward children. *Old Penn Weekly Review, 8,* 98–105.

WITMER, L. (1909f). The study and treatment of retardation: A field of applied psychology. *Psychological Bulletin, 6,* 121–126.

WITMER, L. (1910a). Intelligent imitation and curiosity in a monkey. *The Psychological Clinic, 3,* 224–227.

WITMER, L. (1910b). The irrepressible ego. *The Psychological Clinic, 4,* 193–210.

WITMER, L. (1910c). The restoration of children of the slums. *The Psychological Clinic, 3,* 266–280.

WITMER, L. (1910d). What is meant by retardation? *The Psychological Clinic, 4,* 121–131.

WITMER, L. (1911a). Courses in psychology at the summer school of the University of Pennsylvania. *The Psychological Clinic, 4*, 245–273.

WITMER, L. (1911b). Criminals in the making. *The Psychological Clinic, 4*, 221–238.

WITMER, L. (1911c). *The special class for backward children.* Philadelphia: Psychological Clinic Press. (Described as reported rather than edited, by Witmer)

WITMER, L. (1913). Children with mental defects distinguished from mentally defective children. *The Psychological Clinic, 7*, 173–181.

WITMER, L. (1914a). Dr. George W. Twitmyer died February 21, 1914. *The Psychological Clinic, 8*, 26–28.

WITMER, L. (1914b). The Montessori method. *The Psychological Clinic, 8*, 1–5.

WITMER, L. (1914c). Progress in education of exceptional children in public schools during the year 1912–13. In *Report of the Commissioner of Education for the year ended June 30, 1913* (Vol. 1, Whole No. 532), 435–452. Washington, DC: U.S. Government Printing Office.

WITMER, L. (1914d). The scope of education as a university department. *The Psychological Clinic, 7*, 237–249.

WITMER, L. (1915a). Clinical records. *The Psychological Clinic, 9*, 1–17.

WITMER, L. (1915b). The exceptional child and the training of teachers for exceptional children. *School and Society, 2*, 217–229.

WITMER, L. (1915c). The exceptional child at home and in school. In *University of Pennsylvania: Lectures by members of the faculty* (pp. 535–555). Philadelphia: Published by the University of Pennsylvania.

WITMER, L. (1915d). *The Nearing case.* New York: Huebsch.

WITMER, L. (1915e). On the relation of intelligence to efficiency. *The Psychological Clinic, 9*, 61–86.

WITMER, L. (1916a). Congenital aphasia and feeblemindedness—A clinical diagnosis. *The Psychological Clinic, 10*, 181–191.

WITMER, L. (1916b). A formboard demonstration. *The Psychological Clinic, 10*, 199–202.

WITMER, L. (1917a). Diagnostic education—An education for the fortunate few. *The Psychological Clinic, 11*, 69–78.

WITMER, L. (1917b). A fettered mind. *The Psychological Clinic, 10*, 241–249.

WITMER, L. (1917c). [Reference to his reading of paper titled "The diagnostic method of training intelligence: An education for the fortunate few (with a demonstration)"]. *Proceedings of the American Philosophical Society, 56*, v.

WITMER, L. (1917d). Two feebleminded maidens—A clinical lecture. *The Psychological Clinic, 10*, 224–234.

WITMER, L. (1919a). "Dick": A case of atavism [Transcript of a lecture]. *The Psychological Clinic, 12*, 285–286.

WITMER, L. (1919b). Efficiency and other factors of success. *The Psychological Clinic, 12*, 241–247.

WITMER, L. (1919c). Performance and success: An outline of psychology for diagnostic testing and teaching. *The Psychological Clinic, 12*, 145–170.

WITMER, L. (1919d). The problem of educability. *The Psychological Clinic, 12*, 174–178.

WITMER, L. (1919e). Reference book in clinical psychology for diagnostic teaching. *The Psychological Clinic, 12*, 145–288.

WITMER, L. (1919f). The training of very bright children. *The Psychological Clinic, 13*, 88–96.

WITMER, L. (1919g, April). What I did with Don. *Ladies Home Journal*, pp. 51, 122–123.

WITMER, L. (1920a). Introduction [Title only]: Symposium on Psychology In War and Education. In *Proceedings of the American Philosophical Society, 59*, viii. (Also reported in *Psychological Bulletin* [1920], *17*, 240)

WITMER, L. (1920b). Orthogenic cases, XIV-Don: A curable case of arrested development due to a fear psychosis the result of shock in a three-year-old infant. *The Psychological Clinic, 13*, 97–111.

WITMER, L. (1922a). The analytical diagnosis. *The Psychological Clinic, 14*, 129–135.

WITMER, L. (1922b). Intelligence—A definition. *The Psychological Clinic, 14*, 65–67.

WITMER, L. (1922c). What is intelligence and who has it? *The Scientific Monthly, 15*, 57–67.

WITMER, L. (1925a). The analytical vs. the general diagnosis in clinical psychology [Title only]. *Psychological Bulletin, 22*, 341.

WITMER, L. (1925b). Clinical psychology—Its origin and future [Abstract]. *Psychological Bulletin, 22*, 129.

WITMER, L. (1925c). Psychological diagnosis and the psychonomic orientation of analytic science: An epitome. *The Psychological Clinic, 16*, 1–18.

WITMER, L. (1927a). *The breviary of proficiency and progress in surpassing venture* [3-page summary statement]. Privately printed. AHAP.

WITMER, L. (1927b). Preterficient nature—A psychonomic orientation [Abstract]. *Psychological Bulletin, 24*, 169.

WITMER, L. (1930). Psychonomic personeering. *The Psychological Clinic, 19*, 74.

WITMER, L. (1932). Excerpts from the remarks on demonstration of superior children. In M. L. Sylvester, "A clinical demonstration of superior children." *The Psychological Clinic, 21*, 124–125.

WITMER, L. (1937). *The Witmer School* [Brochure]. Publisher not listed. AHAP.

WITMER, L., & AMBLER, M. E. (1929). Orthogenic cases—XVII—Jack: Feebleminded or normal. *The Psychological Clinic, 17*, 217–225.

WITMER, L., & PHILLIPS, A. (1929). Studies in diagnostic education—A case of intermittent imbecility. *The Psychological Clinic, 18*, 165–169.

Index

ABOUT THE AUTHOR

Paul McReynolds is Emeritus Professor of Psychology at the University of Nevada, Reno. A clinical psychologist, he has published widely in the areas of assessment and psychopathology. He has also had a long interest in the history of psychology, especially of clinical and personality psychology, and has authored and edited a number of historical contributions. With this background, it was only natural that his interest should turn to the life of Lightner Witmer, clinical psychology's founder.

McReynolds received his doctorate in clinical and personality psychology at Stanford University in 1949. He accepted a position at the Veterans Affairs Medical Center, Palo Alto, California, where he founded, and for many years headed, the facility's Behavioral Research Laboratory. During this period, he also taught at Stanford and the University of California, Berkeley. In 1969, he moved to the University of Nevada, Reno, where he established an outstanding doctoral program in clinical psychology.